eat pray love

One Woman's Search
for Everything

ELIZABETH GILBERT

BLOOMSBURY
LONDON OXFORD NEW YORK NEW DELHI SYDNEY

First published in Great Britain in 2006
This paperback edition published 2007
Also available as an audio edition

Copyright © by Elizabeth Gilbert 2006

The moral right of the author has been asserted

Bloomsbury Publishing Plc,
50 Bedford Square,
London WC1B 3DP

A CIP catalogue record is available from the British Library

ISBN 978-0-7475-8566-4

51

Printed and bound by CPI Group (UK) Ltd., Croydon CR0 4YY

Bloomsbury Publishing, London, New Delhi, New York and Sydney

www.bloomsbury.com/elizabethgilbert

Bloomsbury is a trade mark of Bloomsbury Publishing Plc

MIX
Paper from
responsible sources
FSC® C020471

For Susan Bowen—

who provided refuge
even from 12,000 miles away

Tell the truth, tell the truth, tell the truth.*

—Sheryl Louise Moller

---

* *Except when attempting to solve emergency Balinese real estate transactions, such as described in Book 3.*

INTRODUCTION

Or

How This Book Works

Or

The 109th Bead

When you're traveling in India—especially through holy sites and Ashrams—you see a lot of people wearing beads around their necks. You also see a lot of old photographs of naked, skinny and intimidating Yogis (or sometimes even plump, kindly and radiant Yogis) wearing beads, too. These strings of beads are called *japa malas*. They have been used in India for centuries to assist devout Hindus and Buddhists in staying focused during prayerful meditation. The necklace is held in one hand and fingered in a circle—one bead touched for every repetition of mantra. When the medieval Crusaders drove East for the holy wars, they witnessed worshippers praying with these *japa malas*, admired the technique, and brought the idea home to Europe as rosary.

The traditional *japa mala* is strung with 108 beads. Amid the more esoteric circles of Eastern philosophers, the number 108 is held to be most auspicious, a perfect three-digit multiple of three, its components adding up to nine, which is three threes. And three, of course, is the number representing supreme balance, as anyone who has ever studied either the Holy Trinity or a simple barstool can plainly see. Being as this whole book is about my efforts to find balance, I have decided to structure it like a *japa mala*, dividing my story into 108 tales, or beads. This string of 108 tales is further divided into three sections about Italy, India and Indonesia—the three countries I visited during this year of self-inquiry. This division means that there are 36 tales in each section, which appeals to me on a personal level because I am writing all this during my thirty-sixth year.

Now before I get too Louis Farrakhan here with this numerology business, let me conclude by saying that I also like the idea of stringing these stories along the structure of a *japa mala* because it is so . . . structured. Sincere spiritual investigation is, and always has been, an endeavor of methodical discipline. Looking for Truth is not some kind of spazzy free-for-all, not even during this, the great age of the spazzy free-for-all. As both a seeker and a writer, I find it helpful to hang on to the beads as much as possible, the better to keep my attention focused on what it is I'm trying to accomplish.

In any case, every *japa mala* has a special, extra bead—the 109th bead—which dangles outside that balanced circle of 108 like a pendant. I used to think the 109th bead was an emergency spare, like the extra button on a fancy sweater, or the youngest son in a royal family. But apparently there is an even higher purpose. When your fingers reach this marker during prayer, you are meant to pause from your absorption in meditation and thank your teachers. So here, at my own 109th bead, I pause before I even begin. I offer thanks to all my teachers, who have appeared before me this year in so many curious forms.

But most especially I thank my Guru, who is compassion's very heartbeat, and who so generously permitted me to study at her Ashram while I was in India. This is also the moment where I would like to clarify that I write about my experiences in India purely from a personal standpoint and not as a theological scholar or as anybody's official spokesperson. This is why I will not be using my Guru's name throughout this book—because I cannot speak for her. Her teachings speak best for themselves. Nor will I reveal either the name or the location of her Ashram, thereby sparing that fine institution publicity which it may have neither the interest in nor the resources for managing.

One final expression of gratitude: While scattered names throughout this book have been changed for various reasons, I've elected to change the names of every single person I met—both Indian and Western—at this Ashram in India. This is out of respect for the fact that most people don't go on a spiritual pilgrimage in order to appear later as a character in a book. (Unless, of course, they are me.) I've made only one exception to this self-imposed policy of anonymity. Richard from Texas really is named Richard, and he really is from Texas. I wanted to use his real name because he was so important to me when I was in India.

One last thing—when I asked Richard if it was OK with him if I mentioned in my book that he used to be a junkie and a drunk, he said that would be totally fine.

He said, "I'd been trying to figure out how to get the word out about that, anyhow."

But first—Italy . . .

ITALY

Or

'Say It Like You Eat It.'

Or

Thirty-six Tales About the
Pursuit of Pleasure

1

I wish Giovanni would kiss me.

Oh, but there are so many reasons why this would be a terrible idea. To begin with, Giovanni is ten years younger than I am, and—like most Italian guys in their twenties—he still lives with his mother. These facts alone make him an unlikely romantic partner for me, given that I am a professional American woman in my mid-thirties, who has just come through a failed marriage and a devastating, interminable divorce, followed immediately by a passionate love affair that ended in sickening heartbreak. This loss upon loss has left me feeling sad and brittle and about seven thousand years old. Purely as a matter of principle I wouldn't inflict my sorry, busted-up old self on the lovely, unsullied Giovanni. Not to mention that I have finally arrived at that age where a woman starts to question whether the wisest way to get over the loss of one beautiful brown-eyed young man is indeed to promptly invite another one into her bed. This is why I have been alone for many months now. This is why, in fact, I have decided to spend this entire year in celibacy.

To which the savvy observer might inquire: "Then why did you come to *Italy*?"

To which I can only reply—especially when looking across the table at handsome Giovanni—"Excellent question."

Giovanni is my Tandem Exchange Partner. That sounds like an innuendo, but unfortunately it's not. All it really means is that we meet a few evenings a week here in Rome to practice each other's languages. We speak first in Italian, and he is patient with me; then we speak in English, and I am patient with him. I discovered Giovanni a few weeks after I'd arrived in Rome, thanks to that big Internet café at the Piazza Barbarini, across the street from that fountain with the sculpture of that sexy merman blowing into his conch shell. He (Giovanni, that is—not the merman) had posted a flier on the bulletin board explaining that a native Italian speaker was seeking a native English speaker for conversational language practice. Right beside his appeal was another flier with the same request, word-for-word identical in every way, right down to the typeface. The only difference was the contact information. One flier listed an e-mail address for somebody named Giovanni; the other introduced somebody named Dario. But even the home phone number was the same.

Using my keen intuitive powers, I e-mailed both men at the same time, asking in Italian, "Are you perhaps brothers?"

It was Giovanni who wrote back this very *provocativo* message: "Even better. Twins!"

Yes—much better. Tall, dark and handsome identical twenty-five-year-old twins, as it turned out, with those giant brown liquid-center Italian eyes that just unstitch me. After meeting the boys in person, I began to wonder if perhaps I should adjust my rule somewhat about remaining celibate this year. For instance, perhaps I could remain totally celibate *except* for keeping a pair of handsome twenty-five-year-old Italian twin brothers as lovers. Which was slightly reminiscent of a friend of mine who is vegetarian except for bacon, but nonetheless . . . I was already composing my letter to *Penthouse*:

In the flickering, candlelit shadows of the Roman café, it was impossible to tell whose hands were caress—

But, no.

No and no.

I chopped the fantasy off in mid-word. This was not my moment to be seeking romance and (as day follows night) to further complicate my already knotty life. This was my moment to look for the kind of healing and peace that can only come from solitude.

Anyway, by now, by the middle of November, the shy, studious Giovanni and I have become dear buddies. As for Dario—the more razzle-dazzle swinger brother of the two—I have introduced him to my adorable little Swedish friend Sofie, and how they've been sharing *their* evenings in Rome is another kind of Tandem Exchange altogether. But Giovanni and I, we only talk. Well, we eat and we talk. We have been eating and talking for many pleasant weeks now, sharing pizzas and gentle grammatical corrections, and tonight has been no exception. A lovely evening of new idioms and fresh mozzarella.

Now it is midnight and foggy, and Giovanni is walking me home to my apartment through these back streets of Rome, which meander organically around the ancient buildings like bayou streams snaking around shadowy clumps of cypress groves. Now we are at my door. We face each other. He gives me a warm hug. This is an improvement; for the first few weeks, he would only shake my hand. I think if I were to stay in Italy for another three years, he might actually get up the juice to kiss me. On the other hand, he might just kiss me right now, tonight, right here by my door . . . there's still a chance . . . I mean we're pressed up against each other's bodies beneath this moonlight . . . and of course it would be a *terrible* mistake . . . but it's still such a wonderful possibility that he might actually do it right now . . . that he might just bend down . . . and . . . and . . .

Nope.

He separates himself from the embrace.

"Good night, my dear Liz," he says.

"*Buona notte, caro mio,*" I reply.

I walk up the stairs to my fourth-floor apartment, all alone. I let myself into my tiny little studio, all alone. I shut the door behind me. Another solitary bedtime in Rome. Another long night's sleep ahead of me, with nobody and nothing in my bed except a pile of Italian phrasebooks and dictionaries.

I am alone, I am all alone, I am completely alone.

Grasping this reality, I let go of my bag, drop to my knees and press my forehead against the floor. There, I offer up to the universe a fervent prayer of thanks.

First in English.

Then in Italian.

And then—just to get the point across—in Sanskrit.

2

And since I am already down there in supplication on the floor, let me hold that position as I reach back in time three years earlier to the moment when this entire story began—a moment which also found me in this exact same posture: on my knees, on a floor, praying.

Everything else about the three-years-ago scene was different, though. That time, I was not in Rome but in the upstairs bathroom of the big house in the suburbs of New York which I'd recently purchased with my husband. It was a cold November, around three o'clock in the morning. My husband was sleeping in our bed. I was hiding in the bathroom for something like the forty-seventh consecutive night, and—just as during all those nights before—I was sobbing. Sobbing so hard, in fact, that a great lake of tears and snot was spreading before me on the bathroom tiles, a veritable Lake Inferior (if you will) of all my shame and fear and confusion and grief.

I don't want to be married anymore.

I was trying so hard not to know this, but the truth kept insisting itself to me.

I don't want to be married anymore. I don't want to live in this big house. I don't want to have a baby.

But I was supposed to want to have a baby. I was thirty-one years old. My husband and I—who had been together for eight years, married for six—had built our entire life around the common expectation that, after passing the doddering old age of thirty, I would want to settle down and have children. By then, we mutually anticipated, I would have grown weary of traveling and would be happy to live in a big, busy household full of children and home-made quilts, with a garden in the backyard and a cozy stew bubbling on the stovetop. (The fact that this was a fairly accurate portrait of my own mother is a quick indicator of how difficult it once was for me to tell the difference between myself and the powerful woman who had raised me.) But I didn't—as I was appalled to be finding out—want any of these things. Instead, as my twenties had come to

10

a close, that deadline of THIRTY had loomed over me like a death sentence, and I discovered that I did not want to be pregnant. I kept waiting to want to have a baby, but it didn't happen. And I know what it feels like to want something, believe me. I well know what desire feels like. But it wasn't there. Moreover, I couldn't stop thinking about what my sister had said to me once, as she was breast-feeding her firstborn: "Having a baby is like getting a tattoo on your face. You really need to be certain it's what you want before you commit."

How could I turn back now, though? Everything was in place. This was supposed to be the year. In fact, we'd been trying to get pregnant for a few months already. But nothing had happened (aside from the fact that—in an almost sarcastic mockery of pregnancy—I was experiencing psychosomatic morning sickness, nervously throwing up my breakfast every day). And every month when I got my period I would find myself whispering furtively in the bathroom: *Thank you, thank you, thank you, thank you for giving me one more month to live . . .*

I'd been attempting to convince myself that this was normal. All women must feel this way when they're trying to get pregnant, I'd decided. ("Ambivalent" was the word I used, avoiding the much more accurate description: "utterly consumed with dread.") I was trying to convince myself that my feelings were customary, despite all evidence to the contrary—such as the acquaintance I'd run into last week who'd just discovered that she was pregnant for the first time, after spending two years and a king's ransom in fertility treatments. She was ecstatic. She had wanted to be a mother forever, she told me. She admitted she'd been secretly buying baby clothes for years and hiding them under the bed, where her husband wouldn't find them. I saw the joy in her face and I recognized it. This was the exact joy my own face had radiated last spring, the day I discovered that the magazine I worked for was going to send me on assignment to New Zealand, to write an article about the search for giant squid. And I thought, "Until I can feel as ecstatic about having a baby as I felt about going to New Zealand to search for a giant squid, I cannot have a baby."

I don't want to be married anymore.

In daylight hours, I refused that thought, but at night it would consume me. What a catastrophe. How could I be such a criminal jerk as to proceed this deep into a marriage, only to leave it? We'd only just bought this house a year ago. Hadn't I wanted this nice house? Hadn't I loved it? So why was I haunting its halls every night now, howling like Medea? Wasn't I proud of all we'd accumulated—the prestigious home in the Hudson Valley, the apartment in Manhattan, the eight phone lines, the friends and the picnics and the parties, the weekends spent roaming the aisles of some box-shaped superstore of our choice, buying ever more appliances on credit? I had actively participated in every moment of the creation of this life—so why did I feel like none of it resembled me? Why did I feel so overwhelmed with duty, tired of being the primary bread-winner and the housekeeper and the social coordinator and the dog-walker and the wife and the soon-to-be mother, and—somewhere in my stolen moments—a writer . . . ?

I don't want to be married anymore.

My husband was sleeping in the other room, in our bed. I equal parts loved him and could not stand him. I couldn't wake him to share in my distress—what would be the point? He'd already been watching me fall apart for months now, watching me behave like a madwoman (we both agreed on that word), and I only exhausted him. We both knew there was *something wrong with me*, and he'd been losing patience with it. We'd been fighting and crying, and we were weary in that way that only a couple whose marriage is collapsing can be weary. We had the eyes of refugees.

The many reasons I didn't want to be this man's wife anymore are too personal and too sad to share here. Much of it had to do with my problems, but a good portion of our troubles were related to his issues, as well. That's only natural; there are always two figures in a marriage, after all—two votes, two opinions, two conflicting sets of decisions, desires and limitations. But I don't think it's appropriate for me to discuss his issues in my book. Nor would I ask anyone to believe that I am capable of reporting an unbiased version of our story, and therefore the chronicle of our marriage's failure will remain untold here. I also will not discuss here all the reasons why I *did* still want to be his wife, or all his wonderfulness, or why I loved him and why I had married him and why I was unable to imagine life without him. I won't open any of that. Let it be sufficient to say that, on this night, he was still my lighthouse and my albatross in equal measure. The only thing more unthinkable than leaving was staying; the only thing more impossible than staying was leaving. I didn't want to destroy anything or anybody. I just wanted to slip quietly out the back door, without causing any fuss or consequences, and then not stop running until I reached Greenland.

This part of my story is not a happy one, I know. But I share it here because something was about to occur on that bathroom floor that would change forever the progression of my life—almost like one of those crazy astronomical super-events when a planet flips over in outer space for no reason whatsoever, and its molten core shifts, relocating its poles and altering its shape radically, such that the whole mass of the planet suddenly becomes oblong instead of spherical. Something like that.

What happened was that I started to pray.

You know—like, to *God*.

3

Now, this was a first for me. And since this is the first time I have introduced that loaded word—GOD—into my book, and since this is a word which will appear many times again throughout these pages, it seems only fair that I pause here for a moment to explain exactly what I mean when I say that word, just so people can decide right away how offended they need to get.

Saving for later the argument about whether God exists at all (no—here's a better idea: let's skip that argument completely), let me first explain why I use the word God, when I could just as easily use the words *Jehovah*, *Allah*, *Shiva*, *Brahma*, *Vishnu* or *Zeus*. Alternatively, I could call God "That," which is how the ancient Sanskrit scriptures say it, and which I think comes close to the all-inclusive and unspeakable entity I have sometimes experienced. But that "That" feels impersonal to me—a thing, not a being—and I myself cannot pray to a That. I need a proper name, in order to fully sense a personal attendance. For this same reason, when I pray, I do not address my prayers to The Universe, The Great Void, The Force, The Supreme Self, The Whole, The Creator, The Light, The Higher Power, or even the most poetic manifestation of God's name, taken, I believe, from the Gnostic gospels: "The Shadow of the Turning."

I have nothing against any of these terms. I feel they are all equal because they are all equally adequate and inadequate descriptions of the indescribable. But we each do need a functional name for this indescribability, and "God" is the name that feels the most warm to me, so that's what I use. I should also confess that I generally refer to God as "Him," which doesn't bother me because, to my mind, it's just a convenient personalizing pronoun, not a precise anatomical description or a cause for revolution. Of course, I don't mind if people call God "Her," and I understand the urge to do so. Again—to me, these are both equal terms, equally adequate and inadequate. Though I do think the capitalization of either pronoun is a nice touch, a small politeness in the presence of the divine.

Culturally, though not theologically, I'm a Christian. I was born a Protestant of the white Anglo-Saxon persuasion. And while I do love that great teacher of peace who was called Jesus, and while I do reserve the right to ask myself in certain trying situations what indeed He would do, I can't swallow that one fixed rule of Christianity insisting that Christ is the *only* path to God. Strictly speaking, then, I cannot call myself a Christian. Most of the Christians I know accept my feelings on this with grace and open-mindedness. Then again, most of the Christians *I* know don't speak very strictly. To those who do speak (and think) strictly, all I can do here is offer my regrets for any hurt feelings and now excuse myself from their business.

Traditionally, I have responded to the transcendent mystics of all religions. I have always responded with breathless excitement to anyone who has ever said that God does not live in a dogmatic scripture or in a distant throne in the sky, but instead abides very close to us indeed—much closer than we can imagine, breathing right through our own hearts. I respond with gratitude to anyone who has ever voyaged to the center of that heart, and who has then returned to the world with a report for the rest of us that God is *an experience of supreme love.* In every religious tradition on earth, there have always been mystical saints and transcendents who report exactly this experience. Unfortunately many of them have ended up arrested and killed. Still, I think very highly of them.

In the end, what I have come to believe about God is simple. It's like this—I used to have this really great dog. She came from the pound. She was a mixture of about ten different breeds, but seemed to have inherited the finest features of them all. She was brown. When people asked me, "What kind of dog is that?" I would always give the same answer: "She's a brown dog." Similarly, when the question is raised, "What kind of God do you believe in?" my answer is easy: "I believe in a magnificent God."

4

Of course, I've had a lot of time to formulate my opinions about divinity since that night on the bathroom floor when I spoke to God directly for the first time. In the middle of that dark November crisis, though, I was not interested in formulating my views on theology. I was interested only in saving my life. I had finally noticed that I seemed to have reached a state of hopeless and life-threatening despair, and it occurred to me that sometimes people in this state will approach God for help. I think I'd read that in a book somewhere.

What I said to God through my gasping sobs was something like this: "Hello, God. How are you? I'm Liz. It's nice to meet you."

That's right—I was speaking to the creator of the universe as though we'd just been introduced at a cocktail party. But we work with what we know in this life, and these are the words I always use at the beginning of a relationship. In fact, it was all I could do to stop myself from saying, "I've always been a big fan of your work . . ."

"I'm sorry to bother you so late at night," I continued. "But I'm in serious trouble. And I'm sorry I haven't ever spoken directly to you before, but I do hope I have always expressed ample gratitude for all the blessings that you've given me in my life."

This thought caused me to sob even harder. God waited me out. I pulled myself together enough to go on: "I am not an expert at praying, as you know. But can you please help me? I am in desperate need of help. I don't know what to do. I need an answer. Please tell me what to do. Please tell me what to do. Please tell me what to do . . ."

And so the prayer narrowed itself down to that simple entreaty—*Please tell me what to do*—repeated again and again. I don't know how many times I begged. I only know that I begged like someone who was pleading for her life. And the crying went on forever.

Until—quite abruptly—it stopped.

Quite abruptly, I found that I was not crying anymore. I'd stopped crying, in fact, in mid-sob. My misery had been completely vacuumed out of me. I lifted my forehead off the floor and sat up in surprise, wondering if I would see now some Great Being who had taken my weeping away. But nobody was there. I was just alone. But not really alone, either. I was surrounded by something I can only describe as a little pocket of silence—a silence so rare that I didn't want to exhale, for fear of scaring it off. I was seamlessly still. I don't know when I'd ever felt such stillness.

Then I heard a voice. Please don't be alarmed—it was not an Old Testament Hollywood Charlton Heston voice, nor was it a voice telling me I must build a baseball field in my backyard. It was merely my own voice, speaking from within my own self. But this was my voice as I had never heard it before. This was my voice, but perfectly wise, calm and compassionate. This was what my voice would sound like if I'd only ever experienced love and certainty in my life. How can I describe the warmth of affection in that voice, as it gave me the answer that would forever seal my faith in the divine?

The voice said: *Go back to bed, Liz.*

I exhaled.

It was so immediately clear that this was the only thing to do. I would not have accepted any other answer. I would not have trusted a great booming voice that said either: *You Must Divorce Your Husband!* or *You Must Not Divorce Your Husband!* Because that's not true wisdom. True wisdom gives the only possible answer at any given moment, and that night, going back to bed was the only possible answer. *Go back to bed,* said this omniscient interior voice, because you don't need to know the final answer right now, at three o'clock in the morning on a Thursday in November. *Go back to bed,* because I love you. *Go back to bed,* because the only thing you need to do for now is get some rest and take good care of yourself until you do know the answer. *Go back to bed* so that, when the tempest comes, you'll be strong enough to deal with it. And the tempest is coming, dear one. Very soon. But not tonight. Therefore:

Go back to bed, Liz.

In a way, this little episode had all the hallmarks of a typical Christian conversion experience—the dark night of the soul, the call for help, the responding voice, the sense of transformation. But I would not say that this was a religious *conversion* for me, not in that traditional manner of being born again or saved. Instead, I would call what happened that night the beginning of a religious *conversation.* The first words of an open and exploratory dialogue that would, ultimately, bring me very close to God, indeed.

5

If I'd had any way of knowing that things were—as Lily Tomlin once said—going to get a whole lot worse before they got worse, I'm not sure how well I would have slept that night. But seven very difficult months later, I did leave my husband. When I finally made that decision, I thought the worst of it was over. This only shows how little I knew about divorce.

There was once a cartoon in *The New Yorker* magazine. Two women talking, one saying to the other: "If you really want to get to know someone, you have to divorce him." Of course, my experience was the opposite. I would say that if you really want to STOP knowing someone, you have to divorce him. Or her. Because this is what happened between me and my husband. I believe that we shocked each other by how swiftly we went from being the people who knew each other best in the world to being a pair of the most mutually incomprehensible strangers who ever lived. At the bottom of that strangeness was the abysmal fact that we were both doing something the other person would never have conceived possible; he never dreamed I would actually leave him, and I never in my wildest imagination thought he would make it so difficult for me to go.

It was my most sincere belief when I left my husband that we could settle our practical affairs in a few hours with a calculator, some common sense and a bit of goodwill toward the person we'd once loved. My initial suggestion was that we sell the house and divide all the assets fifty-fifty; it never occurred to me we'd proceed in any other way. He didn't find this suggestion fair. So I upped my offer, even suggesting this different kind of fifty-fifty split: What if he took all the assets and I took all the blame? But not even that offer would bring a settlement. Now I was at a loss. How do you negotiate once you've offered everything? I could do nothing now but wait for his counterproposal. My guilt at having left him forbade me from thinking I should be allowed to keep even a dime of the money I'd made in the last decade. Moreover, my newfound spirituality made it essential to me that we not battle. So this was my position—I would neither defend myself from him, nor would I fight him. For the longest time, against the counsel of all who cared about me, I resisted even consulting a lawyer, because I considered even that to be an act of war. I wanted to be all Gandhi about this. I wanted to be all Nelson Mandela about this. Not realizing at the time that both Gandhi and Mandela were *lawyers.*

Months passed. My life hung in limbo as I waited to be released, waited to see what the terms would be. We were living separately (he had moved into our Manhattan apartment), but nothing was resolved. Bills piled up, careers stalled, the house fell into ruin and my husband's silences were broken only by his occasional communications reminding me what a criminal jerk I was.

And then there was David.

All the complications and traumas of those ugly divorce years were multiplied by the drama of David—the guy I fell in love with as I was taking leave of my marriage. Did I say that I "fell in love" with David? What I meant to say is that I dove out of my marriage and into David's arms exactly the same way a cartoon circus performer dives off a high platform and into a small cup of water, vanishing completely. I clung to David for escape from marriage as if he were the last helicopter pulling out of Saigon. I inflicted upon him my every hope for my salvation and happiness. And, yes, I did love him. But if I could think of a stronger word than "desperately" to describe how I loved David, I would use that word here, and desperate love is always the toughest way to do it.

I moved right in with David after I left my husband. He was— is—a gorgeous young man. A born New Yorker, an actor and writer, with those brown liquid-center Italian eyes that have always (have I already mentioned this?) unstitched me. Street-smart, independent, vegetarian, foulmouthed, spiritual, seductive. A rebel poet-Yogi from Yonkers. God's own sexy rookie shortstop. Bigger than life. Bigger than big. Or at least he was to me. The first time my best friend Susan heard me talking about him, she took one look at the high fever in my face and said to me, "Oh my God, baby, you are in so much trouble."

David and I met because he was performing in a play based on short stories I'd written. He was playing a character I had invented, which is somewhat telling. In desperate love, it's always like this, isn't it? In desperate love, we always invent the characters of our partners, demanding that they be what we need of them, and then feeling devastated when they refuse to perform the role we created in the first place.

But, oh, we had such a great time together during those early months when he was still my romantic hero and I was still his living dream. It was excitement and compatibility like I'd never imagined. We invented our own language. We went on day trips and road trips. We hiked to the top of things, swam to the bottom of other things, planned the journeys across the world we would take together. We had more fun waiting in line together at the Department of Motor Vehicles than most couples have on their honeymoons. We gave each other the same nickname, so there would be no separation between us. We made goals, vows, promises and dinner together. He read books to me, and he *did my laundry*. (The first time that happened, I called Susan to report the marvel in astonishment, like I'd just seen a camel using a pay phone. I said, "A *man* just did *my* laundry! And he even hand-washed my delicates!" And she repeated: "Oh my God, baby, you are in so much trouble.")

The first summer of Liz and David looked like the falling-in-love montage of every romantic movie you've ever seen, right down to the splashing in the surf and the running hand-in-hand through the golden meadows at twilight. At this time I was still thinking my divorce might actually proceed gracefully, though I was giving my husband the summer off from talking about it so we could both cool down. Anyway, it was so easy not to think about all that loss in the midst of such happiness. Then that summer (otherwise known as "the reprieve") ended.

On September 9, 2001, I met with my husband face-to-face for the last time, not realizing that every future meeting would necessitate lawyers between us, to mediate. We had dinner in a restaurant. I tried to talk about our separation, but all we did was fight. He let me know that I was a liar and a traitor and that he hated me and would never speak to me again. Two mornings later I woke up after a troubled night's sleep to find that hijacked airplanes were crashing into the two tallest buildings of my city, as everything invincible that had once stood together now became a smoldering avalanche of ruin. I called my husband to make sure he was safe and we wept together over this disaster, but I did not go to him. During that week, when everyone in New York City dropped animosity in deference to the larger tragedy at hand, I still did not go back to my husband. Which is how we both knew it was very, very over.

It's not much of an exaggeration to say that I did not sleep again for the next four months.

I thought I had fallen to bits before, but now (in harmony with the apparent collapse of the entire world) my life really turned to smash. I wince now to think of what I imposed on David during those months we lived together, right after 9/11 and my separation from my husband. Imagine his surprise to discover that the happiest, most confident woman he'd ever met was actually—when you got her alone—a murky hole of bottomless grief. Once again, I could not stop crying. This is when he started to retreat, and that's when I saw the other side of my passionate romantic hero—the David who was solitary as a castaway, cool to the touch, in need of more personal space than a herd of American bison.

David's sudden emotional back-stepping probably would've been a catastrophe for me even under the best of circumstances, given that I am the planet's most affectionate life-form (something like a cross between a golden retriever and a barnacle), but this was my very worst of circumstances. I was despondent and dependent, needing more care than an armful of premature infant triplets. His withdrawal only made me more needy, and my neediness only advanced his withdrawals, until soon he was retreating under fire of my weeping pleas of, "Where are you *going*? What *happened* to us?"

(Dating tip: Men LOVE this.)

The fact is, I had become addicted to David (in my defense, he had fostered this, being something of a "man-*fatale*"), and now that his attention was wavering, I was suffering the easily foreseeable consequences. Addiction is the hallmark of every infatuation-based love story. It all begins when the object of your adoration bestows upon you a heady, hallucinogenic dose of something you never even dared to admit that you wanted—an emotional speedball, perhaps, of thunderous love and roiling excitement. Soon you start craving that intense attention, with the hungry obsession of any junkie. When the drug is withheld, you promptly turn sick, crazy and depleted (not to mention resentful of the dealer who encouraged this addiction in the first place but who now refuses to pony up the good stuff anymore—despite the fact that you *know* he has it hidden somewhere, goddamn it, because *he used to give it to you for free*). Next stage finds you skinny and shaking in a corner, certain only that you would sell your soul or rob your neighbors just to have *that thing* even one more time. Meanwhile, the object of your adoration has now become repulsed by you. He looks at you like you're someone he's never met before, much less someone he once loved with high passion. The irony is, you can hardly blame him. I mean, check yourself out. You're a pathetic mess, unrecognizable even to your own eyes.

So that's it. You have now reached infatuation's final destination —the complete and merciless devaluation of self.

The fact that I can even write calmly about this today is mighty evidence of time's healing powers, because I didn't take it well as it was happening. To be losing David right after the failure of my marriage, and right after the terrorizing of my city, and right during the worst ugliness of divorce (a life experience my friend Brian has compared to "having a really bad car accident every single day for about two years") . . . well, this was simply too much.

David and I continued to have our bouts of fun and compatibility during the days, but at night, in his bed, I became the only survivor of a nuclear winter as he *visibly* retreated from me, more every day, as though I were infectious. I came to fear nighttime like it was a torturer's cellar. I would lie there beside David's beautiful, inaccessible sleeping body and I would spin into a panic of loneliness and meticulously detailed suicidal thoughts. Every part of my body pained me. I felt like I was some kind of primitive spring-loaded machine, placed under far more tension than it had ever been built to sustain, about to blast apart at great danger to anyone standing nearby. I imagined my body parts flying off my torso in order to escape the volcanic core of unhappiness that had become: *me.* Most mornings, David would wake to find me sleeping fitfully on the floor beside his bed, huddled on a pile of bathroom towels, like a dog.

"What happened now?" he would ask—another man thoroughly exhausted by me.

I think I lost something like thirty pounds during that time.

6

Oh, but it wasn't *all* bad, those few years . . .

Because God never slams a door in your face without opening a box of Girl Scout cookies (or however the old adage goes), some wonderful things did happen to me in the shadow of all that sorrow. For one thing, I finally started learning Italian. Also, I found an Indian Guru. Lastly, I was invited by an elderly medicine man to come and live with him in Indonesia.

I'll explain in sequence.

To begin with, things started to look up somewhat when I moved out of David's place in early 2002 and found an apartment of my own for the first time in my life. I couldn't afford it, since I was still paying for that big house in the suburbs which nobody was living in anymore and which my husband was forbidding me to sell, and I was still trying to stay on top of all my legal and counseling fees . . . but it was vital to my survival to have a One Bedroom of my own. I saw the apartment almost as a sanatorium, a hospice clinic for my own recovery. I painted the walls in the warmest colors I could find and bought myself flowers every week, as if I were visiting myself in the hospital. My sister gave me a hot water bottle as a house-warming gift (so I wouldn't have to be all alone in a cold bed) and I slept with the thing laid against my heart every night, as though nursing a sports injury.

David and I had broken up for good. Or maybe we hadn't. It's hard to remember now how many times we broke up and joined up over those months. But there emerged a pattern: I would separate from David, get my strength and confidence back, and then (attracted as always by my strength and confidence) his passion for me would rekindle. Respectfully, soberly and intelligently, we would discuss "trying again," always with some sane new plan for minimizing our apparent incompatibilities. We were so committed to solving this thing. Because how could two people who were so in love *not* end up happily ever after? It *had* to work. Didn't it? Reunited with fresh hopes, we'd share a few deliriously happy days together. Or sometimes even weeks. But eventually David would retreat from me once more and I would cling to him (or I would cling to him and he would retreat—we never could figure out how it got triggered) and I'd end up destroyed all over again. And he'd end up gone.

David was catnip and kryptonite to me.

But during those periods when we *were* separated, as hard as it was, I was practicing living alone. And this experience was bringing a nascent interior shift. I was beginning to sense that—even though my life still looked like a multi-vehicle accident on the New Jersey Turnpike during holiday traffic—I was tottering on the brink of becoming a self-governing individual. When I wasn't feeling suicidal about my divorce, or suicidal about my drama with David, I was actually feeling kind of delighted about all the compartments of time and space that were appearing in my days, during which I could ask myself the radical new question: "What do *you* want to do, Liz?"

Most of the time (still so troubled from bailing out of my marriage) I didn't even dare to answer the question, but just thrilled privately to its existence. And when I finally started to answer, I did so cautiously. I would only allow myself to express little baby-step wants. Like:

I want to go to a Yoga class.

I want to leave this party early, so I can go home and read a novel.

I want to buy myself a new pencil box.

Then there would always be that one weird answer, same every time:

I want to learn how to speak Italian.

For years, I'd wished I could speak Italian—a language I find more beautiful than roses—but I could never make the practical justification for studying it. Why not just bone up on the French or Russian I'd already studied years ago? Or learn to speak Spanish, the better to help me communicate with millions of my fellow Americans? What was I going to do with *Italian*? It's not like I was going to *move* there. It would be more practical to learn how to play the accordion.

But why must everything always have a practical application? I'd been such a diligent soldier for years—working, producing, never missing a deadline, taking care of my loved ones, my gums and my credit record, voting, etc. Is this lifetime supposed to be only about duty? In this dark period of loss, did I need any justification for learning Italian other than that it was the only thing I could imagine bringing me any pleasure right now? And it wasn't that outrageous a goal, anyway, to want to study a language. It's not like I was saying, at age thirty-two, "I want to become the principal ballerina for the New York City Ballet." Studying a language is something you can actually *do*. So I signed up for classes at one of those continuing education places (otherwise known as Night School for Divorced Ladies). My friends thought this was hilarious. My friend Nick asked, "Why are you studying Italian? So that—just in case Italy ever invades Ethiopia again, and is actually successful this time—you can brag about knowing a language that's spoken in two whole countries?"

But I loved it. Every word was a singing sparrow, a magic trick, a truffle for me. I would slosh home through the rain after class, draw a hot bath, and lie there in the bubbles reading the Italian dictionary aloud to myself, taking my mind off my divorce pressures and my heartache. The words made me laugh in delight. I started referring to my cell phone as *il mio telefonino* ("my teensy little telephone"). I became one of those annoying people who always say *Ciao!* Only I was extra annoying, since I would always explain where the word *ciao* comes from. (If you must know, it's an abbreviation of a phrase used by medieval Venetians as an intimate salutation: *Sono il suo schiavo!* Meaning: "I am your slave!") Just speaking these words made me feel sexy and happy. My divorce lawyer told me not to worry; she said she had one client (Korean by heritage) who, after a yucky divorce, legally changed her name to something Italian, just to feel sexy and happy again.

Maybe I *would* move to Italy, after all . . .

7

The other notable thing that was happening during that time was the newfound adventure of spiritual discipline. Aided and abetted, of course, by the introduction into my life of an actual living Indian Guru—for whom I will always have David to thank. I'd been introduced to my Guru the first night I ever went to David's apartment. I kind of fell in love with them both at the same time. I walked into David's apartment and saw this picture on his dresser of a radiantly beautiful Indian woman and I asked, "Who's that?"

He said, "That is my spiritual teacher."

My heart skipped a beat and then flat-out tripped over itself and fell on its face. Then my heart stood up, brushed itself off, took a deep breath and announced: "I want a spiritual teacher." I literally mean that it was my *heart* who said this, speaking through my mouth. I felt this weird division in myself, and my mind stepped out of my body for a moment, spun around to face my heart in astonishment and silently asked, *"You DO?"*

"Yes," replied my heart. *"I do."*

Then my mind asked my heart, a tad sarcastically: *"Since WHEN?"*

But I already knew the answer: Since that night on the bathroom floor.

My God, but I wanted a spiritual teacher. I immediately began constructing a fantasy of what it would be like to have one. I imagined that this radiantly beautiful Indian woman would come to my apartment a few evenings a week and we would sit and drink tea and talk about divinity, and she would give me reading assignments and explain the significance of the strange sensations I was feeling during meditation . . .

All this fantasy was quickly swept away when David told me about the international status of this woman, about her tens of thousands of students—many of whom have never met her face-to-face. Still, he said, there was a gathering here in New York City every Tuesday night of the Guru's devotees who came together as a group to meditate and chant. David said, "If you're not too freaked out by the idea of being in a room with several hundred people chanting God's name in Sanskrit, you can come sometime."

I joined him the following Tuesday night. Far from being freaked out by these regular-looking people singing to God, I instead felt my soul rise diaphanous in the wake of that chanting. I walked home that night feeling like the air could move through me, like I was clean linen fluttering on a clothes-line, like New York itself had become a city made of rice paper—and I was light enough to run across every rooftop. I started going to the chants every Tuesday. Then I started meditating every morning on the ancient Sanskrit mantra the Guru gives to all her students (the regal *Om Namah Shivaya*, meaning, "I honor the divinity that resides within me"). Then I listened to the Guru speak in person for the first time, and her words gave me chill bumps over my whole body, even across the skin of my face. And when I heard she had an Ashram in India, I knew I must take myself there as quickly as possible.

8

In the meantime, though, I had to go on this trip to Indonesia.

Which happened, again, because of a magazine assignment. Just when I was feeling particularly sorry for myself for being broke and lonely and caged up in Divorce Internment Camp, an editor from a women's magazine asked if she could pay to send me to Bali to write a story about Yoga vacations. In return I asked her a series of questions, mostly along the line of *Is a bean green?* and *Does James Brown get down?* When I got to Bali (which is, to be brief, a very nice place) the teacher who was running the Yoga retreat asked us, "While you're all here, is there anybody who would like to go visit a ninth-generation Balinese medicine man?" (another question too obvious to even answer), and so we all went over to his house one night.

The medicine man, as it turned out, was a small, merry-eyed, russet-colored old guy with a mostly toothless mouth, whose resemblance in every way to the Star Wars character Yoda cannot be exaggerated. His name was Ketut Liyer. He spoke a scattered and thoroughly entertaining kind of English, but there was a translator available for when he got stuck on a word.

Our Yoga teacher had told us in advance that we could each bring one question or problem to the medicine man, and he would try to help us with our troubles. I'd been thinking for days of what to ask him. My initial ideas were so lame. *Will you make my husband give me a divorce? Will you make David be sexually attracted to me again?* I was rightly ashamed of myself for these thoughts: who travels all the way around the world to meet an ancient medicine man in Indonesia, only to ask him to intercede in *boy trouble*?

So when the old man asked me in person what I really wanted, I found other, truer words.

"I want to have a lasting experience of God," I told him. "Sometimes I feel like I understand the divinity of this world, but then I lose it because I get distracted by my petty desires and fears. I want to be with God all the time. But I don't want to be a monk, or totally give up worldly pleasures. I guess what I want to learn is how to live in this world and enjoy its delights, but also devote myself to God."

Ketut said he could answer my question with a picture. He showed me a sketch he'd drawn once during meditation. It was an androgynous human figure, standing up, hands clasped in prayer. But this figure had four legs, and no head. Where the head should have been, there was only a wild foliage of ferns and flowers. There was a small, smiling face drawn over the heart.

"To find the balance you want," Ketut spoke through his translator, "this is what you must become. You must keep your feet grounded so firmly on the earth that it's like you have four legs, instead of two. That way, you can stay in the world. But you must stop looking at the world through your head. You must look through your heart, instead. That way, you will know God."

Then he asked if he could read my palm. I gave him my left hand and he proceeded to put me together like a three-piece puzzle.

"You're a world traveler," he began.

Which I thought was maybe a little obvious, given that I was in Indonesia at the moment, but I didn't force the point . . .

"You have more good luck than anyone I've ever met. You will live a long time, have many friends, many experiences. You will see the whole world. You only have one problem in your life. You worry too much. Always you get too emotional, too nervous. If I promise you that you will never have any reason in your life to ever worry about anything, will you believe me?"

Nervously I nodded, not believing him.

"For work, you do something creative, maybe like an artist, and you get paid good money for it. Always you will get paid good money for this thing you do. You are generous with money, maybe too generous. Also one problem. You will lose all your money once in your life. I think maybe it will happen soon."

"I think maybe it will happen in the next six to ten months," I said, thinking about my divorce.

Ketut nodded as if to say, *Yeah, that sounds about right.* "But don't worry," he said. "After you lose all your money, you will get it all right back again. Right away you'll be fine. You will have two marriages in your life. One short, one long. And you will have two children . . ."

I waited for him to say, "one short, one long," but he was suddenly silent, frowning at my palm. Then he said, "Strange . . . ," which is something you never want to hear from either your palmreader or your dentist. He asked me to move directly under the hanging lightbulb so he could take a better look.

"I am wrong," he announced. "You will only have only one child. Late in life, a daughter. Maybe. If you decide . . . but there is something else." He frowned, then looked up, suddenly absolutely confident: "Someday soon you will come back here to Bali. You must. You will stay here in Bali for three, maybe four months. You will be my friend. Maybe you will live here with my family. I can practice English with you. I never had anybody to practice English with. I think you are good with words. I think this creative work you do is something about words, yes?"

"Yes!" I said. "I'm a writer. I'm a book writer!"

"You are a book writer from New York," he said, in agreement, in confirmation. "So you will come back here to Bali and live here and teach me English. And I will teach you everything I know."

Then he stood up and brushed off his hands, like: *That's settled.*

I said, "If you're serious, mister, I'm serious."

He beamed at me toothlessly and said, "See you later, alligator."

9

Now, I'm the kind of person who, when a ninth-generation Indonesian medicine man tells you that you're destined to move to Bali and live with him for four months, thinks you should make every effort to do that. And this, finally, was how my whole idea about this year of traveling began to gel. I absolutely needed to get myself back to Indonesia somehow, on my own dime this time. This was evident. Though I couldn't yet imagine how to do it, given my chaotic and disturbed life. (Not only did I still have a pricey divorce to settle, and David-troubles, I still had a magazine job that prevented me from going anywhere for three or four months at a time.) But I *had* to get back there. Didn't I? Hadn't he *foretold* it? Problem was, I also wanted to go to India, to visit my Guru's Ashram, and going to India is an expensive and time-consuming affair, also. To make matters even more confusing, I'd also been dying lately to get over to Italy, so I could practice speaking Italian in context, but also because I was drawn to the idea of living for a while in a culture where pleasure and beauty are revered.

All these desires seemed to be at odds with one another. Especially the Italy/India conflict. What was more important? The part of me that wanted to eat veal in Venice? Or the part of me that wanted to be waking up long before dawn in the austerity of an Ashram to begin a long day of meditation and prayer? The great Sufi poet and philosopher Rumi once advised his students to write down the three things they most wanted in life. If any item on the list clashes with any other item, Rumi warned, you are destined for unhappiness. Better to live a life of single-pointed focus, he taught. But what about the benefits of living harmoniously amid extremes? What if you could somehow create an expansive enough life that you could synchronize seemingly incongruous opposites into a worldview that excludes nothing? My truth was exactly what I'd said to the medicine man in Bali—I wanted to experience *both*. I wanted worldly enjoyment and divine transcendence—the dual glories of a human life. I wanted what the Greeks called *kalos kai agathos*, the singular balance of the good and the beautiful. I'd been missing both during these last hard years, because both pleasure and devotion require a stress-free space in which to flourish and I'd been living in a giant trash compactor of nonstop anxiety. As for how to balance the urge for pleasure against the longing for devotion . . . well, surely there was a way to learn that trick. And it seemed to me, just from my short stay in Bali, that I maybe could learn this from the Balinese. Maybe even from the medicine man himself.

Four feet on the ground, a head full of foliage, looking at the world through the heart . . .

So I stopped trying to choose—Italy? India? or Indonesia?—and eventually just admitted that I wanted to travel to all of them. Four months in each place. A year in total. Of course this was a slightly more ambitious dream than "I want to buy myself a new pencil box." But this is what I wanted. And I knew that I wanted to write about it. It wasn't so much that I wanted to thoroughly explore the countries themselves; this has been done. It was more that I wanted to thoroughly explore one aspect of myself set against the backdrop of each country, in a place that has traditionally done that one thing very well. I wanted to explore the art of pleasure in Italy, the art of devotion in India and, in Indonesia, the art of balancing the two. It was only later, after admitting this dream, that I noticed the happy coincidence that all these countries begin with the letter *I*. A fairly auspicious sign, it seemed, on a voyage of self-discovery.

Imagine now, if you will, all the opportunities for mockery this idea unleashed in my wise-ass friends. I wanted to go to the Three I's, did I? Then why not spend the year in Iran, Ivory Coast and Iceland? Or even better—why not go on pilgrimage to the Great Tri-State "I" Triumvirate of Islip, I-95 and Ikea? My friend Susan suggested that perhaps I should establish a not-for-profit relief organization called "Divorcées Without Borders." But all this joking was moot because "I" wasn't free to go anywhere yet. That divorce—long after I'd walked out of my marriage—was still not happening. I'd started having to put legal pressure on my husband, doing dreadful things out of my worst divorce nightmares, like serving papers and writing damning legal accusations (required by New York State law) of his alleged mental cruelty—documents that left no room for subtlety, no way in which to say to the judge: "Hey, listen, it was a really complicated relationship, and I made huge mistakes, too, and I'm very sorry about that, but all I want is to be allowed to leave."

(Here, I pause to offer a prayer for my gentle reader: May you never, ever, have to get a divorce in New York.)

The spring of 2003 brought things to a boiling point. A year and a half after I'd left, my husband was finally ready to discuss terms of a settlement. Yes, he wanted cash and the house and the lease on the Manhattan apartment—everything I'd been offering the whole while. But he was also asking for things I'd never even considered (a stake in the royalties of books I'd written during the marriage, a cut of possible future movie rights to my work, a share of my retirement accounts, etc.) and here I had to voice my protest at last. Months of negotiations ensued between our lawyers, a compromise of sorts inched its way toward the table and it was starting to look like my husband might actually accept a modified deal. It would cost me dearly, but a fight in the courts would be infinitely more expensive and time-consuming, not to mention soul-corroding. If he signed the agreement, all I had to do was pay and walk away. Which would be fine with me at this point. Our relationship now thoroughly ruined, with even civility destroyed between us, all I wanted anymore was the door.

The question was—would he sign? More weeks passed as he contested more details. If he didn't agree to this settlement, we'd have to go to trial. A trial would almost certainly mean that every remaining dime would be lost in legal fees. Worst of all, a trial would mean another year—at least—of all this mess. So whatever my husband decided (and he still *was* my husband, after all), it was going to determine yet another year of my life. Would I be traveling all alone through Italy, India and Indonesia? Or would I be getting cross-examined somewhere in a courtroom basement during a deposition hearing?

Every day I called my lawyer fourteen times—*any news?*—and every day she assured me that she was doing her best, that she would telephone immediately if the deal was signed. The nervousness I felt during this time was something between waiting to be called into the principal's office and anticipating the results of a biopsy. I'd love to report that I stayed calm and Zen, but I didn't. Several nights, in waves of anger, I beat the life out of my couch with a softball bat. Most of the time I was just achingly depressed.

Meanwhile, David and I had broken up again. This time, it seemed, for good. Or maybe not—we couldn't totally let go of it. Often I was still overcome with a desire to sacrifice everything for the love of him. Other times, I had the quite opposite instinct—to put as many continents and oceans as possible between me and this guy, in the hope of finding peace and happiness.

I had lines in my face now, permanent incisions dug between my eyebrows, from crying and from worry.

And in the middle of all *that*, a book that I'd written a few years earlier was being published in paperback and I had to go on a small publicity tour. I took my friend Iva with me for company. Iva is my age but grew up in Beirut, Lebanon. Which means that, while I was playing sports and auditioning for musicals in a Connecticut middle school, she was cowering in a bomb shelter five nights out of seven, trying not to die. I'm not sure how all this early exposure to violence created somebody who's so steady now, but Iva is one of the calmest souls I know. Moreover, she's got what I call "The Bat Phone to the Universe," some kind of Iva-only, open-round-the-clock special channel to the divine.

So we were driving across Kansas, and I was in my normal state of sweaty disarray over this divorce deal—*will he sign, will he not sign?*—and I said to Iva, "I don't think I can endure another year in court. I wish I could get some divine intervention here. I wish I could write a *petition* to God, asking for this thing to end."

"So why don't you?"

I explained to Iva my personal opinions about prayer. Namely, that I don't feel comfortable petitioning for specific things from God, because that feels to me like a kind of weakness of faith. I don't like asking, "Will you change this or that thing in my life that's difficult for me?" Because—who knows?—God might want me to be facing that particular challenge for a reason. Instead, I feel more comfortable praying for the courage to face whatever occurs in my life with equanimity, no matter how things turn out.

Iva listened politely, then asked, "Where'd you get that stupid idea?"

"What do you mean?"

"Where did you get the idea you aren't allowed to petition the universe with prayer? You are *part* of this universe, Liz. You're a constituent—you have every entitlement to participate in the actions of the universe, and to let your feelings be known. So put your opinion out there. Make your case. Believe me—it will at least be taken into consideration."

"Really?" All this was news to me.

"Really! Listen—if you *were* to write a petition to God right now, what would it say?"

I thought for a while, then pulled out a notebook and wrote this petition:

> *Dear God.*
>
> *Please intervene and help end this divorce. My husband and I have failed at our marriage and now we are failing at our divorce. This poisonous process is bringing suffering to us and to everyone who cares about us.*
>
> *I recognize that you are busy with wars and tragedies and much larger conflicts than the ongoing dispute of one dysfunctional couple. But it is my understanding that the health of the planet is affected by the health of every individual on it. As long as even two souls are locked in conflict, the whole of the world is contaminated by it. Similarly, if even one or two souls can be free from discord, this will increase the general health of the whole world, the way a few healthy cells in a body can increase the general health of that body.*
>
> *It is my most humble request, then, that you help us end this conflict, so that two more people can have the chance to become free and healthy, and so there will be just a little bit less animosity and bitterness in a world that is already far too troubled by suffering.*
>
> *I thank you for your kind attention.*
> *Respectfully,*
> *Elizabeth M. Gilbert*

I read it to Iva, and she nodded her approval.

"I would sign that," she said.

I handed the petition over to her with a pen, but she was too busy driving, so she said, "No, let's say that I *did* just sign it. I signed it in my heart."

"Thank you, Iva. I appreciate your support."

"Now, who else would sign it?" she asked.

"My family. My mother and father. My sister."

"OK," she said. "They just *did*. Consider their names added. I actually felt them sign it. They're on the list now. OK—who else would sign it? Start naming names."

So I started naming names of all the people who I thought would sign this petition. I named all my close friends, then some family members and some people I worked with. After each name, Iva would say with assurance, "Yep. He just signed it," or "She just signed it." Sometimes she would pop in with her own signatories, like: "My parents just signed it. They raised their children during a war. They hate useless conflict. They'd be happy to see your divorce end."

I closed my eyes and waited for more names to come to me.

"I think Bill and Hillary Clinton just signed it," I said.

"I don't doubt it," she said. "Listen, Liz—*anybody* can sign this petition. Do you understand that? Call on anyone, living or dead, and start collecting signatures."

"Saint Francis of Assisi just signed it!"

"Of *course* he did!" Iva smacked her hand against the steering wheel with certainty.

Now I was cooking:

"Abraham Lincoln just signed it! And Gandhi, and Mandela and all the peacemakers. Eleanor Roosevelt, Mother Teresa, Bono, Jimmy Carter, Muhammad Ali, Jackie Robinson and the Dalai Lama . . . and my grandmother who died in 1984 and my grandmother who's still alive . . . and my Italian teacher, and my therapist, and my agent . . . and Martin Luther King Jr. and Katharine Hepburn . . . and Martin Scorsese (which you wouldn't necessarily expect, but it's still nice of him) . . . and my Guru, of course . . . and Joanne Woodward, and Joan of Arc, and Ms. Carpenter, my fourth-grade teacher, and Jim Henson—"

The names spilled from me. They didn't stop spilling for almost an hour, as we drove across Kansas and my petition for peace stretched into page after invisible page of supporters. Iva kept confirming—*yes, he signed it, yes, she signed it*—and I became filled with a grand sense of protection, surrounded by the collective goodwill of so many mighty souls.

The list finally wound down, and my anxiety wound down with it. I was sleepy. Iva said, "Take a nap. I'll drive." I closed my eyes. One last name appeared. "Michael J. Fox just signed it," I murmured, then drifted into sleep. I don't know how long I slept, maybe only for ten minutes, but it was deep. When I woke up, Iva was still driving. She was humming a little song to herself. I yawned.

My cell phone rang.

I looked at that crazy little *telefonino* vibrating with excitement in the ashtray of the rental car. I felt disoriented, kind of stoned from my nap, suddenly unable to remember how a telephone works.

"Go ahead," Iva said, already knowing. "Answer the thing."

I picked up the phone, whispered hello.

"Great news!" my lawyer announced from distant New York City. "He just signed it!"

10

A few weeks later, I am living in Italy.

I have quit my job, paid off my divorce settlement and legal bills, given up my house, given up my apartment, put what belongings I had left into storage in my sister's place and packed up two suitcases. My year of traveling has commenced. And I can actually *afford* to do this because of a staggering personal miracle: in advance, my publisher has purchased the book I shall write about my travels. It all turned out, in other words, just as the Indonesian medicine man had predicted. I would lose all my money and it would be replaced immediately—or at least enough of it to buy me a year of life.

So now I am a resident of Rome. The apartment I've found is a quiet studio in a historic building, located just a few narrow blocks from the Spanish Steps, draped beneath the graceful shadows of the elegant Borghese Gardens, right up the street from the Piazza del Popolo, where the ancient Romans used to race their chariots. Of course, this district doesn't quite have the sprawling grandeur of my old New York City neighborhood, which overlooked the entrance to the Lincoln Tunnel, but still . . .

It will do.

11

The first meal I ate in Rome was nothing much. Just some home-made pasta (spaghetti carbonara) with a side order of sautéed spinach and garlic. (The great romantic poet Shelley once wrote a horrified letter to a friend in England about cuisine in Italy: "Young women of rank actually eat—you will never guess what—GARLIC!") Also, I had one artichoke, just to try it; the Romans are awfully proud of their artichokes. Then there was a pop-surprise bonus side order brought over by the waitress for free—a serving of fried zucchini blossoms with a soft dab of cheese in the middle (prepared so delicately that the blossoms probably didn't even notice they weren't on the vine anymore). After the spaghetti, I tried the veal. Oh, and also I drank a bottle of house red, just for me. And ate some warm bread, with olive oil and salt. Tiramisu for dessert.

Walking home after that meal, around 11:00 PM, I could hear noise coming from one of the buildings on my street, something that sounded like a convention of seven-year-olds—a birthday party, maybe? Laughter and screaming and running around. I climbed the stairs to my apartment, lay down in my new bed and turned off the light. I waited to start crying or worrying, since that's what usually happened to me with the lights off, but I actually felt OK. I felt fine. I felt the early symptoms of contentment.

My weary body asked my weary mind: "Was this all you needed, then?"

There was no response. I was already fast asleep.

12

In every major city in the Western World, some things are always the same. The same African men are always selling knockoffs of the same designer handbags and sunglasses, and the same Guatemalan musicians are always playing "I'd rather be a sparrow than a snail" on their bamboo windpipes. But some things are only in Rome. Like the sandwich counterman so comfortably calling me "beautiful" every time we speak. *You want this panino grilled or cold, bella*? Or the couples making out all over the place, like there is some contest for it, twisting into each other on benches, stroking each other's hair and crotches, nuzzling and grinding ceaselessly . . .

And then there are the fountains. Pliny the Elder wrote once: "If anyone will consider the abundance of Rome's public supply of water, for baths, cisterns, ditches, houses, gardens, villas; and take into account the distance over which it travels, the arches reared, the mountains pierced, the valleys spanned—he will admit that there never was anything more marvelous in the whole world."

A few centuries later, I already have a few contenders for my favorite fountain in Rome. One is in the Villa Borghese. In the center of this fountain is a frolicking bronze family. Dad is a faun and Mom is a regular human woman. They have a baby who enjoys eating grapes. Mom and Dad are in a strange position—facing each other, grabbing each other's wrists, both of them leaning back. It's hard to tell whether they are yanking against each other in strife or swinging around merrily, but there's lots of energy there. Either way, Junior sits perched atop their wrists, right between them, unaffected by their merriment or strife, munching on his bunch of grapes. His little cloven hoofs dangle below him as he eats. (He takes after his father.)

It is early September, 2003. The weather is warm and lazy. By this, my fourth day in Rome, my shadow has still not darkened the doorway of a church or a museum, nor have I even looked at a guidebook. But I have been walking endlessly and aimlessly, and I did finally find a tiny little place that a friendly bus driver informed me sells The Best Gelato in Rome. It's called "Il Gelato di San

Crispino." I'm not sure, but I think this might translate as "the ice cream of the crispy saint." I tried a combination of the honey and the hazelnut. I came back later that same day for the grapefruit and the melon. Then, after dinner that same night, I walked all the way back over there one last time, just to sample a cup of the cinnamon-ginger.

I've been trying to read through one newspaper article every day, no matter how long it takes. I look up approximately every third word in my dictionary. Today's news was fascinating. Hard to imagine a more dramatic headline than *"Obesità! I Bambini Italiani Sono i Più Grassi d'Europa!"* Good God! Obesity! The article, I think, is declaring that Italian babies are the fattest babies in Europe! Reading on, I learn that Italian babies are significantly fatter than German babies and very significantly fatter than French babies. (Mercifully, there was no mention of how they measure up against American babies.) Older Italian children are dangerously obese these days, too, says the article. (The pasta industry defended itself.) These alarming statistics on Italian child fatness were unveiled yesterday by—no need to translate here—*"una task force internazionale."* It took me almost an hour to decipher this whole article. The entire time, I was eating a pizza and listening to one of Italy's children play the accordion across the street. The kid didn't look very fat to me, but that may have been because he was a gypsy. I'm not sure if I misread the last line of the article, but it seemed there was some talk from the government that the only way to deal with the obesity crisis in Italy was to implement a tax on the over-weight . . . ? Could this be true? After a few months of eating like this, will they come after me?

It's also important to read the newspaper every day to see how the pope is doing. Here in Rome, the pope's health is recorded daily in the newspaper, very much like weather, or the TV schedule. Today the pope is tired. Yesterday, the pope was less tired than he is today. Tomorrow, we expect that the pope will not be quite so tired as he was today.

It's kind of a fairyland of language for me here. For someone who has always wanted to speak Italian, what could be better than Rome? It's like somebody invented a city just to suit my specifications, where everyone (even the children, even the taxi drivers, even the actors on the commercials!) speaks this magical language. It's like the whole society is conspiring to teach me Italian. They'll even print their newspapers in Italian while I'm here; they don't mind! They have bookstores here that *only sell books written in Italian*! I found such a bookstore yesterday morning and felt I'd entered an enchanted palace. Everything was in Italian—even Dr. Seuss. I wandered through, touching all the books, hoping that anyone watching me might think I was a native speaker. Oh, how I want Italian to open itself up to me! This feeling reminded me of when I was four years old and couldn't read yet, but was dying to learn. I remember sitting in the waiting room of a doctor's office with my mother, holding a *Good Housekeeping* magazine in front of my face, turning the pages slowly, staring at the text, and hoping the grown-ups in the waiting room would think I was actually reading. I haven't felt so starved for comprehension since then. I found some works by American poets in that bookstore, with the original English version printed on one side of the page and the Italian translation on the other. I bought a volume by Robert Lowell, another by Louise Glück.

There are spontaneous conversation classes everywhere. Today, I was sitting on a park bench when a tiny old woman in a black dress came over, roosted down beside me and started bossing me around about something. I shook my head, muted and confused. I apologized, saying in very nice Italian, "I'm sorry, but I don't speak Italian," and she looked like she would've smacked me with a wooden spoon, if she'd had one. She insisted: "You do understand!" (Interestingly, she was correct. That sentence, I *did* understand.) Now she wanted to know where I was from. I told her I was from New York, and asked where she was from. Duh—she was from Rome. Hearing this, I clapped my hands like a baby. *Ah, Rome! Beautiful Rome! I love Rome! Pretty Rome!* She listened to my primitive rhapsodies with skepticism. Then she got down to it and asked me if I was married. I told her I was divorced. This was the first time I'd said it to anyone, and here I was, saying it in Italian. Of course she demanded, *"Perché?"* Well ... "why" is a hard question to answer in any language. I stammered, then finally came up with *"L'abbiamo rotto"* (We broke it).

She nodded, stood up, walked up the street to her bus stop, got on her bus and did not even turn around to look at me again. Was she mad at me? Strangely, I waited for her on that park bench for twenty minutes, thinking against reason that she might come back and continue our conversation, but she never returned. Her name was Celeste, pronounced with a sharp *ch,* as in *cello.*

Later in the day, I found a library. Dear me, how I love a library. Because we are in Rome, this library is a beautiful old thing, and within it there is a courtyard garden which you'd never have guessed existed if you'd only looked at the place from the street. The garden is a perfect square, dotted with orange trees and, in the center, a fountain. This fountain was going to be a contender for my favorite in Rome, I could tell immediately, though it was unlike any I'd seen so far. It was not carved of imperial marble, for starters. This was a small green, mossy, organic fountain. It was like a shaggy, leaking bush of ferns. (It looked, actually, exactly like the wild foliage growing out of the head of that praying figure which the old medicine man in Indonesia had drawn for me.) The water shot up out of the center of this flowering shrub, then rained back down on the leaves, making a melancholy, lovely sound throughout the whole courtyard.

I found a seat under an orange tree and opened one of the poetry books I'd purchased yesterday. Louise Glück. I read the first poem in Italian, then in English, and stopped short at this line:

Dal centro della mia vita venne una grande fontana . . .

"From the center of my life, there came a great fountain . . ."

I set the book down in my lap, shaking with relief.

13

Truthfully, I'm not the best traveler in the world.

I know this because I've traveled a lot and I've met people who are great at it. Real naturals. I've met travelers who are so physically sturdy they could drink a shoebox of water from a Calcutta gutter and never get sick. People who can pick up new languages where others of us might only pick up infectious diseases. People who know how to stand down a threatening border guard or cajole an uncooperative bureaucrat at the visa office. People who are the right height and complexion that they kind of look halfway normal wherever they go—in Turkey they just might be Turks, in Mexico they are suddenly Mexican, in Spain they could be mistaken for a Basque, in Northern Africa they can sometimes pass for Arab . . .

I don't have these qualities. First off, I don't blend. Tall and blond and pink-complexioned, I am less a chameleon than a flamingo. Everywhere I go but Dusseldorf, I stand out garishly. When I was in China, women used to come up to me on the street and point me out to their children as though I were some escaped zoo animal. And their children—who had never seen anything quite like this pink-faced yellow-headed phantom person—would often burst into tears at the sight of me. I really hated that about China.

I'm bad (or, rather, lazy) at researching a place before I travel, tending just to show up and see what happens. When you travel this way, what typically "happens" is that you end up spending a lot of time standing in the middle of the train station feeling confused, or dropping way too much money on hotels because you don't know better. My shaky sense of direction and geography means I have explored six continents in my life with only the vaguest idea of where I am at any given time. Aside from my cockeyed internal compass, I also have a shortage of personal coolness, which can be a liability in travel. I have never learned how to arrange my face into that blank expression of competent invisibility that is so useful when traveling in dangerous, foreign places. You know—that super-relaxed, totally-in-charge expression which makes you look like you belong there, anywhere, everywhere, even in the middle of a riot in Jakarta. Oh, no. When I don't know what I'm doing, I look like I don't know what I'm doing. When I'm excited or nervous, I look excited or nervous. And when I am lost, which is frequently, I look lost. My face is a transparent transmitter of my every thought. As David once put it, "You have the opposite of poker face. You have, like . . . miniature golf face."

And, oh, the woes that traveling has inflicted on my digestive tract! I don't really want to open that (forgive the expression) *can of worms*, but suffice it to say I've experienced every extreme of digestive emergency. In Lebanon I became so explosively ill one night that I could only imagine I'd somehow contracted a Middle Eastern version of the Ebola virus. In Hungary, I suffered from an entirely different kind of bowel affliction, which changed forever the way I feel about the term "Soviet Bloc." But I have other bodily weaknesses, too. My back gave out on my first day traveling in Africa, I was the only member of my party to emerge from the jungles of Venezuela with infected spider bites, and I ask you—I beg of you!— who gets sunburned in *Stockholm*?

Still, despite all this, traveling is the great true love of my life. I have always felt, ever since I was sixteen years old and first went to Russia with my saved-up babysitting money, that to travel is worth any cost or sacrifice. I am loyal and constant in my love for travel, as I have not always been loyal and constant in my other loves. I feel about travel the way a happy new mother feels about her impossible, colicky, restless newborn baby—I just don't *care* what it puts me through. Because I adore it. Because it's mine. Because it looks exactly like me. It can barf all over me if it wants to I just don't care.

Anyway, for a flamingo, I'm not completely helpless out there in the world. I have my own set of survival techniques. I am patient. I know how to pack light. I'm a fearless eater. But my one mighty travel talent is that I can make friends with *anybody*. I can make friends with the dead. I once made friends with a war criminal in Serbia, and he invited me to go on a mountain holiday with his family. Not that I'm proud to list Serbian mass murderers amongst my nearest and dearest (I had to befriend him for a story, and also so he wouldn't punch me), but I'm just saying—I can do it. If there isn't anyone else around to talk to, I could probably make friends with a four-foot-tall pile of Sheetrock. This is why I'm not afraid to travel to the most remote places in the world, not if there are human beings there to meet. People asked me before I left for Italy, "Do you have friends in Rome?" and I would just shake my head no, thinking to myself, *But I will.*

Mostly, you meet your friends when traveling by accident, like by sitting next to them on a train, or in a restaurant, or in a holding cell.

But these are chance encounters, and you should never rely entirely on chance. For a more systematic approach, there is still the grand old system of the "letter of introduction" (today more likely to be an e-mail), presenting you formally to the acquaintance of an acquaintance. This is a terrific way to meet people, if you're shameless enough to make the cold call and invite yourself over for dinner. So before I left for Italy, I asked everyone I knew in America if *they* had any friends in Rome, and I'm happy to report that I have been sent abroad with a substantial list of Italian contacts.

Among all the nominees on my Potential New Italian Friends List, I am most intrigued to meet a fellow named . . . brace yourself . . . Luca Spaghetti. Luca Spaghetti is a good friend of my buddy Patrick McDevitt, whom I know from my college days. And that is honestly his name, I swear to God, I'm not making it up. It's too crazy. I mean—just think of it. Imagine going through life with a name like *Patrick McDevitt*?

Anyhow, I plan to get in touch with Luca Spaghetti just as soon as possible.

14

First, though, I must get settled into school. My classes begin today at the Leonardo da Vinci Academy of Language Studies, where I will be studying Italian five days a week, four hours a day. I'm so excited about school. I'm such a shameless *student*. I laid my clothes out last night, just like I did before my first day of first grade, with my patent leather shoes and my new lunch box. I hope the teacher will like me.

We all have to take a test on the first day at Leonardo da Vinci, in order to be placed in the proper level of Italian class for our abilities. When I hear this, I immediately start hoping I don't place into a Level One class, because that would be humiliating, given that I already took a whole entire semester of Italian at my Night School for Divorced Ladies in New York, and that I spent the summer memorizing flash cards, and that I've already been in

Rome a week, and have been practicing the language in person, even conversing with old grandmothers about divorce. The thing is, I don't even know how many levels this school has, but as soon as I heard the word *level*, I decided that I must test into Level Two—at *least*.

So it's hammering down rain today, and I show up to school early (like I always have—*geek!*) and I take the test. It's such a hard test! I can't get through even a tenth of it! I know so much Italian, I know *dozens* of words in Italian, but they don't ask me anything that I know. Then there's an oral exam, which is even worse. There's this skinny Italian teacher interviewing me and speaking way too fast, in my opinion, and I should be doing so much better than this but I'm nervous and making mistakes with stuff I already know (like, why did I say *Vado a scuola* instead of *Sono andata a scuola*? I know that!).

In the end, it's OK, though. The skinny Italian teacher looks over my exam and selects my class level:

Level TWO!

Classes begin in the afternoon. So I go eat lunch (roasted endive) then saunter back to the school and smugly walk past all those Level One students (who must be *molto stupido*, really) and enter my first class. With my peers. Except that it becomes swiftly evident that these are not my peers and that I have no business being here because Level Two is really impossibly *hard*. I feel like I'm swimming, but barely. Like I'm taking in water with every breath. The teacher, a skinny guy (why are the teachers so skinny here? I don't trust skinny Italians), is going way too fast, skipping over whole chapters of the textbook, saying, "You already know this, you already know that . . ." and keeping up a rapid-fire conversation with my apparently fluent classmates. My stomach is gripped in horror and I'm gasping for air and praying he won't call on me. Just as soon as the break comes, I run out of that classroom on wobbling legs and I scurry all the way over to the administrative office almost in tears, where I beg in very clear English if they could please move me down to a Level One class. And so they do. And now I am here.

This teacher is plump and speaks slowly. This is much better.

15

The interesting thing about my Italian class is that nobody really needs to be there. There are twelve of us studying together, of all ages, from all over the world, and everybody has come to Rome for the same reason—to study Italian just because they feel like it. Not one of us can identify a single practical reason for being here. Nobody's boss has said to anyone, "It is vital that you learn to speak Italian in order for us to conduct our business overseas." Everybody, even the uptight German engineer, shares what I thought was my own personal motive: we all want to speak Italian because we love the way it makes us feel. A sad-faced Russian woman tells us she's treating herself to Italian lessons because "I think I deserve something beautiful." The German engineer says, "I want Italian because I love the *dolce vita*"—the sweet life. (Only, in his stiff Germanic accent, it ends up sounding like he said he loved "the *deutsche vita*"— the German life—which I'm afraid he's already had plenty of.)

As I will find out over the next few months, there are actually some good reasons that Italian is the most seductively beautiful language in the world, and why I'm not the only person who thinks so. To understand why, you have to first understand that Europe was once a pandemonium of numberless Latin-derived dialects that gradually, over the centuries, morphed into a few separate languages—French, Portuguese, Spanish, Italian. What happened in France, Portugal and Spain was an organic evolution: the dialect of the most prominent city gradually became the accepted language of the whole region. Therefore, what we today call French is really a version of medieval Parisian. Portuguese is really Lisboan. Spanish is essentially Madrileño. These were capitalist victories; the strongest city ultimately determined the language of the whole country.

Italy was different. One critical difference was that, for the longest time, Italy wasn't even a country. It didn't get itself unified until quite late in life (1861) and until then was a peninsula of warring city-states dominated by proud local princes or other European powers. Parts of Italy belonged to France, parts to Spain, parts to the Church, parts to whoever could grab the local fortress or palace. The Italian people were alternatively humiliated and cavalier about all this domination. Most didn't much like being colonized by their fellow Europeans, but there was always that apathetic crowd that said, *"Franza o Spagna, purchè se magna,"* which means, in dialect, "France or Spain, as long as I can eat."

All this internal division meant that Italy never properly coalesced, and Italian didn't either. So it's not surprising that, for centuries, Italians wrote and spoke in local dialects that were mutually unfathomable. A scientist in Florence could barely communicate with a poet in Sicily or a merchant in Venice (except in Latin, of course, which was hardly considered the national language). In the sixteenth century, some Italian intellectuals got together and decided that this was absurd. This Italian peninsula needed an *Italian* language, at least in the written form, which everyone could agree upon. So this gathering of intellectuals proceeded to do something unprecedented in the history of Europe; they handpicked the most beautiful of all the local dialects and crowned it *Italian.*

In order to find the most beautiful dialect ever spoken in Italy, they had to reach back in time two hundred years to fourteenth-century Florence. What this congress decided would henceforth be considered proper Italian was the personal language of the great Florentine poet Dante Alighieri. When Dante published his *Divine Comedy* back in 1321, detailing a visionary progression through Hell, Purgatory and Heaven, he'd shocked the literate world by not writing in Latin. He felt that Latin was a corrupted, elitist language, and that the use of it in serious prose had "turned literature into a harlot" by making universal narrative into something that could only be bought with money, through the privilege of an aristocratic education. Instead, Dante turned back to the streets, picking up the real Florentine language spoken by the residents of his city (who included such luminous contemporaries as Boccaccio and Petrarch) and using that language to tell his tale.

He wrote his masterpiece in what he called *dolce stil nuovo*, the "sweet new style" of the vernacular, and he shaped that vernacular even as he was writing it, affecting it as personally as Shakespeare would someday affect Elizabethan English. For a group of nationalist intellectuals much later in history to have sat down and decided that Dante's Italian would now be the official language of Italy would be very much as if a group of Oxford dons had sat down one day in the early nineteenth century and decided that—from this point forward—everybody in England was going to speak pure Shakespeare. And it actually *worked*.

The Italian we speak today, therefore, is not Roman or Venetian (though these were the powerful military and merchant cities) nor even really entirely Florentine. Essentially, it is *Dantean*. No other European language has such an artistic pedigree. And perhaps no language was ever more perfectly ordained to express human emotions than this fourteenth-century Florentine Italian, as embellished by one of Western civilization's greatest poets. Dante wrote his *Divine Comedy* in *terza rima*, triple rhyme, a chain of rhymes with each rhyme repeating three times every five lines, giving his pretty Florentine vernacular what scholars call "a cascading rhythm"—a rhythm which still lives in the tumbling, poetic cadences spoken by Italian cabdrivers and butchers and government administrators even today. The last line of the *Divine Comedy*, in which Dante is faced with the vision of God Himself, is a sentiment that is still easily understandable by anyone familiar with so-called modern Italian. Dante writes that God is not merely a blinding vision of glorious light, but that He is, most of all, *l'amor che move il sole e l'altre stelle . . .*

"The love that moves the sun and the other stars."

So it's really no wonder that I want so desperately to learn this language.

16

Depression and Loneliness track me down after about ten days in Italy. I am walking through the Villa Borghese one evening after a happy day spent in school, and the sun is setting gold over St. Peter's Basilica. I am feeling contented in this romantic scene, even if I am all by myself, while everyone else in the park is either fondling a lover or playing with a laughing child. But I stop to lean against a balustrade and watch the sunset, and I get to thinking a little too much, and then my thinking turns to brooding, and that's when they catch up with me.

They come upon me all silent and menacing like Pinkerton Detectives, and they flank me—Depression on my left, Loneliness on my right. They don't need to show me their badges. I know these guys very well. We've been playing a cat-and-mouse game for years now. Though I admit that I am surprised to meet them in this elegant Italian garden at dusk. This is no place they belong.

I say to them, "How did you find me here? Who told you I had come to Rome?"

Depression, always the wise guy, says, "What—you're not happy to see us?"

"Go away," I tell him.

Loneliness, the more sensitive cop, says, "I'm sorry, ma'am. But I might have to tail you the whole time you're traveling. It's my assignment."

"I'd really rather you didn't," I tell him, and he shrugs almost apologetically, but only moves closer.

Then they frisk me. They empty my pockets of any joy I had been carrying there. Depression even confiscates my identity; but he always does that. Then Loneliness starts interrogating me, which I dread because it always goes on for hours. He's polite but relentless, and he always trips me up eventually. He asks if I have any reason to be happy that I know of. He asks why I am all by myself tonight, yet again. He asks (though we've been through this line of questioning hundreds of times already) why I can't keep a relationship going, why I ruined my marriage, why I messed things up with David, why I messed things up with every man I've ever been with. He asks me where I was the night I turned thirty, and why things have gone so sour since then. He asks why I can't get my act together, and why I'm not at home living in a nice house and raising nice children like any respectable woman my age should be. He asks why, exactly, I think I deserve a vacation in Rome when I've made such a rubble of my life. He asks me why I think that running away to Italy like a college kid will make me happy. He asks where I think I'll end up in my old age, if I keep living this way.

I walk back home, hoping to shake them, but they keep following me, these two goons. Depression has a firm hand on my shoulder and Loneliness harangues me with his interrogation. I don't even bother eating dinner; I don't want them watching me. I don't want to let them up the stairs to my apartment, either, but I know Depression, and he's got a billy club, so there's no stopping him from coming in if he decides that he wants to.

"It's not fair for you to come here," I tell Depression. "I paid you off already. I served my time back in New York."

But he just gives me that dark smile, settles into my favorite chair, puts his feet on my table and lights a cigar, filling the place with his awful smoke. Loneliness watches and sighs, then climbs into my bed and pulls the covers over himself, fully dressed, shoes and all. He's going to make me sleep with him again tonight, I just know it.

17

I'd stopped taking my medication only a few days earlier. It had just seemed *crazy* to be taking antidepressants in Italy. How could I be depressed here?

I'd never wanted to be on the medication in the first place. I'd fought taking it for so long, mainly because of a long list of personal objections (e.g.: Americans are overmedicated; we don't know the long-term effects of this stuff yet on the human brain; it's a crime that even American children are on antidepressants these days; we are treating the symptoms and not the causes of a national mental health emergency . . .). Still, during the last few years of my life, there was no question that I was in grave trouble and that this trouble was not lifting quickly. As my marriage dissolved and my drama with David evolved, I'd come to have all the symptoms of a major depression—loss of sleep, appetite and libido, uncontrollable weeping, chronic backaches and stomachaches, alienation and despair, trouble concentrating on work, inability to even get upset that the Republicans had just stolen a presidential election . . . it went on and on.

When you're lost in those woods, it sometimes takes you a while to realize that you *are* lost. For the longest time, you can convince yourself that you've just wandered a few feet off the path, that you'll find your way back to the trailhead any moment now. Then night falls again and again, and you still have no idea where you are, and it's time to admit that you have bewildered yourself so far off the path that you don't even know from which direction the sun rises anymore.

I took on my depression like it was the fight of my life, which, of course, it was. I became a student of my own depressed experience, trying to unthread its causes. What was the root of all this despair? Was it psychological? (Mom and Dad's fault?) Was it just temporal, a "bad time" in my life? (When the divorce ends, will the depression end with it?) Was it genetic? (Melancholy, called by many names, has run through my family for generations, along with its sad bride, Alcoholism.) Was it cultural? (Is this just the fallout of a post-feminist American career girl trying to find balance in an increasingly stressful and alienating urban world?) Was it astrological? (Am I so sad because I'm a thin-skinned Cancer whose major signs are all ruled by unstable Gemini?) Was it artistic? (Don't creative people always suffer from depression because we're so supersensitive and *special* ?) Was it evolutionary? (Do I carry in me the residual panic that comes after millennia of my species' attempting to survive a brutal world?) Was it karmic? (Are all these spasms of grief just the consequences of bad behavior in previous lifetimes, the last obstacles before liberation?) Was it hormonal? Dietary? Philosophical? Seasonal? Environmental? Was I tapping into a universal yearning for God? Did I have a chemical imbalance? Or did I just need to get laid?

What a large number of factors constitute a single human being! How very many layers we operate on, and how very many influences we receive from our minds, our bodies, our histories, our families, our cities, our souls and our lunches! I came to feel that my depression was probably some ever-shifting assortment of all those factors, and probably also included some stuff I couldn't name or claim. So I faced the fight at every level. I bought all those embarrassingly titled self-help books (always being certain to wrap up the books in the latest issue of *Hustler*, so that strangers wouldn't know what I was really reading). I commenced to getting professional help with a therapist who was as kind as she was insightful. I prayed liked a novice nun. I stopped eating meat (for a short time, anyway) after someone told me that I was "eating the fear of the animal at the moment of its death." Some spacey new age massage therapist told me I should wear orange-colored panties, to rebalance my sexual chakras, and, brother—I actually did it. I drank enough of that damn Saint-John's-wort tea to cheer up whole a Russian gulag, to no noticeable effect. I exercised. I exposed myself to the uplifting arts and carefully protected myself from sad movies, books and songs (if anyone even mentioned the words *Leonard* and *Cohen* in the same sentence, I would have to leave the room).

I tried so hard to fight the endless sobbing. I remember asking myself one night, while I was curled up in the same old corner of my same old couch in tears yet again over the same old repetition of sorrowful thoughts, "Is there *anything* about this scene you can change, Liz?" And all I could think to do was stand up, while still sobbing, and try to balance on one foot in the middle of my living room. Just to prove that—while I couldn't stop the tears or change my dismal interior dialogue—I was not yet totally out of control: at least I could cry hysterically while balanced on one foot. Hey, it was a start.

I crossed the street to walk in the sunshine. I leaned on my support network, cherishing my family and cultivating my most enlightening friendships. And when those officious women's magazines kept telling me that my low self-esteem wasn't helping depression matters at all, I got myself a pretty haircut, bought some fancy makeup and a nice dress. (When a friend complimented my new look, all I could say, grimly, was, "Operation Self-Esteem—Day Fucking One.")

The last thing I tried, after about two years of fighting this sorrow, was medication. If I may impose my opinions here, I think it should always be the last thing you try. For me, the decision to go the route of "Vitamin P" happened after a night when I'd sat on the floor of my bedroom for many hours, trying very hard to talk myself out of cutting into my arm with a kitchen knife. I won the argument against the knife that night, but barely. I had some other good ideas around that time—about how jumping off a building or blowing my brains out with a gun might stop the suffering. But something about spending a night with a knife in my hand did it.

The next morning I called my friend Susan as the sun came up, begged her to help me. I don't think a woman in the whole history of my family had ever done that before, had ever sat down in the middle of the road like that and said, in the middle of her life, "I cannot walk another step further—somebody has to help me." It wouldn't have served those women to have stopped walking. Nobody would have, or could have, helped them. The only thing that would've happened was that they and their families would have starved. I couldn't stop thinking about those women.

And I will never forget Susan's face when she rushed into my apartment about an hour after my emergency phone call and saw me in a heap on the couch. The image of my pain mirrored back at me through her visible fear for my life is still one of the scariest memories for me out of all those scary years. I huddled in a ball while Susan made the phone calls and found me a psychiatrist who would give me a consultation that very day, to discuss the possibility of prescribing antidepressants. I listened to Susan's one-sided conversation with the doctor, listened to her say, "I'm afraid my friend is going to seriously hurt herself." I was afraid, too.

When I went to see the psychiatrist that afternoon, he asked me what had taken me so long to get help—as if I hadn't been trying to help myself already for so long. I told him my objections and reservations about antidepressants. I laid copies of the three books I'd already published on his desk, and I said, "I'm a writer. Please don't do anything to harm my brain." He said, "If you had a kidney disease, you wouldn't hesitate to take medication for it—why are you hesitating with this?" But, see, that only shows how ignorant he was about my family; a Gilbert might very well *not* medicate a kidney disease, seeing that we're a family who regard any sickness as a sign of personal, ethical, moral failure.

He put me on a few different drugs—Xanax, Zoloft, Wellbutrin, Busperin—until we found the combination that didn't make me nauseated or turn my libido into a dim and distant memory. Quickly, in less than a week, I could feel an extra inch of daylight opening in my mind. Also, I could finally sleep. And this was the real gift, because when you cannot sleep, you cannot get yourself out of the ditch—there's not a chance. The pills gave me those recuperative night hours back, and also stopped my hands from shaking and released the vise grip around my chest and the panic alert button from inside my heart.

Still, I never relaxed into taking those drugs, though they helped immediately. It never mattered who told me these medications were a good idea and perfectly safe; I always felt conflicted about it. Those drugs were part of my bridge to the other side, there's no question about it, but I wanted to be off them as soon as possible. I'd started taking the medication in January of 2003. By May, I was already diminishing my dosage significantly. Those had been the toughest months, anyhow—the last months of the divorce, the last ragged months with David. Could I have endured that time without the drugs, if I'd just held out a little longer? Could I have survived myself, by myself? I don't know. That's the thing about a human life—there's no control group, no way to ever know how any of us would have turned out if any variables had been changed.

I do know these drugs made my misery feel less catastrophic. So I'm grateful for that. But I'm still deeply ambivalent about mood-altering medications. I'm awed by their power, but concerned by their prevalence. I think they need to be prescribed and used with much more restraint in this country, and never without the parallel treatment of psychological counseling. Medicating the symptom of any illness without exploring its root cause is just a classically hare-brained Western way to think that anyone could ever get truly better. Those pills might have saved my life, but they did so only in conjunction with about twenty other efforts I was making simulta-neously during that same period to rescue myself, and I hope to never have to take such drugs again. Though one doctor did suggest that I might have to go on and off antidepressants many times in my life because of my "tendency toward melancholy." I hope to God he's wrong. I intend to do everything I can to prove him wrong, or at least to fight that melancholic tendency with every tool in the shed. Whether this makes me self-defeatingly stubborn, or self-preservingly stubborn, I cannot say.

But there I am.

18

Or, rather—here I am. I am in Rome, and I am in trouble. The goons of Depression and Loneliness have barged into my life again, and I just took my last Wellbutrin three days ago. There are more pills in my bottom drawer, but I don't want them. I want to be free of them forever. But I don't want Depression or Loneliness around, either, so I don't know what to do, and I'm spiraling in panic, like I always spiral when I don't know what to do. So what I do for tonight is reach for my most private notebook, which I keep next to my bed in case I'm ever in emergency trouble. I open it up. I find the first blank page. I write:

"I need your help."

Then I wait. After a little while, a response comes, in my own handwriting:

I'm right here. What can I do for you?

And here recommences my strangest and most secret conversation. Here, in this most private notebook, is where I talk to myself. I talk to that same voice I met that night on my bathroom floor when I first prayed to God in tears for help, when something (or somebody) had said, "Go back to bed, Liz." In the years since then, I've found that voice again in times of code-orange distress, and have learned that the best way for me to reach it is written conversation. I've been surprised to find that I can almost always access that voice, too, no matter how black my anguish may be. Even during the worst of suffering, that calm, compassionate, affectionate and infinitely wise voice (who is maybe me, or maybe not exactly me) is always available for a conversation on paper at any time of day or night.

I've decided to let myself off the hook from worrying that conversing with myself on paper means I'm a schizo. Maybe the voice I am reaching for is God, or maybe it's my Guru speaking through me, or maybe it's the angel who was assigned to my case, or maybe it's my Highest Self, or maybe it is indeed just a construct of my subconscious, invented in order to protect me from my own torment. Saint Teresa called such divine internal voices "locutions"—words from the supernatural that enter the mind spontaneously, translated into your own language and offering you heavenly consolation. I do know what Freud would have said about such spiritual consolations, of course—that they are irrational and "deserve no trust. Experience teaches us that the world is no nursery." I agree—the world isn't a nursery. But the very fact that this world is so challenging is exactly *why* you sometimes must reach out of its jurisdiction for help, appealing to a higher authority in order to find your comfort.

At the beginning of my spiritual experiment, I didn't always have such faith in this internal voice of wisdom. I remember once reaching for my private notebook in a bitter fury of rage and sorrow, and scrawling a message to my inner voice—to my divine interior comfort—that took up an entire page of capital letters:

"I DO NOT FUCKING BELIEVE IN YOU!!!!!!!!"

After a moment, still breathing heavily, I felt a clear pinpoint of light ignite within me, and then I found myself writing this amused and ever-calm reply:

Who are you talking to, then?

I haven't doubted its existence again since. So tonight I reach for that voice again. This is the first time I've done this since I came to Italy. What I write in my journal tonight is that I am weak and full of fear. I explain that Depression and Loneliness have shown up, and I'm scared they will never leave. I say that I don't want to take the drugs anymore, but I'm frightened I will have to. I'm terrified that I will never really pull my life together.

In response, somewhere from within me, rises a now-familiar presence, offering me all the certainties I have always wished another person would say to me when I was troubled. This is what I find myself writing to myself on the page:

I'm here. I love you. I don't care if you need to stay up crying all night long, I will stay with you. If you need the medication again, go ahead and take it—I will love you through that, as well. If you don't need the medication, I will love you, too. There's nothing you can ever do to lose my love. I will protect you until you die, and after your death I will <u>still</u> protect you. I am stronger than Depression and I am braver than Loneliness and nothing will ever exhaust me.

Tonight, this strange interior gesture of friendship—the lending of a hand from me to myself when nobody else is around to offer solace—reminds me of something that happened to me once in New York City. I walked into an office building one afternoon in hurry, dashed into the waiting elevator. As I rushed in, I caught an unexpected glimpse of myself in a security mirror's reflection. In that moment my brain did an odd thing—it fired off this split-second message: "Hey! You know her! That's a friend of yours!" And I actually ran forward toward my own reflection with a smile, ready to welcome that girl whose name I had lost but whose face was so familiar. In a flash instant, of course, I realized my mistake and laughed in embarrassment at my almost doglike confusion over how a mirror works. But for some reason that incident comes to mind again tonight during my sadness in Rome, and I find myself writing this comforting reminder at the bottom of the page:

Never forget that once upon a time, in an unguarded moment, you recognized yourself as a friend.

I fall asleep holding my notebook pressed against my chest, open to this most recent assurance. In the morning when I wake up, I can still smell a faint trace of Depression's lingering smoke, but he himself is nowhere to be seen. Somewhere during the night, he got up and left. And his buddy Loneliness beat it, too.

19

Here's what's strange, though. I haven't seemed to be able to do any Yoga since getting to Rome. For years I've had a steady and serious practice, and I even brought my Yoga mat with me, along with my best intentions. But it just isn't happening here. I mean, when am I going to do my Yoga stretches? Before my Italian speed-ball breakfast of chocolate pastries and double cappuccino? Or after? The first few days I was here, I would gamely roll out my Yoga mat every morning, but found I could only look at it and laugh. Once I even said aloud to myself, in the character of the Yoga mat: "OK, little Miss *Penne ai Quattro Formaggi* . . . let's see what you got today." Abashed, I stashed the Yoga mat away in the bottom of my suitcase (never to be unrolled again, it would turn out, until India). Then I went for a walk and ate some pistachio gelato. Which Italians consider a perfectly reasonable thing to be eating at 9:30 am, and I frankly could not agree with them more.

The culture of Rome just doesn't match the culture of Yoga, not as far as I can see. In fact, I've decided that Rome and Yoga don't have anything in common at all. Except for the way they both kind of remind you of the word *toga*.

20

I needed to make some friends. So I got busy with it, and now it is October and I have a nice assortment of them. I know two Elizabeths in Rome now, besides myself. Both are American, both are writers. The first Elizabeth is a novelist and the second Elizabeth is a food writer. With an apartment in Rome, a house in Umbria, an Italian husband and a job that requires her to travel around Italy eating food and writing about it for *Gourmet*, it appears that the second Elizabeth must have saved a lot of orphans from drowning during a previous lifetime. Unsurprisingly, she knows all the best places to eat in Rome, including a *gelateria* that serves a frozen rice pudding (and if they don't serve this kind of thing in heaven, then I really don't want to go there). She took me out to lunch the other day, and what we ate included not only lamb and truffles and carpaccio rolled around hazelnut mousse but an exotic little serving of pickled *lampascione*, which is—as everyone knows—the bulb of the wild hyacinth.

Of course, by now I've also made friends with Giovanni and Dario, my Tandem Language Exchange fantasy twins. Giovanni's sweetness, in my opinion, makes him a national treasure of Italy. He endeared himself to me forever the first night we met, when I was getting frustrated with my inability to find the words I wanted in Italian, and he put his hand on my arm and said, "Liz, you must be very polite with yourself when you are learning something new." Sometimes I feel like he's older than me, what with his solemn brow and his philosophy degree and his serious political opinions. I like to try to make him laugh, but Giovanni doesn't always get my jokes. Humor is hard to catch in a second language. Especially when you're as serious a young man as Giovanni. He said to me the other night, "When you are ironic, I am always behind you. I am slower. It is like you are the lightning and I am the thunder."

And I thought, *Yeah, baby! And you are the magnet and I am the steel! Bring to me your leather, take from me my lace!*

But still, he has not kissed me.

I don't very often see Dario, the other twin, though he does spend a lot of his time with Sofie. Sofie is my best friend from my language class, and she's definitely somebody you'd want to spend your time with, too, if you were Dario. Sofie is Swedish and in her late twenties and so damn cute you could put her on a hook and use her as bait to catch men of all different nationalities and ages. Sofie has just taken a four-month leave of absence from her good job in a Swedish bank, much to the horror of her family and bewilderment of her colleagues, only because she wanted to come to Rome and learn how to speak beautiful Italian. Every day after class, Sofie and I go sit by the Tiber, eating our gelato and studying with each other. You can't even rightly call it "studying," the thing that we do. It's more like a shared relishing of the Italian language, an almost worshipful ritual, and we're always offering each other new wonderful idioms. Like, for instance, we just learned the other day that *un'amica stretta* means "a close friend." But *stretta* literally means tight, as in clothing, like a tight skirt. So a close friend, in Italian, is one you that can wear tightly, snug against your skin, and that is what my little Swedish friend Sofie is becoming to me.

At the beginning, I liked to think that Sofie and I looked like sisters. Then we were taking a taxi through Rome the other day and the guy driving the cab asked if Sofie was my daughter. Now, folks—the girl is only about seven years younger than I am. My mind went into such a spin-control mode, trying to explain away what he'd said. (For instance, I thought, *Maybe this native Roman cabdriver doesn't speak Italian very well, and meant to ask if we were* sisters.) But, no. He said daughter and he meant daughter. Oh, what can I say? I've been through a lot in the last few years. I must look so beat-up and old after this divorce. But as that old country-western song out of Texas goes, "I've been screwed and sued and tattooed, and I'm still standin' here in front of you . . ."

I've also become friends with a cool couple named Maria and Giulio, introduced to me by my friend Anne—an American painter who lived in Rome a few years back. Maria is from America, Giulio's from the south of Italy. He's a filmmaker, she works for an international agricultural policy organization. He doesn't speak great English, but she speaks fluent Italian (and also fluent French and Chinese, so *that's* not intimidating). Giulio wants to learn English, and asked if he could practice conversing with me in another Tandem Exchange. In case you're wondering why he couldn't just study English with his American-born wife, it's because they're married and they fight too much whenever one tries to teach anything to the other one. So Giulio and I now meet for lunch twice a week to practice our Italian and English; a good task for two people who don't have any history of irritating each other.

Giulio and Maria have a beautiful apartment, the most impressive feature of which is, to my mind, the wall that Maria once covered with angry curses against Giulio (scrawled in thick black magic marker) because they were having an argument and "he yells louder than me" and she wanted to get a word in edgewise.

I think Maria is terrifically sexy, and this burst of passionate graffiti is only further evidence of it. Interestingly, though, Giulio sees the scrawled-upon wall as a sure sign of Maria's repression, because she wrote her curses against him in Italian, and Italian is her second language, a language she has to think about for a moment before she can choose her words. He said if Maria had truly allowed herself to be overcome by anger—which she *never* does, because she's a good Anglo-Protestant—then she would have written all over that wall in her native English. He says all Americans are like this: repressed. Which makes them dangerous and potentially deadly when they do blow up.

"A savage people," he diagnoses.

What I love is that we all had this conversation over a nice relaxed dinner, while looking at the wall itself.

"More wine, honey?" asked Maria.

But my newest best friend in Italy is, of course, Luca Spaghetti. Even in Italy, by the way, it's considered a very funny thing to have a last name like Spaghetti. I'm grateful for Luca because he has finally allowed me to get even with my friend Brian, who was lucky enough to have grown up next door to a Native American kid named Dennis Ha-Ha, and therefore could always boast that he had the friend with the coolest name. Finally, I can offer competition.

Luca also speaks perfect English and is a good eater (in Italian, *una buona forchetta*—a good fork), so he's terrific company for the hungry likes of me. He often calls in the middle of the day to say, "Hey, I'm in your neighborhood—want to meet up for a quick cup of coffee? Or a plate of oxtail?" We spend a lot of time in these dirty little dives in the back streets of Rome. We like the restaurants with the fluorescent lighting and no name listed outside. Plastic red-checkered tablecloths. Homemade *limoncello* liqueur. Homemade red wine. Pasta served in unbelievable quantities by what Luca calls "little Julius Caesars"—proud, pushy, local guys with hair on the backs of their hands and passionately tended pompadours. I once said to Luca, "It seems to me these guys consider themselves Romans first, Italians second and Europeans third." He corrected me. "No—they are Romans first, Romans second and Romans third. And every one of them is an Emperor."

Luca is a tax accountant. An *Italian* tax accountant, which means that he is, in his own description, "an artist," because there are several hundred tax laws on the books in Italy and all of them contradict each other. So filing a tax return here requires jazzlike improvisation. I think it's funny that he's a tax accountant, because it seems like such stiff work for such a lighthearted guy. On the other hand, Luca thinks it's funny that there's another side of me—this Yoga side—that he's never seen. He can't imagine why I would want to go to India—and to an Ashram, of all places!—when I could just stay in Italy all year, which is obviously where I belong. Whenever he watches me sopping up the leftover gravy from my plate with a hunk of bread and then licking my fingers, he says, "What are you going to *eat* when you go to India?" Sometimes he calls me Gandhi, in a most ironic tone, generally when I'm opening the second bottle of wine.

Luca has traveled a fair amount, though he claims he could never live anywhere but in Rome, near his mother, since he is an Italian man, after all—what can he say? But it's not just his *mamma* who keeps him around. He's in his early thirties, and has had the same girlfriend since he was a teenager (the lovely Giuliana, whom Luca describes fondly and aptly as *acqua e sapone*—"soap and water" in her sweet innocence). All his friends are the same friends he's had since childhood, and all from the same neighborhood. They watch the soccer matches together every Sunday—either at the stadium or in a bar (if the Roman teams are playing away)—and then they all return separately to the homes where they grew up, in order to eat the big Sunday afternoon meals cooked by their respective mothers and grandmothers.

I wouldn't move from Rome, either, if I were Luca Spaghetti.

Luca has visited America a few times, though, and likes it. He finds New York City fascinating but thinks that people work too hard there, though he admits they seem to enjoy it. Whereas Romans work hard and resent it massively. What Luca Spaghetti doesn't like is American food, which he says can be described in two words: "Amtrak Pizza."

I was with Luca the first time I ever tried eating the intestines of a newborn lamb. This is a Roman specialty. Food-wise, Rome is actually a pretty rough town, known for its coarse traditional fare like guts and tongues—all the parts of the animal the rich people up north throw away. My lamb intestines tasted OK, as long as I didn't think too much about what they were. They were served in a heavy, buttery, savory gravy that itself was terrific, but the intestines had a kind of . . . well . . . *intestinal* consistency. Kind of like liver, but mushier. I did well with them until I started trying to think how I would describe this dish, and I thought, *It doesn't look like intestines. It actually looks like tapeworms.* Then I pushed it aside and asked for a salad.

"You don't like it?" asked Luca, who loves the stuff.

"I bet Gandhi never ate lamb intestines in his life," I said.

"He could have."

"No, he couldn't have, Luca. Gandhi was a vegetarian."

"But vegetarians *can* eat this," Luca insisted. "Because intestines aren't even meat, Liz. They're just shit."

21

Sometimes I wonder what I'm doing here, I admit it.

While I have come to Italy in order to experience pleasure, during the first few weeks I was here, I felt a bit of panic as to how one should do that. Frankly, pure pleasure is not my cultural paradigm. I come from a long line of superconscientious people. My mother's family were Swedish immigrant farmers, who look in their photographs like, if they'd ever even seen something pleasurable, they might have stomped on it with their hobnailed boots. (My uncle calls the whole lot of them "oxen.") My father's side of the family were English Puritans, those great goofy lovers of fun. If I look on my dad's family tree all the way back to the seventeenth century, I can actually find Puritan relatives with names like Diligence and Meekness.

My own parents have a small farm, and my sister and I grew up working. We were taught to be dependable, responsible, the top of our classes at school, the most organized and efficient babysitters in town, the very miniature models of our hardworking farmer/nurse of a mother, a pair of junior Swiss Army knives, born to multitask. We had a lot of enjoyment in my family, a lot of laughter, but the walls were papered with to-do lists and I never experienced or witnessed idleness, not once in my whole entire life.

Generally speaking, though, Americans have an inability to relax into sheer pleasure. Ours is an entertainment-seeking nation, but not necessarily a pleasure-seeking one. Americans spend billions to keep themselves amused with everything from porn to theme parks to wars, but that's not exactly the same thing as quiet enjoyment. Americans work harder and longer and more stressful hours than anyone in the world today. But as Luca Spaghetti pointed out, we seem to like it. Alarming statistics back this observation up, showing that many Americans feel more happy and fulfilled in their offices than they do in their own homes. Of course, we all inevitably work too hard, then we get burned out and have to spend the whole weekend in our pajamas, eating cereal straight out of the box and staring at the TV in a mild coma (which is the opposite of working, yes, but not exactly the same thing as pleasure). Americans don't really know how to do *nothing*. This is the cause of that great sad American stereotype—the overstressed executive who goes on vacation, but who cannot relax.

I once asked Luca Spaghetti if Italians on vacation have that same problem. He laughed so hard he almost drove his motorbike into a fountain.

"Oh, no!" he said. "We are the masters of *bel far niente*."

This is a sweet expression. *Bel far niente* means "the beauty of doing nothing." Now listen—Italians have traditionally always been hard workers, especially those long-suffering laborers known as *braccianti* (so called because they had nothing but the brute strength of their arms—*braccie*—to help them survive in this world). But even against that backdrop of hard work, *bel far niente* has always been a cherished Italian ideal. The beauty of doing nothing is the goal of all your work, the final accomplishment for which you are most highly congratulated. The more exquisitely and delightfully you can do nothing, the higher your life's achievement. You don't necessarily need to be rich in order to experience this, either. There's another wonderful Italian expression: *l'arte d'arrangiarsi*—the art of making something out of nothing. The art of turning a few simple ingredients into a feast, or a few gathered friends into a festival. Anyone with a talent for happiness can do this, not only the rich.

For me, though, a major obstacle in my pursuit of pleasure was my ingrained sense of Puritan guilt. Do I really deserve this pleasure? This is very American, too—the insecurity about whether we have earned our happiness. Planet Advertising in America orbits completely around the need to convince the uncertain consumer that yes, you *have* actually warranted a special treat. This Bud's for You! You Deserve a Break Today! Because You're Worth It! You've Come a Long Way, Baby! And the insecure consumer thinks, *Yeah! Thanks! I am gonna go buy a six-pack, damn it! Maybe even two six-packs!* And then comes the reactionary binge. Followed by the remorse. Such advertising campaigns would probably not be as effective in the Italian culture, where people already know that they are entitled to enjoyment in this life. The reply in Italy to "You Deserve a Break Today" would probably be, *Yeah, no duh. That's why I'm planning on taking a break at noon, to go over to your house and sleep with your wife.*

Which is probably why, when I told my Italian friends that I'd come to their country in order to experience four months of pure pleasure, they didn't have any hang-ups about it. *Complimenti! Vai avanti!* Congratulations, they would say. Go ahead. Knock yourself out. Be our guest. Nobody once said, "How completely irresponsible of you," or "What a self-indulgent luxury." But while the Italians have given me full permission to enjoy myself, I still can't quite let go. During my first few weeks in Italy, all my Protestant synapses were zinging in distress, looking for a task. I wanted to take on pleasure like a homework assignment, or a giant science fair project. I pondered such questions as, "How is pleasure most efficiently maximized?" I wondered if maybe I should spend all my time in Italy in the library, doing research on the history of pleasure. Or maybe I should interview Italians who've experienced a lot of pleasure in their lives, asking them what their pleasures feel like, and then writing a report on this topic. (Double-spaced and with one-inch margins, perhaps? To be turned in first thing Monday morning?)

When I realized that the only question at hand was, "How do *I* define pleasure?" and that I was truly in a country where people would permit me to explore that question freely, everything changed. Everything became . . . delicious. All I had to do was ask myself every day, for the first time in my life, "What would *you* enjoy doing today, Liz? What would bring you pleasure right now?" With nobody else's agenda to consider and no other obligations to worry about, this question finally became distilled and absolutely self-specific.

It was interesting for me to discover what I did not want to do in Italy, once I'd given myself executive authorization to enjoy my experience there. There are so many manifestations of pleasure in Italy, and I didn't have time to sample them all. You have to kind of declare a pleasure major here, or you'll get overwhelmed. That being the case, I didn't get into fashion, or opera, or cinema, or fancy automobiles, or skiing in the Alps. I didn't even want to look at that much art. I am a bit ashamed to admit this, but I did not visit a single museum during my entire four months in Italy. (Oh, man—it's even worse than that. I have to confess that I did go to *one* museum: the National Museum of Pasta, in Rome.) I found that all I really wanted was to eat beautiful food and to speak as much beautiful Italian as possible. That was it. So I declared a double major, really—in speaking and in eating (with a concentration on gelato).

The amount of pleasure this eating and speaking brought to me was inestimable, and yet so simple. I passed a few hours once in the middle of October that might look like nothing much to the outside observer, but which I will always count amongst the happiest of my life. I found a market near my apartment, only a few streets over from me, which I'd somehow never noticed before. There I approached a tiny vegetable stall with one Italian woman and her son selling a choice assortment of their produce—such as rich, almost algae-green leaves of spinach, tomatoes so red and bloody they looked like a cow's organs, and champagne-colored grapes with skins as tight as a showgirl's leotard.

I selected a bunch of thin, bright asparagus. I was able to ask the woman, in comfortable Italian, if I could possibly just take half this asparagus home? There was only one of me, I explained to her—I didn't need much. She promptly took the asparagus from my hands and halved it. I asked her if I could find this market every day in the same place, and she said, yes, she was here every day, from 7:00 AM. Then her son, who was very cute, gave me a sly look and said, "Well, she *tries* to be here at seven . . ." We all laughed. This whole conversation was conducted in Italian—a language I could not speak a word of only a few months earlier.

I walked home to my apartment and soft-boiled a pair of fresh brown eggs for my lunch. I peeled the eggs and arranged them on a plate beside the seven stalks of the asparagus (which were so slim and snappy they didn't need to be cooked at all). I put some olives on the plate, too, and the four knobs of goat cheese I'd picked up yesterday from the *formaggeria* down the street, and two slices of pink, oily salmon. For dessert—a lovely peach, which the woman at the market had given to me for free and which was still warm from the Roman sunlight. For the longest time I couldn't even touch this food because it was such a masterpiece of lunch, a true expression of the art of making something out of nothing. Finally, when I had fully absorbed the prettiness of my meal, I went and sat in a patch of sunbeam on my clean wooden floor and ate every bite of it, with my fingers, while reading my daily newspaper article in Italian. Happiness inhabited my every molecule.

Until—as often happened during those first months of travel, whenever I would feel such happiness—my guilt alarm went off. I heard my ex-husband's voice speaking disdainfully in my ear: *So this is what you gave up everything for? This is why you gutted our entire life together? For a few stalks of asparagus and an Italian newspaper?*

I replied aloud to him. "First of all," I said, "I'm very sorry, but this isn't your business anymore. And secondly, to answer your question . . . *yes.*"

22

One obvious topic still needs to be addressed concerning my whole pursuit of pleasure thing in Italy: *What about sex?*

To answer that question simply: I don't want to have any while I'm here.

To answer it more thoroughly and honestly—of course, sometimes I do desperately want to have some, but I've decided to sit this particular game out for a while. I don't want to get involved with anybody. Of course I do miss being kissed because I love kissing. (I complain about this so much to Sofie that the other day she finally said in exasperation, "For God's sake, Liz—if it gets bad enough, *I'll* kiss you.") But I'm not going to do anything about it for now. When I get lonely these days, I think: *So be lonely, Liz. Learn your way around loneliness. Make a map of it. Sit with it, for once in your life. Welcome to the human experience. But never again use another person's body or emotions as a scratching post for your own unfulfilled yearnings.*

It's a kind of emergency life-saving policy, more than anything else. I got started early in life with the pursuit of sexual and romantic pleasure. I barely had an adolescence before I had my first boyfriend, and I have consistently had a boy or a man (or sometimes both) in my life ever since I was fifteen years old. That was—oh, let's see—about nineteen years ago, now. That's almost two solid decades I have been entwined in some kind of drama with some kind of guy. Each overlapping the next, with never so much as a week's breather in between. And I can't help but think that's been something of a liability on my path to maturity.

Moreover, I have boundary issues with men. Or maybe that's not fair to say. To have issues with boundaries, one must *have* boundaries in the first place, right? But I disappear into the person I love. I am the permeable membrane. If I love you, you can have everything. You can have my time, my devotion, my ass, my money, my family, my dog, my dog's money, my dog's time— *everything*. If I love you, I will carry for you all your pain, I will assume for you all your debts (in every definition of the word), I will protect you from your own insecurity, I will project upon you all sorts of good qualities that you have never actually cultivated in yourself and I will buy Christmas presents for your entire family. I will give you the sun and the rain, and if they are not available, I will give you a sun check and a rain check. I will give you all this and more, until I get so exhausted and depleted that the only way I can recover my energy is by becoming infatuated with someone else.

I do not relay these facts about myself with pride, but this is how it's always been.

Some time after I'd left my husband, I was at a party and a guy I barely knew said to me, "You know, you seem like a completely different person, now that you're with this new boyfriend. You used to look like your husband, but now you look like David. You even dress like him and talk like him. You know how some people look like their dogs? I think maybe you always look like your men."

Dear God, I could use a little break from this cycle, to give myself some space to discover what I look like and talk like when I'm not trying to merge with someone. And also, let's be honest—it might be a generous public service for me to leave intimacy alone for a while. When I scan back on my romantic record, it doesn't look so good. It's been one catastrophe after another. How many more different types of men can I keep trying to love, and continue to fail? Think of it this way—if you'd had ten serious traffic accidents in a row, wouldn't they eventually take your driver's license away? Wouldn't you kind of *want* them to?

There's a final reason I'm hesitant to get involved with someone else. I still happen to be in love with David, and I don't think that's fair to the next guy. I don't even know if David and I are totally broken up yet. We were still hanging around each other a lot before I left for Italy, though we hadn't slept together in a long time. But we were still admitting that we both harbored hopes that maybe someday . . .

I don't know.

This much I do know—I'm exhausted by the cumulative consequences of a lifetime of hasty choices and chaotic passions. By the time I left for Italy, my body and my spirit were depleted. I felt like the soil on some desperate sharecropper's farm, sorely overworked and needing a fallow season. So that's why I've quit.

Believe me, I am conscious of the irony of going to Italy in pursuit of pleasure during a period of self-imposed celibacy. But I do think abstinence is the right thing for me at the moment. I was especially sure of it the night I could hear my upstairs neighbor (a very pretty Italian girl with an amazing collection of high-heeled boots) having the longest, loudest, flesh-smackingest, bed-thumpingest, back-breakingest session of lovemaking I'd ever heard, in the company of the latest lucky visitor to her apartment. This slam-dance went on for well over an hour, complete with hyperventilating sound effects and wild animal calls. I lay there only one floor below them, alone and tired in my bed, and all I could think was, *That sounds like an awful lot of work . . .*

Of course sometimes I really do become overcome with lust. I walk past an average of about a dozen Italian men a day whom I could easily imagine in my bed. Or in theirs. Or wherever. To my taste, the men in Rome are ridiculously, hurtfully, stupidly beautiful. More beautiful even than Roman women, to be honest. Italian men are beautiful in the same way as French women, which is to say—no detail spared in the quest for perfection. They're like show poodles. Sometimes they look so good I want to applaud. The men here, in their beauty, force me to call upon romance novel rhapsodies in order to describe them. They are "devilishly attractive," or "cruelly handsome," or "surprisingly muscular."

However, if I may admit something not entirely flattering to myself, these Romans on the street aren't really giving me any second looks. Or even many first looks, for that matter. I found this kind of alarming at first. I'd been to Italy once before, back when I was nineteen, and what I remember is being constantly harassed by men on the street. And in the pizzerias. And at the movies. And in the Vatican. It was endless and awful. It used to be a real liability about traveling in Italy, something that could almost even spoil your appetite. Now, at the age of thirty-four, I am apparently invisible. Sure, sometimes a man will speak to me in a friendly way, "You look beautiful today, *signorina*," but it's not all that common and it never gets aggressive. And while it's certainly nice, of course, to not get pawed by a disgusting stranger on the bus, one does have one's feminine pride, and one must wonder, *What has changed here? Is it me? Or is it them?*

So I ask around, and everybody agrees that, yes, there's been a true shift in Italy in the last ten to fifteen years. Maybe it's a victory of feminism, or an evolution of culture, or the inevitable modernizing effects of having joined the European Union. Or maybe it's just simple embarrassment on the part of young men about the infamous lewdness of their fathers and grandfathers. Whatever the cause, though, it seems that Italy has decided as a society that this sort of stalking, pestering behavior toward women is no longer acceptable. Not even my lovely young friend Sofie gets harassed on the streets, and those milkmaid-looking Swedish girls used to really get the worst of it.

In conclusion—it seems Italian men have earned themselves the Most Improved Award.

Which is a relief, because for a while there I was afraid it was *me*. I mean, I was afraid maybe I wasn't getting any attention because I was no longer nineteen years old and pretty. I was afraid that maybe my friend Scott was correct last summer when he said, "Ah, don't worry, Liz—those Italian guys won't bother you anymore. It ain't like France, where they dig the old babes."

23

Yesterday afternoon I went to the soccer game with Luca Spaghetti and his friends. We were there to watch Lazio play. There are two soccer teams in Rome—Lazio and Roma. The rivalry between the teams and their fans is immense, and can divide otherwise happy families and peaceful neighborhoods into civil war zones. It's important that you choose early in life whether you are a Lazio fan or a Roma fan, because this will determine, to a large part, whom you hang out with every Sunday afternoon for the rest of time.

Luca has a group of about ten close friends who all love each other like brothers. Except that half of them are Lazio fans and half of them are Roma fans. They can't really help it; they were all born into families where the loyalty was already established. Luca's grandfather (who I hope is known as Nonno Spaghetti) gave him his first sky-blue Lazio jersey when the boy was just a toddler. Luca, likewise, will be a Lazio fan until he dies.

"We can change our wives," he said. "We can change our jobs, our nationalities and even our religions, but we can never change our team."

By the way, the word for "fan" in Italian is *tifoso*. Derived from the word for typhus. In other words—one who is mightily fevered.

My first soccer game with Luca Spaghetti was, for me, a delirious banquet of Italian language. I learned all sorts of new and interesting words in that stadium which they don't teach you in school. There was an old man sitting behind me, stringing together such a gorgeous flower-chain of curses as he screamed down at the players on the field. I don't know all that much about soccer, but I sure didn't waste any time asking Luca inane questions about what was going on in the game. All I kept demanding was, "Luca, what did the guy behind me just say? What does *cafone* mean?" And Luca— never taking his eyes from the field—would reply, "Asshole. It means asshole."

I would write it down. Then shut my eyes and listen to some more of the old man's rant, which went something like:

Dai, dai, dai, Albertini, dai . . . va bene, va bene, ragazzo mio, perfetto, bravo, bravo . . . Dai! Dai! Via! Via! Nella porta! Eccola, eccola, eccola, mio bravo ragazzo, caro mio, eccola, eccola, ecco—AAAHHH-HHHHHH!!! VAFFANCULO!!! FIGLIO DI MIGNOTTA!! STRONZO! CAFONE! TRADI-TORE! Madonna . . . Ah, Dio mio, perché, perché, perché, questo è stupido, è una vergogna, la vergogna . . . Che casino, che bordello . . . NON HAI UN CUORE, ALBERTINI! FAI FINTA! Guarda, non è successo niente . . . Dai, dai, ah. . . . Molto migliore, Albertini, molto migliore, sì sì sì, eccola, bello, bravo, anima mia, ah, ottimo, eccola adesso . . . nella porta, nella porta, nell—VAFFANCULO!!!!!!!

Which I can attempt to translate as:

Come on, come on, come on, Albertini, come on . . .
OK, OK, my boy, perfect, brilliant, brilliant . . .
Come on! Come on! Go! Go! In the goal! There it is,
there it is, there it is, my brilliant boy, my dear, there it
is, there it is, there—AHHHH! GO FUCK YOUR-
SELF! YOU SON OF A BITCH! SHITHEAD!
ASSHOLE! TRAITOR! . . . Mother of God . . . Oh
my God, why, why, why, this is stupid, this is shame-
ful, the shame of it . . . What a mess . . . [Author's
note: Unfortunately there's no good way to translate
into English the fabulous Italian expressions che
casino *and* che bordello, *which literally mean "what*
a casino," and "what a whorehouse," but essentially
mean "what a friggin' mess."] . . . YOU DON'T
HAVE A HEART, ALBERTINI!!!! YOU'RE A
FAKER! Look, nothing happened . . . Come on,
come on, hey, yes . . . Much better, Albertini, much
better, yes yes yes, there it is, beautiful, brilliant, oh,
excellent, there it is now . . . in the goal, in the goal, in
the—FUUUUUCK YOUUUUUUU!!!

Oh, it was such an exquisite and lucky moment in my life to be
sitting right in front of this man. I loved every word out of his
mouth. I wanted to lean my head back into his old lap and let him
pour his eloquent curses into my ears forever. And it wasn't just
him! The whole stadium was full of such soliloquies. At such high
fervor! Whenever there was some grave miscarriage of justice on the
field, the entire stadium would rise to its feet, every man waving his
arms in outrage and cursing, as if all 20,000 of them had just been in
a traffic altercation. The Lazio players were no less dramatic than
their fans, rolling on the ground in pain like death scenes from
Julius Caesar, totally playing to the back row, then jumping up on
their feet two seconds later to lead another attack on the goal.

Lazio lost, though.

Needing to be cheered up after the game, Luca Spaghetti asked
his friends, "Should we go out?"

I assumed this meant, "Should we go out to a bar?" That's what sports fans in America would do if their team had just lost. They'd go to a bar and get good and drunk. And not just Americans would do this—so would the English, the Australians, the Germans . . . everyone, right? But Luca and his friends didn't go out to a bar to cheer themselves up. They went to a bakery. A small, innocuous bakery hidden in a basement in a nondescript district in Rome. The place was crowded that Sunday night. But it always is crowded after the games. The Lazio fans always stop here on their way home from the stadium to stand in the street for hours, leaning up against their motorcycles, talking about the game, looking macho as anything, and eating *cream puffs*.

I love Italy.

24

I am learning about twenty new Italian words a day. I'm always studying, flipping through my index cards while I walk around the city, dodging local pedestrians. Where am I getting the brain space to store these words? I'm hoping that maybe my mind has decided to clear out some old negative thoughts and sad memories and replace them with these shiny new words.

I work hard at Italian, but I keep hoping it will one day just be revealed to me, whole, perfect. One day I will open my mouth and be magically fluent. Then I will be a real Italian girl, instead of a total American who still can't hear someone call across the street to his friend Marco without wanting instinctively to yell back *"Polo!"* I wish that Italian would simply take up residence within me, but there are so many glitches in this language. Like, why are the Italian words for "tree" and "hotel" (*albero* vs. *albergo*) so very similar? This causes me to keep accidentally telling people that I grew up on "a Christmas hotel farm" instead of the more accurate and slightly less surreal description: "Christmas tree farm." And then there are words with double or even triple meanings. For instance: *tasso*. Which can mean either interest rate, badger, or yew tree. Depending on the context, I suppose. Most upsetting to me is when I stumble on Italian words that are actually—I hate to say it—ugly. I take this as almost a personal affront. I'm sorry, but I didn't come all the way to Italy to learn how to say a word like *schermo* (screen).

Still, overall it's so worthwhile. It's mostly a pure pleasure. Giovanni and I have such a good time teaching each other idioms in English and Italian. We were talking the other evening about the phrases one uses when trying to comfort someone who is in distress. I told him that in English we sometimes say, "I've been there." This was unclear to him at first—*I've been where?* But I explained that deep grief sometimes is almost like a specific location, a coordinate on a map of time. When you are standing in that forest of sorrow, you cannot imagine that you could ever find your way to a better place. But if someone can assure you that they themselves have stood in that same place, and now have moved on, sometimes this will bring hope.

"So sadness is a place?" Giovanni asked.

"Sometimes people live there for years," I said.

In return, Giovanni told me that empathizing Italians say *L'ho provato sulla mia pelle*, which means "I have experienced that on my own skin." Meaning, I have also been burned or scarred in this way, and I know exactly what you're going through.

So far, though, my favorite thing to say in all of Italian is a simple, common word:

Attraversiamo.

It means, "Let's cross over." Friends say it to each other constantly when they're walking down the sidewalk and have decided it's time to switch to the other side of the street. Which is to say, this is literally a pedestrian word. Nothing special about it. Still, for some reason, it goes right through me. The first time Giovanni said it to me, we were walking near the Colosseum. I suddenly heard him speak that beautiful word, and I stopped dead, demanding, "What does that mean? What did you just say?"

"Attraversiamo."

He couldn't understand why I liked it so much. *Let's cross the street?* But to my ear, it's the perfect combination of Italian sounds. The wistful *ah* of introduction, the rolling trill, the soothing *s*, that lingering "ee-ah-moh" combo at the end. I love this word. I say it all the time now. I invent any excuse to say it. It's making Sofie nuts. *Let's cross over! Let's cross over!* I'm constantly dragging her back and forth across the crazy traffic of Rome. I'm going to get us both killed with this word.

Giovanni's favorite word in English is *half-assed.*

Luca Spaghetti's is *surrender.*

25

There's a power struggle going on across Europe these days. A few cities are competing against each other to see who shall emerge as the great twenty-first-century European metropolis. Will it be London? Paris? Berlin? Zurich? Maybe Brussels, center of the young union? They all strive to outdo one another culturally, architecturally, politically, fiscally. But Rome, it should be said, has not bothered to join the race for status. Rome doesn't compete. Rome just watches all the fussing and striving, completely unfazed, exuding an air like: *Hey—do whatever you want, but I'm still Rome.* I am inspired by the regal self-assurance of this town, so grounded and rounded, so amused and monumental, knowing that she is held securely in the palm of history. I would like to be like Rome when I am an old lady.

I take myself on a six-hour walk through town today. This is easy to do, especially if you stop frequently to fuel up on espresso and pastries. I start at my apartment door, then wander through the cosmopolitan shopping center that is my neighborhood. (Though I wouldn't exactly call this a *neighborhood*, not in the traditional sense. I mean, if it is a neighborhood, then my neighbors are those just-plain-regular-folk with names like the Valentinos, the Guccis and the Armanis.) This has always been an upscale district. Rubens, Tennyson, Stendhal, Balzac, Liszt, Wagner, Thackeray, Byron, Keats—they all stayed here. I live in what they used to call "The English Ghetto," where all the posh aristocrats rested on their European grand tours. One London touring club was actually called

"The Society of Dilettanti"—imagine *advertising* that you're a dilettante! Oh, the glorious shamelessness of it . . .

I walk over to the Piazza del Popolo, with its grand arch, carved by Bernini in honor of the historic visit of Queen Christina of Sweden (who was really one of history's neutron bombs. Here's how my Swedish friend Sofie describes the great queen: "She could ride, she could hunt, she was a scholar, she became a Catholic and it was a huge scandal. Some say she was a man, but at least she was probably a lesbian. She dressed in pants, she went on archaeological excavations, she collected art and she refused to leave an heir"). Next to the arch is a church where you can walk in for free and see two paintings by Caravaggio depicting the martyrdom of Saint Peter and the conversion of Saint Paul (so overcome by grace that he has fallen to the ground in holy rapture; not even his horse can believe it). Those Caravaggio paintings always make me feel weepy and overwhelmed, but I cheer myself up by moving to the other side of the church and enjoying a fresco which features the happiest, goofiest, giggliest little baby Jesus in all of Rome.

I start walking south again. I pass the Palazzo Borghese, a building that has known many famous tenants, including Pauline, Napoleon's scandalous sister, who kept untold numbers of lovers there. She also liked to use her maids as footstools. (One always hopes that one has read this sentence wrong in one's *Companion Guide to Rome*, but, no—it is accurate. Pauline also liked to be carried to her bath, we are told, by "a giant Negro.") Then I stroll along the banks of the great, swampy, rural-looking Tiber, all the way down to the Tiber Island, which is one of my favorite quiet places in Rome. This island has always been associated with healing. A Temple of Aesculapius was built there after a plague in 291 BC; in the Middle Ages a hospital was constructed there by a group of monks called the Fatebenefratelli (which can groovily be translated as "The Do-Good Brothers"); and there is a hospital on the island even to this day.

I cross over the river to Trastevere—the neighborhood that claims to be inhabited by the truest Romans, the workers, the guys who have, over the centuries, built all the monuments on the other side of the Tiber. I eat my lunch in a quiet trattoria here, and I linger over my food and wine for many hours because nobody in

Trastevere is ever going to stop you from lingering over your meal if that's what you would like to do. I order an assortment of *bruschette*, some *spaghetti cacio e pepe* (that simple Roman specialty of pasta served with cheese and pepper) and then a small roast chicken, which I end up sharing with the stray dog who has been watching me eat my lunch the way only a stray dog can.

Then I walk back over the bridge, through the old Jewish ghetto, a sorely tearful place that survived for centuries until it was emptied by the Nazis. I head back north, past the Piazza Navona with its mammoth fountain honoring the four great rivers of Planet Earth (proudly, if not totally accurately, including the sluggish Tiber in that list). Then I go have a look at the Pantheon. I try to look at the Pantheon every chance I get, since I am here in Rome after all, and an old proverb says that anyone who goes to Rome without seeing the Pantheon "goes and comes back an ass."

On my way back home I take a little detour and stop at the address in Rome I find most strangely affecting—the Augusteum. This big, round, ruined pile of brick started life as a glorious mausoleum, built by Octavian Augustus to house his remains and the remains of his family for all of eternity. It must have been impossible for the emperor to have imagined at the time that Rome would ever be anything but a mighty Augustus-worshipping empire. How could he possibly have foreseen the collapse of the realm? Or known that, with all the aqueducts destroyed by barbarians and with the great roads left in ruin, the city would empty of citizens, and it would take almost twenty centuries before Rome ever recovered the population she had boasted during her height of glory?

Augustus's mausoleum fell to ruins and thieves during the Dark Ages. Somebody stole the emperor's ashes—no telling who. By the twelfth century, though, the monument had been renovated into a fortress for the powerful Colonna family, to protect them from assaults by various warring princes. Then the Augusteum was transformed somehow into a vineyard, then a Renaissance garden, then a bullring (we're in the eighteenth century now), then a fireworks depository, then a concert hall. In the 1930s, Mussolini seized the property and restored it down to its classical foundations, so that it could someday be the final resting place for *his* remains. (Again, it must have been impossible back then to imagine that Rome could ever be anything but a Mussolini-worshipping empire.) Of course, Mussolini's fascist dream did not last, nor did he get the imperial burial he'd anticipated.

Today the Augusteum is one of the quietest and loneliest places in Rome, buried deep in the ground. The city has grown up around it over the centuries. (One inch a year is the general rule of thumb for the accumulation of time's debris.) Traffic above the monument spins in a hectic circle, and nobody ever goes down there—from what I can tell—except to use the place as a public bathroom. But the building still exists, holding its Roman ground with dignity, waiting for its next incarnation.

I find the endurance of the Augusteum so reassuring, that this structure has had such an erratic career, yet always adjusted to the particular wildness of the times. To me, the Augusteum is like a person who's led a totally crazy life—who maybe started out as a housewife, then unexpectedly became a widow, then took up fan-dancing to make money, ended up somehow as the first female dentist in outer space, and then tried her hand at national politics—yet who has managed to hold an intact sense of herself throughout every upheaval.

I look at the Augusteum, and I think that perhaps my life has not actually been *so* chaotic, after all. It is merely this world that is chaotic, bringing changes to us all that nobody could have anticipated. The Augusteum warns me not to get attached to any obsolete ideas about who I am, what I represent, whom I belong to, or what function I may once have intended to serve. Yesterday I might have been a glorious monument to somebody, true enough—but tomorrow I could be a fireworks depository. Even in the Eternal City, says the silent Augusteum, one must always be prepared for riotous and endless waves of transformation.

26

I had shipped ahead a box of books to myself, right before I left New York to move to Italy. The box was guaranteed to arrive at my

Roman apartment within four to six days, but I think the Italian post office must have misread that instruction as "forty-six days," for two months have passed now, and I have seen no sign of my box. My Italian friends tell me to put the box out of my mind completely. They say that the box may arrive or it may not arrive, but such things are out of our hands.

"Did someone maybe steal it?" I ask Luca Spaghetti. "Did the post office lose it?"

He covers his eyes. "Don't ask these questions," he says. "You'll only make yourself upset."

The mystery of my missing box prompts a long discussion one night between me, my American friend Maria and her husband, Giulio. Maria thinks that in a civilized society one should be able to rely on such things as the post office delivering one's mail in a prompt manner, but Giulio begs to differ. He submits that the post office belongs not to man, but to the fates, and that delivery of mail is not something anybody can guarantee. Maria, annoyed, says this is only further evidence of the Protestant-Catholic divide. This divide is best proven, she says, by the fact that Italians—including her own husband—can never make plans for the future, not even a week in advance. If you ask a Protestant from the American Midwest to commit to a dinner date next week, that Protestant, believing that she is the captain of her own destiny, will say, "Thursday night works fine for me." But if you ask a Catholic from Calabria to make the same commitment, he will only shrug, turn his eyes to God, and ask, "How can any of us know whether we will be free for dinner next Thursday night, given that everything is in God's hands and none of us can know our fate?"

Still, I go to the post office a few times to try to track down my box, to no avail. The Roman postal employee is not at all happy to have her phone call to her boyfriend interrupted by my presence. And my Italian—which *has* been getting better, honestly—fails me in such stressful circumstances. As I try to speak logically about my missing box of books, the woman looks at me like I'm blowing spit bubbles.

"Maybe it will be here next week?" I ask her in Italian.

She shrugs: *"Magari."*

Another untranslatable bit of Italian slang, meaning something between "hopefully" and "in your dreams, sucker."

Ah, maybe it's for the best. I can't even remember now what books I'd packed in the box in the first place. Surely it was some stuff I thought I should study, if I were to truly understand Italy. I'd packed that box full of all sorts of due-diligence research material about Rome that just seems unimportant now that I'm here. I think I even loaded the complete unabridged text of Gibbon's *History of the Decline and Fall of the Roman Empire* into that box. Maybe I'm happier without it, after all. Given that life is so short, do I really want to spend one-ninetieth of my remaining days on earth reading Edward Gibbon?

27

I met a young Australian girl last week who was backpacking through Europe for the first time in her life. I gave her directions to the train station. She was heading up to Slovenia, just to check it out. When I heard her plans, I was stricken with such a dumb spasm of jealousy, thinking, *I want to go to Slovenia! How come I never get to travel anywhere?*

Now, to the innocent eye it might appear that I already *am* traveling. And longing to travel while you are already traveling is, I admit, a kind of greedy madness. It's kind of like fantasizing about having sex with your favorite movie star while you're having sex with your *other* favorite movie star. But the fact that this girl asked directions from me (clearly, in her mind, a civilian) suggests that I am not technically traveling in Rome, but living here. However temporary it may be, I am a civilian. When I ran into the girl, in fact, I was just on my way to pay my electricity bill, which is not something travelers worry about. Traveling-to-a-place energy and living-in-a-place energy are two fundamentally different energies, and something about meeting this Australian girl on her way to Slovenia just gave me such a jones to hit the road.

And that's why I called my friend Sofie and said, "Let's go down to Naples for the day and eat some pizza!"

Immediately, just a few hours later, we are on the train, and then—like magic—we are there. I instantly love Naples. Wild, raucous, noisy, dirty, balls-out Naples. An anthill inside a rabbit warren, with all the exoticism of a Middle Eastern bazaar and a touch of New Orleans voodoo. A tripped-out, dangerous and cheerful nuthouse. My friend Wade came to Naples in the 1970s and was mugged . . . in a *museum*. The city is all decorated with the laundry that hangs from every window and dangles across every street; everybody's fresh-washed undershirts and brassieres flapping in the wind like Tibetan prayer flags. There is not a street in Naples in which some tough little kid in shorts and mismatched socks is not screaming up from the sidewalk to some other tough little kid on a rooftop nearby. Nor is there a building in this town that doesn't have at least one crooked old woman seated at her window, peering suspiciously down at the activity below.

The people here are so insanely psyched to be from Naples, and why shouldn't they be? This is a city that gave the world pizza *and* ice cream. The Neapolitan women in particular are such a gang of tough-voiced, loud-mouthed, generous, nosy dames, all bossy and annoyed and right up in your face and just trying to friggin' *help* you for chrissake, you dope—*why they gotta do everything around here?* The accent in Naples is like a friendly cuff on the ear. It's like walking through a city of short-order cooks, everybody hollering at the same time. They still have their own dialect here, and an ever-changing liquid dictionary of local slang, but somehow I find that the Neapolitans are the easiest people for me to understand in Italy. Why? Because they *want* you to understand, damn it. They talk loud and emphatically, and if you can't understand what they're actually saying out of their mouths, you can usually pick up the inference from the gesture. Like that punk little grammar-school girl on the back of her older cousin's motorbike, who flipped me the finger *and* a charming smile as she drove by, just to make me understand, "Hey, no hard feelings, lady. But I'm only seven, and I can already tell you're a complete moron, but that's cool—I think you're halfway OK despite yourself and I kinda like your dumb-ass face. We both know you would love to be me, but sorry—you can't. Anyhow, here's my middle finger, enjoy your stay in Naples, and *ciao!*"

As in every public space in Italy, there are always boys, teenagers and grown men playing soccer, but here in Naples there's something extra, too. For instance, today I found kids—I mean, a group of eight-year-old boys—who had gathered up some old chicken crates to create makeshift chairs and a table, and they were playing *poker* in the piazza with such intensity I feared one of them might get shot.

Giovanni and Dario, my Tandem Exchange twins, are originally from Naples. I cannot picture it. I cannot imagine shy, studious, sympathetic Giovanni as a young boy amongst this—and I don't use the word lightly—mob. But he is Neapolitan, no question about it, because before I left Rome he gave me the name of a pizzeria in Naples that I had to try, because, Giovanni informed me, it sold the best pizza in Naples. I found this a wildly exciting prospect, given that the best pizza in Italy is from Naples, and the best pizza in the world is from Italy, which means that this pizzeria must offer . . . I'm almost too superstitious to say it . . . *the best pizza in the world?* Giovanni passed along the name of the place with such seriousness and intensity, I almost felt I was being inducted into a secret society. He pressed the address into the palm of my hand and said, in gravest confidence, "Please go to this pizzeria. Order the margherita pizza with double mozzarella. If you do not eat this pizza when you are in Naples, please lie to me later and tell me that you did."

So Sofie and I have come to Pizzeria da Michele, and these pies we have just ordered—one for each of us—are making us lose our minds. I love my pizza so much, in fact, that I have come to believe in my delirium that my pizza might actually love me, in return. I am having a relationship with this pizza, almost an affair. Meanwhile, Sofie is practically in tears over hers, she's having a metaphysical crisis about it, she's begging me, "Why do they even *bother* trying to make pizza in Stockholm? Why do we even bother eating food at *all* in Stockholm?"

Pizzeria da Michele is a small place with only two rooms and one non-stop oven. It's about a fifteen-minute walk from the train station in the rain, don't even worry about it, just go. You need to get there fairly early in the day because sometimes they run out of dough, which will break your heart. By 1:00 PM, the streets outside the pizzeria have become jammed with Neapolitans trying to get into the place, shoving for access like they're trying to get space on a lifeboat. There's not a menu. They have only two varieties of pizza here—regular and extra cheese. None of this new age southern California olives-and-sun-dried-tomato wannabe pizza twaddle. The dough, it takes me half my meal to figure out, tastes more like Indian *nan* than like any pizza dough I ever tried. It's soft and chewy and yielding, but incredibly thin. I always thought we only had two choices in our lives when it came to pizza crust—thin and crispy, or thick and doughy. How was I to have known there could be a crust in this world that was thin *and* doughy? Holy of holies! Thin, doughy, strong, gummy, yummy, chewy, salty pizza paradise. On top, there is a sweet tomato sauce that foams up all bubbly and creamy when it melts the fresh buffalo mozzarella, and the one sprig of basil in the middle of the whole deal somehow infuses the entire pizza with herbal radiance, much the same way one shimmering movie star in the middle of a party brings a contact high of glamour to everyone around her. It's technically impossible to eat this thing, of course. You try to take a bite off your slice and the gummy crust folds, and the hot cheese runs away like topsoil in a landslide, makes a mess of you and your surroundings, but just deal with it.

The guys who make this miracle happen are shoveling the pizzas in and out of the wood-burning oven, looking for all the world like the boilermen in the belly of a great ship who shovel coal into the raging furnaces. Their sleeves are rolled up over their sweaty forearms, their faces red with exertion, one eye squinted against the heat of the fire and a cigarette dangling from the lips. Sofie and I each order another pie—another whole pizza each—and Sofie tries to pull herself together, but really, the pizza is so good we can barely cope.

A word about my body. I am gaining weight every day, of course. I am doing rude things to my body here in Italy, taking in such ghastly amounts of cheese and pasta and bread and wine and chocolate and pizza dough. (Elsewhere in Naples, I'd been told, you can actually get something called chocolate pizza. What kind of nonsense is that? I mean, later I did go find some, and it's delicious, but honestly—*chocolate pizza*?) I'm not exercising, I'm not eating enough fiber, I'm not taking any vitamins. In my real life, I have been known to eat organic goat's milk yoghurt sprinkled with wheat germ for breakfast. My real-life days are long gone. Back in America, my friend Susan is telling people I'm on a "No Carb Left Behind" tour. But my body is being such a good sport about all this. My body is turning a blind eye to my misdoings and my overindulgences, as if to say, "OK, kid, live it up, I recognize that this is just temporary. Let me know when your little experiment with pure pleasure is over, and I'll see what I can do about damage control."

Still, when I look at myself in the mirror of the best pizzeria in Naples, I see a bright-eyed, clear-skinned, happy and healthy face. I haven't seen a face like that on me for a long time.

"Thank you," I whisper. Then Sofie and I run out in the rain to look for pastries.

28

It is this happiness, I suppose (which is really a few months old by now), that gets me to thinking upon my return to Rome that I need to do something about David. That maybe it's time for us to end our story forever. We were already separated, that was official, but there was still a window of hope left open that perhaps someday (maybe after my travels, maybe after a year apart) we could give things another try. We loved each other. That was never the question. It's just that we couldn't figure out how to stop making each other desperately, shriekingly, soul-punishingly miserable.

Last spring David had offered this crazy solution to our woes, only half in jest: "What if we just acknowledged that we have a bad relationship, and we stuck it out, anyway? What if we admitted that we make each other nuts, we fight constantly and hardly ever have sex, but we can't live without each other, so we deal with it? And then we could spend our lives together—in misery, but happy to not be apart."

Let it be a testimony to how desperately I love this guy that I have spent the last ten months giving that offer serious consideration.

The other alternative in the backs of our minds, of course, was that one of us might change. He might become more open and affectionate, not withholding himself from anyone who loves him on the fear that she will eat his soul. Or I might learn how to . . . stop trying to eat his soul.

So many times I had wished with David that I could behave more like my mother does in her marriage—independent, strong, self-sufficient. A self-feeder. Able to exist without regular doses of romance or flattery from my solitary farmer of a father. Able to cheerfully plant gardens of daisies among the inexplicable stone walls of silence that my dad sometimes builds up around himself. My dad is quite simply my favorite person in the world, but he is a bit of an odd case. An ex-boyfriend of mine once described him this way: "Your father only has one foot on this earth. And really, really long legs . . ."

What I grew up watching in my household was a mother who would receive her husband's love and affection whenever he thought to offer it, but would then step aside and take care of herself whenever he drifted off into his own peculiar universe of low-grade oblivious neglect. This is how it looked to me, anyway, taking into account that nobody (and especially not the children) ever knows the secrets of a marriage. What I believed I grew up seeing was a mother who asked nothing of anybody. This was my mom, after all—a woman who had taught herself how to swim as an adolescent, alone in a cold Minnesota lake, with a book she'd borrowed from the local library entitled *How to Swim.* To my eye, there was nothing this woman could not do on her own.

But then I'd had a revelatory conversation with my mother, not long before I'd left for Rome. She'd come into New York to have one last lunch with me, and she'd asked me frankly—breaking all the rules of communication in our family's history—what had happened between me and David. Further disregarding the Gilbert Family Standard Communications Rulebook, I actually told her. I told her everything. I told her how much I loved David, but how lonely and heartsick it made me to be with this person who was always disappearing from the room, from the bed, from the planet.

"He sounds kind of like your father," she said. A brave and generous admission.

"The problem is," I said, "I'm not like my mother. I'm not as tough as you, Mom. There's a constant level of closeness that I really need from the person I love. I wish I could be more like you, then I could have this love story with David. But it just destroys me to not be able to count on that affection when I need it."

Then my mother shocked me. She said, "All those things that you want from your relationship, Liz? I have always wanted those things, too."

In that moment, it was as if my strong mother reached across the table, opened her fist and finally showed me the handful of bullets she'd had to bite over the decades in order to stay happily married (and she *is* happily married, all considerations weighed) to my father. I had never seen this side of her before, not ever. I had never imagined what she might have wanted, what she might have been missing, what she might have decided not to fight for in the larger scheme of things. Seeing all this, I could feel my worldview start to make a radical shift.

If even she wants what I want, then . . . ?

Continuing with this unprecedented string of intimacies, my mother said, "You have to understand how little I was raised to expect that I deserved in life, honey. Remember—I come from a different time and place than you do."

I closed my eyes and saw my mother, ten years old on the family farm in Minnesota, working like a hired hand, raising her younger brothers, wearing the clothes of her older sister, saving dimes to get herself out of there . . .

"And you have to understand how much I love your father," she concluded.

My mother has made choices in her life, as we all must, and she is at peace with them. I can see her peace. She did not cop out on herself. The benefits of her choices are massive—a long, stable marriage to a man she still calls her best friend; a family that has extended now into grandchildren who adore her; a certainty in her own strength. Maybe some things were sacrificed, and my dad made his sacrifices, too—but who amongst us lives without sacrifice?

And the question now for me is, What are *my* choices to be? What do I believe that I deserve in this life? Where can I accept sacrifice, and where can I not? It has been so hard for me to imagine living a life without David in it. Even just to imagine that there will never be another road trip with my favorite traveling companion, that I will never again pull up at his curb with the windows down and Springsteen playing on the radio, a lifetime supply of banter and snacks between us, and an ocean destination looming down the highway. But how can I accept that bliss when it comes with this dark underside—bone-crushing isolation, corrosive insecurity, insidious resentment and, of course, the complete dismantling of self that inevitably occurs when David ceases to giveth, and commences to taketh away. I can't do it anymore. Something about my recent joy in Naples has made me certain that I not only *can* find happiness without David, but *must*. No matter how much I love him (and I do love him, in stupid excess), I have to say good-bye to this person now. And I have to make it stick.

So I write him an e-mail.

It's November. We haven't had any communication since July. I'd asked him not to get in touch with me while I was traveling, knowing that my attachment to him was so strong it would be impossible for me to focus on my journey if I were also tracking his. But now I'm entering his life again with this e-mail.

I tell him that I hope he's well, and I report that I am well. I make a few jokes. We always were good with the jokes. Then I explain that I think we need to put an end to this relationship for good. That maybe it's time to admit that it will never happen, that it *should* never happen. The note isn't overly dramatic. Lord knows we've had enough drama together already. I keep it short and simple. But there's one more thing I need to add. Holding my breath, I type, "If you want to look for another partner in your life, of course you have nothing but my blessings." My hands are shaking. I sign off with love, trying to keep as cheerful a tone as possible.

I feel like I just got hit in the chest with a stick.

I don't sleep much that night, imagining him reading my words. I run back to the Internet café a few times throughout the next day, looking for a response. I'm trying to ignore the part of me that is dying to find that he has replied: "COME BACK! DON'T GO! I'LL CHANGE!" I'm trying to disregard the girl in me who would happily drop this whole grand idea of traveling around the world in simple exchange for the keys to David's apartment. But around ten o'clock that night, I finally get my answer. A wonderfully written e-mail, of course. David always wrote wonderfully. He agrees that, yes, it's time we really said good-bye forever. He's been thinking along the same lines himself, he says. He couldn't be more gracious in his response, and he shares his own feelings of loss and regret with that high tenderness he was sometimes so achingly capable of reaching. He hopes that I know how much he adores me, beyond even his ability to find words to express it. "But we are not what the other one needs," he says. Still, he is certain that I will find great love in my life someday. He's sure of it. After all, he says, "beauty attracts beauty."

Which is a lovely thing to say, truly. Which is just about the loveliest thing that the love of your life could ever possibly say, when he's not saying, "COME BACK! DON'T GO! I'LL CHANGE!"

I sit there staring at the computer screen in silence for a long, sad time. It's all for the best, I know it is. I'm choosing happiness over suffering, I know I am. I'm making space for the unknown future to fill up my life with yet-to-come surprises. I know all this. But still . . .

It's *David.* Lost to me now.

I drop my face in my hands for a longer and even sadder time. Finally I look up, only to see that one of the Albanian women who work at the Internet café has paused from her night-shift mopping of the floor to lean against the wall and watch me. We hold our tired gazes on each other for a moment. Then I give her a grim shake of my head and say aloud, "This blows ass." She nods sympathetically. She doesn't understand, but of course, in her way, she understands completely.

My cell phone rings.

It's Giovanni. He sounds confused. He says he's been waiting for me for over an hour in the Piazza Fiume, which is where we always meet on Thursday nights for language exchange. He's bewildered, because normally *he's* the one who's late or who forgets to show up for our appointments, but he got there right on time tonight for once and he was pretty sure—didn't we have a date?

I'd forgotten. I tell him where I am. He says he'll come pick me up in his car. I'm not in the mood for seeing anybody, but it's too hard to explain this over the *telefonino*, given our limited language skills. I go wait outside in the cold for him. A few minutes later, his little red car pulls up and I climb in. He asks me in slangy Italian what's up. I open my mouth to answer and collapse into tears. I mean—wailing. I mean—that terrible, ragged breed of bawling my friend Sally calls "double-pumpin' it," when you have to inhale two desperate gasps of oxygen with every sob. I never even saw this grief-quake coming, got totally blindsided by it.

Poor Giovanni! He asks in halting English if he did something wrong. Am I mad at him, maybe? Did he hurt my feelings? I can't answer, but only shake my head and keep howling. I'm so mortified with myself and so sorry for dear Giovanni, trapped here in this car with this sobbing, incoherent old woman who is totally *a pezzi*—in pieces.

I finally manage to rasp out an assurance that my distress has nothing to do with him. I choke forth an apology for being such a mess. Giovanni takes charge of the situation in a manner far beyond his years. He says, "Do not apologize for crying. Without this emotion, we are only robots." He gives me some tissues from a box in the back of the car. He says, "Let's drive."

He's right—the front of this Internet café is far too public and brightly lit a place to fall apart. He drives for a bit, then pulls the car over in the center of the Piazza della Repubblica, one of Rome's more noble open spaces. He parks in front of that gorgeous fountain with the bodacious naked nymphs cavorting so pornographically with their phallic flock of stiff-necked giant swans. This fountain was built fairly recently, by Roman standards. According to my guidebook, the women who modeled for the nymphs were a pair of sisters, two popular burlesque dancers of their day. They gained a fair bit of notoriety when the fountain was completed; the church tried for months to prevent the thing from being unveiled because it was too sexy. The sisters lived well into old age, and even as late as the 1920s these two dignified old ladies could be seen walking together every day into the piazza to have a look at "their" fountain. And every year, once a year, for as long as he lived, the French sculptor who had captured them in marble during their prime would come to Rome and take the sisters out to lunch, where they would reminisce together about the days when they were all so young and beautiful and wild.

So Giovanni parks there, and waits for me to get a hold of myself. All I can do is press the heels of my palms against my eyes, trying to push the tears back in. We have never once had a personal conversation, me and Giovanni. All these months, all these dinners together, all we have ever talked about is philosophy and art and culture and politics and food. We know nothing of each other's private lives. He does not even know that I am divorced or that I have left love behind in America. I do not know a thing about him except that he wants to be a writer and that he was born in Naples. My crying, though, is about to force a whole new level of conversation between these two people. I wish it wouldn't. Not under these dreadful circumstances.

He says, "I'm sorry, but I don't understand. Did you lose something today?"

But I'm still having trouble figuring out how to talk. Giovanni smiles and says encouragingly, *"Parla come magni."* He knows this is one of my favorite expressions in Roman dialect. It means, "Speak the way you eat," or, in my personal translation: "Say it like you eat it." It's a reminder—when you're making a big deal out of explaining something, when you're searching for the right words—to keep your language as simple and direct as Roman food. Don't make a big production out of it. Just lay it on the table.

I take a deep breath and offer a heavily abridged (yet somehow totally complete) Italian-language version of my situation:

"It's about a love story, Giovanni. I had to say good-bye to someone today."

Then my hands are slapped over my eyes again, tears spraying through my clamped fingers. Bless his heart, Giovanni doesn't try to put a reassuring arm around me, nor does he express the slightest discomfort about my explosion of sadness. Instead, he just sits through my tears in silence, until I've calmed down. At which point he speaks with perfect empathy, choosing each word with care (as his English teacher, I was so *proud* of him that night!), saying slowly and clearly and kindly: "I understand, Liz. I have been there."

29

My sister's arrival in Rome a few days later helped nudge my attention away from lingering sadness over David and bring me back up to speed. My sister does everything fast, and energy twists up around her in miniature cyclones. She's three years older than me and three inches taller than me. She's an athlete and a scholar and a mother and a writer. The whole time she was in Rome, she was training for a marathon, which means she would wake up at dawn and run eighteen miles in the time it generally takes me to read one article in the newspaper and drink two cappuccinos. She actually looks like a deer when she runs. When she was pregnant with her first child, she swam across an entire lake one night in the dark. I wouldn't join her, and I wasn't even pregnant. I was too scared. But my sister doesn't really get scared. When she was pregnant with her second child, a midwife asked if Catherine had any unspoken fears about anything that could go wrong with the baby—such as genetic defects or complications during the birth. My sister said, "My only fear is that he might grow up to become a Republican."

That's my sister's name—Catherine. She's my one and only sibling. When we were growing up in rural Connecticut, it was just the two of us, living in a farmhouse with our parents. No other kids nearby. She was mighty and domineering, the commander of my whole life. I lived in awe and fear of her; nobody else's opinion mattered but hers. I cheated at card games with her in order to *lose*, so she wouldn't get mad at me. We were not always friends. She was annoyed by me, and I was scared of her, I believe, until I was twenty-eight years old and got tired of it. That was the year I finally stood up to her, and her reaction was something along the lines of, "What took you so long?"

We were just beginning to hammer out the new terms of our relationship when my marriage went into a skid. It would have been so easy for Catherine to have gained victory from my defeat. I'd always been the loved and lucky one, the favorite of both family and destiny. The world had always been a more comfortable and welcoming place for me than it was for my sister, who pressed so sharply against life and who was hurt by it fairly hard sometimes in return. It would have been so easy for Catherine to have responded to my divorce and depression with a: "Ha! Look at Little Mary Sunshine now!" Instead, she held me up like a champion. She answered the phone in the middle of the night whenever I was in distress and made comforting noises. And she came along with me when I went searching for answers as to why I was so sad. For the longest time, my therapy was almost vicariously shared by her. I'd call her after every session with a debriefing of everything I'd realized in my therapist's office, and she'd put down whatever she was doing and say, "Ah . . . that explains a lot." Explains a lot about *both* of us, that is.

Now we speak to each other on the phone almost every day—or at least we did, before I moved to Rome. Before either of us gets on an airplane now, the one always calls the other and says, "I know this is morbid, but I just wanted to tell you that I love you. You know . . . just in case . . ." And the other one always says, "I know . . . just in case."

She arrives in Rome prepared, as ever. She brings five guidebooks, all of which she has read already, and she has the city pre-mapped in her head. She was completely oriented before she even left Philadelphia. And this is a classic example of the differences between us. I am the one who spent my first weeks in Rome wandering about, 90 percent lost and 100 percent happy, seeing everything around me as an unexplainable beautiful mystery. But this is how the world kind of always looks to me. To my sister's eyes, there is nothing which cannot be explained if one has access to a proper reference library. This is a woman who keeps *The Columbia Encyclopedia* in her kitchen next to the cookbooks and *reads* it, for pleasure.

There's a game I like to play with my friends sometimes called "Watch This!" Whenever anybody's wondering about some obscure fact (for instance: "Who *was* Saint Louis?") I will say, "Watch this!" then pick up the nearest phone and dial my sister's number. Sometimes I'll catch her in the car, driving her kids home from school in the Volvo, and she will muse: "Saint Louis . . . well, he was a hair-shirt-wearing French king, actually, which is interesting because . . ."

So my sister comes to visit me in Rome—in my new city—and then shows it to me. This is Rome, Catherine-style. Full of facts and dates and architecture that I do not see because my mind does not work in that way. The only thing I ever want to know about any place or any person is the *story*, this is the only thing I watch for—never for aesthetic details. (Sofie came to my apartment a month after I'd moved into the place and said, "Nice pink bathroom," and this was the *first time* I'd noticed that it was, indeed, pink. Bright pink, from floor to ceiling, bright pink tile everywhere—I honestly hadn't seen it before.) But my sister's trained eye picks up the Gothic, or Romanesque, or Byzantine features of a building, the pattern of the church floor, or the dim sketch of the unfinished fresco hidden behind the altar. She strides across Rome on her long legs (we used to call her "Catherine-of-the-Three-Foot-Long-Femurs") and I hasten after her, as I have since toddlerhood, taking two eager steps to her every one.

"See, Liz?" she says, "See how they just slapped that nineteenth-century façade over that brickwork? I bet if we turn the corner we'll find . . . yes! . . . see, they *did* use the original Roman monoliths as supporting beams, probably because they didn't have the manpower to move them . . . yes, I quite like the jumble-sale quality of this basilica. . . ."

Catherine carries the map and her Michelin Green Guide, and I carry our picnic lunch (two of those big softball-sized rolls of bread, spicy sausage, pickled sardines wrapped around meaty green olives, a mushroom pâté that tastes like a forest, balls of smoked moz-zarella, peppered and grilled arugula, cherry tomatoes, pecorino cheese, mineral water and a split of cold white wine), and while I wonder when we're going to eat, she wonders aloud, "Why *don't* people talk more about the Council of Trent?"

She takes me into dozens of churches in Rome, and I can't keep them straight—St. This and St. That, and St. Somebody of the Barefoot Penitents of Righteous Misery ... but just because I cannot remember the names or details of all these buttresses and cornices is not to say that I do not love to be inside these places with my sister, whose cobalt eyes miss nothing. I don't remember the name of the church that had those frescoes that looked so much like American WPA New Deal heroic murals, but I do remember Catherine pointing them out to me and saying, "You gotta love those Franklin Roosevelt popes up there ..." I also remember the morning we woke early and went to mass at St. Susanna, and held each other's hands as we listened to the nuns there chanting their daybreak Gregorian hymns, both of us in tears from the echoing haunt of their prayers. My sister is not a religious person. Nobody in my family really is. (I've taken to calling myself the "white sheep" of the family.) My spiritual investigations interest my sister mostly from a point of intellectual curiosity. "I think that kind of faith is so beautiful," she whispers to me in the church, "but I can't do it, I just can't ..."

Here's another example of the difference in our worldviews. A family in my sister's neighborhood was recently stricken with a double tragedy, when both the young mother and her three-year-old son were diagnosed with cancer. When Catherine told me about this, I could only say, shocked, "Dear God, that family needs grace." She replied firmly, "That family needs *casseroles*," and then proceeded to organize the entire neighborhood into bringing that family dinner, in shifts, every single night, for an entire year. I do not know if my sister fully recognizes that this *is* grace.

We walk out of St. Susanna, and she says, "Do you know why the popes needed city planning in the Middle Ages? Because basically you had two million Catholic pilgrims a year coming from all over the Western World to make that walk from the Vatican to St. John Lateran—sometimes on their knees—and you had to have *amenities* for those people."

My sister's faith is in learning. Her sacred text is the *Oxford English Dictionary*. As she bows her head in study, fingers speeding across the pages, she is with her God. I see my sister in prayer again later that same day—when she drops to her knees in the middle of the Roman Forum, clears away some litter off the face of the soil (as though erasing a blackboard), then takes up a small stone and draws for me in the dirt a blueprint of a classic Romanesque basilica. She points from her drawing to the ruin before her, leading me to understand (even visually challenged *me* can understand!) what that building once must have looked like eighteen centuries earlier. She sketches with her finger in the empty air the missing arches, the nave, the windows long gone. Like Harold with his Purple Crayon, she fills in the absent cosmos with her imagination and makes whole the ruined.

In Italian there is a seldom-used tense called the *passato remoto*, the remote past. You use this tense when you are discussing things in the far, far distant past, things that happened so long ago they have no personal impact whatsoever on you anymore—for example, ancient history. But my sister, if she spoke Italian, would not use this tense to discuss ancient history. In her world, the Roman Forum is not remote, nor is it past. It is exactly as present and close to her as I am.

She leaves the next day.

"Listen," I say, "be sure to call me when your plane lands safely, OK? Not to be morbid, but . . ."

"I know, sweetie," she says. "I love you, too."

30

I am so surprised sometimes to notice that my sister is a wife and a mother, and I am not. Somehow I always thought it would be the opposite. I thought it would be me who would end up with a houseful of muddy boots and hollering kids, while Catherine would be living by herself, a solo act, reading alone at night in her bed. We grew up into different adults than anyone might have foretold when we were children. It's better this way, though, I think. Against all predictions, we've each created lives that tally with us. Her solitary nature means she needs a family to keep her from loneliness; my gregarious nature means I will never have to worry about being alone, even when I am single. I'm happy that she's going back home to her family and also happy that I have another nine months of traveling ahead of me, where all I have to do is eat and read and pray and write.

I still can't say whether I will ever want children. I was so astonished to find that I did not want them at thirty; the remembrance of that surprise cautions me against placing any bets on how I will feel at forty. I can only say how I feel now—grateful to be on my own. I also know that I won't go forth and have children just in case I might regret missing it later in life; I don't think this is a strong enough motivation to bring more babies onto the earth. Though I suppose people do reproduce sometimes for that reason—for insurance against later regret. I think people have children for all manner of reasons—sometimes out of a pure desire to nurture and witness life, sometimes out of an absence of choice, sometimes in order to hold on to a partner or create an heir, sometimes without thinking about it in any particular way. Not all the reasons to have children are the same, and not all of them are necessarily unselfish. Not all the reasons *not* to have children are the same, either, though. Nor are all those reasons necessarily selfish.

I say this because I'm still working out that accusation, which was leveled against me many times by my husband as our marriage was collapsing—*selfishness*. Every time he said it, I agreed completely, accepted the guilt, bought everything in the store. My God, I hadn't even had the babies yet, and I was already neglecting them, already choosing myself over them. I was already a bad mother. These babies—these phantom babies—came up a lot in our arguments. Who would take care of the babies? Who would stay home with the babies? Who would financially support the babies? Who would feed the babies in the middle of the night? I remember saying once to my friend Susan, when my marriage was becoming intolerable, "I don't want my children growing up in a household like this." Susan said, "Why don't you leave those so-called children out of the discussion? They don't even exist yet, Liz. Why can't you just admit that *you* don't want to live in unhappiness anymore? That neither of you does. And it's better to realize it now, by the way, than in the delivery room when you're at five centimeters."

I remember going to a party in New York around that time. A couple, a pair of successful artists, had just had a baby, and the mother was celebrating a gallery opening of her new paintings. I remember watching this woman, the new mother, my friend, the artist, as she tried to be hostess to this party (which was in her loft) at the same time as taking care of her infant and trying to discuss her work professionally. I never saw somebody look so sleep-deprived in my life. I can never forget the image of her standing in her kitchen after midnight, elbows-deep in a sink full of dishes, trying to clean up after this event. Her husband (I am sorry to report it, and I fully realize this is not *at all* representational of every husband) was in the other room, feet literally on the coffee table, watching TV. She finally asked him if he would help clean the kitchen, and he said, "Leave it, hon—we'll clean up in the morning." The baby started crying again. My friend was leaking breast milk through her cocktail dress.

Almost certainly, other people who attended this party came away with different images than I did. Any number of the other guests could have felt great envy for this beautiful woman with her healthy new baby, for her successful artistic career, for her marriage to a nice man, for her lovely apartment, for her cocktail dress. There were people at this party who would probably have traded lives with her in an instant, given the chance. This woman herself probably looks back on that evening—if she ever thinks of it at all—as one tiring but totally worth-it night in her overall satisfying life of motherhood and marriage and career. All I can say for myself, though, is that I spent that whole party trembling in panic, thinking, *If you don't recognize that this is your future, Liz, then you are out of your mind. Do not let it happen.*

But did I have a responsibility to have a family? Oh, Lord—*responsibility*. That word worked on me until I worked on it, until I looked at it carefully and broke it down into the two words that make its true definition: the *ability* to *respond*. And what I ultimately had to respond to was the reality that every speck of my being was telling me to get out of my marriage. Somewhere inside me an early-warning system was forecasting that if I kept trying to white-knuckle my way through this storm, I would end up getting cancer. And that if I brought children into the world anyway, just because I didn't want to deal with the hassle or shame of revealing some impractical facts about myself—*this* would be an act of grievous irresponsibility.

In the end, though, I was most guided by something my friend Sheryl said to me that very night at that very party, when she found me hiding in the bathroom of our friend's fancy loft, shaking in fear, splashing water on my face. Sheryl didn't know then what was going on in my marriage. Nobody did. And I didn't tell her that night. All I could say was, "I don't know what to do." I remember her taking me by the shoulders and looking me in the eye with a calm smile and saying simply, "Tell the truth, tell the truth, tell the truth."

So that's what I tried to do.

Getting out of a marriage is rough, though, and not just for the legal/financial complications or the massive lifestyle upheaval. (As my friend Deborah once advised me wisely: "Nobody ever died from splitting up furniture.") It's the emotional recoil that kills you, the shock of stepping off the track of a conventional lifestyle and losing all the embracing comforts that keep so many people on that track forever. To create a family with a spouse is one of the most fundamental ways a person can find continuity and meaning in American (or any) society. I rediscover this truth every time I go to a big reunion of my mother's family in Minnesota and I see how everyone is held so reassuringly in their positions over the years. First you are a child, then you are a teenager, then you are a young married person, then you are a parent, then you are retired, then you are a grandparent—at every stage you know who you are, you know what your duty is and you know where to sit at the reunion. You sit with the other children, or teenagers, or young parents, or retirees. Until at last you are sitting with the ninety-year-olds in the shade, watching over your progeny with satisfaction. Who are you? No problem—you're the person who created all *this*. The satisfaction of this knowledge is immediate, and moreover, it's universally recognized. How many people have I heard claim their children as the greatest accomplishment and comfort of their lives? It's the thing they can always lean on during a metaphysical crisis, or a moment of doubt about their relevancy—*If I have done nothing else in this life, then at least I have raised my children well.*

But what if, either by choice or by reluctant necessity, you end up not participating in this comforting cycle of family and continuity? What if you step out? Where do you sit at the reunion? How do you mark time's passage without the fear that you've just frittered away your time on earth without being relevant? You'll need to find another purpose, another measure by which to judge whether or not you have been a successful human being. I love children, but what if I don't have any? What kind of person does that make me?

Virginia Woolf wrote, "Across the broad continent of a woman's life falls the shadow of a sword." On one side of that sword, she said, there lies convention and tradition and order, where "all is correct." But on the other side of that sword, if you're crazy enough to cross it and choose a life that does not follow convention, "all is confusion. Nothing follows a regular course." Her argument was that the crossing of the shadow of that sword may bring a far more interesting existence to a woman, but you can bet it will also be more perilous.

I'm lucky that at least I have my writing. This is something people can understand. *Ah, she left her marriage in order to preserve her art.* That's sort of true, though not completely so. A lot of writers have families. Toni Morrison, just to name an example, didn't let the raising of her son stop her from winning a little trinket we call the Nobel Prize. But Toni Morrison made her own path, and I must make mine. The Bhagavad Gita—that ancient Indian Yogic text— says that it is better to live your own destiny imperfectly than to live an imitation of somebody else's life with perfection. So now I have started living my own life. Imperfect and clumsy as it may look, it is resembling me now, thoroughly.

Anyway, I bring all this up only to admit that—in comparison to my sister's existence, to her home and to her good marriage and to her children—I'm looking pretty unstable these days. I don't even have an address, and that's kind of a crime against normality at this ripe old age of thirty-four. Even at this very moment, all my belongings are stored in Catherine's home and she's given me a temporary bedroom on the top floor of her house (which we call "The Maiden Aunt's Quarters," as it includes a garret window through which I can stare out at the moors while dressed in my old wedding gown, grieving my lost youth). Catherine seems to be fine with this arrangement, and it's certainly convenient for me, but I'm wary of the danger that if I drift about this world randomly for too long, I may someday become The Family Flake. Or it may have already happened. Last summer, my five-year-old niece had a little friend over to my sister's house to play. I asked the child when her birthday was. She told me it was January 25.

"Uh-oh!" I said. "You're an Aquarius! I've dated enough Aquarians to know that they are *trouble.*"

Both the five-year-olds looked at me with bewilderment and a bit of fearful uncertainty. I had a sudden horrifying image of the woman I might become if I'm not careful: Crazy Aunt Liz. The divorcée in the muumuu with the dyed orange hair who doesn't eat dairy but smokes menthols, who's always just coming back from her astrology cruise or breaking up with her aroma-therapist boyfriend, who reads the Tarot cards of kindergarteners and says things like, "Bring Aunty Liz another wine cooler, baby, and I'll let you wear my mood ring. . . ."

Eventually I may have to become a more solid citizen again, I'm aware of this.

But not yet . . . *please.* Not just yet.

31

Over the next six weeks, I travel to Bologna, to Florence, to Venice, to Sicily, to Sardinia, once more down to Naples, then over to Calabria. These are short trips, mostly—a week here, a weekend there—just the right amount of time to get the feel for a place, to look around, to ask people on the street where the good food is and then to go eat it. I drop out of my Italian language school, having come to feel that it was interfering with my efforts to learn Italian, since it was keeping me stuck in the classroom instead of wandering around Italy, where I could practice with people in person.

These weeks of spontaneous travel are such a glorious twirl of time, some of the loosest days of my life, running to the train station and buying tickets left and right, finally beginning to flex my freedom for real because it has finally sunk in that *I can go wherever I want.* I don't see my friends in Rome for a while. Giovanni tells me over the phone, *"Sei una trottola"* ("You're a spinning top"). One night in a town somewhere on the Mediterranean, in a hotel room by the ocean, the sound of my own laughter actually wakes me up the middle of my deep sleep. I am startled. *Who is that laughing in my bed?* The realization that it is only me just makes me laugh again. I can't remember now what I was dreaming. I think maybe it had something to do with boats.

32

Florence is just a weekend, a quick train ride up on a Friday morning to visit my Uncle Terry and Aunt Deb, who have flown in from Connecticut to visit Italy for the first time in their lives, and to see their niece, of course. It is evening when they arrive, and I take them on a walk to look at the Duomo, always such an impressive sight, as evidenced by my uncle's reaction:

"Oy vey!" he says, then pauses and adds, "Or maybe that's the wrong word for praising a Catholic church . . ."

We watch the Sabines getting raped right there in the middle of the sculpture garden with nobody doing a damn thing to stop it, and pay our respects to Michelangelo, to the science museum, to the views from the hillsides around town. Then I leave my aunt and uncle to enjoy the rest of their vacation without me, and I go on alone to wealthy, ample Lucca, that little Tuscan town with its celebrated butcher shops, where the finest cuts of meat I've seen in all of Italy are displayed with a "you know you want it" sensuality in shops across town. Sausages of every imaginable size, color and derivation are stuffed like ladies' legs into provocative stockings, swinging from the ceilings of the butcher shops. Lusty buttocks of hams hang in the windows, beckoning like Amsterdam's high-end hookers. The chickens look so plump and contented even in death that you imagine they offered themselves up for sacrifice proudly, after competing among themselves in life to see who could become the moistest and the fattest. But it's not just the meat that's wonderful in Lucca; it's the chestnuts, the peaches, the tumbling displays of figs, dear God, the figs . . .

The town is famous, too, of course, for having been the birthplace of Puccini. I know I should probably be interested in this, but I'm much more interested in the secret a local grocer has shared with me—that the best mushrooms in town are served in a restaurant *across* from Puccini's birthplace. So I wander through Lucca, asking directions in Italian, "Can you tell me where is the house of Puccini?" and a kind civilian finally leads me right to it, and then is probably very surprised when I say *"Grazie,"* then turn on my heel and march in the exact opposite direction of the museum's entrance, entering a restaurant across the street and waiting out the rain over my serving of *risotto ai funghi.*

I don't recall now if it was before or after Lucca that I went to Bologna—a city so beautiful that I couldn't stop singing, the whole time I was there: "My Bologna has a first name! It's P-R-E-T-T-Y." Traditionally Bologna—with its lovely brick architecture and famous wealth—has been called "The Red, The Fat and The Beautiful." (And, yes, that was an alternate title for this book.) The food is definitely better here than in Rome, or maybe they just use more butter. Even the gelato in Bologna is better (and I feel somewhat disloyal saying that, but it's true). The mushrooms here are like big thick sexy tongues, and the prosciutto drapes over pizzas like a fine lace veil draping over a fancy lady's hat. And of course there is the Bolognese sauce, which laughs disdainfully at any other idea of a *ragù.*

It occurs to me in Bologna that there is no equivalent in English for the term *buon appetito.* This is a pity, and also very telling. It occurs to me, too, that the train stops of Italy are a tour through the names of the world's most famous foods and wines: next stop, *Parma* . . . next stop, *Bologna* . . . next stop, approaching *Montepulciano* . . . Inside the trains there is food, too, of course—little sandwiches and good hot chocolate. If it's raining outside, it's even nicer to snack and speed along. For one long ride, I share a train compartment with a good-looking young Italian guy who sleeps for hours through the rain as I eat my octopus salad. The guy wakes up shortly before we arrive in Venice, rubs his eyes, looks me over carefully from foot to head and pronounces under his breath: *"Carina."* Which means: Cute.

"Grazie mille," I tell him with exaggerated politeness. A thousand thanks.

He's surprised. He didn't realize I spoke Italian. Neither did I, actually, but we talk for about twenty minutes and I realize for the first time that I *do*. Some line has been crossed and I'm actually speaking Italian now. I'm not translating; I'm talking. Of course, there's a mistake in every sentence, and I only know three tenses, but I can communicate with this guy without much effort. *Me la cavo,* is how you would say it in Italian, which basically means, "I can get by," but comes from the same verb you use to talk about uncorking a bottle of wine, meaning, "I can use this language to extract myself from tight situations."

He's hitting on me, this kid! It's not entirely unflattering. He's not entirely unattractive. Though he's not remotely uncocky, either. At one point he says to me in Italian, meaning to be complimentary, of course, "You're not too fat, for an American woman."

I reply in English, "And you're not too greasy, for an Italian man."

"Come?"

I repeat myself, in slightly modified Italian: "And you're so gracious, just like all Italian men."

I can speak this language! The kid thinks I like him, but it's the words I'm flirting with. My God—I have decanted myself! I have uncorked my tongue, and Italian is pouring forth! He wants me to meet him later in Venice, but I don't have the first interest in him. I'm just lovesick over the language, so I let him slide away. Anyhow, I've already got a date in Venice. I'm meeting my friend Linda there.

Crazy Linda, as I like to call her, even though she isn't, is coming to Venice from Seattle, another damp and gray town. She wanted to come see me in Italy, so I invited her along on this leg of my trip because I refuse—I absolutely decline—to go to the most romantic city on earth by myself, no, not now, not this year. I could just picture myself all alone, in the butt end of a gondola, getting dragged through the mist by a crooning gondolier as I . . . read a magazine? It's a sad image, rather like the idea of humping up a hill all by yourself on a bicycle-built-for-two. So Linda will provide me with company, and good company, at that.

I met Linda (and her dreadlocks, and her piercings) in Bali almost two years ago, when I went for that Yoga retreat. Since then, we've done a trip to Costa Rica together, too. She's one of my favorite traveling companions, an unflappable and entertaining and surprisingly organized little pixie in tight red crushed-velvet pants. Linda is the owner of one of the world's more intact psyches, with an incomprehension for depression and a self-esteem that has never even considered being anything but high. She said to me once, while regarding herself in a mirror, "Admittedly, I am not the one who looks fantastic in everything, but still I cannot help loving myself." She's got this ability to shut me up when I start fretting over metaphysical questions, such as, "What is the nature of the universe?" (Linda's reply: "My only question is: Why ask?") Linda would like to someday grow her dreadlocks so long she could weave them into a wire-supported structure on the top of her head "like a topiary" and maybe store a bird there. The Balinese loved Linda. So did the Costa Ricans. When she's not taking care of her pet lizards and ferrets, she is managing a software development team in Seattle and making more money than any of us.

So we find each other there in Venice, and Linda frowns at our map of the city, turns it upside down, locates our hotel, orients herself and announces with characteristic humility: "We are the mayors of this town's ass."

Her cheer, her optimism—they in no way match this stinky, slow, sinking, mysterious, silent, weird city. Venice seems like a wonderful city in which to die a slow and alcoholic death, or to lose a loved one, or to lose the murder weapon with which the loved one was lost in the first place. Seeing Venice, I'm grateful that I chose to live in Rome instead. I don't think I would have gotten off the anti-depressants quite so quick here. Venice is beautiful, but like a Bergman movie is beautiful; you can admire it, but you don't really want to live in it.

The whole town is peeling and fading like those suites of rooms that once-rich families will barricade away in the backs of their mansions when it gets too expensive to keep the maintenance up and it's easier to just nail the doors shut and forget about the dying treasures on the other side—this is Venice. Greasy streams of Adriatic backwash nudge up against the long-suffering foundations of these buildings, testing the endurance of this fourteenth-century science fair experiment—*Hey, what if we built a city that sits in water all the time?*

Venice is spooky under its grainy November skies. The city creaks and sways like a fishing pier. Despite Linda's initial confidence that we can govern this town, we get lost every day, and most especially at night, taking wrong turns toward dark corners that dead-end dangerously and directly into canal water. One foggy night, we pass an old building that seems to actually be groaning in pain. "Not to worry," chirps Linda. "That's just Satan's hungry maw." I teach her my favorite Italian word—*attraversiamo* ("let's cross over")—and we backtrack nervously out of there.

The beautiful young Venetian woman who owns the restaurant near where we are staying is miserable with her fate. She hates Venice. She swears that everyone who lives in Venice regards it as a tomb. She'd fallen in love once with a Sardinian artist, who'd promised her another world of light and sun, but had left her, instead, with three children and no choice but to return to Venice and run the family restaurant. She is my age but looks even older than I do, and I can't imagine the kind of man who could do *that* to a woman so attractive. ("He was powerful," she says, "and I died of love in his shadow.") Venice is conservative. The woman has had some affairs here, maybe even with some married men, but it always ends in sorrow. The neighbors talk about her. People stop speaking when she walks into the room. Her mother begs her to wear a wedding ring just for appearances—saying, *Darling, this is not Rome, where you can live as scandalously as you like.* Every morning when Linda and I come for breakfast and ask our sorrowful young/old Venetian proprietress about the weather report for the day, she cocks the fingers of her right hand like a gun, puts it to her temple, and says, "More rain."

Yet I don't get depressed here. I can cope with, and even somehow enjoy, the sinking melancholy of Venice, just for a few days.

Somewhere in me I am able to recognize that this is not *my* melancholy; this is the city's *own* indigenous melancholy, and I am healthy enough these days to be able to feel the difference between me and it. This is a sign, I cannot help but think, of healing, of the coagulation of my self. There were a few years there, lost in borderless despair, when I used to experience all the world's sadness as my own. Everything sad leaked through me and left damp traces behind.

Anyhow, it's hard to be depressed with Linda babbling beside me, trying to get me to buy a giant purple fur hat, and asking of the lousy dinner we ate one night, "Are these called Mrs. Paul's Veal Sticks?" She is a firefly, this Linda. In Venice in the Middle Ages there was once a profession for a man called a *codega*—a fellow you hired to walk in front of you at night with a lit lantern, showing you the way, scaring off thieves and demons, bringing you confidence and protection through the dark streets. This is Linda—my temporary, special-order, travel-sized Venetian *codega*.

33

I step off the train a few days later to a Rome full of hot, sunny, eternal disorder, where—immediately upon walking out into the street—I can hear the soccer-stadium-like cheers of a nearby *manifestazione*, another labor demonstration. What they are striking about this time, my taxi driver cannot tell me, mainly because, it seems, he doesn't care. " *'Sti cazzi*," he says about the strikers. (Literal translation: "These balls," or, as we might say: "I don't give a shit.") It's nice to be back. After the staid sobriety of Venice, it's nice to be back where I can see a man in a leopard-skin jacket walking past a pair of teenagers making out right in the middle of the street. The city is so awake and alive, so dolled-up and sexy in the sunshine.

I remember something that my friend Maria's husband, Giulio, said to me once. We were sitting in an outdoor café, having our conversation practice, and he asked me what I thought of Rome. I told him I really loved the place, of course, but somehow knew it was not my city, not where I'd end up living for the rest of my life. There was something about Rome that didn't belong to me, and I couldn't quite figure out what it was. Just as we were talking, a helpful visual aid walked by. It was the quintessential Roman woman—a fantastically maintained, jewelry-sodden forty-something dame wearing four-inch heels, a tight skirt with a slit as long as your arm, and those sunglasses that look like race cars (and probably cost as much). She was walking her little fancy dog on a gem-studded leash, and the fur collar on her tight jacket looked as if it had been made out of the pelt of her former little fancy dog. She was exuding an unbelievably glamorous air of: "You will look at me, but I will refuse to look at you." It was hard to imagine she had ever, even for ten minutes of her life, not worn mascara. This woman was in every way the opposite of me, who dresses in a style my sister refers to as "Stevie Nicks Goes to Yoga Class in Her Pajamas."

I pointed that woman out to Giulio, and I said, "See, Giulio— *that* is a Roman woman. Rome cannot be her city and my city, too. Only one of us really belongs here. And I think we both know which one."

Giulio said, "Maybe you and Rome just have different words."

"What do you mean?"

He said, "Don't you know that the secret to understanding a city and its people is to learn—what is the word of the street?"

Then he went on to explain, in a mixture of English, Italian and hand gestures, that every city has a single word that defines it, that identifies most people who live there. If you could read people's thoughts as they were passing you on the streets of any given place, you would discover that most of them are thinking the same thought. Whatever that majority thought might be—that is the word of the city. And if your personal word does not match the word of the city, then you don't really belong there.

"What's Rome's word?" I asked.

"SEX," he announced.

"But isn't that a stereotype about Rome?"

"No."

"But surely there are *some* people in Rome thinking about other things than sex?"

Giulio insisted: "No. All of them, all day, all they are thinking about is SEX."

"Even over at the Vatican?"

"That's different. The Vatican isn't part of Rome. They have a different word over there. Their word is POWER."

"You'd think it would be FAITH."

"It's POWER," he repeated. "Trust me. But the word in Rome—it's SEX."

Now if you are to believe Giulio, that little word—SEX—cobbles the streets beneath your feet in Rome, runs through the fountains here, fills the air like traffic noise. Thinking about it, dressing for it, seeking it, considering it, refusing it, making a sport and game out of it—that's all anybody is doing. Which would make a bit of sense as to why, for all its gorgeousness, Rome doesn't quite feel like my hometown. Not at this moment in my life. Because SEX isn't my word right now. It has been at other times of my life, but it isn't right now. Therefore, Rome's word, as it spins through the streets, just bumps up against me and tumbles off, leaving no impact. I'm not participating in the word, so I'm not fully living here. It's a kooky theory, impossible to prove, but I sort of like it.

Giulio asked, "What's the word in New York City?"

I thought about this for a moment, then decided. "It's a verb, of course. I think it's ACHIEVE."

(Which is subtly but significantly different from the word in Los Angeles, I believe, which is also a verb: SUCCEED. Later, I will share this whole theory with my Swedish friend Sofie, and she will offer her opinion that the word on the streets of Stockholm is CONFORM, which depresses both of us.)

I asked Giulio, "What's the word in Naples?" He knows the south of Italy well.

"FIGHT," he decides. "What was the word in your family when you were growing up?"

That one was difficult. I was trying to think of a single word that somehow combines both FRUGAL and IRREVERENT. But Giulio was already on to the next and most obvious question: "What's your word?"

Now *that,* I definitely could not answer.

And still, after a few weeks of thinking about it, I can't answer it any better now. I know some words that it definitely isn't. It's not MARRIAGE, that's evident. It's not FAMILY (though this was the word of the town I'd lived in for a few years with my husband, and since I did not fit with that word, this was a big cause of my suffering). It's not DEPRESSION anymore, thank heavens. I'm not concerned that I share Stockholm's word of CONFORM. But I don't feel that I'm entirely inhabiting New York City's ACHIEVE anymore, either, though that had indeed been my word all throughout my twenties. My word might be SEEK. (Then again, let's be honest—it might just as easily be HIDE.) Over the last months in Italy, my word has largely been PLEASURE, but that word doesn't match every single part of me, or I wouldn't be so eager to get myself to India. My word might be DEVOTION, though this makes me sound like more of a goody-goody than I am and doesn't take into account how much wine I've been drinking.

I don't know the answer, and I suppose that's what this year of journeying is about. Finding my word. But one thing I can say with all assurance—it ain't SEX.

Or so I claim, anyhow. You tell me, then, why today my feet led me almost of their own accord to a discreet boutique off the Via Condotti, where—under the expert tutelage of the silky young Italian shop girl—I spent a few dreamy hours (and a transcontinental airline ticket's worth of money) buying enough lingerie to keep a sultan's consort outfitted for 1,001 nights. I bought bras of every shape and formation. I bought filmy, flimsy camisoles and sassy bits of panty in every color of the Easter basket, and slips that came in creamy satins and hush-now-baby silks, and handmade little bits of string and things and basically just one velvety, lacy, crazy valentine after another.

I have never owned things like this in my life. So why now? As I was walking out of the store, hauling my cache of tissue-wrapped naughties under my arm, I suddenly thought of the anguished demand I'd heard a Roman soccer fan yell the other night at the Lazio game, when Lazio's star player Albertini at a critical moment had passed the ball right into the middle of nowhere, for no reason whatsoever, totally blowing the play.

"Per chi???" the fan had shouted in near-madness. *"Per chi???"*

For WHOM??? For whom are you passing this ball, Albertini? Nobody's *there!*

Out on the street after my delirious hours of lingerie shopping, I remembered this line and repeated it to myself in a whisper: *"Per chi?"*

For whom, Liz? For whom all this decadent sexiness? Nobody's *there.* I had only a few weeks left in Italy and absolutely no intention of knocking boots with anyone. Or did I? Had I finally been affected by the word on the streets in Rome? Was this some final effort to become Italian? Was this a gift to myself, or was it a gift for some as yet not even imagined lover? Was this an attempt to start healing my libido after the sexual self-confidence disaster of my last relationship?

I asked myself, "You gonna bring all this stuff to *India?"*

34

Luca Spaghetti's birthday falls this year on America's Thanksgiving Day, so he wants to do a turkey for his birthday party. He's never eaten a big, fat, roasted American Thanksgiving turkey, though he's seen them in pictures. He thinks it should be easy to replicate such a feast (especially with the help of me, a real American). He says we can use the kitchen of his friends Mario and Simona, who have a nice big house in the mountains outside Rome, and who always host Luca's birthday parties.

So here was Luca's plan for the festivities—he would pick me up at around seven o'clock at night, after he'd finished work, and then we would drive north out of Rome for an hour or so to his friends' house (where we would meet the other attendees of the birthday party) and we'd drink some wine and all get to know each other, and then, probably around 9:00 PM, we would commence to roasting a twenty-pound turkey . . .

I had to do some explaining to Luca about how much time it takes to roast a twenty-pound turkey. I told him his birthday feast would probably be ready to eat, at that rate, around dawn the next day. He was destroyed. "But what if we bought a very small turkey? A just-born turkey?"

I said, "Luca—let's make it easy and have pizza, like every other good dysfunctional American family does on Thanksgiving."

But he's still sad about it. Though there's a general sadness around Rome right now, anyway. The weather has turned cold. The sanitation workers and the train employees and the national airline all went on strike on the same day. A study has just been released saying that 36 percent of Italian children have an allergy to the gluten needed to make pasta, pizza and bread, so there goes Italian culture. Even worse, I recently saw an article with the shocking headline: *"Insoddisfatte 6 Donne su 10!"* Meaning that six out of ten Italian women are sexually unsatisfied. Moreover, 35 percent of Italian men are reporting difficulty maintaining *un'erezione*, leaving researchers feeling very *perplessi* indeed, and making me wonder if SEX should be allowed to be Rome's special word anymore, after all.

In more serious bad news, nineteen Italian soldiers have recently been killed in The Americans' War (as it is called here) in Iraq—the largest number of military deaths in Italy since World War II. The Romans were shocked by these deaths and the city closed down the day the boys were buried. The wide majority of Italians want nothing to do with George Bush's war. The involvement was the decision of Silvio Berlusconi, Italy's prime minister (more commonly referred to around these parts as *l'idiota*). This intellect-free, soccer-club-owning businessman, with his oily film of corruption and sleaze, who regularly embarrasses his fellow citizens by making lewd gestures in the European parliament, who has mastered the art of speaking *l'aria fritta* ("fried air"), who expertly manipulates the media (not difficult when you own it), and who generally behaves not at all like a proper world leader but rather like a Waterbury mayor (that's an inside joke for Connecticut residents only—sorry), has now engaged the Italians in a war they see as none of their business whatsoever.

"They died for freedom," Berlusconi said at the funeral of the nineteen Italian soldiers, but most Romans have a different opinion: *They died for George Bush's personal vendetta.* In this political climate, one might think it would be difficult to be a visiting American. Indeed, when I came to Italy, I expected to encounter a certain amount of resentment, but have received instead empathy from most Italians. In any reference to George Bush, people only nod to Berlusconi, saying, "We understand how it is—we have one, too."

We've been there.

It is odd, then, that Luca would want to use this birthday to celebrate an American Thanksgiving, given these circumstances, but I do like the idea of it. Thanksgiving is a nice holiday, something an American can freely be proud of, our one national festival that has remained relatively uncommodified. It's a day of grace and thanks and community and—yes—*pleasure.* It might be what we all need right now.

My friend Deborah has come to Rome from Philadelphia for the weekend, to celebrate the holiday with me. Deborah's an internationally respected psychologist, a writer and a feminist theorist, but I still think of her as my favorite regular customer, back from the days when I was a diner waitress in Philly and she would come in for lunch and drink Diet Coke with no ice and say clever things to me over the counter. She really classed up that joint. We've been friends now for over fifteen years. Sofie will be coming to Luca's party, too. Sofie and I have been friends for about fifteen weeks. Everybody is always welcome on Thanksgiving. Especially when it also happens to be Luca Spaghetti's birthday.

We drive out of tired, stressed-out Rome late in the evening, up into the mountains. Luca loves American music, so we're blasting the Eagles and singing "Take it . . . to the limit . . . one more time!!!!!!" which adds an oddly Californian sound track to our drive through olive groves and ancient aqueducts. We arrive at the house of Luca's old friends Mario and Simona, parents of the twin twelve-year-old girls Giulia and Sara. Paolo—a friend of Luca's whom I'd met before at soccer games—is there, too, along with his girlfriend. Of course, Luca's own girlfriend, Giuliana, is there, as well, having driven up earlier in the evening. It's an exquisite house, hidden away in a grove of olive and clementine and lemon trees. The fireplace is lit. The olive oil is homemade.

No time to roast a twenty-pound turkey, obviously, but Luca sautés up some lovely cuts of turkey breast and I preside over a whirlwind group effort to make a Thanksgiving stuffing, as best as I can remember the recipe, made from the crumbs of some high-end Italian bread, with necessary cultural substitutions (dates instead of apricots; fennel instead of celery). Somehow it comes out great. Luca had been worried about how the conversation would proceed tonight, given that half the guests can't speak English and the other half can't speak Italian (and only Sofie can speak Swedish), but it seems to be one of those miracle evenings where everyone can understand each other perfectly, or at least your neighbor can help translate when the odd word gets lost.

I lose count of how many bottles of Sardinian wine we drink before Deborah introduces to the table the suggestion that we follow a nice American custom here tonight by joining hands and—each in turn—saying what we are most grateful for. In three languages, then, this montage of gratitude comes forth, one testimony at a time.

Deborah starts by saying she is grateful that America will soon get a chance to pick a new president. Sofie says (first in Swedish, then in Italian, then in English) that she is grateful for the benevolent hearts of Italy and for these four months she's been allowed to experience such pleasure in this country. The tears begin when Mario—our host—weeps in open gratitude as he thanks God for the work in his life that has enabled him to have this beautiful home for his family and friends to enjoy. Paolo gets a laugh when he says that he, too, is grateful that America will soon have the chance to elect a new president. We fall into a silence of collective respect for little Sara, one of the twelve-year-old twins, when she bravely shares that she is grateful to be here tonight with such nice people because she's been having a hard time at school lately—some of the other students are being mean to her—"so thank you for being sweet to me tonight and not mean to me, like they are." Luca's girlfriend says she is grateful for the years of loyalty Luca has shown to her, and for how warmly he has taken care of her family through difficult times. Simona—our hostess—cries even more openly than her husband had, as she expresses her gratitude that a new custom of celebration and thankfulness has been brought into her home by these strangers from America, who are not really strangers at all, but friends of Luca's and therefore friends of peace.

When it comes my turn to speak, I begin *"Sono grata . . ."* but then find I cannot say my real thoughts. Namely, that I am so grateful to be free tonight from the depression that had been gnawing at me like a rat over the years, a depression that had chewed such perforations in my soul that I would not, at one time, have been able to enjoy even such a lovely night as this. I don't mention any of this because I don't want to alarm the children. Instead, I say a simpler truth—that I am grateful for old and new friends. That I am grateful, most especially tonight, for Luca Spaghetti. That I hope he has a happy thirty-third birthday, and I hope he lives a long life, in order to stand as an example to other men of how to be a generous, loyal and loving human being. And that I hope nobody minds that I'm crying as I say all this, though I don't think they do mind, since everyone else is crying, too.

Luca is so clutched by emotion that he cannot find words except to say to all of us: "Your tears are my prayers."

The Sardinian wine keeps on coming. And while Paolo washes the dishes and Mario puts his tired daughters to bed and Luca plays the guitar and everyone sings drunken Neil Young songs in various accents, Deborah the American feminist psychologist says quietly to me, "Look around at these good Italian men. See how open they are to their feelings and how lovingly they participate in their families. See the regard and the respect they hold for the women and children in their lives. Don't believe what you read in the papers, Liz. This country is doing very well."

Our party doesn't end until almost dawn. We could have roasted that twenty-pound turkey, after all, and eaten it for breakfast. Luca Spaghetti drives me and Deborah and Sofie all the way back home. We try to help him stay awake as the sun comes up by singing Christmas carols. *Silent night, sainted night, holy night,* we sing over and over in every language we know, as we all head back into Rome together.

35

I couldn't hold out. None of my pants, after almost four months in Italy, fit me anymore. Not even the new clothes I just bought last month (when I'd already outgrown my "Second Month in Italy" pants) fit me anymore. I can't afford to buy a new wardrobe every few weeks, and I am aware that soon I will be in India, where the pounds will just *melt away*, but still—I cannot walk in these pants anymore. I can't stand it.

Which all makes sense, given that I recently stepped on a scale in a fancy Italian hotel and learned that I have gained twenty-three pounds in my four months of Italy—a truly admirable statistic. About fifteen pounds of that I actually needed to gain because I had become so skeletal during these last hard years of divorce and depression. The next five pounds, I just gained for fun. As for the final three? Just to prove a point, I suppose.

But so it is that I find myself shopping for an item of clothing I will always keep in my life as a cherished souvenir: "My Last Month in Italy Jeans." The young lady in the shop is nice enough to keep bringing me bigger and bigger sizes, handing them through the curtain one after another without commentary, only asking with concern each time if *this* is closer to a fit. Several times, I have needed to poke my head out of this curtain and ask, "Excuse me— do you have a pair that is *slightly* bigger?" Until the nice young lady finally gives me a pair of jeans with a waist measurement that verily hurts my eyes to witness. I step out of the dressing room, presenting myself to the salesgirl.

She doesn't blink. She looks at me like an art curator trying to assess the value of a vase. A rather large vase.

"Carina," she decides finally. Cute.

I ask her in Italian if she could please tell me honestly whether these jeans are causing me to resemble a cow.

No, *signorina*, I am told. You do not resemble a cow.

"Do I resemble a pig, then?"

No, she assures me with great seriousness. Nor do I resemble a pig in the least.

"Perhaps a buffalo?"

This is becoming good vocabulary practice. I'm also trying to get a smile out of the salesclerk, but she's too intent on remaining professional.

I try one more time: "Maybe I resemble a buffalo mozzarella?"

Okay, *maybe*, she concedes, smiling only slightly. Maybe you do look a *little* like a buffalo mozzarella . . .

36

I have only a week left here. I'm planning to go back to America for Christmas before flying to India, not only because I can't stand the thought of spending Christmas without my family but also because the next eight months of my journey—India and Indonesia— require a complete repacking of gear. Very little of the stuff you need when you are living in Rome is the same stuff you need when you are wandering around India.

And maybe it's in preparation for my trip to India that I decide to spend this last week traveling through Sicily—the most third-world section of Italy, and therefore not a bad place to go if you need to prepare yourself to experience extreme poverty. Or maybe I only want to go to Sicily because of what Goethe said: "Without seeing Sicily one cannot get a clear idea of what Italy is."

But it's not easy getting to or around Sicily. I have to use all my finding-out skills to find a train that runs on Sunday all the way down the coast and then to find the correct ferryboat to Messina (a scary and suspicious Sicilian port town that seems to howl from behind barricaded doors, "It's not my fault I'm ugly! I've been earthquaked and carpet-bombed and raped by the Mafia, too!") Once I've arrived in Messina, I have to find a bus station (grimy as a smoker's lung) and find the man whose job it is to sit there in the ticket booth, mourning his life, and see if he will please sell me a ticket to the coastal town of Taormina. Then I rattle along the cliffs and beaches of Sicily's stupendous and hard-edged east coast until I get to Taormina, and then I have to find a taxi and then I have to find a hotel. Then I have to find the right person of whom to ask my favorite question in Italian: "Where is the best food in this town?" In Taormina, that person turns out to be a sleepy policeman. He gives me one of the greatest things anyone can ever give me in life—a tiny piece of paper with the name of an obscure restaurant written on it, a hand-drawn map of how to find the place.

Which turns out to be a little trattoria where the friendly elderly proprietress is getting ready for her evening's customers by standing on a table in her stocking feet, trying not to knock over the Christmas crèche as she polishes the restaurant windows. I tell her that I don't need to see the menu but could she just bring me the best food possible because this is my first night in Sicily. She rubs her hands together in pleasure and yells something in Sicilian dialect to her even-more-elderly mother in the kitchen, and within the space of twenty minutes I am busily eating the hands-down most amazing meal I've eaten yet in all of Italy. It's pasta, but a shape of pasta I've never before seen—big, fresh, sheets of pasta folded ravioli-like into the shape (if not exactly the size) of the pope's hat, stuffed with a hot, aromatic puree of crustaceans and octopus and squid, served tossed like a hot salad with fresh cockles and strips of julienned vegetables, all swimming in an olivey, oceany broth. Followed by the rabbit, stewed in thyme.

But Syracuse, the next day, is even better. The bus coughs me up on a street corner here in the cold rain, late in the day. I love this town immediately. There are three thousand years of history under my feet in Syracuse. It's a place of such ancient civilization that it makes Rome look like Dallas. Myth says that Daedalus flew here from Crete and that Hercules once slept here. Syracuse was a Greek colony that Thucydides called "a city not in the least inferior to Athens itself." Syracuse is the link between ancient Greece and ancient Rome. Many great playwrights and scientists of antiquity lived here. Plato thought it would be the ideal location for a utopian experiment where perhaps "by some divine fate" rulers might become philosophers, and philosophers might become rulers. Historians say that rhetoric was invented in Syracuse, and also (and this is just a minor thing) *plot*.

I walk through the markets of this crumbly town and my heart tumbles with a love I can't answer or explain as I watch an old guy in a black wool hat gut a fish for a customer (he has stuck his cigarette in his lips for safekeeping the way a seamstress keeps her pins in her mouth as she sews; his knife works with devotional perfection on the fillets). Shyly, I ask this fisherman where I should eat tonight, and I leave our conversation clutching yet another little piece of paper, directing me to a little restaurant with no name, where—as soon as I sit down that night—the waiter brings me airy clouds of ricotta sprinkled with pistachio, bread chunks floating in aromatic oils, tiny plates of sliced meats and olives, a salad of chilled oranges tossed in a dressing of raw onion and parsley. This is before I even hear about the calamari house specialty.

"No town can live peacefully, whatever its laws," Plato wrote, "when its citizens . . . do nothing but feast and drink and tire themselves out in the cares of love."

But is it such a bad thing to live like this for just a little while? Just for a few months of one's life, is it so awful to travel through time with no greater ambition than to find the next lovely meal? Or to learn how to speak a language for no higher purpose than that it pleases your ear to hear it? Or to nap in a garden, in a patch of sunlight, in the middle of the day, right next to your favorite fountain? And then to do it again the next day?

Of course, one can't live like this forever. Real life and wars and traumas and mortality will interfere eventually. Here in Sicily with its dreadful poverty, real life is never far from anyone's mind. The Mafia has been the only successful business in Sicily for centuries (running the business of protecting citizens from itself), and it still keeps its hand down everybody's pants. Palermo—a city Goethe once claimed was possessed of an impossible-to-describe beauty— may now be the only city in Western Europe where you can still find yourself picking your steps through World War II rubble, just to give a sense of development here. The town has been systematically uglified beyond description by the hideous and unsafe apartment blocks the Mafia constructed in the 1980s as money-laundering operations. I asked one Sicilian if those buildings were made from cheap concrete and he said, "Oh, no—this is very expensive concrete. In each batch, there are a few bodies of people who were killed by the Mafia, and that costs money. But it does make the concrete stronger to be reinforced with all those bones and teeth."

In such an environment, is it maybe a little shallow to be thinking only about your next wonderful meal? Or is it perhaps the best you can do, given the harder realities? Luigi Barzini, in his 1964 masterwork *The Italians* (written when he'd finally grown tired of foreigners writing about Italy and either loving it or hating it too much) tried to set the record straight on his own culture. He tried to answer the question of why the Italians have produced the greatest artistic, political and scientific minds of the ages, but have still never become a major world power. Why are they the planet's masters of verbal diplomacy, but still so inept at home government? Why are they so individually valiant, yet so collectively unsuccessful as an army? How can they be such shrewd merchants on the personal level, yet such inefficient capitalists as a nation?

His answers to these questions are more complex than I can fairly encapsulate here, but have much to do with a sad Italian history of corruption by local leaders and exploitation by foreign dominators, all of which has generally led Italians to draw the seemingly accurate conclusion that nobody and nothing in this world can be trusted. Because the world is so corrupted, misspoken, unstable, exaggerated and unfair, one should trust only what one can experience with one's own senses, and *this* makes the senses stronger in Italy than anywhere in Europe. This is why, Barzini says, Italians will tolerate hideously incompetent generals, presidents, tyrants, professors, bureaucrats, journalists and captains of industry, but will never tolerate incompetent "opera singers, conductors, ballerinas, courtesans, actors, film directors, cooks, tailors . . ." In a world of disorder and disaster and fraud, sometimes only beauty can be trusted. Only artistic excellence is incorruptible. Pleasure cannot be bargained down. And sometimes the meal is the only currency that is real.

To devote yourself to the creation and enjoyment of beauty, then, can be a serious business—not always necessarily a means of escaping reality, but sometimes a means of holding on to the real when everything else is flaking away into . . . rhetoric and plot. Not too long ago, authorities arrested a brotherhood of Catholic monks in

Sicily who were in tight conspiracy with the Mafia, so who can you trust? What can you believe? The world is unkind and unfair. Speak up against this unfairness and in Sicily, at least, you'll end up as the foundation of an ugly new building. What can you do in such an environment to hold a sense of your individual human dignity? Maybe nothing. Maybe nothing except, perhaps, to pride yourself on the fact that you always fillet your fish with perfection, or that you make the lightest ricotta in the whole town?

I don't want to insult anyone by drawing too much of a comparison between myself and the long-suffering Sicilian people. The tragedies in my life have been of a personal and largely self-created nature, not epically oppressive. I went through a divorce and a depression, not a few centuries of murderous tyranny. I had a crisis of identity, but I also had the resources (financial, artistic and emotional) with which to try to work it out. Still, I will say that the same thing which has helped generations of Sicilians hold their dignity has helped me begin to recover mine—namely, the idea that the appreciation of pleasure can be an anchor of one's humanity. I believe this is what Goethe meant by saying that you have to come here, to Sicily, in order to understand Italy. And I suppose this is what I instinctively felt when I decided that I needed to come here, to Italy, in order to understand myself.

It was in a bathtub back in New York, reading Italian words aloud from a dictionary, that I first started mending my soul. My life had gone to bits and I was so unrecognizable to myself that I probably couldn't have picked me out of a police lineup. But I felt a glimmer of happiness when I started studying Italian, and when you sense a faint potentiality for happiness after such dark times you must grab onto the ankles of that happiness and not let go until it drags you face-first out of the dirt—this is not selfishness, but obligation. You were given life; it is your duty (and also your entitlement as a human being) to find something beautiful within life, no matter how slight.

I came to Italy pinched and thin. I did not know yet what I deserved. I still maybe don't fully know what I deserve. But I do know that I have collected myself of late—through the enjoyment of harmless pleasures—into somebody much more intact. The easiest, most fundamentally human way to say it is that *I have put on weight.* I exist more now than I did four months ago. I will leave Italy noticeably bigger than when I arrived here. And I will leave with the hope that the expansion of one person—the magnification of one life—is indeed an act of worth in this world. Even if that life, just this one time, happens to be nobody's but my own.

INDIA

Or

'Congratulations to Meet You.'

Or

Thirty-six Tales About the Pursuit of Devotion

37

When I was growing up, my family kept chickens. We always had about a dozen of them at any given time and whenever one died off—taken away by hawk or fox or by some obscure chicken illness—my father would replace the lost hen. He'd drive to a nearby poultry farm and return with a new chicken in a sack. The thing is, you must be very careful when introducing a new chicken to the general flock. You can't just toss it in there with the old chickens, or they will see it as an invader. What you must do instead is to slip the new bird into the chicken coop in the middle of the night while the others are asleep. Place her on a roost beside the flock and tiptoe away. In the morning, when the chickens wake up, they don't notice the newcomer, thinking only, "She must have been here all the time since I didn't see her arrive." The clincher of it is, awaking within this flock, the newcomer herself doesn't even remember that she's a newcomer, thinking only, "I must have been here the whole time . . ."

This is exactly how I arrive in India.

My plane lands in Mumbai around 1:30 AM. It is December 30. I find my luggage, then find the taxi that will take me hours and hours out of the city to the Ashram, located in a remote rural village. I doze on the drive through nighttime India, sometimes waking to look out the window, where I can see strange haunted shapes of thin women in saris walking alongside the road with bundles of firewood on their heads. *At this hour?* Buses with no headlights pass us, and we pass oxcarts. The banyan trees spread their elegant roots throughout the ditches.

We pull up to the front gate of the Ashram at 3:30 AM, right in front of the temple. As I'm getting out of the taxi, a young man in Western clothes and a wool hat steps out of the shadows and introduces himself—he is Arturo, a twenty-four-year-old journalist from Mexico and a devotee of my Guru, and he's here to welcome me. As we're exchanging whispered introductions, I can hear the first familiar bars of my favorite Sanskrit hymn coming from inside. It's the morning *arati*, the first morning prayer, sung every day at 3:30 AM as the Ashram wakes. I point to the temple, asking Arturo, "May I . . . ?" and he makes a be-my-guest gesture. So I pay my taxi driver, tuck my backpack behind a tree, slip off my shoes, kneel and touch my forehead to the temple step and then ease myself inside, joining the small gathering of mostly Indian women who are singing this beautiful hymn.

This is the hymn I call "The Amazing Grace of Sanskrit," filled with devotional longing. It is the one devotional song I have memorized, not so much from effort as from love. I begin to sing the familiar words in Sanskrit, from the simple introduction about the sacred teachings of Yoga to the rising tones of worship ("I adore the cause of the universe . . . I adore the one whose eyes are the sun, the moon and fire . . . you are everything to me, O god of gods . . .") to the last gemlike summation of all faith ("This is perfect, that is perfect, if you take the perfect from the perfect, the perfect remains").

The women finish singing. They bow in silence, then move out a side door across a dark courtyard and into a smaller temple, barely lit by one oil lamp and perfumed with incense. I follow them. The room is filled with devotees—Indian and Western—wrapped in woolen shawls against the predawn cold. Everyone is seated in meditation, roosted there, you might say, and I slip in beside them, the new bird in the flock, completely unnoticed. I sit cross-legged, place my hands on my knees, close my eyes.

I have not meditated in four months. I have not even *thought* about meditating in four months. I sit there. My breath quiets. I say the mantra to myself once very slowly and deliberately, syllable by syllable.

Om.
Na.
Mah.
Shi.
Va.
Ya.
Om Namah Shivaya.
I honor the divinity that resides within me.

Then I repeat it again. Again. And again. It's not so much that I'm meditating as unpacking the mantra carefully, the way you would unpack your grandmother's best china if it had been stored in a box for a long time, unused. I don't know if I fall asleep or if I drop into some kind of spell or even how much time passes. But when the sun finally comes up that morning in India and everyone opens their eyes and looks around, Italy feels ten thousand miles away from me now, and it is as if I have been here in this flock forever.

38

"Why do we practice Yoga?"

I had a teacher once ask that question during a particularly challenging Yoga class, back in New York. We were all bent into these exhausting sideways triangles, and the teacher was making us hold the position longer than any of us would have liked.

"Why do we practice Yoga?" he asked again. "Is it so we can become a little *bendier* than our neighbors? Or is there perhaps some higher purpose?"

Yoga, in Sanskrit, can be translated as "union." It originally comes from the root word *yuj,* which means "to yoke," to attach yourself to a task at hand with ox-like discipline. And the task at hand in Yoga is to find union—between mind and body, between the individual and her God, between our thoughts and the source of our thoughts, between teacher and student, and even between ourselves and our sometimes hard-to-bend neighbors. In the West, we've mainly come to know Yoga through its now-famous pretzel-like exercises for the body, but this is only Hatha Yoga, one limb of the philosophy. The ancients developed these physical stretches not for personal fitness, but to loosen up their muscles and minds in order to prepare them for meditation. It is difficult to sit in stillness for many hours, after all, if your hip is aching, keeping you from contemplating your intrinsic divinity because you are too busy contemplating, "Wow . . . my hip really aches."

But Yoga can also mean trying to find God through meditation, through scholarly study, through the practice of silence, through devotional service or through mantra—the repetition of sacred words in Sanskrit. While some of these practices tend to look rather Hindu in their derivation, Yoga is not synonymous with Hinduism, nor are all Hindus Yogis. True Yoga neither competes with nor precludes any other religion. You may use your Yoga—your disciplined practices of sacred union—to get closer to Krishna, Jesus, Muhammad, Buddha or Yahweh. During my time at the Ashram, I met devotees who identified themselves as practicing Christians, Jews, Buddhists, Hindus and even Muslims. I have met others who would rather not talk about their religious affiliation at all, for which, in this contentious world, you can hardly blame them.

The Yogic path is about disentangling the built-in glitches of the human condition, which I'm going to over-simply define here as the heartbreaking inability to sustain contentment. Different schools of thought over the centuries have found different explanations for man's apparently inherently flawed state. Taoists call it imbalance, Buddhism calls it ignorance, Islam blames our misery on rebellion against God, and the Judeo-Christian tradition attributes all our suffering to original sin. Freudians say that unhappiness is the inevitable result of the clash between our natural drives and civilization's needs. (As my friend Deborah the psychologist explains it: "Desire is the design flaw.") The Yogis, however, say that human discontentment is a simple case of mistaken identity. We're miserable because we think that we are mere individuals, alone with our fears and flaws and resentments and mortality. We wrongly believe that our limited little egos constitute our whole entire nature. We have failed to recognize our deeper divine character. We don't realize that, somewhere within us all, there does exist a supreme Self who is eternally at peace. That supreme Self is our true identity, universal and divine. Before you realize this truth, say the Yogis, you will always be in despair, a notion nicely expressed in this exasperated line from the Greek stoic philosopher Epictetus: "You bear God within you, poor wretch, and know it not."

Yoga is the effort to experience one's divinity personally and then to hold on to that experience forever. Yoga is about self-mastery and the dedicated effort to haul your attention away from your endless brooding over the past and your nonstop worrying about the future so that you can seek, instead, a place of eternal *presence* from which you may regard yourself and your surroundings with poise. Only from that point of even-mindedness will the true nature of the world (and yourself) be revealed to you. True Yogis, from their seat of equipoise, see all this world as an equal manifestation of God's creative energy—men, women, children, turnips, bedbugs, coral: it's all God in disguise. But the Yogis believe a human life is a very special opportunity, because only in a human form and only with a human mind can God-realization ever occur. The turnips, the bedbugs, the coral—they never get a chance to find out who they really are. But we do have that chance.

"Our whole business therefore in this life," wrote Saint Augustine, rather Yogically, "is to restore to health the eye of the heart whereby God may be seen."

Like all great philosophical ideas, this one is simple to understand but virtually impossible to imbibe. OK—so we are all one, and divinity abides within us all equally. No problem. Understood. But now try living from that place. Try putting that understanding into practice twenty-four hours a day. It's not so easy. Which is why in India it is considered a given that you need a teacher for your Yoga. Unless you were born one of those rare shimmering saints who come into life already fully actualized, you're going to need some guidance along your journey toward enlightenment. If you're lucky enough, you will find a living Guru. This is what pilgrims have been coming to India to seek for ages. Alexander the Great sent an ambassador to India in the fourth century BC, with a request to find one of these famous Yogis and return with him to court. (The ambassador did report finding a Yogi, but couldn't convince the gentleman to travel.) In the first century AD, Apollonius of Tyrana, another Greek ambassador, wrote of his journey through India: "I saw Indian Brahmans living upon the earth and yet not on it, and fortified without fortifications, and possessing nothing, yet having the richness of all men." Gandhi himself always wanted to study with a Guru, but never, to his regret, had the time or opportunity to find one. "I think there is a great deal of truth," he wrote, "in the doctrine that true knowledge is impossible without a Guru."

A great Yogi is anyone who has achieved the permanent state of enlightened bliss. A Guru is a great Yogi who can actually pass that state on to others. The word *Guru* is composed of two Sanskrit syllables. The first means "darkness," the second means "light." Out of the darkness and into the light. What passes from the master into the disciple is something called *mantravirya*: "The potency of the enlightened consciousness." You come to your Guru, then, not only to receive lessons, as from any teacher, but to actually receive the Guru's state of grace.

Such transfers of grace can occur in even the most fleeting of encounters with a great being. I once went to see the great Vietnamese monk, poet and peacemaker Thich Nhat Hanh speak in New York. It was a characteristically hectic weeknight in the city, and as the crowd pushed and shoved its way into the auditorium, the very air in the place was whisked into a nerve-racking urgency of everyone's collective stress. Then the monk came on stage. He sat in stillness for a good while before he began to speak, and the audience—you could feel it happening, one row of high-strung New Yorkers at a time—became *colonized* by his stillness. Soon, there was not a flutter in the place. In the space of maybe ten minutes, this small Vietnamese man had drawn every single one of us into his silence. Or maybe it's more accurate to say that he drew us each into our *own* silence, into that peace which we each inherently possessed, but had not yet discovered or claimed. His ability to bring forth this state in all of us, merely by his presence in the room—this is divine power. And this is why you come to a Guru: with the hope that the merits of your master will reveal to you your own hidden greatness.

The classical Indian sages wrote that there are three factors which indicate whether a soul has been blessed with the highest and most auspicious luck in the universe:

1. To have been born a human being, capable of conscious inquiry.
2. To have been born with—or to have developed—a yearning to understand the nature of the universe.
3. To have found a living spiritual master.

There is a theory that if you yearn sincerely enough for a Guru, you will find one. The universe will shift, destiny's molecules will get themselves organized and your path will soon intersect with the path of the master you need. It was only one month after my first night of desperate prayer on my bathroom floor—a night spent tearfully begging God for answers—that I found mine, having walked into David's apartment and encountered a photograph of this stunning Indian woman. Of course, I was more than a bit ambivalent about the concept of having a Guru. As a general rule, Westerners aren't comfortable with that word. We have a kind of sketchy recent history with it. In the 1970s a number of wealthy, eager, susceptible young Western seekers collided with a handful of charismatic but dubious Indian Gurus. Most of the chaos has settled down now, but the echoes of mistrust still resonate. Even for me, even after all this time, I still find myself sometimes balking at the word *Guru*. This is not a problem for my friends in India; they grew up with the Guru principle, they're relaxed with it. As one young Indian girl told me, "Everybody in India almost has a Guru!" I know what she meant to say (that *almost* everyone in India has a Guru) but I related more to her unintentional statement, because that's how I feel sometimes— like I *almost* have a Guru. Sometimes I just can't seem to admit it because, as a good New Englander, skepticism and pragmatism are my intellectual heritage. Anyhow, it's not like I consciously went shopping for a Guru. She just arrived. And the first time I saw her, it was as though she looked at me through her photograph—those dark eyes smoldering with intelligent compassion—and she said, "You called for me and now I'm here. So do you want to do this thing, or not?"

Setting aside all nervous jokes and cross-cultural discomforts, I must always remember what I replied that night: a straightforward and bottomless YES.

39

One of my first roommates at the Ashram was a middle-aged African-American devout Baptist and meditation instructor from

South Carolina. My other roommates, over time, would include an Argentinean dancer, a Swiss homeopath, a Mexican secretary, an Australian mother of five, a young Bangladeshi computer programmer, a pediatrician from Maine and a Filipino accountant. Others would come and go, too, as devotees cycled in and out of their residencies.

This Ashram is not a place you can casually drop by and visit. First of all, it's not wildly accessible. It's located far away from Mumbai, on a dirt road in a rural river valley near a pretty and scrappy little village (composed of one street, one temple, a handful of shops and a population of cows who wander about freely, sometimes walking into the tailor's shop and lying down there). One evening I noticed a naked sixty-watt lightbulb hanging from a wire on a tree in the middle of town; this is the town's one streetlamp. The Ashram essentially creates the local economy, such as it is, and also stands as the town's pride. Outside the walls of the Ashram, it is all dust and poverty. Inside, it's all irrigated gardens, beds of flowers, hidden orchids, birdsong, mango trees, jackfruit trees, cashew trees, palm trees, magnolias, banyans. The buildings are nice, though not extravagant. There's a simple dining hall, cafeteria-style. There's a comprehensive library of spiritual writings from the world's religious traditions. There are a few temples for different types of gatherings. There are two meditation "caves"—dark and silent basements with comfortable cushions, open all day and night, to be used only for meditation practice. There's a covered outdoor pavilion, where Yoga classes are held in the morning, and there's a kind of a park with an oval walking path around it, where students can jog for exercise. I'm sleeping in a concrete dormitory.

During my stay at the Ashram, there were never more than a few hundred residents at any time. If the Guru herself had been in residence, those numbers would have swollen considerably, but she was never in India when I was there. I'd sort of expected that; she'd been spending a fair bit of time lately in America, but you never knew when she might show up anywhere by surprise. It's not considered essential to be in her literal presence in order to keep up your studies with her. There is, of course, the irreplaceable high of actually being around a living Yogic master, and I've experienced that before. But many longtime devotees agree that it can also sometimes be a distraction—if you're not careful, you can get all caught up in the celebrity buzz of excitement that surrounds the Guru and lose the focus of your true intention. Whereas, if you just go to one of her Ashrams and discipline yourself to keep to the austere schedule of practices, you will sometimes find that it is easier to communicate with your teacher from within these private meditations than to push your way through crowds of eager students and get a word in edgewise in person.

There are some long-term paid staffers at the Ashram, but most of the work here is done by the students themselves. Some of the local villagers also work here on salary. Other locals are devotees of the Guru and live here as students. One teenage Indian boy around the Ashram somehow really provoked my fascination. There was something about his (pardon the word, but . . .) *aura* that was so compelling to me. For one thing, he was incredibly skinny (though this is a fairly typical sight around here; if there's anything in this world skinnier than an Indian teenage boy, I'd be afraid to see it). He dressed the way the computer-interested boys in my junior high school used to dress for band concerts—dark trousers and an ironed white button-down shirt that was far too big for him, his thin, stemlike neck sticking out of the opening like a single daisy popping out of a giant flowerpot. His hair was always combed neatly with water. He wore an older man's belt wrapped almost twice around what had to be a sixteen-inch waist. He wore the same clothes every day. This was his only outfit, I realized. He must have been washing his shirt by hand every night and ironing it in the mornings. (Though this attention to polite dress is also typical around here; the Indian teenagers with their starched outfits quickly shamed me out of my wrinkled peasant dresses and put me into tidier, more modest clothes.) So what was it about this kid? Why was I so moved every time I saw his face—a face so drenched with luminescence it looked like he'd just come back from a long vacation in the Milky Way? I finally asked another Indian teenager who he was. She replied matter-of-factly: "This is the son of one of the local shopkeepers. His family is very poor. The Guru invited him to stay here. When he plays the drums, you can hear God's voice."

There is one temple in the Ashram that is open to the general public, where many Indians come throughout the day to pay tribute to a statue of the Siddha Yogi (or "perfected master") who established this lineage of teaching back in the 1920s and who is still revered across India as a great saint. But the rest of the Ashram is for students only. It's not a hotel or a tourist location. It's more like a university. You must apply to come here, and in order to be accepted for a residency, you must show that you've been studying this Yoga seriously for a good long while. A minimum stay of one month is required. (I've decided to stay here for six weeks, and then to travel around India on my own, exploring other temples, Ashrams and devotional sites.)

The students here are about equally divided between Indians and Westerners (and the Westerners are about evenly divided between Americans and Europeans). Courses are taught in both Hindi and English. On your application, you must write an essay, gather references, and answer questions about your mental and physical health, about any possible history of drug or alcohol abuse and also about your financial stability. The Guru doesn't want people to use her Ashram as an escape from whatever bedlam they may have created in their real lives; this will not benefit anyone. She also has a general policy that if your family and loved ones for some reason deeply object to the idea of your following a Guru and living in an Ashram, then you shouldn't do it, it's not worth it. Just stay home in your normal life and be a good person. There's no reason to make a big dramatic production over this.

The level of this woman's practical sensibilities are always comforting to me.

To come here, then, you must demonstrate that you are also a sensible and practical human being. You must show that you can work because you'll be expected to contribute to the overall operation of the place with about five hours a day of *seva*, or "selfless service." The Ashram management also asks, if you have gone through a major emotional trauma in the last six months (divorce; death in the family) that you please postpone your visit to another time because chances are you won't be able to concentrate on your studies, and, if you have a meltdown of some sort, you'll only bring distraction to your fellow students. I just made the post-divorce cutoff myself. And when I think of the mental anguish I was going through right after I left my marriage, I have no doubt that I would have been a great drain on everyone at this Ashram had I come here at that moment. Far better to have rested first in Italy, gotten my strength and health back, and then showed up. Because I will need that strength now.

They want you to come here strong because Ashram life is rigorous. Not just physically, with days that begin at 3:00 AM and end at 9:00 PM, but also psychologically. You're going to be spending hours and hours a day in silent meditation and contemplation, with little distraction or relief from the apparatus of your own mind. You will be living in close quarters with strangers, in rural India. There are bugs and snakes and rodents. The weather can be extreme—sometimes torrents of rain for weeks on end, sometimes 100 degrees in the shade before breakfast. Things can get deeply real around here, very fast.

My Guru always says that only one thing will happen when you come to the Ashram—that you will discover who you really are. So if you're hovering on the brink of madness already, she'd really rather you didn't come at all. Because, frankly, nobody wants to have to carry you out of this place with a wooden spoon clenched between your teeth.

40

My arrival coincides nicely with the arrival of a new year. I have barely one day to get myself oriented to the Ashram, and then it is already New Year's Eve. After dinner, the small courtyard starts to fill with people. We all sit on the ground—some of us on the cool marble floor and some on grass mats. The Indian women have all dressed as though for a wedding. Their hair is oiled and dark and braided down their backs. They are wearing their finest silk saris and gold bracelets, and each woman has a brightly jeweled bindi in the center of her forehead, like a dim echo of the starlight above us.

The plan is to chant outside in this courtyard until midnight, until the year changes over.

Chanting is a word I do not love for a practice that I love dearly. To me, the word *chant* connotes a kind of dronelike and scary monotony, like something male druids would do around a sacrificial fire. But when we chant here at the Ashram, it's a kind of angelic singing. Generally, it's done in a call-and-response manner. A handful of young men and women with the loveliest voices begin by singing one harmonious phrase, and the rest of us repeat it. It's a meditative practice—the effort is to hold your attention on the music's progression and blend your voice together with your neighbor's voice so that eventually all are singing as one. I'm jetlagged and afraid it will be impossible for me to stay awake until midnight, much less to find the energy to sing for so long. But then this evening of music begins, with a single violin in the shadows playing one long note of longing. Then comes the harmonium, then the slow drums, then the voices . . .

I'm sitting in the back of the courtyard with all the mothers, the Indian women who are so comfortably cross-legged, their children sleeping across them like little human lap rugs. The chant tonight is a lullaby, a lament, an attempt at gratitude, written in a *raga* (a tune) that is meant to suggest compassion and devotion. We are singing in Sanskrit, as always (an ancient language that is extinct in India, except for prayer and religious study), and I'm trying to become a vocal mirror for the voices of the lead singers, picking up their inflections like little strings of blue light. They pass the sacred words to me, I carry the words for a while, then pass the words back, and this is how we are able to sing for miles and miles of time without tiring. All of us are swaying like kelp in the dark sea current of night. The children around me are wrapped in silks, like gifts.

I'm so tired, but I don't drop my little blue string of song, and I drift into such a state that I think I might be calling God's name in my sleep, or maybe I am only falling down the well shaft of this universe. By 11:30, though, the orchestra has picked up the tempo of the chant and kicked it up into sheer joy. Beautifully dressed women in jingly bracelets are clapping and dancing and attempting to tambourine with their whole bodies. The drums are slamming, rhythmic, exciting. As the minutes pass, it feels to me like we are collectively pulling the year 2004 toward us. Like we have roped it with our music, and now we are hauling it across the night sky like it's a massive fishing net, brimming with all our unknown destinies. And what a heavy net it is, indeed, carrying as it does all the births, deaths, tragedies, wars, love stories, inventions, transformations and calamities that are destined for all of us this coming year. We keep singing and we keep hauling, hand-over-hand, minute-by-minute, voice after voice, closer and closer. The seconds drop down to midnight and we sing with our biggest effort yet and in this last brave exertion we finally pull the net of the New Year *over* us, covering both the sky and ourselves with it. God only knows what the year might contain, but now it is here, and we are all beneath it.

This is the first New Year's Eve I can ever remember in my life where I haven't known any of the people I was celebrating with. In all this dancing and singing, there is nobody for me to embrace at midnight. But I wouldn't say that anything about this night has been lonely.

No, I would definitely not say that.

41

We are all given work here, and it turns out that my work assignment is to scrub the temple floors. So that's where you can find me for several hours a day now—down on my knees on the cold marble with a brush and a bucket, working away like a fairy-tale stepsister. (By the way, I'm aware of the metaphor—the scrubbing clean of the temple that is my heart, the polishing of my soul, the everyday mundane effort that must be applied to spiritual practice in order to purify the self, etc., etc.)

My fellow floor-scrubbers are mainly a bunch of Indian teenagers. They always give teenagers this job because it requires high physical energy but not enormous reserves of responsibility; there's a limit to how much damage you can do if you mess up. I like my coworkers. The girls are fluttery little butterflies who seem so much younger than American eighteen-year-old girls, and the boys are serious little autocrats who seem so much older than American eighteen-year-old boys. Nobody's supposed to talk in the temples, but these are teenagers, so there's a constant chatter going on all the time as we're working. It's not all idle gossip. One of the boys spends all day scrubbing beside me, lecturing me earnestly on how to best perform my work here: "Take seriously. Make punctual. Be cool and easy. Remember—everything you do, you do for God. And everything God does, He do for you."

It's tiring physical labor, but my daily hours of work are considerably easier than my daily hours of meditation. The truth is, I don't think I'm good at meditation. I know I'm out of practice with it, but honestly I was never good at it. I can't seem to get my mind to hold still. I mentioned this once to an Indian monk, and he said, "It's a pity you're the only person in the history of the world who ever had this problem." Then the monk quoted to me from the Bhagavad Gita, the most sacred ancient text of Yoga: "Oh Krishna, the mind is restless, turbulent, strong and unyielding. I consider it as difficult to subdue as the wind."

Meditation is both the anchor and the wings of Yoga. Meditation is the *way*. There's a difference between meditation and prayer, though both practices seek communion with the divine. I've heard it said that prayer is the act of talking to God, while meditation is the act of listening. Take a wild guess as to which comes easier for me. I can prattle away to God about all my feelings and my problems all the livelong day, but when it comes time to descend into silence and *listen* . . . well, that's a different story. When I ask my mind to rest in stillness, it is astonishing how quickly it will turn (1) bored, (2) angry, (3) depressed, (4) anxious or (5) all of the above.

Like most humanoids, I am burdened with what the Buddhists call the "monkey mind"—the thoughts that swing from limb to limb, stopping only to scratch themselves, spit and howl. From the distant past to the unknowable future, my mind swings wildly through time, touching on dozens of ideas a minute, unharnessed and undisciplined. This in itself is not necessarily a problem; the problem is the emotional attachment that goes along with the thinking. Happy thoughts make me happy, but—*whoop!*—how quickly I swing again into obsessive worry, blowing the mood; and then it's the remembrance of an angry moment and I start to get hot and pissed off all over again; and then my mind decides it might be a good time to start feeling sorry for itself, and loneliness follows promptly. You are, after all, what you think. Your emotions are the slaves to your thoughts, and you are the slave to your emotions.

The other problem with all this swinging through the vines of thought is that you are never where you *are*. You are always digging in the past or poking at the future, but rarely do you rest in this moment. It's something like the habit of my dear friend Susan, who—whenever she sees a beautiful place—exclaims in near panic, "It's so beautiful here! I want to come back here someday!" and it takes all of my persuasive powers to try to convince her that she is *already* here. If you're looking for union with the divine, this kind of forward/backward whirling is a problem. There's a reason they call God a *presence*—because God is right *here*, right *now*. In the present is the only place to find Him, and now is the only time.

But to stay in the present moment requires dedicated one-pointed focus. Different meditation techniques teach one-pointedness in different ways—for instance, by focusing your eyes on a single point of light, or by observing the rise and fall of your breath. My Guru teaches meditation with the help of a mantra, sacred words or syllables to be repeated in a focused manner. Mantra has a dual function. For one thing, it gives the mind something to do. It's as if you've given the monkey a pile of 10,000 buttons and said, "Move these buttons, one at time, into a new pile." This is a considerably easier task for the monkey than if you just plopped him in a corner and asked him not to move. The other purpose of mantra is to transport you to another state, rowboatlike, through the choppy waves of the mind. Whenever your attention gets pulled into a cross-current of thought, just return to the mantra, climb back into the boat and keep going. The great Sanskrit mantras are said to contain unimaginable powers, the ability to row you, if you can stay with one, all the way to the shorelines of divinity.

Among my many, many problems with meditation is that the mantra I have been given—*Om Namah Shivaya*—doesn't sit comfortably in my head. I love the sound of it and I love the meaning of it, but it does not glide me into meditation. It never has, not in the two years I've been practicing this Yoga. When I try to repeat *Om Namah Shivaya* in my head, it actually gets stuck in my throat, making my chest clench tightly, making me nervous. I can never match the syllables to my breathing.

I end up asking my roommate Corella about this one night. I'm shy to admit to her how much trouble I have keeping my mind focused on mantra repetition, but she is a meditation teacher. Maybe she can help me. She tells me that her mind used to wander during meditation, too, but that now her practice is the great, easy, transformative joy of her life.

"Seems I just sit down and shut my eyes," she says, "and all I have to do is *think* of the mantra and I vanish right into heaven."

Hearing this, I am nauseated with envy. Then again, Corella has been practicing Yoga for almost as many years as I've been alive. I ask her if she can show me *how* exactly she uses *Om Namah Shivaya* in her meditation practice. Does she take one inhale for every syllable? (When I do this, it feels really interminable and annoying.) Or is it one word for every breath? (But the words are all different lengths! So how do you even it out?) Or does she say the whole mantra once on the inhale, then once again on the exhale? (Because when I try to do that, it gets all speeded up and I get anxious.)

"I don't know," Corella says. "I just kind of . . . say it."

"But do you sing it?" I push, desperate now. "Do you put a beat on it?"

"I just say it."

"Can you maybe speak aloud for me the way you say it in your head when you're meditating?"

Indulgently, my roommate closes her eyes and starts saying the mantra aloud, the way it appears in her head. And, indeed, she's just . . . saying it. She says it quietly, normally, smiling slightly. She says it a few times, in fact, until I get restless and cut her off.

"But don't you get bored?" I ask.

"Ah," says Corella and opens her eyes, smiling. She looks at her watch. "Ten seconds have passed, Liz. Bored already, are we?"

42

The following morning, I arrive right on time for the 4:00 am meditation session which always starts the day here. We are meant to sit for an hour in silence, but I log the minutes as if they are miles—sixty brutal miles that I have to endure. By mile/minute fourteen, my nerves have started to go, my knees are breaking down and I'm overcome with exasperation. Which is understandable, given that the conversations between me and my mind during meditation generally go something like this:

> **Me:** OK, we're going to meditate now. Let's draw our attention to our breath and focus on the mantra. *Om Namah Shivaya. Om Namah Shiv—*

> **Mind:** I can help you out with this, you know!

> **Me:** OK, good, because I need your help. Let's go. *Om Namah Shivaya. Om Namah Shi—*

> **Mind:** I can help you think of nice meditative images. Like—hey, here's a good one. Imagine you are a temple. A temple on an island! And the island is in the ocean!

> **Me:** Oh, that *is* a nice image.

> **Mind:** Thanks. I thought of it myself.

> **Me:** But what ocean are we picturing here?

Mind: The Mediterranean. Imagine you're one of those Greek islands, with an old Greek temple on it. No, never mind, that's too touristy. You know what? Forget the ocean. Oceans are too dangerous. Here's a better idea— imagine you're an island in a *lake*, instead.

Me: Can we meditate now, please? *Om Namah Shiv*—

Mind: Yes! Definitely! But try not to picture that the lake is covered with . . . what are those things called—

Me: Jet Skis?

Mind: Yes! Jet Skis! Those things consume so much fuel! They're really a menace to the environment. Do you know what else uses a lot of fuel? Leaf blowers. You wouldn't think so, but—

Me: OK, but let's MEDITATE now, please? *Om Namah*—

Mind: Right! I definitely want to help you meditate! And that's why we're going to skip the image of an island on a lake or an ocean, because that's obviously not working. So let's imagine that you're an island in . . . a river!

Me: Oh, you mean like Bannerman Island, in the Hudson River?

Mind: Yes! Exactly! Perfect. Therefore, in conclusion, let's meditate on this image—envision that you are an island in a river. All the thoughts that float by as you're meditating, these are just the river's natural currents and you can ignore them because you are an island.

Me: Wait, I thought you said I was a temple.

Mind: That's right, sorry. You're a temple *on* an island. In fact, you are both the temple *and* the island.

Me: Am I also the river?

Mind: No, the river is just the thoughts.

Me: Stop! Please stop! YOU'RE MAKING ME CRAZY!!!

Mind (wounded): Sorry. I was only trying to help.

Me: *Om Namah Shivaya . . . Om Namah Shivaya . . . Om Namah Shivaya . . .*

Here there is a promising eight-second pause in thoughts. But then—

Mind: Are you mad at me now?

—and then with a big gasp, like I am coming up for air, my mind wins, my eyes fly open and I *quit*. In tears. An Ashram is supposed to be a place where you come to deepen your meditation, but this is a disaster. The pressure is too much for me. I can't do it. But what should I do? Run out of the temple crying after fourteen minutes, every day?

This morning, though, instead of fighting it, I just stopped. I gave up. I let myself slump against the wall behind me. My back hurt, I had no strength, my mind was quivering. My posture collapsed like a bridge crumbling down. I took the mantra off the top of my head (where it had been pressing down on me like an invisible anvil) and set it on the floor beside me. And then I said to God, "I'm really sorry, but this is the closest I could get to you today."

The Lakota Sioux say that a child who cannot sit still is a half-developed child. And an old Sanskrit text says, "By certain signs you can tell when meditation is being rightly performed. One of them is that a bird will sit on your head, thinking you are an inert thing." This has not exactly happened to me yet. But for the next forty minutes or so, I tried to stay as quiet as possible, trapped in that meditation hall and ensnared in my own shame and inadequacy, watching the devotees around me as they sat in their perfect postures, their perfect eyes closed, their smug faces emanating calmness as they surely transported themselves into some perfect heaven. I was full of a hot, powerful sadness and would have loved to burst into the comfort of tears, but tried hard not to, remembering something my Guru once said—that you should never give yourself a chance to fall apart because, when you do, it becomes a tendency and it happens over and over again. You must practice staying strong, instead.

But I didn't feel strong. My body ached in diminished worthlessness. I wondered who is the "me" when I am conversing with my mind, and who is the "mind." I thought about the relentless thought-processing, soul-devouring machine that is my brain, and wondered how on earth I was ever going to master it. Then I remembered that line from *Jaws* and couldn't help smiling:

"We're gonna need a bigger boat."

43

Dinnertime. I'm sitting alone, trying to eat slowly. My Guru is always encouraging us to practice discipline when it comes to eating. She encourages us to eat in moderation and without desperate gulps, to not extinguish the sacred fires of our bodies by dumping too much food into our digestive tracts too fast. (My Guru, I'm fairly certain, has never been to Naples.) When students come to her complaining that they're having trouble meditating, she always asks how their digestion has been lately. It only stands to reason that you'll have trouble gliding lightly into transcendence when your guts are struggling to churn through a sausage calzone, a pound of buffalo wings and half a coconut cream pie. Which is why they don't serve that kind of stuff here. The food at the Ashram is vegetarian, light and healthy. But still delicious. Which is why it's difficult for me not to wolf it down like a starving orphan. Plus, meals are served buffet-style, and it never has been easy for me to resist taking a second or third turn at-bat when beautiful food is just lying out there in the open, smelling good and costing nothing.

So I'm sitting at the dinner table all by myself, making an effort to restrain my fork, when I see a man walk over with his dinner tray, looking for an open chair. I nod to him that he is welcome to join me. I haven't seen this guy around here yet. He must be a new arrival. The stranger's got a cool, ain't-no-big-hurry kind of walk, and he moves with the authority of a border town sheriff, or maybe a lifelong high-rolling poker player. He looks like he's in his fifties, but walks like he's lived a few centuries longer than that. He's got white hair and a white beard and a plaid flannel shirt. Wide shoulders and giant hands that look like they could do some damage, but a totally relaxed face.

He sits down across from me and drawls, "Man, they got mosquitoes 'round this place big enough to rape a chicken."

Ladies and Gentlemen, Richard from Texas has arrived.

44

Among the many jobs that Richard from Texas has held in his life—
and I know I'm leaving a lot of them out—are oil-field worker;
eighteen-wheeler truck driver; the first authorized dealer of
Birkenstocks in the Dakotas; sack-shaker in a midwestern landfill
(I'm sorry, but I really don't have time to explain what a "sack-
shaker" is); highway construction worker; used-car salesman;
soldier in Vietnam; "commodities broker" (that commodity generally being Mexican narcotics); junkie and alcoholic (if you can call
this a profession); then reformed junkie and alcoholic (a much more
respectable profession); hippie farmer on a commune; radio voice-
over announcer; and, finally, successful dealer in high-end medical
equipment (until his marriage fell apart and he gave the whole business to his ex and got left "scratchin' my broke white ass again").
Now he renovates old houses in Austin.

"Never did have much of a career path," he says. "Never could
do anything but the hustle."

Richard from Texas is not a guy who worries about a lot of stuff. I
wouldn't call him a neurotic person, no sir. But I am a bit neurotic,
and that's why I've come to adore him. Richard's presence at this
Ashram becomes my great and amusing sense of security. His giant
ambling confidence hushes down all my inherent nervousness and
reminds me that everything really is going to be OK. (And if not
OK, then at least comic.) Remember the cartoon rooster Foghorn
Leghorn? Well, Richard is kind of like that, and I become his chatty
little sidekick, the Chickenhawk. In Richard's own words: "Me and
Groceries, we steady be laughin' the whole damn time."

Groceries.

That's the nickname Richard has given me. He bestowed it upon
me the first night we met, when he noticed how much I could eat. I
tried to defend myself ("I was purposefully eating with discipline
and intention!") but the name stuck.

Maybe Richard from Texas doesn't seem like a typical Yogi.
Though my time in India has cautioned me against deciding what a
typical Yogi is. (Don't get me started on the dairy farmer from rural

Ireland I met here the other day, or the former nun from South Africa.) Richard came to this Yoga through an ex-girlfriend, who drove him up from Texas to the Ashram in New York to hear the Guru speak. Richard says, "I thought the Ashram was the weirdest thing I ever saw, and I was wondering where the room was where you have to give 'em all your money and turn over the deed to your house and car, but that never did happen . . ."

After that experience, which was about ten years ago, Richard found himself praying all the time. His prayer was always the same. He kept begging God, "Please, please, please open my heart." That was all he wanted—an open heart. And he would always finish the prayer for an open heart by asking God, "And please send me a sign when the event has occurred." Now he says, recollecting that time, "Be careful what you pray for, Groceries, cuz you just might get it." After a few months of praying constantly for an open heart, what do you think Richard got? That's right—emergency open-heart surgery. His chest was literally cracked open, his ribs cleaved away from each other to allow some daylight to finally reach into his heart, as though God were saying, "How's *that* for a sign?" So now Richard is always cautious with his prayers, he tells me. "Whenever I pray for anything these days, I always wrap it up by saying, 'Oh, and God? Please be gentle with me, OK?' "

"What should I do about my meditation practice?" I ask Richard one day, as he's watching me scrub the temple floors. (He's lucky—he works in the kitchen, doesn't even have to show up there until an hour before dinner. But he likes watching me scrub the temple floors. He thinks it's funny.)

"Why do you have to do anything about it, Groceries?"

"Because it stinks."

"Says who?"

"I can't get my mind to sit still."

"Remember what the Guru teaches us—if you sit down with the pure intention to meditate, whatever happens next is none of your business. So why are you judging your experience?"

"Because what's happening in my meditations *cannot* be the point of this Yoga."

"Groceries, baby—you got no *idea* what's happening in there."

"I never see visions, I never have transcendent experiences—"

"You wanna see pretty colors? Or you wanna know the truth about yourself? What's your intention?"

"All I seem to do is argue with myself when I try to meditate."

"That's just your ego, trying to make sure it stays in charge. This is what your ego *does*. It keeps you feeling separate, keeps you with a sense of duality, tries to convince you that you're flawed and broken and alone instead of whole."

"But how does that serve me?"

"It *doesn't* serve you. Your ego's job isn't to serve you. Its only job is to keep itself in power. And right now, your ego's scared to death cuz it's about to get downsized. You keep up this spiritual path, baby, and that bad boy's days are numbered. Pretty soon your ego will be out of work, and your heart'll be making all the decisions. So your ego's fighting for its life, playing with your mind, trying to assert its authority, trying to keep you cornered off in a holding pen away from the rest of the universe. Don't listen to it."

"How do you not listen to it?"

"Ever try to take a toy away from a toddler? They don't like that, do they? They start kicking and screaming. Best way to take a toy away from a toddler is distract the kid, give him something else to play with. Divert his attention. Instead of trying to forcefully take thoughts out of your mind, give your mind something better to play with. Something healthier."

"Like what?"

"Like love, Groceries. Like pure divine love."

45

Going into that meditation cave every day is supposed to be this time of divine communion, but I've been walking in there lately flinching the way my dog used to flinch when she walked into the vet's office (knowing that no matter how friendly everybody might be acting now, this whole thing was going to end with a sharp poke with a medical instrument). But after my last conversation with

Richard from Texas, I'm trying a new approach this morning. I sit down to meditate and I say to my mind, "Listen—I understand you're a little frightened. But I promise, I'm not trying to annihilate you. I'm just trying to give you a place to rest. I love you."

The other day a monk told me, "The resting place of the mind is the heart. The only thing the mind hears all day is clanging bells and noise and argument, and all it wants is quietude. The only place the mind will ever find peace is inside the silence of the heart. That's where you need to go."

I'm trying a different mantra, too. It's one I've had luck with in the past. It's simple, just two syllables:

Ham-sa.

In Sanskrit it means "I am That."

The Yogis say that *Ham-sa* is the most natural mantra, the one we are all given by God before birth. It is the sound of our own breath. *Ham* on the inhale, *sa* on the exhale. (*Ham*, by the way, is pronounced softly, openly, like *hahhhm*, not like the meat you put on a sandwich. And *sa* rhymes with "Ahhhh . . .") As long as we live, every time we breathe in or out, we are repeating this mantra. I am That. I am divine, I am with God, I am an expression of God, I am not separate, I am not alone, I am not this limited illusion of an individual. I've always found *Ham-sa* easy and relaxing. Easier to meditate with than *Om Namah Shivaya*, the—how would you say this—"official" mantra of this Yoga. But I was talking to this monk the other day and he told me to go ahead and use *Ham-sa* if it helped my meditation. He said, "Meditate on whatever causes a revolution in your mind."

So I'll sit with it here today.

Ham-sa.

I am That.

Thoughts come, but I don't pay much attention to them, other than to say to them in an almost motherly manner, "Oh, I know *you* jokers . . . go outside and play now . . . Mommy's listening to God."

Ham-sa.

I am That.

I fall asleep for a while. (Or whatever. In meditation, you can never really be sure if what you think is sleep is actually sleep; sometimes it's just another level of consciousness.) When I awake, or whatever, I can feel this soft blue electrical energy pulsing through my body, in waves. It's a little alarming, but also amazing. I don't know what to do, so I just speak internally to this energy. I say to it, "I believe in you," and it magnifies, volumizes, in response. It's frighteningly powerful now, like a kidnapping of the senses. It's humming up from the base of my spine. My neck feels like it wants to stretch and twist, so I let it, and then I'm sitting there in the strangest position—perched upright like a good Yogi, but with my left ear pressed hard against my left shoulder. I don't know why my head and neck want to do this, but I'm not going to argue with them; they are insistent. The pounding blue energy keeps pitching through my body, and I can hear a sort of thrumming sound in my ears, and it's so mighty now that I actually can't deal with it anymore. It scares me so much that I say to it, "I'm not ready yet!" and snap open my eyes. It all goes away. I'm back in a room again, back in my surroundings. I look at my watch. I've been here—or somewhere—for almost an hour.

I am panting, literally panting.

46

To understand what that experience was, what happened in there (by which I mean both "in the meditation cave" and "in me") brings up a topic rather esoteric and wild—namely, the subject of *kundalini shakti*.

Every religion in the world has had a subset of devotees who seek a direct, transcendent experience with God, excusing themselves from fundamentalist scriptural or dogmatic study in order to personally encounter the divine. The interesting thing about these mystics is that, when they describe their experiences, they all end up describing exactly the same occurrence. Generally, their union with God occurs in a meditative state, and is delivered through an energy source that fills the entire body with euphoric, electric light. The Japanese call this energy *ki*, the Chinese Buddhists call it *chi*, the

Balinese call it *taksu*, the Christians call it The Holy Spirit, the Kalahari Bushmen call it *n/um* (their holy men describe it as a snakelike power that ascends the spine and blows a hole in the head through which the gods then enter). The Islamic Sufi poets called that God-energy "The Beloved," and wrote devotional poems to it. The Australian aborigines describe a serpent in the sky that descends into the medicine man and gives him intense, other-worldly powers. In the Jewish tradition of Kabbalah this union with the divine is said to occur through stages of spiritual ascension, with energy that runs up the spine along a series of invisible meridians.

Saint Teresa of Avila, that most mystical of Catholic figures, described her union with God as a physical ascension of light through seven inner "mansions" of her being, after which she burst into God's presence. She used to go into meditative trances so deep that the other nuns couldn't feel her pulse anymore. She would beg her fellow nuns not to tell anyone what they had witnessed, as it was "a most extraordinary thing and likely to arouse considerable talk." (Not to mention a possible interview with the Inquisitor.) The most difficult challenge, the saint wrote in her memoirs, was to not stir up the intellect during meditation, for any thoughts of the mind—even the most fervent prayers—will extinguish the fire of God. Once the troublesome mind "begins to compose speeches and dream up arguments, especially if these are clever, it will soon imagine it is doing important work." But if you can surpass those thoughts, Teresa explained, and ascend toward God, "it is a glorious bewilderment, a heavenly madness, in which true wisdom is acquired." Unknowingly echoing the poems of the Persian Sufi mystic Hafiz, who demanded why, with a God so wildly loving, are we not all screaming drunks, Teresa cried out in her autobiography that, if these divine experiences were mere madness, then "I beseech you, Father, let us all be mad!"

Then, in the next sentences of her book, it's like she catches her breath. Reading Saint Teresa today, you can almost feel her coming out of that delirious experience, then looking around at the political climate of medieval Spain (where she lived under one of the most repressive religious tyrannies of history) and soberly, dutifully, apologizing for her excitement. She writes, "Forgive me if I have been very bold," and reiterates that all her idiot babbling should be ignored because, of course, she is just a woman and a worm and despicable vermin, etc., etc. You can almost see her smoothing back her nun's skirts and tucking away those last loose strands of hair—her divine secret a blazing, hidden bonfire.

In Indian Yogic tradition, this divine secret is called *kundalini shakti* and is depicted as a snake who lies coiled at the base of the spine until it is released by a master's touch or by a miracle, and which then ascends up through seven chakras, or wheels (which you might also call the seven mansions of the soul), and finally through the head, exploding into union with God. These chakras do not exist in the gross body, say the Yogis, so don't look for them there; they exist only in the subtle body, in the body that the Buddhist teachers are referring to when they encourage their students to pull forth a new self from the physical body the way you pull a sword from its sheath. My friend Bob, who is both a student of Yoga and a neuroscientist, told me that he was always agitated by this idea of the chakras, that he wanted to actually see them in a dissected human body in order to believe they existed. But after a particularly transcendent meditative experience, he came away with a new understanding of it. He said, "Just as there exists in writing a literal truth and a poetic truth, there also exists in a human being a literal anatomy and a poetic anatomy. One, you can see; one, you cannot. One is made of bones and teeth and flesh; the other is made of energy and memory and faith. But they are both equally true."

I like it when science and devotion find places of intersection. I found an article in *The New York Times* recently about a team of neurologists who had wired up a volunteer Tibetan monk for experimental brain-scanning. They wanted to see what happens to a transcendent mind, scientifically speaking, during moments of enlightenment. In the mind of a normal thinking person, an electrical storm of thoughts and impulses whirls constantly, registering on a brain scan as yellow and red flashes. The more angry or impassioned the subject becomes, the hotter and deeper those red flashes burn. But mystics across time and cultures have all described a stilling of the brain during meditation, and say that the ultimate union with God is a blue light which they can feel radiating from the center of their skulls. In Yogic tradition, this is called "the blue pearl," and it is the goal of every seeker to find it. Sure enough, this Tibetan monk, monitored during meditation, was able to quiet his mind so completely that no red or yellow flashes could be seen. In fact, all the neurological energy of this gentleman pooled and collected at last into the center of his brain—you could see it happening right there on the monitor—into a small, cool, blue pearl of light. Just like the Yogis have always described.

This is the destination of the *kundalini shakti*.

In mystical India, as in many shamanistic traditions, *kundalini shakti* is considered a dangerous force to play around with if you are unsupervised; the inexperienced Yogi could quite literally blow his mind with it. You need a teacher—a Guru—to guide you on this path, and ideally a safe place—an Ashram—from which to practice. It is said to be the Guru's touch (either literally in person, or through a more supernatural encounter, like a dream) which releases the bound *kundalini* energy from its coil at the base of the spine and allows it to begin journeying upward toward God. This moment of release is called *shaktipat*, divine initiation, and it is the greatest gift of an enlightened master. After that touch, the student might still labor for years toward enlightenment, but the journey has at least begun. The energy has been freed.

I received *shaktipat* initiation two years ago, when I met my Guru for the first time, back in New York. It was during a weekend retreat at her Ashram in the Catskills. To be honest, I felt nothing special afterward. I was kind of hoping for a dazzling encounter with God, maybe some blue lightning or a prophetic vision, but I searched my body for special effects and felt only vaguely hungry, as usual. I remember thinking that I probably didn't have enough faith to ever experience anything really wild like unleashed *kundalini shakti*. I remember thinking that I was too brainy, not intuitive enough, and that my devotional path was probably going to be more intellectual than esoteric. I would pray, I would read books, I would think interesting thoughts, but I would probably never ascend into the kind of divine meditative bliss Saint Teresa describes. But that was OK. I still loved devotional practice. It's just that *kundalini shakti* wasn't for me.

The next day, though, something interesting did happen. We were all gathered with the Guru once more. She led us into meditation, and in the middle of it all, I fell asleep (or whatever the state was) and had a dream. In this dream, I was on a beach, at the ocean. The waves were massive and terrifying and they were building fast. Suddenly, a man appeared beside me. It was my Guru's own master—a great charismatic Yogi I will refer to here only as "Swamiji" (which is Sanskrit for "beloved monk"). Swamiji had died in 1982. I knew him only from photographs around the Ashram. Even through these photographs—I must admit—I'd always found the guy to be a little too scary, a little too powerful, a little too much on fire for my taste. I'd been dodging the idea of him for a long time, and generally avoiding his gaze as it stared down at me from the walls. He seemed overwhelming. He wasn't my kind of Guru. I'd always preferred my lovely, compassionate, feminine living master to this deceased (but still fierce) character.

But now Swamiji was in my dream, standing beside me on the beach in all his power. I was terrified. He pointed to the approaching waves and said sternly, "I want you to figure out a way to stop *that* from happening." Panicked, I whipped out a notebook and tried to draw inventions that would stop the ocean waves from advancing. I drew massive seawalls and canals and dams. All my designs were so stupid and pointless, though. I knew I was way out of my league here (I'm not an engineer!) but I could feel Swamiji watching me, impatient and judgmental. Finally I gave up. None of my inventions were clever or strong enough to keep those waves from breaking.

That's when I heard Swamiji laugh. I looked up at this tiny Indian man in his orange robes, and he was veritably busting a gut in laughter, bent over double in delight, wiping mirthful tears from his eyes.

"Tell me, dear one," he said, and he pointed out toward the colossal, powerful, endless, rocking ocean. "Tell me, if you would be so kind—how exactly were *you* planning on stopping *that*?"

47

Two nights in a row now I've had dreams of a snake entering my room. I've read that this is spiritually auspicious (and not just in Eastern religions; Saint Ignatius had serpent visions all throughout his mystical experiences), but it doesn't make the snakes any less vivid or scary. I've been waking up sweating. Even worse, once I am awake, my mind has been two-timing me again, betraying me into a state of panic like I haven't felt since the worst of the divorce years. My thoughts keep flying back to my failed marriage, and to all the attendant shame and anger of that event. Worse, I'm again dwelling on David. I'm arguing with him in my mind, I'm mad and lonely and remembering every hurtful thing he ever said or did to me. Plus I can't stop thinking about all our happiness together, the thrilling delirium when times were good. It's all I can do not to jump out of this bed and call him from India in the middle of the night and just—I don't know what—just hang up on him, probably. Or beg him to love me again. Or read him such a ferocious indictment on all his character flaws.

Why is all this stuff coming up again now?

I know what they would say, all the old-timers at this Ashram. They would say this is perfectly *normal*, that everyone goes *through* this, that intense meditation brings everything *up*, that you're just clearing out all your residual *demons* . . . but I'm in such an emotional state I can't stand it and I don't want to hear anyone's hippie *theories*. I recognize that everything is coming up, thank you very much. Like *vomit* it's coming up.

Somehow I manage to fall asleep again, lucky me, and I have another dream. No snakes this time, but a rangy, evil dog who chases me and says, "I will kill you. I will kill you and eat you!"

I wake up crying and shaking. I don't want to disturb my room-mates, so I go hide in the bathroom. The bathroom, always the bathroom! Heaven help me, but there I am in a bathroom again, in the middle of the night again, weeping my heart out on the floor in loneliness. Oh, cold world—I have grown so weary of you and all your horrible bathrooms.

When the crying doesn't stop, I go get myself a notebook and a pen (last refuge of a scoundrel) and I sit once more beside the toilet. I open to a blank page and scrawl my now-familiar plea of desperation:

"I NEED YOUR HELP."

Then a long exhale of relief comes as, in my own handwriting, my own constant friend (who *is* it?) commences loyally to my own rescue:

"I'm right here. It's OK. I love you. I will never leave you . . ."

48

The next morning's meditation is a disaster. Desperate, I beg my mind to please step aside and let me find God, but my mind stares at me with steely power and says, "I will *never* let you pass me by."

That whole next day, in fact, I'm so hateful and angry that I fear for the life of anyone who crosses my path. I snap at this poor German woman because she doesn't speak English well and she can't understand when I tell her where the bookstore is. I'm so ashamed of my rage that I go hide in (yet another!) bathroom and cry, and then I'm so mad at myself for crying as I remember my Guru's counsel not to fall apart all the time or else it becomes a habit . . . but what does *she* know about it? She's *enlightened*. She can't help me. She doesn't understand *me*.

I don't want anyone to talk to me. I can't tolerate anyone's face right now. I even manage to dodge Richard from Texas for a while, but he eventually finds me at dinner and sits down—brave man—in my black smoke of self-loathing.

"What's got you all wadded up?" he drawls, toothpick in mouth, as usual.

"Don't ask," I say, but then I start talking and tell him every bit of it, concluding with, "And worst of all, I can't stop obsessing over David. I thought I was over him, but it's all coming up again."

He says, "Give it another six months, you'll feel better."

"I've already given it twelve months, Richard."

"Then give it six more. Just keep throwin' six months at it till it goes away. Stuff like this takes time."

I exhale hotly through my nose, bull-like.

"Groceries," Richard says, "listen to me. Someday you're gonna look back on this moment of your life as such a sweet time of grieving. You'll see that you were in mourning and your heart was broken, but your life was changing and you were in the best possible place in the world for it—in a beautiful place of worship, surrounded by grace. Take this time, every minute of it. Let things work themselves out here in India."

"But I really loved him."

"Big deal. So you fell in love with someone. Don't you see what happened? This guy touched a place in your heart deeper than you thought you were capable of reaching, I mean you got *zapped*, kiddo. But that love you felt, that's just the beginning. You just got a taste of love. That's just limited little rinky-dink mortal love. Wait till you see how much more deeply you can love than that. Heck, Groceries—you have the capacity to someday love the whole world. It's your destiny. Don't laugh."

"I'm not laughing." I was actually crying. "And please don't laugh at me now, but I think the reason it's so hard for me to get over this guy is because I seriously believed David was my soul mate."

"He probably was. Your problem is you don't understand what that word means. People think a soul mate is your perfect fit, and that's what everyone wants. But a true soul mate is a mirror, the person who shows you everything that's holding you back, the person who brings you to your own attention so you can change your life. A true soul mate is probably the most important person you'll ever meet, because they tear down your walls and smack you awake. But to live with a soul mate forever? Nah. Too painful. Soul mates, they come into your life just to reveal another layer of yourself to you, and then they leave. And thank God for it. Your problem is, you just can't let this one go. It's over, Groceries. David's purpose was to shake you up, drive you out of that marriage that you needed to leave, tear apart your ego a little bit, show you your obstacles and addictions, break your heart open so new light could get in, make you so desperate and out of control that you *had* to transform your life, then introduce you to your spiritual master and *beat it*. That was his job, and he did great, but now it's over. Problem is, you can't accept that this relationship had a real short shelf life. You're like a dog at the dump, baby—you're just lickin' at an empty tin can, trying to get more nutrition out of it. And if you're not careful, that can's gonna get stuck on your snout forever and make your life miserable. So drop it."

"But I love him."

"So love him."

"But I miss him."

"So miss him. Send him some love and light every time you think about him, and then drop it. You're just afraid to let go of the last bits of David because then you'll really be alone, and Liz Gilbert is scared to death of what will happen if she's really alone. But here's what you gotta understand, Groceries. If you clear out all that space in your mind that you're using right now to obsess about this guy, you'll have a vacuum there, an open spot—a *doorway*. And guess what the universe will do with that doorway? It will rush in—God will rush in—and fill you with more love than you ever dreamed. So stop using David to block that door. Let it go."

"But I wish me and David could—"

He cuts me off. "See, now that's your problem. You're wishin' too much, baby. You gotta stop wearing your wishbone where your backbone oughtta be."

This line gives me the first laugh of the day.

Then I ask Richard, "So how long will it be before all this grieving passes?"

"You want an exact date?"

"Yes."

"Somethin' you can circle on your calendar?"

"Yes."

"Lemme tell you something, Groceries—you got some serious control issues."

My rage at this statement consumes me like fire. *Control issues? ME?* I actually consider slapping Richard for this insult. And then, from right down inside the intensity of my offended outrage comes the truth. The immediate, obvious, laughable truth.

He's totally right.

The fire passes out of me, fast as it came.

"You're totally right," I say.

"I *know* I'm right, baby. Listen, you're a powerful woman and you're used to getting what you want out of life, and you didn't get what you wanted in your last few relationships and it's got you all jammed up. Your husband didn't behave the way you wanted him to and David didn't either. Life didn't go your way for once. And nothing pisses off a control freak more than life not goin' her way."

"Don't call me a control freak, please."

"You have got *control issues*, Groceries. Come on. Nobody ever told you this before?"

(Well . . . *yeah*. But the thing about divorcing someone is that you kind of stop listening to all the mean stuff they say about you after a while.)

So I buck up and admit it. "OK, I think you're probably right. Maybe I do have a problem with control. It's just weird that you noticed. Because I don't think it's that obvious on the surface. I mean—I bet most people can't see my control issues when they first look at me."

Richard from Texas laughs so hard he almost loses his toothpick.

"They *can't*? Honey—Ray Charles could see your control issues!"

"OK, I think I'm done with this conversation now, thank you."

"You gotta learn how to let go, Groceries. Otherwise you're gonna make yourself sick. Never gonna have a good night's sleep again. You'll just toss and turn forever, beatin' on yourself for being such a fiasco in life. *What's wrong with me? How come I screw up all my relationships? Why am I such a failure?* Lemme guess—that's probably what you were up at all hours doin' to yourself again last night."

"All right, Richard, that's enough," I say. "I don't want you walking around inside my head anymore."

"Shut the door, then," says my big Texas Yogi.

49

When I was nine years old, going on ten, I experienced a true metaphysical crisis. Maybe this seems young for such a thing, but I was always a precocious child. It all happened over the summer between fourth and fifth grade. I was going to be turning ten years old in July, and there was something about the transition from nine to ten— from single digit to double digits—that shocked me into a genuine existential panic, usually reserved for people turning fifty. I remember thinking that life was passing me by *so fast*. It seemed like only yesterday I was in kindergarten, and here I was, about to turn ten. Soon I would be a teenager, then middle-aged, then elderly, then dead. And everyone else was aging in hyperspeed, too. Everybody was going to be dead soon. My parents would die. My friends would die. My cat would die. My older sister was almost in *high school* already; I could remember her going off to first grade only moments ago, it seemed, in her little knee socks, and now she was in *high school*? Obviously it wouldn't be long before she was dead. What was the point of all this?

The strangest thing about this crisis was that nothing in particular had spurred it. No friend or relative had died, giving me my first taste of mortality, nor had I read or seen anything particular about death; I hadn't even read *Charlotte's Web* yet. This panic I was feeling at age ten was nothing less than a spontaneous and full-out realization of mortality's inevitable march, and I had no spiritual vocabulary with which to help myself manage it. We were Protestants, and not even devout ones, at that. We said grace only before Christmas and Thanksgiving dinner and went to church sporadically. My dad chose to stay home on Sunday mornings, finding his devotional practice in farming. I sang in the choir because I liked singing; my pretty sister was the angel in the Christmas pageant. My mother used the church as a headquarters from which to organize good works of volunteer service for the community. But even in that church, I don't remember there being a lot of talking about God. This was New England, after all, and the word *God* tends to make Yankees nervous.

My sense of helplessness was overwhelming. What I wanted to do was pull some massive emergency brake on the universe, like the brakes I'd seen on the subways during our school trip to New York City. I wanted to call a time out, to demand that everybody just STOP until I could understand everything. I suppose this urge to force the entire universe to stop in its tracks until I could get a grip on myself might have been the beginning of what my dear friend Richard from Texas calls my "control issues." Of course, my efforts and worry were futile. The closer I watched time, the faster it spun, and that summer went by so quickly that it made my head hurt, and at the end of every day I remember thinking, "Another one gone," and bursting into tears.

I have a friend from high school who now works with the mentally handicapped, and he says his autistic patients have a particularly heartbreaking awareness of time's passage, as if they never got the mental filter that allows the rest of us to forget about mortality every once in a while and just live. One of Rob's patients always asks him the date at the beginning of every day, and at the end of the day will ask, "Rob—when will it be February fourth again?" And before Rob can answer, the guy shakes his head in sorrow and says, "I know, I know, never mind . . . not until *next year*, right?"

I know this feeling all too intimately. I know the sad longing to delay the end of another February 4. This sadness is one of the great trials of the human experiment. As far as we know, we are the only species on the planet who have been given the gift—or curse, perhaps—of awareness about our own mortality. Everything here eventually dies; we're just the lucky ones who get to think about this fact every day. How are you going to cope with this information? When I was nine, I couldn't do a thing with it except cry. Later, over the years, my hypersensitive awareness of time's speed led me to push myself to experience life at a maximum pace. If I were going to have such a short visit on earth, I had to do everything possible to experience it now. Hence all the traveling, all the romances, all the ambition, all the pasta. My sister had a friend who used to think that Catherine had two or three younger sisters, because she was always hearing stories about the sister who was in Africa, the sister who was working on a ranch in Wyoming, the sister who was the bartender in New York, the sister who was writing a book, the sister who was getting married—surely this could not all be the same person? Indeed, if I could have split myself into many Liz Gilberts, I would willingly have done so, in order to not miss a moment of life. What am I saying? I *did* split myself into many Liz Gilberts, all of whom simultaneously collapsed in exhaustion on a bathroom floor in the suburbs one night, somewhere around the age of thirty.

I should say here that I'm aware not everyone goes through this kind of metaphysical crisis. Some of us are hardwired for anxiety about mortality, while some of us just seem more comfortable with the whole deal. You meet lots of apathetic people in this world, of course, but you also meet some people who seem to be able to gracefully accept the terms upon which the universe operates and who genuinely don't seem troubled by its paradoxes and injustices. I have a friend whose grandmother used to tell her, "There's no trouble in this world so serious that it can't be cured with a hot bath, a glass of whiskey and the Book of Common Prayer." For some people, that's truly enough. For others, more drastic measures are required.

And now I *will* mention my friend the dairy farmer from Ireland—on the surface, a most unlikely character to meet in an Indian Ashram. But Sean is one of those people like me who were born with the itch, the mad and relentless urge to understand the workings of existence. His little parish in County Cork didn't seem to have any of these answers, so he left the farm in the 1980s to go traveling through India, looking for inner peace through Yoga. A few years later, he returned home to the dairy farm in Ireland. He was sitting in the kitchen of the old stone house with his father—a lifelong farmer and a man of few words—and Sean was telling him all about his spiritual discoveries in the exotic East. Sean's father listened with mild interest, watching the fire in the hearth, smoking his pipe. He didn't speak at all until Sean said, "Da—this meditation stuff, it's crucial for teaching serenity. It can really save your life. It teaches you how to quiet your mind."

His father turned to him and said kindly, "I *have* a quiet mind already, son," then resumed his gaze on the fire.

But I *don't*. Nor does Sean. Many of us don't. Many of us look into the fire and see only inferno. I need to actively learn how to do what Sean's father, it seems, was born knowing—how to, as Walt Whitman once wrote, stand "apart from the pulling and hauling . . . amused, complacent, compassionating, idle, unitary . . . both in and out of the game and watching and wondering at it all." Instead of being amused, though, I'm only anxious. Instead of watching, I'm always probing and interfering. The other day in prayer I said to God, "Look—I understand that an unexamined life is not worth living, but do you think I could someday have an unexamined *lunch*?"

Buddhist lore has a story about the moments that followed the Buddha's transcendence into enlightenment. When—after thirty-nine days of meditation—the veil of illusion finally fell away and the true workings of the universe were revealed to the great master, he was reported to have opened his eyes and said immediately, "This cannot be taught." But then he changed his mind, decided that he would go out into the world, after all, and attempt to teach the practice of meditation to a small handful of students. He knew there would be only a meager percentage of people who would be served by (or interested in) his teachings. Most of humanity, he said, have eyes that are so caked shut with the dust of deception they will never see the truth, no matter who tries to help them. A few others (like Sean's Da, perhaps) are so naturally clear-eyed and calm already that they need no instruction or assistance whatsoever. But then there are those whose eyes are just slightly caked with dust, and who might, with the help of the right master, be taught to see more clearly someday. The Buddha decided he would become a teacher for the benefit of that minority—"for those of little dust."

I dearly hope that I am one of these mid-level dust-caked people, but I don't know. I only know that I have been driven to find inner peace with methods that might seem a bit drastic for the general populace. (For instance, when I told one friend back in New York City that I was going to India to live in an Ashram and search for divinity, he sighed and said, "Oh, there's a part of me that *so* wishes I wanted to do that . . . but I really have no desire for it whatsoever.") I don't know that I have much of a choice, though. I have searched frantically for contentment for so many years in so many ways, and all these acquisitions and accomplishments—they run you down in the end. Life, if you keep chasing it so hard, will drive you to death. Time—when pursued like a bandit—will behave like one; always remaining one county or one room ahead of you, changing its name and hair color to elude you, slipping out the back door of the motel just as you're banging through the lobby with your newest search warrant, leaving only a burning cigarette in the ashtray to taunt you. At some point you have to stop because *it won't*. You have to admit that you can't catch it. That you're not supposed to catch it. At some point, as Richard keeps telling me, you gotta let go and sit still and allow contentment to come to *you*.

Letting go, of course, is a scary enterprise for those of us who believe that the world revolves only because it has a handle on the top of it which we personally turn, and that if we were to drop this handle for even a moment, well—that would be the end of the universe. *But try dropping it, Groceries.* This is the message I'm getting. Sit quietly for now and cease your relentless participation. Watch what happens. The birds do not crash dead out of the sky in mid-flight, after all. The trees do not wither and die, the rivers do not run red with blood. Life continues to go on. Even the Italian post office will keep limping along, doing its own thing without you—why are you so sure that your micromanagement of every moment in this whole world is so essential? Why don't you let it be?

I hear this argument and it appeals to me. I believe in it, intellectually. I really do. But then I wonder—with all my restless yearning, with all my hyped-up fervor and with this stupidly hungry nature of mine—what should I do with my energy, instead?

That answer arrives, too:

Look for God, suggests my Guru. *Look for God like a man with his head on fire looks for water.*

50

The next morning in meditation, all my caustic old hateful thoughts come up again. I'm starting to think of them as irritating telemarketers, always calling at the most inopportune moments. What I'm alarmed to find in meditation is that my mind is actually not that interesting a place, after all. In actuality I really only think about a few things, and I think about them constantly. I believe the official term is "brooding." I brood about my divorce, and all the pain of my marriage, and all the mistakes I made, and all the mistakes my husband made, and then (and there's no return from this dark topic) I start brooding about David . . .

Which is getting embarrassing, to be quite honest. I mean—here I am in this sacred place of study in the middle of India, and all I can think about is my *ex-boyfriend*? What am I, in eighth grade?

And then I remember a story my friend Deborah the psychologist told me once. Back in the 1980s, she was asked by the city of Philadelphia if she could volunteer to offer psychological counseling to a group of Cambodian refugees—boat people—who had recently arrived in the city. Deborah is an exceptional psychologist, but she was terribly daunted by this task. These Cambodians had suffered the worst of what humans can inflict on each other—genocide, rape, torture, starvation, the murder of their relatives before their eyes, then long years in refugee camps and dangerous boat trips to the West where people died and corpses were fed to sharks—what could *Deborah* offer these people in terms of help? How could she possibly relate to their suffering?

"But don't you know," Deborah reported to me, "what all these people wanted to talk about, once they could see a counselor?"

It was all: *I met this guy when I was living in the refugee camp, and we fell in love. I thought he really loved me, but then we were separated on different boats, and he took up with my cousin. Now he's married to her, but he says he really loves me, and he keeps calling me, and I know I should tell him to go away, but I still love him and I can't stop thinking about him. And I don't know what to do . . .*

This is what we are *like*. Collectively, as a species, this is our emotional landscape. I met an old lady once, almost one hundred years old, and she told me, "There are only two questions that human beings have ever fought over, all through history. *How much do you love me?* And *Who's in charge?*" Everything else is somehow manageable. But these two questions of love and control undo us all, trip us up and cause war, grief and suffering. And both of them, unfortunately (or maybe obviously), are what I'm dealing with at this Ashram. When I sit in my silence and look at my mind, it is only questions of longing and control that emerge to agitate me, and this agitation is what keeps me from evolving forward.

When I tried this morning, after an hour or so of unhappy thinking, to dip back into my meditation, I took a new idea with me: compassion. I asked my heart if it could please infuse my soul with a more generous perspective on my mind's workings. Instead of thinking that I was a failure, could I perhaps accept that I am only a human being—and a normal one, at that? The thoughts came up as usual—OK, so it will be—and then the attendant emotions rose, too. I began feeling frustrated and judgmental about myself, lonely and angry. But then a fierce response boiled up from somewhere in the deepest caverns of my heart, and I told myself, "I will *not* judge you for these thoughts."

My mind tried to protest, said, "Yeah, but you're such a failure, you're such a loser, you'll never amount to anything—"

But suddenly it was like a lion was roaring from within my chest, drowning all this claptrap out. A voice bellowed in me like nothing I had ever heard before. It was so internally, eternally loud that I actually clamped my hand over my mouth because I was afraid that if I opened my mouth and let this sound out, it would shake the foundations of buildings as far away as Detroit.

And this is what it roared:

YOU HAVE NO <u>IDEA</u> HOW STRONG MY LOVE IS!!!!!!!!!

The chattering, negative thoughts in my mind scattered in the wind of this statement like birds and jackrabbits and antelopes—they hightailed it out of there, terrified. Silence followed. An intense, vibrating, awed silence. The lion in the giant savannah of my heart surveyed his newly quiet kingdom with satisfaction. He licked his great chops once, closed his yellow eyes and went back to sleep.

And then, in that regal silence, finally—I began to meditate on (and with) God.

51

Richard from Texas has some cute habits. Whenever he passes me in the Ashram and notices by my distracted face that my thoughts are a million miles away, he says, "How's David doing?"

"Mind your own business," I always say. "You don't know what I'm thinking about, mister."

Of course, he's always right.

Another habit he has is to wait for me when I come out of the meditation hall because he likes to see how wigged out and spazzy I look when I crawl out of there. Like I've been wrestling alligators and ghosts. He says he's never watched anybody fight so hard against herself. I don't know about *that*, but it's true that what goes on in that dark meditation room for me can get pretty intense. The most fierce experiences come when I let go of some last fearful reserve and permit a veritable turbine of energy to unleash itself up my spine. It amuses me now that I ever dismissed these ideas of the *kundalini shakti* as mere myth. When this energy rides through me, it rumbles like a diesel engine in low gear, and all it asks of me is this one simple request—*Would you kindly turn yourself inside out, so that your lungs and heart and offal will be on the outside and the whole universe will be on the inside? And emotionally, will you do the same?* Time gets all screwy in this thunderous space, and I am taken—numbed, dumbed and stunned—to all sorts of worlds, and I experience every intensity of sensation: fire, cold, hatred, lust, fear . . . When it's all over, I wobble to my feet and stagger out into the daylight in such a state—ravenously hungry, desperately thirsty, randier than a sailor on a three-day shore leave. Richard is usually there waiting for me, ready to start laughing. He always teases me with the same line when he sees my confounded and exhausted face: "Think you'll ever amount to anything, Groceries?"

But this morning in meditation, after I heard the lion roar YOU HAVE NO IDEA HOW STRONG MY LOVE IS, I came out of that meditation cave like a warrior queen. Richard didn't even have time to ask if I thought I'd ever amount to anything in this life before I looked him eye to eye and said, "I already have, mister."

"Check *you* out," Richard said. "This is cause for celebration. Come on, kiddo—I'll take you into town, buy you a Thumbs-Up."

Thumbs-Up is an Indian soft drink, sort of like Coca-Cola, but with about nine times the corn syrup and triple that of caffeine. I think it might have methamphetamines in it, too. It makes me see double. A few times a week, Richard and I wander into town and share one small bottle of Thumbs-Up—a radical experience after the purity of vegetarian Ashram food—always being careful not to actually touch the bottle with our lips. Richard's rule about traveling in India is a sound one: "Don't touch anything but yourself." (And, yes, that was also a tentative title for this book.)

We have our favorite visits in town, always stopping to pay respects to the temple, and to say hello to Mr. Panicar, the tailor, who shakes our hands and says, "Congratulations to meet you!" every time. We watch the cows mill about enjoying their sacred status (I think they actually abuse the privilege, lying right in the middle of the road just to drive home the point that they are holy), and we watch the dogs scratch themselves like they're wondering how the heck they ever ended up here. We watch the women doing road work, busting up rocks under the sweltering sun, swinging sledgehammers, barefoot, looking so strangely beautiful in their jewel-colored saris and their necklaces and bracelets. They give us dazzling smiles which I can't begin to understand—how can they be happy doing this rough work under such terrible conditions? Why don't they all faint and die after fifteen minutes in the boiling heat with those sledgehammers? I ask Mr. Panicar the tailor about it and he says it's like this with the villagers, that people in this part of the world were born to this kind of hard labor and work is all they are used to.

"Also," he adds casually, "we don't live very long around here."

It is a poor village, of course, but not desperate by the standards of India; the presence (and charity) of the Ashram and some Western currency floating around makes a significant difference. Not that there's so much to buy here, though Richard and I like to look around in all the shops that sell the beads and the little statues. There are some Kashmiri guys—very shrewd salesmen, indeed— who are always trying to unload their wares on us. One of them really came after me today, asking if madam would perhaps like to buy a fine Kashmiri rug for her home?

This made Richard laugh. He enjoys, among other sports, making fun of me for being homeless.

"Save your breath, brother," he said to the rug salesman. "This old girl ain't got any floors to put a rug on."

Undaunted, the Kashmiri salesman suggested, "Then perhaps madam would like to hang a rug on her wall?"

"See, now," said Richard, "that's the thing—she's a little short on walls these days, too."

"But I have a brave heart!" I piped up, in my own defense.

"And other sterling qualities," added Richard, tossing me a bone for once in his life.

52

The biggest obstacle in my Ashram experience is not meditation, actually. That's difficult, of course, but not murderous. There's something even harder for me here. The murderous thing is what we do every morning after meditation and before breakfast (my God, but these mornings are long)—a chant called the Gurugita. Richard calls it "The Geet." I have so much trouble with The Geet. I do not like it at all, never have, not since the first time I heard it sung at the Ashram in upstate New York. I love all the other chants and hymns of this Yogic tradition, but the Gurugita feels long, tedious, sonorous and insufferable. That's just my opinion, of course; other people claim to love it, though I can't fathom why.

The Gurugita is 182 verses long, for crying out loud (and sometimes I do), and each verse is a paragraph of impenetrable Sanskrit. Together with the preamble chant and the wrap-up chorus, the entire ritual takes about an hour and half to perform. This is before breakfast, remember, and after we have already had an hour of meditation and a twenty-minute chanting of the first morning hymn. The Gurugita is basically the reason you have to get up at 3:00 AM around here.

I don't like the tune, and I don't like the words. Whenever I tell anyone around the Ashram this, they say, "Oh, but it's so sacred!" Yes, but so is the Book of Job, and I don't choose to sing the thing aloud every morning before breakfast.

The Gurugita does have an impressive spiritual lineage; it's an excerpt from a holy ancient scripture of Yoga called the Skanda Purana, most of which has been lost, and little of which has been translated out of Sanskrit. Like much of Yogic scripture, it's written in the form of a conversation, an almost Socratic dialogue. The conversation is between the goddess Parvati and the almighty, all-encompassing god Shiva. Parvati and Shiva are the divine embodiment of creativity (the feminine) and consciousness (the masculine). She is the generative energy of the universe; he is its formless wisdom. Whatever Shiva imagines, Parvati brings to life. He dreams it; she materializes it. Their dance, their union (their *Yoga*), is both the cause of the universe and its manifestation.

In the Gurugita, the goddess is asking the god for the secrets of worldly fulfillment, and he is telling her. It bugs me, this hymn. I had hoped my feelings about the Gurugita would change during my stay at the Ashram. I'd hoped that putting it in an Indian context would cause me to learn how to love the thing. In fact, the opposite has happened. Over the few weeks that I've been here, my feelings about the Gurugita have shifted from simple dislike to solid dread. I've started skipping it and doing other things with my morning that I think are much better for my spiritual growth, like writing in my journal, or taking a shower, or calling my sister back in Pennsylvania and seeing how her kids are doing.

Richard from Texas always busts me for skipping out. "I noticed you were absent from The Geet this morning," he'll say, and I'll say, "I am communicating with God in other ways," and he'll say, "By sleeping in, you mean?"

But when I try to go to the chant, all it does is agitate me. I mean, physically. I don't feel like I'm singing it so much as being dragged behind it. It makes me sweat. This is very odd because I tend to be one of life's chronically cold people, and it's cold in this part of India in January before the sun comes up. Everyone else sits in the chant huddled in wool blankets and hats to stay warm, and I'm peeling layers off myself as the hymn drones on, foaming like an overworked farm horse. I come out of the temple after the Gurugita and the sweat rises off my skin in the cold morning air like fog—like horrible, green, stinky fog. The physical reaction is mild compared to the hot waves of emotion that rock me as I try to sing the thing. And I can't even sing it. I can only croak it. Resentfully.

Did I mention that it has 182 verses?

So a few days ago, after a particularly yucky session of chanting, I decided to seek advice from my favorite teacher around here—a monk with a wonderfully long Sanskrit name which translates as "He Who Dwells in the Heart of the Lord Who Dwells Within His Own Heart." This monk is American, in his sixties, smart and educated. He used to be a classical theater professor at NYU, and he still carries himself with a rather venerable dignity. He took his monastic vows almost thirty years ago. I like him because he's no-nonsense and funny. In a dark moment of confusion about David, I'd once confided my heartache to this monk. He listened respectfully, offered up the most compassionate advice he could find, and then said, "And now I'm kissing my robes." He lifted a corner of his saffron robes and gave a loud smack. Thinking this was probably some super-arcane religious custom, I asked what he was doing. He said, "Same thing I always do whenever anyone comes to me for relationship advice. I'm just thanking God I'm a monk and I don't have to deal with this stuff anymore."

So I knew I could trust him to let me speak frankly about my problems with the Gurugita. We went for a walk in the gardens together one night after dinner, and I told him how much I disliked the thing and asked if he could please excuse me from having to sing it anymore. He immediately started laughing. He said, "You don't have to sing it if you don't want to. Nobody around here is ever going to make you do anything you don't want to do."

"But people say it's a vital spiritual practice."

"It is. But I'm not going to tell you that you're going to go to hell if you don't do it. The only thing I'll tell you is that your Guru has been very clear about this—the Gurugita is the one essential text of this Yoga, and maybe the most important practice you can do, next to meditation. If you're staying at the Ashram, she expects you to get up for the chant every morning."

"It's not that I mind getting up early in the morning . . ."

"What is it, then?"

I explained to the monk why I had come to dread the Gurugita, how tortuous it feels.

He said, "Wow—look at you. Even just talking about it you're getting all bent out of shape."

It was true. I could feel cold, clammy sweat accumulating in my armpits. I asked, "Can't I use that time to do other practices, instead? I find sometimes that if I go to the meditation cave during the Gurugita I can get a nice vibe going for meditation."

"Ah—Swamiji would've yelled at you for that. He would've called you a chanting thief for riding on the energy of everyone else's hard work. Look, the Gurugita isn't supposed to be a fun song to sing. It has a different function. It's a text of unimaginable power. It is a mighty purifying practice. It burns away all your junk, all your negative emotions. And I think it's probably having a positive effect on you if you're experiencing such strong emotions and physical reactions while you're chanting it. This stuff can be painful, but it's awfully beneficial."

"How do you keep the motivation to stay with it?"

"What's the alternative? To quit whenever something gets challenging? To futz around your whole life, miserable and incomplete?"

"Did you really just say 'futz around'?"

"Yes. Yes, I did."

"What should I do?"

"You have to decide for yourself. But my advice—since you asked—is that you stick to chanting the Gurugita while you're here, *especially* because you're having such an extreme reaction to it. If something is rubbing so hard against you, you can be sure it's working on you. This is what the Gurugita does. It burns away the ego, turns you into pure ash. It's supposed to be arduous, Liz. It has power beyond what can be rationally understood. You're only staying at the Ashram another week, right? And then you're free to go traveling and have fun. So just chant the thing seven more times, then you never have to do it again. Remember what our Guru says—be a scientist of your own spiritual experience. You're not here as a tourist or a journalist; you're here as a seeker. So explore it."

"So you're not letting me off the hook?"

"You can let yourself off the hook anytime you want, Liz. That's the divine contract of a little something we call *free will*."

53

So I went to the chant the next morning, all full of resolve, and the Gurugita kicked me down a twenty-foot flight of cement stairs—or anyway, that's how it felt. The following day it was even worse. I woke up in a fury, and before I even got to the temple I was already sweating, boiling, *teeming*. I kept thinking: "It's only an hour and a half—you can do anything for an hour and a half. For God's sake, you have friends who were in *labor* for fourteen hours . . ." But still, I could not have been less comfortable in this chair if I had been stapled to it. I kept feeling fireballs of, like, *menopausal* heat pulsing over me, and I thought I might faint, or bite somebody in my fury.

My anger was giant. It took in everyone in this world, but it was most specifically directed at Swamiji—my Guru's master, who had instituted this ritual chanting of the Gurugita in the first place. This was not my first difficult encounter with the great and now-deceased Yogi. He was the one who had come to me in my dream on the beach, demanding to know how I intended to stop the tide, and I always felt like he was riding me.

Swamiji had been, all throughout his life, relentless, a spiritual firebrand. Like Saint Francis of Assisi, Swamiji had been born into a wealthy family and had been expected to enter the family business. But when he was just a young boy, he met a holy man in a small village near his, and had been deeply touched by the experience. Still in his teens, Swamiji left home in a loincloth and spent years making pilgrimages to every holy spot in India, searching for a true spiritual master. He was said to have met over sixty saints and Gurus, never finding the teacher he wanted. He starved, wandered on foot, slept outside in Himalayan snowstorms, suffered from malaria, dysentery—and called these the happiest years of his life, just searching for somebody who would show God to him. Over those years, Swamiji became a Hatha Yogi, an expert in ayurvedic medicine and cooking, an architect, a gardener, a musician and a swordfighter (this I love). By his middle years, he had still not found a Guru, until one day he encountered a naked, mad sage who told him to go back home, back to the village where he had met the holy man as a child, and to study with that great saint.

Swamiji obeyed, returned home, and became the holy man's most devoted student, finally achieving enlightenment through his master's guidance. Ultimately, Swamiji would become a Guru himself. Over time, his Ashram in India grew from three rooms on a barren farm to the lush garden it is today. Then he got the inspiration to go traveling and incite a worldwide meditation revolution. He came to America in 1970 and blew everybody's mind. He gave divine initiation—*shaktipat*—to hundreds and thousands of people a day. He had a power that was immediate and transformative. The Reverend Eugene Callender (a respected civil rights leader, a colleague of Martin Luther King Jr. and still the pastor of a Baptist church in Harlem) remembers meeting Swamiji in the 1970s and dropping on his knees before the Indian man in amazement and thinking to himself, "There's no time for shuckin' and jivin' now, this is *it* . . . This man knows everything there is to know about you."

Swamiji demanded enthusiasm, commitment, self-control. He was always scolding people for being *jad*, the Hindi word for "inert." He brought ancient concepts of discipline to the lives of his often rebellious young Western followers, commanding them to stop wasting their own (and everyone else's) time and energy with their freewheeling hippie nonsense. He would throw his walking stick at you one minute, hug you the next. He was complicated, often controversial, but truly world-changing. The reason we have access now in the West to many ancient Yogic scriptures is that Swamiji presided over the translation and revitalization of philosophical texts that had long been forgotten even in much of India.

My Guru was Swamiji's most devoted student. She was literally born to be his disciple; her Indian parents were amongst his earliest followers. When she was only a child, she would often chant for eighteen hours a day, tireless in her devotion. Swamiji recognized her potential, and he took her on when she was still a teenager to be his translator. She traveled all over the world with him, paying such close attention to her Guru, she said later, that she could even feel him speaking to her with his knees. She became his successor in 1982, still in her twenties.

All true Gurus are alike in the fact that they exist in a constant state of self-realization, but external characteristics differ. The apparent differences between my Guru and her master are vast— she's a feminine, multilingual, university-educated and savvy professional woman; he was a sometimes-capricious, sometimes-kingly South Indian old lion. For a nice New England girl like me, it is easy to follow my living teacher, who is so reassuring in her propriety— exactly the kind of Guru you could take home to meet Mom and Dad. But Swamiji . . . he was such a wild card. And from the first time I came to this Yogic path and saw photographs of him, and heard stories about him, I've thought, "I'm just going to stay clear of this character. He's too big. He makes me nervous."

But now that I am here in India, here in the Ashram that was his home, I'm finding that all I want is Swamiji. All I feel is Swamiji. The only person I talk to in my prayers and meditations is Swamiji. It's the Swamiji channel, round the clock. I am in the furnace of Swamiji here and I can feel him working on me. Even in his death, there's something so earthy and present about him. He's the master I need when I'm really struggling, because I can curse him and show him all my failures and flaws and all he does is laugh. Laugh, and love me. His laughter makes me angrier and the anger motivates me to act. And I never feel him closer to me than when I'm struggling through the Gurugita, with its unfathomable Sanskrit verses. I'm arguing with Swamiji the whole time in my head, making all kinds of blowhard proclamations, like, "You better be doing something for me because I'm doing this for you! I better see some *results* here! This better be purifying!" Yesterday, I got so incensed when I looked down at my chanting book and realized we were only on Verse Twenty-five and I was already burning in discomfort, already sweating (and not like a person sweats, either, but rather like a cheese sweats), that I actually expelled a loud: "You gotta be *kidding* me!" and a few women turned and looked at me in alarm, expecting, no doubt, to see my head start spinning demonically on my neck.

Every once in a while I recall that I used to live in Rome and spend my leisurely mornings eating pastries and drinking cappuccino and reading the newspaper.

That sure was nice.

Though it seems very far away now.

54

This morning, I overslept. Which is to say—sloth that I am, I dozed until the ungodly hour of 4:15 AM. I woke up only minutes before the Gurugita was to begin, motivated myself reluctantly to get out of bed, splashed some water on my face, dressed and—feeling so crusty and cranky and resentful—went to leave my room in the predawn pitch-black . . . only to find that my roommate had left the room before me and had locked me in.

This was a really difficult thing for her to have done. It's not that big a room and it's hard not to notice that your roommate is still sleeping in the next bed. And she's a really responsible, practical woman—a mother of five from Australia. This is not her style. But she did it. She literally padlocked me in the room.

My first thought, was: *If there were ever a good excuse not to go to the Gurugita, this would be it.* My second thought, though? Well—it wasn't even a thought. It was an action.

I jumped out the window.

To be specific, I crawled outside over the railing, gripping it with my sweaty palms and dangling there from two stories up over the darkness for a moment, only then asking myself the reasonable question, "Why are you jumping out of this building?" My reply came with a fierce, impersonal determination: *I have to get to the Gurugita.* Then I let go and dropped backward maybe twelve or fifteen feet through the dark air to the concrete sidewalk below, hitting something on the way down that peeled a long strip of skin off my right shin, but I didn't care. I picked myself up and ran bare-foot, my pulse slamming in my ears, all the way to the temple, found a seat, opened up my prayer book just as the chant was beginning and—bleeding down my leg the whole while—I started to sing the Gurugita.

It was only after a few verses that I caught my breath and was able to think my normal, instinctive morning thought: *I don't want to be here.* After which I heard Swamiji burst out laughing in my head, saying: *That's funny—you sure act like somebody who wants to be here.*

And I replied to him, *OK, then. You win.*

I sat there, singing and bleeding and thinking that it was maybe time for me to change my relationship with this particular spiritual practice. The Gurugita is meant to be a hymn of pure love, but something had been stopping me short from offering up that love in sincerity. So as I chanted each verse I realized that I needed to find something—or somebody—to whom I could devote this hymn, in order to find a place of pure love within me. By Verse Twenty, I had it: *Nick.*

Nick, my nephew, is an eight-year-old boy, skinny for his age, scarily smart, frighteningly astute, sensitive and complex. Even minutes after his birth, amid all the squalling newborns in the nursery, he alone was not crying, but looking around with adult, worldly and worried eyes, looking as though he'd done all this before so many times and wasn't sure how excited he felt about having to do it again. This is a child for whom life is never simple, a child who hears and sees and feels everything intensely, a child who can be overcome by emotion so fast sometimes that it unnerves us all. I love this boy so deeply and protectively. I realized—doing the math on the time difference between India and Pennsylvania—that it was nearing his bedtime back home. So I sang the Gurugita to my nephew Nick, to help him sleep. Sometimes he has trouble sleeping because he cannot still his mind. So each devotional word of this hymn, I dedicated to Nick. I filled the song with everything I wished I could teach him about life. I tried to reassure him with every line about how the world is hard and unfair sometimes, but that it's all OK because he is so loved. He is surrounded by souls who would do anything to help him. And not only that—he has wisdom and patience of his own, buried deep inside his being, which will only reveal themselves over time and will always carry him through any trial. He is a gift from God to all of us. I told him this fact through this old Sanskrit scripture, and soon I noticed that I was weeping cool tears. But before I could wipe the tears away the Gurugita was over. The hour and a half was finished. It felt like ten minutes had passed. I realized what had happened—that Nicky had carried *me* through it. The little soul I'd wanted to help had actually been helping me.

I walked to the front of the temple and bowed flat on my face in gratitude to my God, to the revolutionary power of love, to myself, to my Guru and to my nephew—briefly understanding on a molecular level (not an intellectual level) that there was no difference whatsoever between any of these words or any of these ideas or any of these people. Then I slid into the meditation cave, where I skipped breakfast and sat for almost two hours, humming with stillness.

Needless to say, I never missed the Gurugita again, and it became the most holy of my practices at the Ashram. Of course Richard from Texas went to great lengths to tease me about having jumped out of the dormitory, being sure to say to me every night after dinner, "See you at The Geet tomorrow morning, Groceries. And, hey—try using the stairs this time, OK?" And, of course, I called my sister the next week and she said that—for reasons nobody could understand—Nick suddenly wasn't having trouble falling asleep anymore. And naturally I was reading in the library a few days later from a book about the Indian saint Sri Ramakrishna, and I stumbled upon a story about a seeker who once came to see the great master and admitted to him that she feared she was not a good enough devotee, feared that she did not love God enough. And the saint said, "Is there nothing you love?" The woman admitted that she adored her young nephew more than anything on earth. The saint said, "There, then. He is your Krishna, your beloved. In your service to your nephew, you are serving God."

But all this is inconsequential. The really amazing thing happened the same day I'd jumped out of the building. That afternoon, I ran into Delia, my roommate. I told her that she had padlocked me into our room. She was aghast. She said, "I can't imagine why I would've done that! Especially because you've been on my mind all morning. I had this really vivid dream about you last night. I haven't been able to stop thinking about it all day."

"Tell me," I said.

"I dreamt that you were on fire," Delia said, "and that your bed was on fire, too. I jumped up to try to help you, but by the time I got there, you were nothing but white ash."

55

It was then I decided I needed to stay here at the Ashram. This was so totally not my original plan. My original plan had been to stay here for just six weeks, have a bit of transcendental experience, then continue traveling all over India . . . um . . . looking for God. I had maps and guidebooks and hiking boots and everything! I had specific temples and mosques and holy men I was all lined up to meet. I mean—it's India! There's so much to see and experience here. I've got a lot of mileage to cover, temples to explore, elephants and camels to ride. And I'd be devastated to miss the Ganges, the great Rajasthani desert, the nutty Mumbai movie houses, the Himalayas, the old tea plantations, the Calcutta rickshaws racing against each other like the chariot scene from *Ben-Hur*. And I was even planning on meeting the Dalai Lama in March, up in Daramsala. I was hoping *he* could teach me about God.

But to stay put, to immobilize myself in a small Ashram in a tiny little village in the middle of nowhere—no, this was not my plan.

On the other hand, the Zen masters always say that you cannot see your reflection in running water, only in still water. So something was telling me it would be spiritually negligent to run off now, when so much was happening right here in this small, cloistered place where every minute of the day is organized to facilitate self-exploration and devotional practice. Did I really need to get on a bunch of trains and pick up intestinal parasites and hang around backpackers right now? Couldn't I do that later? Couldn't I meet the

Dalai Lama some other time? Won't the Dalai Lama always be there? (And, if he should die, heaven forbid, won't they just find another one?) Don't I already have a passport that looks like a tattooed circus lady? Is more travel really going to bring me any closer to revelatory contact with divinity?

I didn't know what to do. I spent a day wavering over the decision. As usual, Richard from Texas had the last word.

"Stay put, Groceries," he said. "Forget about sightseeing—you got the rest of your life for that. You're on a spiritual journey, baby. Don't cop out and only go halfway to your potential. You got a personal invitation from God here—you really gonna turn that away?"

"But what about all those beautiful things to see in India?" I asked. "Isn't it kind of a pity to travel halfway around the world just to stay in a little Ashram the whole time?"

"Groceries, baby, listen your friend Richard. You go set your lily-white ass down in that meditation cave every day for the next three months and I promise you this—you're gonna start seeing some stuff that's so damn beautiful it'll make you wanna throw rocks at the Taj Mahal."

56

Here's what I caught myself thinking about in meditation this morning.

I was wondering where I should live once this year of traveling has ended. I don't want to move back to New York just out of reflex. Maybe a new town, instead. Austin is supposed to be nice. And Chicago has all that beautiful architecture. Horrible winters, though. Or maybe I'll live abroad. I've heard good things about Sydney . . . If I lived somewhere cheaper than New York, maybe I could afford an extra bedroom and then I could have a special meditation room! That'd be nice. I could paint it gold. Or maybe a rich blue. No, gold. No, blue . . .

Finally noticing this train of thought, I was aghast. I thought: *Here you are in India, in an Ashram in one of the holiest pilgrimage sites on earth. And instead of communing with the divine, you're trying to plan where you'll be meditating a year from now in a home that doesn't yet exist in a city yet to be determined. How about this, you spastic fool—how about you try to meditate right here, right now, right where you actually are?*

I pulled my attention back to the silent repetition of the mantra.

A few moments later, I paused to take back that mean comment about calling myself a spastic fool. I decided maybe that wasn't very loving.

Still, I thought in the next moment, *a gold meditation room would be nice.*

I opened my eyes and sighed. Is this really the best I can do?

So, that evening, I tried something new. I'd recently met a woman at the Ashram who'd been studying Vipassana meditation. Vipassana is an ultra-orthodox, stripped-down and very intensive Buddhist meditation technique. Basically, it's just *sitting*. An introductory Vipassana course lasts for ten days, during which time you sit for ten hours a day in stretches of silence that last two to three hours at a time. It's the Extreme Sports version of transcendence. Your Vipassana master won't even give you a mantra; this is considered a kind of cheating. Vipassana meditation is the practice of pure regarding, witnessing your mind and offering your complete consideration to your thought patterns, but allowing nothing to move you from your seat.

It's physically grueling too. You are forbidden to shift your body at all once you have been seated, no matter how severe your discomfort. You just sit there and tell yourself, "There's no reason I need to move at all during the next two hours." If you are feeling discomfort then you are supposed to meditate upon that discomfort, watching the effect that physical pain has on you. In our real lives, we are constantly hopping around to adjust ourselves around discomfort—physical, emotional and psychological—in order to evade the reality of grief and nuisance. Vipassana meditation teaches that grief and nuisance are inevitable in this life, but if you can plant yourself in stillness long enough, you will, in time, experience the truth that everything (both uncomfortable and lovely) does eventually pass.

"The world is afflicted with death and decay, therefore the wise do not grieve, knowing the terms of the world," says an old Buddhist teaching. In other words: Get used to it.

I don't think Vipassana is necessarily the path for me. It's far too austere for my notions of devotional practice, which generally revolve around compassion and love and butterflies and bliss and a friendly God (what my friend Darcey calls "Slumber Party Theology"). There isn't even any talk about "God" in Vipassana, since the notion of God is considered by some Buddhists to be the final object of dependency, the ultimate fuzzy security blanket, the last thing to be abandoned on the path to pure detachment. Now, I have my own personal issues with the very word *detachment*, having met spiritual seekers who already seem to live in a state of complete emotional disconnect from other human beings and who, when they talk about the sacred pursuit of detachment, make me want to shake them and holler, "Buddy, that is the *last* thing you need to practice!"

Still, I can see where cultivating a measure of intelligent detachment in your life can be a valuable instrument of peace. And after reading about Vipassana meditation in the library one afternoon, I got to thinking about how much time I spend in my life crashing around like a great gasping fish, either squirming away from some uncomfortable distress or flopping hungrily toward ever more pleasure. And I wondered whether it might serve me (and those who are burdened with the task of loving me) if I could learn to stay still and endure a bit more without always getting dragged along on the pot-holed road of circumstance.

All these questions came back to me this evening, when I found a quiet bench in one of the Ashram gardens and decided to sit in meditation for an hour—Vipassana-style. No movement, no agitation, not even mantra—just pure regarding. Let's see what comes up. Unfortunately, I had forgotten about what "comes up" at dusk in India: mosquitoes. As I soon as I sat down on that bench in the lovely gloaming, I could hear the mosquitoes coming at me, brushing against my face and landing—in a group assault—on my head, ankles, arms. And then their fierce little burns. I didn't like this. I thought, "This is a bad time of day to practice Vipassana meditation."

On the other hand—when *is* it a good time of day, or life, to sit in detached stillness? When *isn't* there something buzzing about, trying to distract you and get a rise out of you? So I made a decision (inspired again by my Guru's instruction that we are to become scientists of our own inner experience). I presented myself with an experiment—*what if I sat through this for once?* Instead of slapping and griping, what if I sat through the discomfort, just for one hour of my long life?

So I did it. In stillness, I watched myself get eaten by mosquitoes. To be honest, part of me was wondering what this little macho experiment was meant to prove, but another part of me well knew—it was a beginner's attempt at self-mastery. If I could sit through this nonlethal physical discomfort, then what other discomforts might I someday be able to sit through? What about emotional discomforts, which are even harder for me to endure? What about jealousy, anger, fear, disappointment, loneliness, shame, boredom?

The itch was maddening at first but eventually it just melded into a general burning feeling and I rode that heat to a mild euphoria. I allowed the pain to lose its specific associations and become pure sensation—neither good nor bad, just intense—and that intensity lifted me out of myself and into meditation. I sat there for two hours. A bird might very well have landed on my head; I wouldn't have noticed.

Let me be clear about one thing. I recognize that this experiment wasn't the most stoic act of fortitude in the history of mankind, and I'm not asking for a Congressional Medal of Honor here. But there was something mildly thrilling for me about realizing that in my thirty-four years on earth I have *never* not slapped at a mosquito when it was biting me. I've been a puppet to this and to millions of other small and large signals of pain or pleasure throughout my life. Whenever something happens, I always react. But here I was—disregarding the reflex. I was doing something I'd never done before. A small thing, granted, but how often do I get to say that? And what will I be able to do tomorrow that I cannot yet do today?

When it was all over, I stood up, walked to my room and assessed the damage. I counted about twenty mosquito bites. But within a half an hour, all the bites had diminished. It all goes away. Eventually, everything goes away.

57

The search for God is a reversal of the normal, mundane worldly order. In the search for God, you revert from what attracts you and swim toward that which is difficult. You abandon your comforting and familiar habits with the hope (the mere hope!) that something greater will be offered you in return for what you've given up. Every religion in the world operates on the same common understandings of what it means to be a good disciple—get up early and pray to your God, hone your virtues, be a good neighbor, respect yourself and others, master your cravings. We all agree that it would be easier to sleep in, and many of us do, but for millennia there have been others who choose instead to get up before the sun and wash their faces and go to their prayers. And then fiercely try to hold on to their devotional convictions throughout the lunacy of another day.

The devout of this world perform their rituals without guarantee that anything good will ever come of it. Of course there are plenty of scriptures and plenty of priests who make plenty of promises as to what your good works will yield (or threats as to the punishments awaiting you if you lapse), but to even believe all this is an act of faith, because nobody amongst us is shown the endgame. Devotion is diligence without assurance. Faith is a way of saying, "Yes, I pre-accept the terms of the universe and I embrace in advance what I am presently incapable of understanding." There's a reason we refer to "leaps of faith"—because the decision to consent to any notion of divinity is a mighty jump from the rational over to the unknowable, and I don't care how diligently scholars of every religion will try to sit you down with their stacks of books and prove to you through scripture that their faith is indeed rational; it isn't. If faith were rational, it wouldn't be—by definition—faith. Faith is belief in what you cannot see or prove or touch. Faith is walking face-first and full-speed into the dark. If we truly knew all the answers in advance as to the meaning of life and the nature of God and the destiny of our souls, our belief would not be a leap of faith and it would not be a courageous act of humanity; it would just be . . . a prudent insurance policy.

I'm not interested in the insurance industry. I'm tired of being a skeptic, I'm irritated by spiritual prudence and I feel bored and parched by empirical debate. I don't want to hear it anymore. I couldn't care less about evidence and proof and assurances. I just want God. I want God inside me. I want God to play in my bloodstream the way sunlight amuses itself on water.

58

My prayers are becoming more deliberate and specific. It has occurred to me that it's not much use to send prayers out to the universe that are lazy. Every morning before meditation, I kneel in the temple and talk for a few minutes to God. I found during the beginning of my stay here at the Ashram that I was often dull-witted during those divine conversations. Tired, confused and bored, my prayers sounded the same. I remember kneeling down one morning, touching my forehead to the floor and muttering to my creator, "Oh, I dunno what I need . . . but you must have some ideas . . . so just do something about it, would you?"

Similar to the way I have oftentimes spoken to my hairdresser.

And, I'm sorry, but that's a little lame. You can imagine God regarding that prayer with an arched eyebrow, and sending back this message: "Call me again when you decide to get serious about this."

Of *course* God already knows what I need. The question is—do *I* know? Casting yourself at God's feet in helpless desperation is all well and good—heaven knows, I've done it myself plenty of times—but ultimately you're likely to get more out of the experience if you can take some action on your end. There's a wonderful old Italian joke about a poor man who goes to church every day and prays before the statue of a great saint, begging, "Dear saint—please,

please, please . . . give me the grace to win the lottery." This lament goes on for months. Finally the exasperated statue comes to life, looks down at the begging man and says in weary disgust, "My son—please, please, please . . . *buy a ticket.*"

Prayer is a relationship; half the job is mine. If I want transformation, but can't even be bothered to articulate what, exactly, I'm aiming for, how will it ever occur? Half the benefit of prayer is in the asking itself, in the offering of a clearly posed and well-considered intention. If you don't have this, all your pleas and desires are boneless, floppy, inert; they swirl at your feet in a cold fog and never lift. So now I take the time every morning to search myself for specificity about what I am truly asking for. I kneel there in the temple with my face on that cold marble for as long as it takes me to formulate an authentic prayer. If I don't feel sincere, then I will stay there on the floor until I do. What worked yesterday doesn't always work today. Prayers can become stale and drone into the boring and familiar if you let your attention stagnate. In making an effort to stay alert, I am assuming custodial responsibility for the maintenance of my own soul.

Destiny, I feel, is also a relationship—a play between divine grace and willful self-effort. Half of it you have no control over; half of it is absolutely in your hands, and your actions will show measurable consequence. Man is neither entirely a puppet of the gods, nor is he entirely the captain of his own destiny; he's a little of both. We gallop through our lives like circus performers balancing on two speeding side-by-side horses—one foot is on the horse called "fate," the other on the horse called "free will." And the question you have to ask every day is—which horse is which? Which horse do I need to stop worrying about because it's not under my control, and which do I need to steer with concentrated effort?

There is so much about my fate that I cannot control, but other things do fall under my jurisdiction. There are certain lottery tickets I can buy, thereby increasing my odds of finding contentment. I can decide how I spend my time, whom I interact with, whom I share my body and life and money and energy with. I can select what I eat and read and study. I can choose how I'm going to regard unfortunate circumstances in my life—whether I will see them as curses or opportunities (and on the occasions when I can't rise to the most optimistic viewpoint, because I'm feeling too damn sorry for myself, I can choose to keep trying to change my outlook). I can choose my words and the tone of voice in which I speak to others. And most of all, I can choose my thoughts.

This last concept is a radically new idea for me. Richard from Texas brought it to my attention recently, when I was complaining about my inability to stop brooding. He said, "Groceries, you need to learn how to select your thoughts just the same way you select what clothes you're gonna wear every day. This is a power you can cultivate. If you want to control things in your life so bad, work on the mind. That's the only thing you should be trying to control. Drop everything else but that. Because if you can't learn to master your thinking, you're in deep trouble forever."

On first glance, this seems a nearly impossible task. Control your *thoughts*? Instead of the other way around? But imagine if you could? This is not about repression or denial. Repression and denial set up elaborate games to pretend that negative thoughts and feelings are not occurring. What Richard is talking about is instead admitting to the existence of negative thoughts, understanding where they came from and why they arrived, and then—with great forgiveness and fortitude—dismissing them. This is a practice that fits hand-in-glove with any psychological work you do during therapy. You can use the shrink's office to understand why you have these destructive thoughts in the first place; you can use spiritual exercises to help overcome them. It's a sacrifice to let them go, of course. It's a loss of old habits, comforting old grudges and familiar vignettes. Of course this all takes practice and effort. It's not a teaching that you can hear once and then expect to master immediately. It's constant vigilance and I want to do it. I need to do it, for my strength. *Devo farmi le ossa* is how they say it in Italian. "I need to make my bones."

So I've started being vigilant about watching my thoughts all day, and monitoring them. I repeat this vow about 700 times a day: "I will not harbor unhealthy thoughts anymore." Every time a diminishing thought arises, I repeat the vow. *I will not harbor unhealthy thoughts anymore.* The first time I heard myself say this, my inner ear perked up at the word "harbor," which is a noun as well as a verb. A harbor, of course, is a place of refuge, a port of entry. I pictured the harbor of my mind—a little beat-up, perhaps, a little storm-worn, but well situated and with a nice depth. The harbor of my mind is an open bay, the only access to the island of my Self (which is a young and volcanic island, yes, but fertile and promising). This island has been through some wars, it is true, but it is now committed to peace, under a new leader (me) who has instituted new policies to protect the place. And now—let the word go out across the seven seas—there are much, much stricter laws on the books about who may enter this harbor.

You may not come here anymore with your hard and abusive thoughts, with your plague ships of thoughts, with your slave ships of thoughts, with your warships of thoughts—all these will be turned away. Likewise, any thoughts that are filled with angry or starving exiles, with malcontents and pamphleteers, mutineers and violent assassins, desperate prostitutes, pimps and seditious stowaways—you may not come here anymore, either. Cannibalistic thoughts, for obvious reasons, will no longer be received. Even missionaries will be screened carefully, for sincerity. This is a peaceful harbor, the entryway to a fine and proud island that is only now beginning to cultivate tranquillity. If you can abide by these new laws, my dear thoughts, then you are welcome in my mind—otherwise, I shall turn you all back toward the sea from whence you came.

That is my mission, and it will never end.

59

I've made good friends with this seventeen-year-old Indian girl named Tulsi. She works with me scrubbing the temple floors every day. Every evening we take a walk through the gardens of the Ashram together and talk about God and hip-hop music, two subjects for which Tulsi feels equivalent devotion. Tulsi is just about the cutest little bookworm of an Indian girl you ever saw, even cuter since one lens of her "specs" (as she calls her eyeglasses) broke last week in a cartoonish spiderweb design, which hasn't stopped her from wearing them. Tulsi is so many interesting and foreign things to me at once—a teenager, a tomboy, an Indian girl, a rebel in her family, a soul who is so crazy about God that it's almost like she's got a schoolgirl crush on Him. She also speaks a delightful, lilting English—the kind of English you can find only in India—which includes such colonial words as "splendid!" and "nonsense!" and sometimes produces eloquent sentences like: "It is beneficial to walk on the grass in the morning when the dew has already been accumulated, for it lowers naturally and pleasantly the body's temperature." When I told her once that I was going to Mumbai for the day, Tulsi said, "Please stand carefully, as you will find there are many speeding buses everywhere."

She's exactly half my age, and practically half my size.

Tulsi and I have been talking a lot about marriage lately during our walks. Soon she will turn eighteen, and this is the age when she will be regarded as a legitimate marriage prospect. It will happen like this—after her eighteenth birthday, she will be required to attend family weddings dressed in a sari, signaling her womanhood. Some nice Amma ("Aunty") will come and sit beside her, start asking questions and getting to know her: "How old are you? What's your family background? What does your father do? What universities are you applying to? What are your interests? When is your birthday?" Next thing you know, Tulsi's dad will get a big envelope in the mail with a photo of this woman's grandson who is studying computer sciences in Delhi, along with the boy's astrology charts and his university grades and the inevitable question, "Would your daughter care to marry him?"

Tulsi says, "It sucks."

But it means so much to the family, to see their children wedded off successfully. Tulsi has an aunt who just shaved her head as a gesture of thanks to God because her oldest daughter—at the Jurassic age of twenty-eight—finally got married. And this was a difficult girl to marry off, too; she had a lot of strikes against her. I asked Tulsi what makes an Indian girl difficult to marry off, and she said there are any number of reasons.

"If she has a bad horoscope. If she's too old. If her skin is too dark. If she's too educated and you can't find a man with a higher position than hers, and this is a widespread problem these days because a woman cannot be more educated than her husband. Or if she's had an affair with someone and the whole community knows about it, oh, it would be quite difficult to find a husband after that . . ."

I quickly ran through the list, trying to see how marriageable I would appear in Indian society. I don't know whether my horoscope is good or bad, but I'm definitely too old and I'm way too educated, and my morals have been publicly demonstrated to be quite tarnished . . . I'm not a very appealing prospect. At least my skin is fair. I have only this in my favor.

Tulsi had to go to another cousin's wedding last week, and she was saying (in very un-Indian fashion) how much she hates weddings. All that dancing and gossip. All that dressing up. She would rather be at the Ashram scrubbing floors and meditating. Nobody else in her family can understand this; her devotion to God is way beyond anything they consider normal. Tulsi said, "In my family, they have already given up on me as too different. I have established a reputation for being someone who, if you tell her to do one thing, will almost certainly do the other. I also have a temper. And I'm not dedicated to my studies, except that now I will be, because now I'm going to college and I can decide for myself what I'm interested in. I want to study psychology, just as our Guru did when she attended college. I'm considered a difficult girl. I have a reputation for needing to be told a good reason to do something before I will do it. My mother understands this about me and always tries to give good reasons, but my father doesn't. He gives reasons, but I don't think they're good enough. Sometimes I wonder what I'm doing in my family because I don't resemble them at all."

Tulsi's cousin who got married last week is only twenty-one, and her older sister is next on the marriage list at age twenty, which means there will be huge pressure after that for Tulsi herself to find a husband. I asked her if she wanted to ever get married and she said:

"Noooooooooooooooooooooooo . . ."

. . . and the word drew out longer than the sunset we were watching over the gardens.

"I want to roam!" she said. "Like you."

"You know, Tulsi, I couldn't always roam like this. I was married once."

She frowned at me through her cracked specs, studying me with a quizzical look, almost as if I'd just told her I'd once been a brunette and she was trying to imagine it. In the end, she pronounced: "You, married? I cannot picture this."

"But it's true—I was."

"Are you the one who ended the marriage?"

"Yes."

She said, "I think it's most commendable that you ended your marriage. You seem splendidly happy now. But as for me—how did I get here? Why was I born an Indian girl? It's outrageous! Why did I come into this family? Why must I attend so many weddings?"

Then Tulsi ran around in a frustrated circle, shouting (quite loudly for Ashram standards): "I want to live in Hawaii!!!"

60

Richard from Texas was married once, too. He had two sons, both of whom are grown men now, both close to their dad. Sometimes Richard mentions his ex-wife in some anecdote or other, and he always seems to speak of her with fondness. I get a bit envious whenever I hear this, imagining how lucky Richard is to still be friends with his former spouse, even after separating. This is an odd side effect of my terrible divorce; whenever I hear of couples splitting amicably, I get jealous. It's worse than that—I've actually come to think that it's really romantic when a marriage ends civilly. Like, "Aw . . . how sweet . . . they must've really loved each other . . ."

So I asked Richard one day about it. I said, "It seems like you have fond feelings toward your ex-wife. Are you two still close?"

"Nah," he said casually. "She thinks I changed my name to Motherfucker."

Richard's lack of concern about this impressed me. My own ex-spouse happens to think I changed my name too, and it breaks my heart. One of the hardest things about this divorce was the fact that my ex-husband never forgave me for leaving, that it didn't matter how many bushels of apologies or explanations I laid at his feet, how much blame I assumed, or how many assets or acts of contrition I was willing to offer him in exchange for departing—he certainly was never going to congratulate me and say, "Hey, I was so impressed with your generosity and honesty and I just want to tell you it's been a great pleasure being divorced by you." No. I was unredeemable. And this unredeemed dark hole was still inside me. Even in moments of happiness and excitement (especially in moments of happiness and excitement) I could never forget it for long. *I am still hated by him.* And that felt like it would never change, never release.

I was talking about all this one day with my friends at the Ashram—the newest member of whom is a plumber from New Zealand, a guy I'd met because he'd heard I was a writer and he sought me out to tell me that he was one, too. He's a poet who had recently published a terrific memoir in New Zealand called *A Plumber's Progress* about his own spiritual journey. The plumber/poet from New Zealand, Richard from Texas, the Irish dairy farmer, Tulsi the Indian teenage tomboy and Vivian, an older woman with wispy white hair and incandescently humorous eyes (who used to be a nun in South Africa)—this was my circle of close friends here, a most vibrant crowd of characters whom I never would have expected to meet at an Ashram in India.

So, during lunch one day, we were all having this conversation together about marriage, and the plumber/poet from New Zealand said, "I see marriage as an operation that sews two people together, and divorce is a kind of amputation that can take a long time to heal. The longer you were married, or the rougher the amputation, the harder it is to recover."

Which would explain the postdivorce, postamputation sensations I've had for a few years now, of still swinging that phantom limb around, constantly knocking stuff off the shelves.

Richard from Texas was wondering if I was planning on allowing my ex-husband to dictate for the rest of my life how I felt about myself, and I said I wasn't too sure about that, actually—so far, my ex still seemed to have a pretty strong vote, and to be honest I was still halfway waiting for the man to forgive me, to release me and allow me to go forth in peace.

The dairy farmer from Ireland observed, "Waiting for that day to arrive is not exactly a rational use of your time."

"What can I say, guys? I do a lot with guilt. Kind of like the way other women do a lot with beige."

The former Catholic nun (who oughtta know about guilt, after all) wouldn't hear of it. "Guilt's just your ego's way of tricking you into thinking that you're making moral progress. Don't fall for it, my dear."

"What I hate about the way my marriage ended," I said, "is that it's so unresolved. It's just an open wound that never goes away."

"If you insist," said Richard. "If that's how you've decided to think about it, don't let me spoil your party."

"One of these days this has to end," I said. "I just wish I knew how."

When lunch ended, the plumber/poet from New Zealand slipped me a note. It said to meet him after dinner; he wanted to show me something. So after dinner that night I met him over by the meditation caves, and he told me to follow him, that he had a gift for me. He walked me across the Ashram, then led me to a building I'd never been inside before, unlocked a door and took me up a back set of stairs. He knew of this place, I guessed, because he fixes all the air-conditioning units, and some of them are located up there. At the top of the stairs there was a door which he had to unlock with a combination; he did this swiftly, from memory. Then we were up on a gorgeous rooftop, tiled in ceramic chips that glittered in the evening twilight like the bottom of a reflecting pool. He took me across that roof to a little tower, a minaret, really, and showed me another narrow set of stairs, leading to the tippity-top of the tower. He pointed to the tower and said, "I'm going to leave you now. You're going to go up there. Stay up there until it's finished."

"Until what's finished?" I asked.

The plumber just smiled, handed me a flashlight, "for getting down safely when it's over," and also handed me a folded piece of paper. Then he left.

I climbed to the top of the tower. I was now standing at the tallest place in the Ashram, with a view overlooking the entirety of this river valley in India. Mountains and farmland stretched out as far as I could see. I had a feeling this was not a place students were normally allowed to hang out, but it was so lovely up there. Maybe this is where my Guru watches the sun go down, when she's in residence here. And the sun was going down right now. The breeze was warm. I unfolded the piece of paper the plumber/poet had given me.

He had typed:

INSTRUCTIONS FOR FREEDOM

1. *Life's metaphors are God's instructions.*

2. *You have just climbed up and above the roof. There is nothing between you and the Infinite. Now, let go.*

3. *The day is ending. It's time for something that was beautiful to turn into something else that is beautiful. Now, let go.*

4. *Your wish for resolution was a prayer. Your being here is God's response. Let go, and watch the stars come out—on the outside and on the inside.*

5. *With all your heart, ask for grace, and let go.*

6. *With all your heart, forgive him, FORGIVE YOURSELF, and let him go.*

7. *Let your intention be freedom from useless suffering. Then, let go.*

8. *Watch the heat of day pass into the cool night. Let go.*

9. *When the karma of a relationship is done, only love remains. It's safe. Let go.*

10. *When the past has passed from you at last, let go. Then climb down and begin the rest of your life. With great joy.*

For the first few minutes, I couldn't stop laughing. I could see over the whole valley, over the umbrella of the mango trees, and the wind was blowing my hair around like a flag. I watched the sun go down, and then I lay down on my back and watched the stars come out. I sang a small little prayer in Sanskrit, and repeated it every time I saw a new star emerge in the darkening sky, almost like I was calling forth the stars, but then they started popping out too fast and I couldn't keep up with them. Soon the whole sky was a glitzy show of stars. The only thing between me and God was . . . nothing.

Then I shut my eyes and I said, "Dear Lord, please show me everything I need to understand about forgiveness and surrender."

What I had wanted for so long was to have an actual conversation with my ex-husband, but this was obviously never going to happen. What I had been craving was a resolution, a peace summit, from which we could emerge with a united understanding of what had occurred in our marriage, and a mutual forgiveness for the ugliness of our divorce. But months of counseling and mediation had only made us more divided and locked our positions solid, turning us into two people who were absolutely incapable of giving each other any release. Yet it's what we both needed, I was sure of it. And I was sure of this, too—that the rules of transcendence insist that you will not advance even one inch closer to divinity as long as you cling to even one last seductive thread of blame. As smoking is to the lungs, so is resentment to the soul; even one puff of it is bad for you. I mean, what kind of prayer is this to imbibe—"Give us this day our daily grudge"? You might just as well hang it up and kiss God good-bye if you really need to keep blaming somebody else for your own life's limitations. So what I asked of God that night on the Ashram roof was—given the reality that I would probably never speak to my ex-husband again—might there be some level upon which we *could* communicate? Some level on which we could forgive?

I lay up there, high above the world, and I was all alone. I dropped into meditation and waited to be told what to do. I don't know how many minutes or hours passed before I knew what to do. I realized I'd been thinking about all this too literally. I'd been wanting to talk to my ex-husband? So *talk* to him. Talk to him right now. I'd been waiting to be offered forgiveness? Offer it up personally, then. Right now. I thought of how many people go to their graves unforgiven and unforgiving. I thought of how many people have had siblings or friends or children or lovers disappear from their lives before precious words of clemency or absolution could be passed along. How do the survivors of terminated relationships ever endure the pain of unfinished business? From that place of meditation, I found the answer—you can finish the business yourself, from within yourself. It's not only possible, it's essential.

And then, to my surprise, still in meditation, I did an odd thing. I invited my ex-husband to please join me up here on this rooftop in India. I asked him if he would be kind enough to meet me up here for this farewell event. Then I waited until I felt him arrive. And he did arrive. His presence was suddenly absolute and tangible. I could practically smell him.

I said, "Hi, sweetie."

I almost started to cry right then, but quickly realized I didn't need to. Tears are part of this bodily life, and the place where these two souls were meeting that night in India had nothing to do with the body. The two people who needed to talk to each other up there on the roof were not even people anymore. They wouldn't even be talking. They weren't even ex-spouses, not an obstinate midwesterner and a high-strung Yankee, not a guy in his forties and a woman in her thirties, not two limited people who had argued for years about sex and money and furniture—none of this was relevant. For the purposes of this meeting, at the level of this reunion, they were just two cool blue souls who already understood everything. Unbound by their bodies, unbound by the complex history of their past relationship, they came together above this roof (above me, even) in infinite wisdom. Still in meditation, I watched these two cool blue souls circle each other, merge, divide again and regard each other's perfection and similarity. They knew everything. They knew everything long ago and they will always know everything. They didn't need to forgive each other; they were *born* forgiving each other.

The lesson they were teaching me in their beautiful turning was, "Stay out of this, Liz. Your part of this relationship is over. Let *us* work things out from now on. You go on with your life."

Much later I opened my eyes, and I knew it was *over*. Not just my marriage and not just my divorce, but all the unfinished bleak hollow sadness of it . . . it was over. I could feel that I was free. Let me be clear—it's not that I would never again think about my ex-husband, or never again have any emotions attached to the memory of him. It's just that this ritual on the rooftop had finally given me a place where I could house those thoughts and feelings whenever they would arise in the future—and they will always arise. But when they do show up again, I can just send them back *here,* back to this rooftop of memory, back to the care of those two cool blue souls who already and always understand everything.

This is what rituals are for. We do spiritual ceremonies as human beings in order to create a safe resting place for our most complicated feelings of joy or trauma, so that we don't have to haul those feelings around with us forever, weighing us down. We all need such places of ritual safekeeping. And I do believe that if your culture or tradition doesn't have the specific ritual you're craving, then you are absolutely permitted to make up a ceremony of your own devising, fixing your own broken-down emotional systems with all the do-it-yourself resourcefulness of a generous plumber/poet. If you bring the right earnestness to your homemade ceremony, God will provide the grace. And that is why we need God.

So I stood up and did a handstand on my Guru's roof, to celebrate the notion of liberation. I felt the dusty tiles under my hands. I felt my own strength and balance. I felt the easy night breeze on the palms of my bare feet. This kind of thing—a spontaneous hand-stand—isn't something a disembodied cool blue soul can do, but a human being can do it. We have hands; we can stand on them if we want to. That's our privilege. That's the joy of a mortal body. And that's why God needs us. Because God loves to feel things through our hands.

61

Richard from Texas left today. Flew back to Austin. I took the drive with him to the airport, and we were both sad. We stood for a long time on the sidewalk before he went inside.

"What am I gonna do when I don't have Liz Gilbert to kick around anymore?" He sighed. Then he said, "You've had a good experience at the Ashram, haven't you? You look all different from a few months back, like maybe you chucked out some of that sorrow you been hauling around."

"I'm feeling really happy these days, Richard."

"Well, just remember—all your misery will be waiting for you at the door upon your exit, should you care to pick it up again when you leave."

"I won't pick it up again."

"Good girl."

"You've helped me a lot," I told him. "I think of you as an angel with hairy hands and cruddy toenails."

"Yeah, my toenails never really did recover from Vietnam, poor things."

"It could've been worse."

"It *was* worse for a lot of guys. At least I got to keep my legs. Nope, I got a pretty cushy incarnation in this lifetime, kiddo. So did you—never forget that. Next lifetime you might come back as one of those poor Indian women busting up rocks by the side of the road, find out life ain't so much fun. So appreciate what you got now, OK? Keep cultivating gratitude. You'll live longer. And, Groceries? Do me a favor? Move ahead with your life, will ya?"

"I *am*."

"What I mean is—find somebody new to love someday. Take the time you need to heal, but don't forget to eventually share your heart with someone. Don't make your life a monument to David or to your ex-husband."

"I won't," I said. And I knew suddenly that it was true—I *wouldn't*. I could feel all this old pain of lost love and past mistakes attenuating before my eyes, diminishing at last through the famous healing powers of time, patience and the grace of God.

And then Richard spoke again, snapping my thoughts back quickly to the world's more basic realities: "After all, baby, remember what they say—sometimes the best way to get over someone is to get under someone else."

I laughed. "OK, Richard, that'll do. Now you can go back to Texas."

"Might as well," he said, casting a gaze around this desolate Indian airport parking lot. "Cuz I ain't gettin' any prettier just standing around here."

62

On my ride back to the Ashram, after seeing Richard off at the airport, I decide that I've been talking too much. To be honest, I've been talking too much my whole life, but I've really been talking too much during my stay at the Ashram. I have another two months here, and I don't want to waste the greatest spiritual opportunity of my life by being all social and chatty the whole time. It's been amazing for me to discover that even here, even in a sacred environment of spiritual retreat on the other side of the world, I have managed to create a cocktail-party-like vibe around me. It's not just Richard I've been talking to constantly—though we did do the most gabbing—I'm always yakking with somebody. I've even found myself—in an *Ashram*, mind you!—creating appointments to see acquaintances, having to say to somebody, "I'm sorry, I can't hang out with you at lunch today because I promised Sakshi I would eat with her . . . maybe we could make a date for next Tuesday."

This has been the story of my life. It's how I am. But I've been thinking lately that this is maybe a spiritual liability. Silence and solitude are universally recognized spiritual practices, and there are good reasons for this. Learning how to discipline your speech is a way of preventing your energies from spilling out of you through the rupture of your mouth, exhausting you and filling the world with words, words, words instead of serenity, peace and bliss. Swamiji, my Guru's master, was a stickler about silence in the Ashram, heavily enforcing it as a devotional practice. He called silence the only true religion. It's ridiculous how much I've been talking at this Ashram, the one place in the world where silence should—and can—reign.

So I'm not going to be the Ashram social bunny anymore, I've decided. No more scurrying, gossiping, joking. No more spotlight-hogging or conversation-dominating. No more verbal tap-dancing for pennies of affirmation. It's time to change. Now that Richard is gone, I'm going to make the remainder of my stay a completely quiet experience. This will be difficult, but not impossible, because silence is universally respected at the Ashram. The whole community will support it, recognizing your decision as a disciplined act of devotion. In the bookstore they even sell little badges you can wear which read, "I am in Silence."

I'm going to buy four of those little badges.

On the drive back to the Ashram, I really let myself dip into a fantasy about just how silent I am going to become now. I will be so silent that it will make me famous. I imagine myself becoming known as That Quiet Girl. I'll just keep to the Ashram schedule, take my meals in solitude, meditate for endless hours every day and scrub the temple floors without making a peep. My only interaction with others will be to smile beatifically at them from within my self-contained world of stillness and piety. People will talk about me. They'll ask, "Who *is* That Quiet Girl in the Back of the Temple, always scrubbing the floors, down on her knees? She never speaks. She's so elusive. She's so mystical. I can't even imagine what her voice sounds like. You never even hear her coming up behind you on the garden path when she's out walking . . . she moves as silently as the breeze. She must be in a constant state of meditative communion with God. *She's the quietest girl I've ever seen.*"

63

The next morning I was down on my knees in the temple, scrubbing the marble floor again, emanating (I imagined) a holy radiance of silence, when an Indian teenage boy came looking for me with a message—that I needed to report to the Seva Office immediately. *Seva* is the Sanskrit term for the spiritual practice of selfless service (for instance, the scrubbing of a temple floor). The Seva Office administers all the work assignments for the Ashram. So I wandered over there, very curious as to why I'd been summoned, and the nice lady at the desk asked me, "Are you Elizabeth Gilbert?"

I smiled at her with the warmest piety and nodded. Silently.

Then she told me that my work detail had been changed. Due to a special request from management, I was no longer to be part of the floor-scrubbing team. They had a new position in mind for me at the Ashram.

And the title of my new job was—if you will kindly dig this—"Key Hostess."

64

This was so obviously another one of Swamiji's jokes.

You wanted to be The Quiet Girl in the Back of the Temple? Well, guess what . . .

But this is what always happens at the Ashram. You make some big grandiose decision about what you need to do, or who you need to be, and then circumstances arise that immediately reveal to you how little you understood about yourself. I don't know how many times Swamiji said it during his lifetime, and I don't know how many more times my Guru has repeated it since his death, but it seems I have not quite yet absorbed the truth of their most insistent statement:

"God dwells within you, as you."

AS you.

If there is one holy truth of this Yoga, that line encapsulates it. God dwells within you as you *yourself*, exactly the way you are. God isn't interested in watching you enact some performance of personality in order to comply with some crackpot notion you have about how a spiritual person looks or behaves. We all seem to get this idea that, in order to be sacred, we have to make some massive, dramatic change of character, that we have to renounce our individuality. This is a classic example of what they call in the East "wrong-thinking." Swamiji used to say that every day renunciants find something new to renounce, but it is usually depression, not peace, that they attain. Constantly he was teaching that austerity and renunciation—just for their own sake—are not what you need. To know God, you need only to renounce one thing—your sense of division from God. Otherwise, just stay as you were made, within your natural character.

So what is my natural character? I love studying in this Ashram, but my dream of finding divinity by gliding silently through the place with a gentle, ethereal smile—who is that person? That's probably someone I saw on a TV show. The reality is, it's a little sad for me to admit that I will never be that character. I've always been so fascinated by these wraith-like, delicate souls. Always wanted to be the quiet girl. Probably precisely because I'm *not*. It's the same reason I think that thick, dark hair is so beautiful—precisely because I don't have it, because I can't have it. But at some point you have to make peace with what you were given and if God wanted me to be a shy girl with thick, dark hair, He would have made me that way, but He didn't. Useful, then, might be to accept how I was made and embody myself fully therein.

Or, as Sextus, the ancient Pythagorian philospher, said, "The wise man is always similar to himself."

This doesn't mean I cannot be devout. It doesn't mean I can't be thoroughly tumbled and humbled with God's love. This does not mean I cannot serve humanity. It doesn't mean I can't improve myself as a human being, honing my virtues and working daily to minimize my vices. For instance, I'm never going to be a wallflower, but that doesn't mean I can't take a serious look at my talking habits and alter some aspects for the better—working *within* my personality. Yes, I like talking, but perhaps I don't have to curse so much, and perhaps I don't always have to go for the cheap laugh, and maybe I don't need to talk about myself quite so constantly. Or here's a radical concept—maybe I can stop interrupting others when they are speaking. Because no matter how creatively I try to look at my habit of interrupting, I can't find another way to see it than this: "I believe that what I am saying is more important than what you are saying." And I can't find another way to see *that* than: "I believe that I am more important than you." And that must end.

All these changes would be useful to make. But even so, even with reasonable modifications to my speaking habits, I probably won't ever be known as That Quiet Girl. No matter how pretty a picture that is and no matter how hard I try. Because let's be really honest about who we're dealing with here. When the woman at the Ashram Seva Center gave me my new job assignment of Key Hostess, she said, "We have a special nickname for this position, you know. We call it 'Little Suzy Creamcheese,' because whoever does the job needs to be social and bubbly and smiling all the time."

What could I say?

I just stuck out a hand to shake, bade a silent farewell to all my wishful old delusions and announced, "Madam—I'm your girl."

65

What I will be hosting, to be exact, is a series of retreats to be held at the Ashram this spring. During each retreat, about a hundred devotees will come here from all over the world for a period of a week to ten days, to deepen their meditation practices. My role is to take care of these people during their stay here. For most of the retreat, the participants will be in silence. For some of them, it will be the first time they've experienced silence as a devotional practice, and it can be intense. However, I will be the one person in the Ashram they are allowed to talk to if something is going wrong.

That's right—my job *officially* requires me to be the speech-magnet.

I will listen to the problems of the retreat participants and then try to find solutions for them. Maybe they'll need to change room-mates because of a snoring situation, or maybe they'll need to speak to the doctor because of India-related digestive trouble—I'll try to solve it. I'll need to know everybody's name, and where they are from. I'll be walking around with a clipboard, taking notes and following up. I'm Julie McCoy, your Yogic cruise director.

And, yes, the position does come with a beeper.

As the retreats begin, it is so quickly evident how much I am made for this job. I'm sitting there at the Welcome Table with my *Hello, My Name Is* badge, and these people are arriving from thirty different countries, and some of them are old-timers but many of them have never been to India. It's over 100 degrees already at 10:00 AM, and most of these people have been flying all night in coach. Some of them walk into this Ashram looking like they just woke up in the trunk of a car—like they have no idea at all what they're doing here. Whatever desire for transcendence drove them to apply for this spiritual retreat in the first place, they've long ago forgotten it, probably somewhere around the time their luggage got lost in Kuala Lumpur. They're thirsty, but don't know yet if they can drink the water. They're hungry, but don't know what time lunch is, or where the cafeteria can be found. They're dressed all wrong, wearing synthetics and heavy boots in the tropical heat. They don't know if there's anyone here who speaks Russian.

I can speak a teensy bit of Russian . . .

I can help them. I am so equipped to help. All the antennas I've ever sprouted throughout my lifetime that have taught me how to read what people are feeling, all the intuition I developed growing up as the supersensitive younger child, all the listening skills I learned as a sympathetic bartender and an inquisitive journalist, all the proficiency of care I mastered after years of being somebody's wife or girlfriend—it was all accumulated so that I could help ease these good people into the difficult task they've taken on. I see them coming in from Mexico, from the Philippines, from Africa, from Denmark, from Detroit and it feels like that scene in *Close Encounters of the Third Kind* where Richard Dreyfuss and all those other seekers have been pulled to the middle of Wyoming for reasons they don't understand at all, drawn by the arrival of the spaceship. I am so consumed by wonder at their bravery. These people have left their families and lives behind for a few weeks to go into silent retreat amidst a crowd of perfect strangers in India. Not everybody does this in their lifetime.

I love all these people, automatically and unconditionally. I even love the pain-in-the-ass ones. I can see through their neuroses and recognize that they're just horribly afraid of what they're going to face when they go into silence and meditation for seven days. I love the Indian man who comes to me in outrage, reporting that there's a four-inch statue of the Indian god Ganesh in his room which has one foot missing. He's furious, thinks this is a terrible omen and wants that statue removed—ideally by a Brahman priest, during a "traditionally appropriate" cleansing ceremony. I comfort him and listen to his anger, then send my teenage tomboy friend Tulsi over to the guy's room to get rid of the statue while he's at lunch. The next day I pass the man a note, telling him that I hope he's feeling better now that the broken statue is gone, and reminding him that I'm here if he needs anything else whatsoever; he rewards me with a giant, relieved smile. He's just afraid. The French woman who has a near panic attack about her wheat allergies—she's afraid, too. The Argentinean man who wants a special meeting with the entire staff of the Hatha Yoga department in order to be counseled on how to sit properly during meditation so his ankle doesn't hurt; he's just afraid. They're all afraid. They're going into silence, deep into their own minds and souls. Even for an experienced meditator, nothing is more unknown than this territory. Anything can happen in there. They'll be guided during this retreat by a wonderful woman, a monk in her fifties, whose every gesture and word is the embodiment of compassion, but they're still afraid because—as loving as this monk may be—she cannot go with them where they are going. Nobody can.

As the retreat was beginning, I happened to get a letter in the mail from a friend of mine in America who is a wildlife filmmaker for *National Geographic*. He told me he'd just been to a fancy dinner at the Waldorf-Astoria in New York, honoring members of the Explorers' Club. He said it was amazing to be in the presence of such incredibly courageous people, all of whom have risked their lives so many times to discover the world's most remote and dangerous mountain ranges, canyons, rivers, ocean depths, ice fields and volcanoes. He said that so many of them were missing bits of themselves—toes and noses and fingers lost over the years to sharks, frostbite and other dangers.

He wrote, "You have never seen so many brave people gathered in one place at the same time."

I thought to myself, *You ain't seen nothin', Mike.*

66

The topic of the retreat, and its goal, is the *turiya* state—the elusive fourth level of human consciousness. During the typical human experience, say the Yogis, most of us are always moving between three different levels of consciousness—waking, dreaming or deep dreamless sleep. But there is a fourth level, too. This fourth level is the witness of all the other states, the integral awareness that links the other three levels together. This is the pure consciousness, an intelligent awareness that can—for example—report your dreams back to you in the morning when you wake up. You were gone, you were sleeping, but somebody was watching over your dreams while you slept—who was that witness? And who is the one who is always standing outside the mind's activity, observing its thoughts? It's simply God, say the Yogis. And if you can move into that state of witness-consciousness, then you can be present with God all the time. This constant awareness and experience of the God-presence within can only happen on a fourth level of human consciousness, which is called *turiya*.

Here's how you can tell if you've reached the *turiya* state—if you're in a state of constant bliss. One who is living from within *turiya* is not affected by the swinging moods of the mind, nor fearful of time or harmed by loss. "Pure, clean, void, tranquil, breathless, selfless, endless, undecaying, steadfast, eternal, unborn, independent, he abides in his own greatness," say the Upanishads, the ancient Yogic scriptures, describing anyone who has reached the *turiya* state. The great saints, the great Gurus, the great prophets of history—they were all living in the *turiya* state, all the time. As for the rest of us, most of us have been there, too, if only for fleeting moments. Most of us, even if only for two minutes in our lives, have experienced at some time or another an inexplicable and random sense of complete bliss, unrelated to anything that was happening in the outside world. One instant, you're just a regular Joe, schlepping through your mundane life, and then suddenly—what is this?—nothing has changed, yet you feel stirred by grace, swollen with wonder, overflowing with bliss. Everything—for no reason whatsoever—is perfect.

Of course, for most of us this state passes as fast as it came. It's almost like you are shown your inner perfection as a tease and then you tumble back to "reality" very quickly, collapsing into a heap upon all your old worries and desires once again. Over the centuries, people have tried to hold on to that state of blissful perfection through all sorts of external means—through drugs and sex and power and adrenaline and the accumulation of pretty things—but it doesn't keep. We search for happiness everywhere, but we are like Tolstoy's fabled beggar who spent his life sitting on a pot of gold, begging for pennies from every passerby, unaware that his fortune was right under him the whole time. Your treasure—your perfection—is within you already. But to claim it, you must leave the busy commotion of the mind and abandon the desires of the ego and enter into the silence of the heart. The *kundalini shakti*—the supreme energy of the divine—will take you there.

This is what everyone has come here for.

When I initially wrote that sentence, what I meant by it was: "This is why these one hundred retreat participants from all over the world have come to this Ashram in India." But actually, the Yogic saints and philosophers would have agreed with the broadness of my original statement: "This is what *everyone* has come here for." According to the mystics, this search for divine bliss is the entire purpose of a human life. This is why we all chose to be born, and this is why all the suffering and pain of life on earth is worthwhile—just for the chance to experience this infinite love. And once you have found this divinity within, can you hold it? Because if you can . . . *bliss.*

I spend the entire retreat in the back of the temple, watching over the participants as they meditate in the half-dark and total quiet. It is my job to be concerned about their comfort, paying careful attention to see if anyone is in trouble or need. They've all taken vows of silence for the duration of the retreat, and every day I can feel them descending deeper into that silence until the entire Ashram is saturated with their stillness. Out of respect to the retreat participants, we are all tiptoeing through our days now, even eating our meals in silence. All traces of chatter are gone. Even I am quiet. There is a middle-of-the-night silence around here now, the hushed timelessness you generally only experience around 3:00 AM when you're totally alone—yet it's carried through the broad daylight and held by the whole Ashram.

As these hundred souls meditate, I have no idea what they're thinking or feeling, but I know what they want to experience, and I find myself in a constant state of prayer to God on their behalf, making odd bargains for them like, *Please give these wonderful people any blessings you might have originally set aside for me.* It's not my intention to go into meditation at the same time the retreat participants are meditating; I'm supposed to be keeping an eye on them, not worrying about my own spiritual journey. But I find myself every day lifted on the waves of their collective devotional intention, much the same way that certain scavenging birds can ride the thermal heat waves which rise off the earth, taking them much higher in the air than they ever could have flown on their own wing-power. So it's probably not surprising that this is when it happens. One Thursday afternoon in the back of the temple, right in the midst of my Key Hostess duties, wearing my name-tag and everything—I am suddenly transported through the portal of the universe and taken to the center of God's palm.

67

As a reader and seeker, I always get frustrated at this moment in somebody else's spiritual memoirs—that moment in which the soul excuses itself from time and place and merges with the infinite. From the Buddha to Saint Teresa to the Sufi mystics to my own Guru—so many great souls over the centuries have tried to express in so many words what it feels like to become one with the divine, but I'm never quite satisfied by these descriptions. Often you will see the maddening adjective *indescribable* used to describe the event. But even the most eloquent reporters of the devotional experience—like Rumi, who wrote about having abandoned all effort and tied himself to God's sleeve, or Hafiz, who said that he and God had become like two fat men living in a small boat—"we keep bumping into each other and laughing"—even these poets leave me behind. I don't want to read about it; I want to feel it, too. Sri Ramana Maharshi, a beloved Indian Guru, used to give long talks on the transcendental experience to his pupils and then always wrap it up with this instruction: "Now go find out."

So now I have found out. And I don't want to say that what I experienced that Thursday afternoon in India was indescribable, even though it was. I'll try to explain anyway. Simply put, I got pulled through the wormhole of the Absolute, and in that rush I suddenly understood the workings of the universe completely. I left my body, I left the room, I left the planet, I stepped through time and I entered the void. I was inside the void, but I also *was* the void and I was looking at the void, all at the same time. The void was a place of limitless peace and wisdom. The void was conscious and it was intelligent. The void was God, which means that I was inside God. But not in a gross, physical way—not like I was Liz Gilbert stuck inside a chunk of God's thigh muscle. I just was part of God. In addition to being God. I was both a tiny piece of the universe and exactly the same size as the universe. ("All know that the drop merges into the ocean, but few know that the ocean merges into the drop," wrote the sage Kabir—and I can personally attest now that this is true.)

It wasn't hallucinogenic, what I was feeling. It was the most basic of events. It was heaven, yes. It was the deepest love I'd ever experienced, beyond anything I could have previously imagined, but it wasn't euphoric. It wasn't exciting. There wasn't enough ego or passion left in me to create euphoria and excitement. It was just obvious. Like when you've been looking at an optical illusion for a long time, straining your eyes to decode the trick, and suddenly your cognizance shifts and there—now you can clearly see it!—the two vases are actually two faces. And once you've seen through the optical illusion, you can never not see it again.

"So this is God," I thought. "Congratulations to meet you."

The place in which I was standing can't be described like an earthly location. It was neither dark nor light, neither big nor small. Nor was it a place, nor was I technically standing there, nor was I exactly "I" anymore. I still had my thoughts, but they were so modest, quiet and observatory. Not only did I feel unhesitating compassion and unity with everything and everybody, it was vaguely and amusingly strange for me to wonder how anybody could ever feel anything *but* that. I also felt mildly charmed by all my old ideas about who I am and what I'm like. *I'm a woman, I come from America, I'm talkative, I'm a writer*—all this felt so cute and obsolete. Imagine cramming yourself into such a puny box of identity when you could experience your infinitude instead.

I wondered, "Why have I been chasing happiness my whole life when bliss was here the entire time?"

I don't know how long I hovered in this magnificent ether of union before I had a sudden urgent thought: "I want to hold on to this experience forever!" And that's when I started to tumble out of it. Just those two little words—*I want!*—and I began to slide back to earth. Then my mind started to really protest—*No! I don't want to leave here!*—and I slid further still.

I want!
I don't want!
I want!
I don't want!

With each repetition of those desperate thoughts, I could feel myself falling through layer after layer of illusion, like an action-comedy hero crashing through a dozen canvas awnings during his fall from a building. This return of useless longing was bringing me back again into my own small borders, my own mortal confines, my limited comic-strip world. I watched my ego return the way you watch a Polaroid photo develop, instant-by-instant getting clearer—there's the face, there are the lines around the mouth, there are the eyebrows—yes, now it is finished: there is a picture of regular old me. I felt a tremor of panic, mildly heartbroken to have lost this divine experience. But exactly parallel to that panic I could also sense a witness, a wiser and older me, who just shook her head and smiled, knowing this: If I believed that this state of bliss was something that could be taken away from me, then I obviously didn't understand it yet. And therefore, I was not yet ready to inhabit it completely. I would have to practice more. At that moment of realization, that's when God let me go, let me slide through His fingers with this last compassionate, unspoken message:

You may return here once you have fully come to understand that you are always here.

68

The retreat ended two days later, and everyone came out of silence. I got so many hugs from people, thanking me for having helped them.

"Oh, no! Thank *you*," I kept saying, frustrated at how inadequate those words sounded, how impossible it was to express ample gratitude for their having lifted me to such a towering height.

Another one hundred seekers arrived a week later for another retreat, and the teachings and the brave endeavors inward and the all-encompassing silence were all repeated, with new souls in practice. I watched over them, too, and tried to help in every possible way and glided back into *turiya* a few times with them, too. I could only laugh later when many of them came out of their meditations to tell me that I had appeared to them during the retreat as a "silent, gliding, ethereal presence." So this was the Ashram's final joke on me? Once I had learned to accept my loud, chatty, social nature and fully embrace my inner Key Hostess—only then could I become The Quiet Girl in the Back of the Temple, after all?

In my final weeks there, the Ashram was imbibed with a somewhat melancholy last-days-of-summer-camp feeling. Every morning, it seemed, some more people and some more luggage got on a bus and left. There were no new arrivals. It was almost May, the beginning of the hottest season in India, and the place would be slowing down for a while. There would be no more retreats, so I was relocated for work again, now placed in the Office of Registration, where I had the bittersweet job of officially "departing" all my friends off the computer once they had left the Ashram.

I shared the office with a funny former Madison Avenue hairdresser. We'd do our morning prayers together all alone, just the two of us singing our hymn to God.

"Think we could pick up the tempo on this hymn today?" asked the hairdresser one morning. "And maybe raise it to a higher octave? So I don't sound like a spiritual version of Count Basie?"

I'm getting a lot of time alone here now. I'm spending about four or five hours every day in the meditation caves. I can sit in my own company for hours at a time now, at ease in my own presence, undisturbed by my own existence on the planet. Sometimes my meditations are surreal and physical experiences of *shakti*—all spine-twisting, blood-boiling wildness. I try to give in to it with as little resistance as possible. Other times I experience a sweet, quiet contentment, and that is fine, too. The sentences still form in my mind, and thoughts still do their little show-off dance, but I know my thought patterns so well now that they don't bother me anymore. My thoughts have become like old neighbors, kind of bothersome but ultimately rather endearing—Mr. and Mrs. Yakkity-Yak and their three dumb children, Blah, Blah and Blah. But they don't agitate my home. There's room for all of us in this neighborhood.

As for whatever other changes may have occurred within me during these last few months, perhaps I can't even feel them yet. My friends who have been studying Yoga for a long time say you don't really see the impact that an Ashram has had on you until you leave the place and return to your normal life. "Only then," said the former nun from South Africa, "will you start to notice how your interior closets have all been rearranged." Of course at the moment, I'm not entirely sure what my normal life is. I mean, I'm maybe about to go move in with an elderly medicine man in Indonesia—is that my normal life? It may be, who knows? In any case, though, my friends say that the changes appear only later. You may find that lifelong obsessions are gone, or that nasty, indissoluble patterns have finally shifted. Petty irritations that once maddened you are no longer problems, whereas abysmal old miseries you once endured out of habit will no longer be tolerated now for even five minutes. Poisonous relationships get aired out or disposed of, and brighter, more beneficial people start arriving into your world.

Last night I couldn't sleep. Not out of anxiety, but out of thrilled anticipation. I got dressed and went out for a walk through the gardens. The moon was lusciously ripe and full, and it hovered right above me, spilling a pewtery light all around. The air was perfumed with jasmine and also the intoxicating scent from this heady, flowery bush they have around here which only blossoms in the night. The day had been humid and hot, and now it was only slightly less humid and hot. The warm air shifted around me and I realized: "I'm in India!"

I'm in my sandals and I'm in India!

I took off at a run, galloping away from the path and down into the meadow, just tearing across that moonlit bath of grass. My body felt so alive and healthy from all these months of Yoga and vegetarian food and early bedtimes. My sandals on the soft dewy grass made this sound: *shippa-shippa-shippa-shippa,* and that was the only sound in the whole valley. I was so exultant I ran straight to the clump of eucalyptus trees in the middle of the park (where they say an ancient temple used to stand, honoring the god Ganesh—the remover of obstacles) and I threw my arms around one of those trees, which was still warm from the day's heat, and I kissed it with such passion. I mean, I kissed that tree with all my heart, not even thinking at the time that this is the worst nightmare of every American parent whose child has ever run away to India to find herself—that she will end up having orgies with trees in the moonlight.

But it was pure, this love that I was feeling. It was godly. I looked around the darkened valley and I could see nothing that was not God. I felt so deeply, terribly happy. I thought to myself, "Whatever this feeling is—this is what I have been praying for. And this is also what I have been praying *to.*"

69

By the way, I found my word.

I found it in the library, of course, bookworm that I am. I'd been wondering about my word ever since that afternoon back in Rome when my Italian friend Giulio had told me that Rome's word is SEX, and had asked me what mine was. I didn't know the answer then, but kind of figured my word would show up eventually, and that I'd recognize it when I saw it.

So I saw it during my last week at the Ashram. I was reading through an old text about Yoga, when I found a description of ancient spiritual seekers. A Sanskrit word appeared in the paragraph: ANTEVASIN. It means "one who lives at the border." In ancient times this was a literal description. It indicated a person who had left the bustling center of worldly life to go live at the edge of the forest where the spiritual masters dwelled. The *antevasin* was not one of the villagers anymore—not a householder with a conventional life. But neither was he yet a transcendent—not one of those sages who live deep in the unexplored woods, fully realized. The *antevasin* was an in-betweener. He was a border-dweller. He lived in sight of both worlds, but he looked toward the unknown. And he was a scholar.

When I read this description of the *antevasin*, I got so excited I gave a little bark of recognition. That's my word, baby! In the modern age, of course, that image of an unexplored forest would have to be figurative, and the border would have to be figurative, too. But you can still live there. You can still live on that shimmering line between your old thinking and your new understanding, always in a state of learning. In the figurative sense, this is a border that is always moving—as you advance forward in your studies and realizations, that mysterious forest of the unknown always stays a few feet ahead of you, so you have to travel light in order to keep following it. You have to stay mobile, movable, supple. Slippery, even. Which is funny, because just the day before, my friend the poet/plumber from New Zealand had left the Ashram, and on his way out the door, he'd handed me a friendly little good-bye poem about my journey. I remembered this verse:

> *Elizabeth, betwixt and between*
> *Italian phrases and Bali dreams,*
> *Elizabeth, between and betwixt,*
> *Sometimes as slippery as a fish . . .*

I've spent so much time these last years wondering what I'm supposed to be. A wife? A mother? A lover? A celibate? An Italian? A glutton? A traveler? An artist? A Yogi? But I'm not any of these things, at least not completely. And I'm not Crazy Aunt Liz, either. I'm just a slippery *antevasin*—betwixt and between—a student on the ever-shifting border near the wonderful, scary forest of the new.

70

I believe that all the world's religions share, at their core, a desire to find a transporting metaphor. When you want to attain communion with God, what you're really trying to do is move away from the worldly into the eternal (from the village to the forest, you might say, keeping with the theme of the *antevasin*) and you need some kind of magnificent idea to convey you there. It has be a big one, this metaphor—really big and magic and powerful, because it needs to carry you across a mighty distance. It has to be the biggest boat imaginable.

Religious rituals often develop out of mystical experimentation. Some brave scout goes looking for a new path to the divine, has a transcendent experience and returns home a prophet. He or she brings back to the community tales of heaven and maps of how to get there. Then others repeat the words, the works, the prayers, or the acts of this prophet, in order to cross over, too. Sometimes this is successful—sometimes the same familiar combination of syllables and devotional practices repeated generation after generation might carry many people to the other side. Sometimes it doesn't work, though. Inevitably even the most original new ideas will eventually harden into dogma or stop working for everybody.

The Indians around here tell a cautionary fable about a great saint who was always surrounded in his Ashram by loyal devotees. For hours a day, the saint and his followers would meditate on God. The only problem was that the saint had a young cat, an annoying creature, who used to walk through the temple meowing and purring and bothering everyone during meditation. So the saint, in all his practical wisdom, commanded that the cat be tied to a pole outside for a few hours a day, only during meditation, so as to not disturb anyone. This became a habit—tying the cat to the pole and then meditating on God—but as years passed, the habit hardened into religious ritual. Nobody could meditate unless the cat was tied to the pole first. Then one day the cat died. The saint's followers were panic-stricken. It was a major religious crisis—how could they meditate now, without a cat to tie to a pole? How would they reach God? In their minds, the cat had become the means.

Be very careful, warns this tale, not to get too obsessed with the repetition of religious ritual just for its own sake. Especially in this divided world, where the Taliban and the Christian Coalition continue to fight out their international trademark war over who owns the rights to the word *God* and who has the proper rituals to reach that God, it may be useful to remember that it is not the tying of the cat to the pole that has ever brought anyone to transcendence, but only the constant desire of an individual seeker to experience the eternal compassion of the divine. Flexibility is just as essential for divinity as is discipline.

Your job, then, should you choose to accept it, is to keep searching for the metaphors, rituals and teachers that will help you move ever closer to divinity. The Yogic scriptures say that God responds to the sacred prayers and efforts of human beings *in any way whatsoever* that mortals choose to worship—just so long as those prayers are sincere. As one line from the Upanishads suggests: "People follow different paths, straight or crooked, according to their temperament, depending on which they consider best, or most appropriate—and all reach You, just as rivers enter the ocean."

The other objective of religion, of course, is to try to make sense of our chaotic world and explain the inexplicabilities we see playing out here on earth every day: the innocent suffer, the wicked are rewarded—what are we to make of all this? The Western tradition says, "It'll all get sorted out after death, in heaven and hell." (All justice to be doled out, of course, by what James Joyces used to call the "Hangman God"—a paternal figure who sits upon His strict seat of judgment punishing the evil and rewarding the good.) Over in the East, though, the Upanishads shrug away any attempt to make sense of the world's chaos. They're not even so sure that the world *is* chaotic, but suggest that it may only appear so to us, because of our limited vision. These texts do not promise justice or revenge for anybody, though they do say that there are consequences for every action—so choose your behavior accordingly. You might not see those consequences any time soon, though. Yoga takes the long view, always. Furthermore, the Upanishads suggest that so-called chaos may have an actual divine function, even if you personally can't recognize it right now: "The gods are fond of the cryptic and dislike the evident." The best we can do, then, in response to our incomprehensible and dangerous world, is to practice holding equilibrium *internally*—no matter what insanity is transpiring out there.

Sean, my Yogic Irish dairy farmer, explained it to me this way. "Imagine that the universe is a great spinning engine," he said. "You want to stay near the core of the thing—right in the hub of the wheel—not out at the edges where all the wild whirling takes place, where you get can frayed and crazy. The hub of calmness—that's your heart. That's where God lives within you. So stop looking for answers in the world. Just keep coming back to that center and you'll always find peace."

Nothing has ever made more sense to me, spiritually speaking, than this idea. It works for me. And if I ever find anything that works better, I assure you—I will use it.

I have many friends in New York who are not religious people. Most, I would say. Either they fell away from the spiritual teachings of their youth or they never grew up with any God to begin with. Naturally, some of them are a bit freaked out by my newfound efforts to reach holiness. Jokes are made, of course. As my friend Bobby quipped once while he was trying to fix my computer: "No offense to your *aura*, but you still don't know shit about downloading software." I roll with the jokes. I think it's all funny, too. Of course it is.

What I'm seeing in some of my friends, though, as they are aging, is a longing to have *something* to believe in. But this longing chafes against any number of obstacles, including their intellect and common sense. Despite all their intellect, though, these people still live in a world that careens about in a series of wild and devastating and completely nonsensical lurches. Great and horrible experiences of either suffering or joy occur in the lives of all these people, just as with the rest of us, and these mega-experiences tend to make us long for a spiritual context in which to express either lament or gratitude, or to seek understanding. The problem is—what to worship, whom to pray to?

I have a dear friend whose first child was born right after his beloved mother died. After this confluence of miracle and loss, my friend felt a desire to have some kind of sacred place to go, or some ritual to perform, in order to sort through all the emotion. My friend was a Catholic by upbringing, but couldn't stomach returning to the church as an adult. ("I can't buy it anymore," he said, "knowing what I know.") Of course, he'd be embarrassed to become a Hindu or a Buddhist or something wacky like that. So what could he do? As he told me, "You don't want to go cherry-picking a religion."

Which is a sentiment I completely respect except for the fact that I totally disagree. I think you have every right to cherry-pick when it comes to moving your spirit and finding peace in God. I think you are free to search for any metaphor whatsoever which will take you across the worldly divide whenever you need to be transported or comforted. It's nothing to be embarrassed about. It's the history of mankind's search for holiness. If humanity never evolved in its exploration of the divine, a lot of us would still be worshipping golden Egyptian statues of cats. And this evolution of religious thinking does involve a fair bit of cherry-picking. You take whatever works from wherever you can find it, and you keep moving toward the light.

The Hopi Indians thought that the world's religions each contained one spiritual thread, and that these threads are always seeking each other, wanting to join. When all the threads are finally woven together they will form a rope that will pull us out of this dark cycle of history and into the next realm. More contemporarily, the Dalai Lama has repeated the same idea, assuring his Western students repeatedly that they needn't become Tibetan Buddhists in order to be his pupils. He welcomes them to take whatever ideas they like out of Tibetan Buddhism and integrate these ideas into their own religious practices. Even in the most unlikely and conservative of places, you can find sometimes this glimmering idea that God might be bigger than our limited religious doctrines have taught us. In 1954, Pope Pius XI, of all people, sent some Vatican delegates on a trip to Libya with these written instructions: "Do NOT think that you are going among Infidels. Muslims attain salvation, too. The ways of Providence are infinite."

But doesn't that make sense? That the infinite would be, indeed . . . infinite? That even the most holy amongst us would only be able to see scattered pieces of the eternal picture at any given time? And that maybe if we could collect those pieces and compare them, a story about God would begin to emerge that resembles and includes everyone? And isn't our individual longing for transcendence all just part of this larger human search for divinity? Don't we each have the right to not stop seeking until we get as close to the source of wonder as possible? Even if it means coming to India and kissing trees in the moonlight for a while?

That's me in the corner, in other words. That's me in the spotlight. Choosing my religion.

71

My flight leaves India at four in the morning, which is typical of how India works. I decide not to go to sleep at all that night, but to spend the whole evening in one of the meditation caves, in prayer. I'm not a late-night person by nature, but something in me wants to stay awake for these last hours at the Ashram. There are many things in my life I've stayed up all night to do—to make love, to argue with someone, to drive long distances, to dance, to cry, to worry (and sometimes all those things, in fact, in the course of one night)—but I've never sacrificed sleep for a night of exclusive prayer. Why not now?

I pack my bag and leave it by the temple gate, so I can be ready to grab it and go when the taxi arrives before dawn. And then I walk up the hill, I go into the meditation cave and I sit. I'm alone in there, but I sit where I can see the big photograph of Swamiji, my Guru's master, the founder of this Ashram, the long-gone lion who is somehow still here. I close my eyes and let the mantra come. I climb down that ladder into my own hub of stillness. When I get there, I can feel the world halt, the way I always wanted it to halt when I was nine years old and panicking about the relentlessness of time. In my heart, the clock stops and the calendar pages quit flying off the wall. I sit in silent wonder at all I understand. I am not actively praying. I have *become* a prayer.

I can sit here all night.

In fact, I do.

I don't know what alerts me when it's time to go meet my taxi, but after several hours of stillness, something gives me a nudge, and when I look at my watch it's exactly time to go. I have to fly to Indonesia now. How funny and strange. So I stand up and bow before the photograph of Swamiji—the bossy, the marvelous, the fiery. And then I slide a piece of paper under the carpet, right below his image. On the paper are the two poems I wrote during my four months in India. These are the first real poems I've ever written. A plumber from New Zealand encouraged me to try poetry for once—that's why it happened. One of these poems I wrote after having been here only a month. The other, I just wrote this morning.

In the space between the two poems, I have found acres of grace.

72

Two Poems from an Ashram in India

First

All this talk of nectar and bliss is starting to piss me off.
I don't know about you, my friend,
but my path to God ain't no sweet waft of incense.
It's a cat set loose in a pigeon pen,
and I'm the cat—but also them who yell like hell when they
get pinned.

My path to God is a worker's uprising,
won't be peace till they unionize.
Their picket is so fearsome
the National Guard won't go near them.

My path was beaten unconscious before me,
by a small brown man I never got to see,
who chased God through India, shin-deep in mud,
barefoot and famined, malarial blood,
sleeping in doorways, under bridges—a hobo.
(Which is short for "homeward bound," you know)
And he now chases me, saying: "Got it yet, Liz?
What HOMEWARD means? What BOUND really is?"

Second

However.
If they'd let me wear pants made out of the
fresh-mown grass from this place,
I'd do it.

If they'd let me make out
with every single Eucalyptus tree in Ganesh's Grove,
I swear, I'd do it.

I've sweated out dew these days,
worked out the dregs,
rubbed my chin on tree bark,
mistaking it for my master's leg.

I can't get far enough in.

If they'd let me eat the soil of this place
served on a bed of birds' nests,
I'd finish only half my plate,
Then sleep all night on the rest.

INDONESIA

Or

'Even in My Underpants I Feel Different.'

Or

Thirty-six Tales About the
Pursuit of Balance

73

I've never had less of a plan in my life than I do upon arrival in Bali. In all my history of careless travels, this is the most carelessly I've ever landed anyplace. I don't know where I'm going to live, I don't know what I'm going to do, I don't know what the exchange rate is, I don't know how to get a taxi at the airport—or even where to ask that taxi to take me. Nobody is expecting my arrival. I have no friends in Indonesia, or even friends-of-friends. And here's the problem about traveling with an out-of-date guidebook, and then not reading it anyway: I didn't realize that I'm actually not allowed to stay in Indonesia for four months, even if I want to. I find this out only upon entry into the country. Turns out I'm allowed only a one-month tourist visa. It hadn't occurred to me that the Indonesian government would be anything less than delighted to host me in their country for just as long as I pleased to stay.

As the nice immigration official is stamping my passport with permission to stay in Bali for only and exactly thirty days, I ask him in my most friendly manner if I can please remain longer.

"No," he says, in his most friendly manner. The Balinese are famously friendly.

"See, I'm supposed to stay here for three or four months," I tell him.

I don't mention that it's a *prophecy*—that my staying here for three or four months was predicted two years ago by an elderly and quite possibly demented Balinese medicine man, during a ten-minute palm-reading. I'm not sure how to explain this.

But what *did* that medicine man tell me, now that I think of it? Did he actually say that I would come back to Bali and spend three or four months living with him? Did he really say "living with" him? Or did he just want me to drop by again sometime if I was in the neighborhood and give him another ten bucks for another palm-reading? Did he say I *would* come back, or that I *should* come back? Did he really say, "See you later, alligator"? Or was it, "In a while, crocodile"?

I haven't had any communication with the medicine man since that one evening. I wouldn't know how to contact him, anyway. What might his address be? "Medicine Man, On His Porch, Bali, Indonesia"? I don't know whether he's dead or alive. I remember that he seemed exceedingly old two years ago when we met; anything could have happened to him since then. All I have for sure is his name—Ketut Liyer—and the memory that he lives in a village just outside the town of Ubud. But I don't remember the name of the village.

Maybe I should have thought all this through better.

74

But Bali is a fairly simple place to navigate. It's not like I've landed in the middle of the Sudan with no idea of what to do next. This is an island approximately the size of Delaware and it's a popular tourist destination. The whole place has arranged itself to help you, the Westerner with the credit cards, get around with ease. English is spoken here widely and happily. (Which makes me feel guiltily relieved. My brain synapses are so overloaded by my efforts to learn modern Italian and ancient Sanskrit during these last few months that I just can't take on the task of trying to learn Indonesian or, even more difficult, Balinese—a language more complex than Martian.) It's really no trouble being here. You can change your money at the airport, find a taxi with a nice driver who will suggest to you a lovely hotel—none of this is hard to arrange. And since the tourism industry collapsed in the wake of the terrorist bombing here two years ago (which happened a few weeks after I'd left Bali the first time), it's even easier to get around now; everyone is desperate to help you, desperate for work.

So I take a taxi to the town of Ubud, which seems like a good place to start my journey. I check into a small and pretty hotel there on the fabulously named Monkey Forest Road. The hotel has a sweet swimming pool and a garden crammed with tropical flowers with blossoms bigger than volleyballs (tended to by a highly organized team of hummingbirds and butterflies). The staff is Balinese, which means they automatically start adoring you and complimenting you on your beauty as soon as you walk in. The room has a view of the tropical treetops and there's a breakfast included every morning with piles of fresh tropical fruit. In short, it's one of the nicest places I've ever stayed and it's costing me less than ten dollars a day. It's good to be back.

Ubud is in the center of Bali, located in the mountains, surrounded by terraced rice paddies and innumerable Hindu temples, with rivers that cut fast through deep canyons of jungle and volcanoes visible on the horizon. Ubud has long been considered the cultural hub of the island, the place where traditional Balinese painting, dance, carving, and religious ceremonies thrive. It isn't near any beaches, so the tourists who come to Ubud are a self-selecting and rather classy crowd; they would prefer to see an ancient temple ceremony than to drink piña coladas in the surf. Regardless of what happens with my medicine man prophecy, this could be a lovely place to live for a while. The town is sort of like a small Pacific version of Santa Fe, only with monkeys walking around and Balinese families in traditional dress all over the place. There are good restaurants and nice little bookstores. I could feasibly spend my whole time here in Ubud doing what nice divorced American women have been doing with their time ever since the invention of the YWCA—signing up for one class after another: batik, drumming, jewelry-making, pottery, traditional Indonesian dance and cooking . . . Right across the road from my hotel there's even something called "The Meditation Shop"—a small storefront with a sign advertising open meditation sessions every night from 6:00 to 7:00. May peace prevail on earth, reads the sign. I'm all for it.

By the time I unpack my bags it's still early afternoon, so I decide to take myself for a walk, get reoriented to this town I haven't seen in two years. And then I'll try to figure out how to start finding my medicine man. I imagine this will be a difficult task, might take days or even weeks. I'm not sure where to start with my search, so I stop at the front desk on my way out and ask Mario if he can help me.

Mario is one of the guys who work at this hotel. I already made friends with him when I checked in, largely on account of his name. Not too long ago I was traveling in a country where many men were named Mario, but not one of them was a small, muscular, energetic Balinese fellow wearing a silk sarong and a flower behind his ear. So I had to ask, "Is your name really Mario? That doesn't sound very Indonesian."

"Not my real name," he said. "My real name is Nyoman."

Ah—I should have known. I should have known that I would have a 25 percent chance of guessing Mario's real name. In Bali, if I may digress, there are only four names that the majority of the population give to their children, regardless of whether the baby is a boy or a girl. The names are Wayan (pronounced "Why-Ann"), Made ("mah-DAY"), Nyoman and Ketut. Translated, these names mean simply First, Second, Third and Fourth, and they connote birth order. If you have a fifth child, you start the name cycle all over again, so that the fifth child is really known as something like: "Wayan to the Second Power." And so forth. If you have twins, you name them in the order they came out. Because there are basically only four names in Bali (higher-caste elites have their own selection of names) it's totally possible (indeed, quite common) that two Wayans would marry each other. And then their firstborn would be named, of course: Wayan.

This gives a slight indication of how important family is in Bali, and how important your placement in that family is. You would think this system could become complicated, but somehow the Balinese work it out. Understandably and necessarily, nicknaming is popular. For instance, one of the most successful business-women in Ubud is a lady named Wayan who has a busy restaurant called Café Wayan, and so she is known as "Wayan Café"— meaning, "The Wayan who owns Café Wayan." Somebody else might be known as "Fat Made," or "Nyoman-Rental-Car" or "Stupid-Ketut-Who-Burned-Down-His-Uncle's-House." My new Balinese friend Mario got around the problem by simply naming himself Mario.

"Why Mario?"

"Because I love everything Italian," he said.

When I told him that I'd recently spent four months in Italy, he found this fact so stupendously amazing that he came out from behind his desk and said, "Come, sit, talk." I came, I sat, we talked. And that's how we became friends.

So this afternoon I decide to start my search for my medicine man by asking my new friend Mario if by any chance he knows a man by the name of Ketut Liyer.

Mario frowns, thinking.

I wait for him to say something like, "Ah, yes! Ketut Liyer! Old medicine man who died just last week—so sad when venerable old medicine man passes away . . ."

Mario asks me to repeat the name, and this time I write it down, assuming I'm pronouncing something wrong. Sure enough, Mario brightens in recognition. "Ketut Liyer!"

Now I wait for him to say something like, "Ah, yes! Ketut Liyer! Insane person! Arrested last week for being a crazy man . . ."

But he says instead, "Ketut Liyer is famous healer."

"Yes! That's him!"

"I know him. I go in his house. Last week I take my cousin, she needs cure for her baby crying all night. Ketut Liyer fixes it. One time I took American girl like you to Ketut Liyer's house. Girl wanted magic to make her more beautiful to men. Ketut Liyer draw magic painting, for help her be more beautiful. I tease her after that. Every day I tell her, 'Painting working! Look how beautiful you are! Painting working!' "

Remembering the image Ketut Liyer had drawn for me a few years ago, I tell Mario that I'd gotten a magic picture myself from the medicine man once.

Mario laughs. "Painting working for you, too!"

"My picture was to help me find God," I explain.

"You don't want to be more beautiful to men?" he asks, understandably confused.

I say, "Hey, Mario—do you think you could take me to visit Ketut Liyer someday? If you're not too busy?"

"Not now," he says.

Just as I'm starting to feel disappointed, he adds, "But maybe in five minutes?"

75

So this is how it comes to pass that—the very afternoon I have arrived in Bali—I'm suddenly on the back of a motorbike, clutching my new friend Mario the Italian-Indonesian, who is speeding me through the rice terraces toward Ketut Liyer's home. For all that I've thought about this reunion with the medicine man over the last two years, I actually have no idea what I'm going to say to him when I arrive. And of course we don't have an appointment. So we show up unannounced. I recognize the sign outside his door, same as last time, saying: "Ketut Liyer—painter." It's a typical, traditional Balinese family compound. A high stone wall surrounds the entire property, there's a courtyard in the middle and a temple in the back. Several generations live out their lives together in the various interconnected small homes within these walls. We enter without knocking (no door, anyway) to the riotous dismay of a some typical Balinese watchdogs (skinny, angry) and there in the courtyard is Ketut Liyer the elderly medicine man, wearing his sarong and his golf shirt, looking precisely the same as he did two years ago when I first met him. Mario says something to Ketut, and I'm not exactly fluent in Balinese, but it sounds like a general introduction, something along the lines of, "Here's a girl from America—go for it."

Ketut turns his mostly toothless smile upon me with the force of a compassionate fire hose, and this is so reassuring: I had remembered correctly, he *is* extraordinary. His face is a comprehensive encyclopedia of kindness. He shakes my hand with an excited and powerful grip.

"I am very happy to meet you," he says.

He has no idea who I am.

"Come, come," he says, and I'm ushered to the porch of his little house, where woven bamboo mats serve as furniture. It looks exactly as it did two years ago. We both sit down. With no hesitation, he takes my palm in his hand—assuming that, like most of his Western visitors, a palm-reading is what I've come for. He gives me a quick reading, which I am reassured to see is an abridged version of exactly what he said to me last time. (He may not remember my face, but my destiny, to his practiced eye, is unchanged.) His English is better than I remembered, and also better than Mario's. Ketut speaks like the wise old Chinamen in classic kung fu movies, a form of English you could call "Grasshopperese," because you could insert the endearment "Grasshopper" into the middle of any sentence and it sounds very wise. "Ah—you have very lucky good fortune, *Grasshopper* . . ."

I wait for a pause in Ketut's predictions, then interrupt to remind him that I had been here to see him already, two years ago.

He looks puzzled. "Not first time in Bali?"

"No, sir."

He thinks hard. "You girl from California?"

"No," I say, my spirits tumbling deeper. "I'm the girl from New York."

Ketut says to me (and I'm not sure what this has to do with anything), "I am not so handsome anymore, lost many teeth. Maybe I will go to dentist someday, get new teeth. But too afraid of dentist."

He opens his deforested mouth and shows me the damage. Indeed, he has lost most of his teeth on the left side of his mouth and on the right side it's all broken, hurtful-looking yellow stubs. He fell down, he tells me. That's how his teeth got knocked out.

I tell him I'm sorry to hear it, then try again, speaking slowly. "I don't think you remember me, Ketut. I was here two years ago with an American Yoga teacher, a woman who lived in Bali for many years."

He smiles, elated. "I know Ann Barros!"

"That's right. Ann Barros is the Yoga teacher's name. But I'm Liz. I came here asking for your help once because I wanted to get closer to God. You drew me a magic picture."

He shrugs amiably, couldn't be less concerned. "Don't remember," he says.

This is such bad news it's almost funny. What am I going to do in Bali now? I don't know exactly what I'd imagined it would be like to meet Ketut again, but I did hope we'd have some sort of super-karmic tearful reunion. And while it's true I had feared he might be dead, it hadn't occurred to me that—if he were still alive—he wouldn't remember me at all. Although now it seems the height of dumbness to have ever imagined that our first meeting would have been as memorable for him as it was for me. Maybe I should have planned this better, for real.

So I describe the picture he had made for me, the figure with the four legs ("so grounded on earth") and the missing head ("not looking at the world through the intellect") and the face in the heart ("looking at the world through the heart") and he listens to me politely, with modest interest, like we're discussing somebody else's life entirely.

I hate to do this because I don't want to put him on the spot, but it's got to be said, so I just lay it out there. I say, "You told me I should come back here to Bali. You told me to stay here for three or four months. You said I could help you learn English and you would teach me the things that you know." I don't like the way my voice sounds—just the teensiest bit desperate. I don't mention anything about the invitation he'd once floated for me to live with his family. That seems way out of line, given the circumstances.

He listens to me politely, smiling and shaking his head, like, *Isn't it so funny the things people say?*

I almost drop it then. But I've come so far, I have to put forth one last effort. I say, "I'm the book writer, Ketut. I'm the book writer from New York."

And for some reason that does it. Suddenly his face goes translucent with joy, turns bright and pure and transparent. A Roman candle of recognition sparks to life in his mind. "YOU!" he says. "YOU! I remember YOU!" He leans forward, takes my shoulders in his hands and starts to shake me happily, the way a child shakes an unopened Christmas present to try to guess what's inside. "You came back! You came BACK!"

"I came back! I came back!" I say.

"You, you, you!"

"Me, me, me!"

I'm all tearful now, but trying not to show it. The depth of my relief—it's hard to explain. It takes even me by surprise. It's like this—it's like I was in a car accident, and my car went over a bridge and sank to the bottom of a river and I'd somehow managed to free myself from the sunken car by swimming through an open window and then I'd been frog-kicking and struggling to swim all the way up to the daylight through the cold, green water and I was almost out of oxygen and the arteries were bursting out of my neck and my cheeks were puffed with my last breath and then—GASP!—I broke through to the surface and took in huge gulps of air. And I survived. That gasp, that breaking through—this is what it feels like when I hear the Indonesian medicine man say, "You came back!" My relief is exactly that big.

I can't believe it worked.

"Yes, I came back," I say. "Of course I came back."

"I so happy!" he says. We're holding hands and he's wildly excited now. "I do not remember you at first! So long ago we meet! You look different now! So different from two years! Last time, you very sad-looking woman. Now—so happy! Like different person!"

The idea of this—the idea of a person looking so different after a mere two years have passed—seems to incite in him a shiver of giggles.

I give up trying to hide my tearfulness and just let it all spill over. "Yes, Ketut. I was very sad before. But life is better now."

"Last time you in bad divorce. No good."

"No good," I confirm.

"Last time you have too much worry, too much sorrow. Last time, you look like sad old woman. Now you look like young girl. Last time you ugly! Now you pretty!"

Mario bursts into ecstatic applause and pronounces victoriously: "See? Painting *working*!"

I say, "Do you still want me to help you with your English, Ketut?"

He tells me I can start helping him right now and hops up nimbly, gnome-like. He bounds into his little house and comes back with a pile of letters he's received from abroad over the last few years (so he *does* have an address!). He asks me to read the letters aloud to him; he can understand English well, but can't read much. I'm his secretary already. I'm a medicine man's secretary. This is fabulous. The letters are from art collectors overseas, from people who have somehow managed to acquire his famous magic drawings and magic paintings. One letter is from a collector in Australia, praising Ketut for his painting skills, saying, "How can you be so clever to paint with such detail?" Ketut answers to me, like giving dictation: "Because I practice many, many years."

When the letters are finished, he updates me on his life over the last few years. Some changes have occurred. Now he has a wife, for instance. He points across the courtyard at a heavyset woman who's been standing in the shadow of her kitchen door, glaring at me like she's not sure if she should shoot me, or poison me first and then shoot me. Last time I was here, Ketut had sadly shown me photographs of his wife who had recently died—a beautiful old Balinese woman who seemed bright and childlike even at her advanced age. I wave across the courtyard to the new wife, who backs away into her kitchen.

"Good woman," Ketut proclaims toward the kitchen shadows. "Very good woman."

He goes on to say that he's been very busy with his Balinese patients, always a lot to do, has to give much magic for new babies, ceremonies for dead people, healing for sick people, ceremonies for marriage. Next time he goes to Balinese wedding, he says, "We can go together! I take you!" The only thing is, he doesn't have very many Westerners visiting him anymore. Nobody comes to visit Bali since the terrorist bombing. This makes him "feel very confusing in my head." This also makes him feel "very empty in my bank." He says, "You come to my house every day to practice English with me now?" I nod happily and he says, "I will teach you Balinese meditation, OK?"

"OK," I say.

"I think three months enough time to teach you Balinese meditation, find God for you this way," he says. "Maybe four months. You like Bali?"

"I love Bali."

"You get married in Bali?"

"Not yet."

"I think maybe soon. You come back tomorrow?"

I promise to. He doesn't say anything about my moving in with his family, so I don't bring it up, stealing one last glance at the scary wife in the kitchen. Maybe I'll just stay in my sweet hotel the whole time, instead. It's more comfortable, anyway. Plumbing, and all that. I'll need a bicycle, though, to come see him every day . . .

So now it's time to go.

"I am very happy to meet you," he says, shaking my hand.

I offer up my first English lesson. I teach him the difference between "happy to meet you," and "happy to see you." I explain that we only say "Nice to meet you" the first time we meet somebody. After that, we say "Nice to see you," every time. Because you only meet someone once. But now we will see each other repeatedly, day after day.

He likes this. He gives it a practice round: "Nice to see you! I am happy to see you! I can see you! I am not deaf!"

This makes us all laugh, even Mario. We shake hands, and agree that I will come by again tomorrow afternoon. Until then, he says, "See you later, alligator."

"In a while, crocodile," I say.

"Let your conscience be your guide. If you have any Western friend come to Bali, send them to me for palm-reading—I am very empty now in my bank since the bomb. I am an autodidact. I am very happy to see you, Liss!"

"I am very happy to see you, too, Ketut."

76

Bali is a tiny Hindu island located in the middle of the two-thousand-mile-long Indonesian archipelago that constitutes the most populous Muslim nation on earth. Bali is therefore a strange and wondrous thing; it should not even exist, yet does. The island's Hinduism was an export from India by way of Java. Indian traders brought the religion east during the fourth century AD. The Javanese kings founded a mighty Hindu dynasty, little of which remains today except the impressive temple ruins at Borobudur. In the sixteenth century, a violent Islamic uprising swept across the region and the Shiva-worshipping Hindu royalty escaped Java, fleeing to Bali in droves during what would be remembered as the Majapahit

Exodus. The high-class, high-caste Javanese brought with them to Bali only their royal families, their craftsmen and their priests—and so it is not a wild exaggeration when people say that everyone in Bali is the descendent of either a king, a priest or an artist, and that this is why the Balinese have such pride and brilliance.

The Javanese colonists brought their Hindu caste system with them to Bali, though caste divisions were never as brutally enforced here as they once were in India. Still, the Balinese recognize a complex social hierarchy (there are five divisions of Brahmans alone) and I would have better luck personally decoding the human genome than trying to understand the intricate, interlocking clan system that still thrives here. (The writer Fred B. Eiseman's many fine essays on Balinese culture go much further into expert detail explaining these subtleties, and it is from his research that I take most of my general information, not only here but throughout this book.) Suffice it to say for our purposes that everyone in Bali is in a clan, that everyone knows which clan he is in, and that everyone knows which clan everyone else is in. And if you get kicked out of your clan for some grave disobedience, you really might as well jump into a volcano, because, honestly, you're as good as dead.

Balinese culture is one of the most methodical systems of social and religious organization on earth, a magnificent beehive of tasks and roles and ceremonies. The Balinese are *lodged*, completely held, within an elaborate lattice of customs. A combination of several factors created this network, but basically we can say that Bali is what happens when the lavish rituals of traditional Hinduism are superimposed over a vast rice-growing agricultural society that operates, by necessity, with elaborate communal cooperation. Rice terraces require an unbelievable amount of shared labor, maintenance and engineering in order to prosper, so each Balinese village has a *banjar*—a united organization of citizens who administer, through consensus, the village's political and economic and religious and agricultural decisions. In Bali, the collective is absolutely more important than the individual, or nobody eats.

Religious ceremonies are of paramount importance here in Bali (an island, don't forget, with seven unpredictable volcanoes on it—

you would pray, too). It has been estimated that a typical Balinese woman spends one-third of her waking hours either preparing for a ceremony, participating in a ceremony or cleaning up after a ceremony. Life here is a constant cycle of offerings and rituals. You must perform them all, in correct order and with the correct intention, or the entire universe will fall out of balance. Margaret Mead wrote about "the incredible busy-ness" of the Balinese, and it's true—there is rarely an idle moment in a Balinese compound. There are ceremonies here which must be performed five times a day and others that must be performed once a day, once a week, once a month, once a year, once every ten years, once every hundred years, once every thousand years. All these dates and rituals are kept organized by the priests and holy men, who consult a byzantine system of three separate calendars.

There are thirteen major rites of passage for every human being in Bali, each marked by a highly organized ceremony. Elaborate spiritual appeasement ceremonies are conducted all throughout life, in order to protect the soul from the 108 vices (108—there's that number again!), which include such spoilers as violence, stealing, laziness and lying. Every Balinese child passes through a momentous puberty ceremony in which the canine teeth, or "fangs," are filed down to a flat level, for aesthetic improvement. The worst thing you can be in Bali is coarse and animalistic, and these fangs are considered to be reminders of our more brutal natures and therefore must go. It is dangerous in such a close-knit culture for people to be brutal. A village's entire web of cooperation could be sliced through by one person's murderous intent. Therefore the best thing you can be in Bali is *alus*, which means "refined," or even "prettified." Beauty is good in Bali, for men and women. Beauty is revered. Beauty is safety. Children are taught to approach all hardship and discomfort with "a shining face," a giant smile.

The whole idea of Bali is a matrix, a massive and invisible grid of spirits, guides, paths and customs. Every Balinese knows exactly where he or she belongs, oriented within this great, intangible map. Just look at the four names of almost every Balinese citizen—First, Second, Third, Fourth—reminding them all of when they were born in the family, and where they belong. You couldn't have a clearer social mapping system if you called your kids North, South, East and West. Mario, my new Italian-Indonesian friend, told me that he is only happy when he can maintain himself—mentally and spiritually—at the intersection between a vertical line and horizontal one, in a state of perfect balance. For this, he needs to know exactly where he is located at every moment, both in his relationship to the divine and to his family here on earth. If he loses that balance, he loses his power.

It's not a ludicrous hypothesis, therefore, to say that the Balinese are the global masters of balance, the people for whom the maintenance of perfect equilibrium is an art, a science and a religion. For me, on a personal search for balance, I had hoped to learn much from the Balinese about holding steady in this chaotic world. But the more I read and see about this culture, the more I realize how far off the grid of balance I've fallen, at least from the Balinese perspective. My habit of wandering through this world oblivious to my physical orientation, in addition to my decision to have stepped outside the containing network of marriage and family, makes me—for Balinese purposes—something like a ghost. I enjoy living this way, but it's a nightmare of a life by the standards of any self-respecting Balinese. If you don't know where you are or whose clan you belong to, then how can you possibly find balance?

Given all this, I'm not so sure how much of the Balinese worldview I'm going to be able to incorporate into my own worldview, since at the moment I seem to be taking a more modern and Western definition of the word *equilibrium*. (I'm currently translating it as meaning "equal freedom," or the equal possibility of falling in any direction at any given time, depending on . . . you know . . . how things go.) The Balinese don't wait and see "how things go." That would be terrifying. They *organize* how things go, in order to keep things from falling apart.

When you are walking down the road in Bali and you pass a stranger, the very first question he or she will ask you is, "Where are you going?" The second question is, "Where are you coming from?" To a Westerner, this can seem like a rather invasive inquiry from a perfect stranger, but they're just trying to get an orientation on you, trying to insert you into the grid for the purposes of security and comfort. If you tell them that you don't know where you're going, or that you're just wandering about randomly, you might instigate a bit of distress in the heart of your new Balinese friend. It's far better to pick some kind of specific direction—*anywhere*—just so everybody feels better.

The third question a Balinese will almost certainly ask you is, "Are you married?" Again, it's a positioning and orienting inquiry. It's necessary for them to know this, to make sure that you are completely in order in your life. They really want you to say yes. It's such a relief to them when you say yes. If you're single, it's better not to say so directly. And I really recommend that you not mention your divorce at all, if you happen to have had one. It just makes the Balinese so worried. The only thing your solitude proves to them is your perilous dislocation from the grid. If you are a single woman traveling through Bali and somebody asks you, "Are you married?" the best possible answer is: "Not yet." This is a polite way of saying, "No," while indicating your optimistic intentions to get that taken care of just as soon as you can.

Even if you are eighty years old, or a lesbian, or a strident feminist, or a nun, or an eighty-year-old strident feminist lesbian nun who has never been married and never intends to get married, the politest possible answer is still: "Not yet."

77

In the morning, Mario helps me buy a bicycle. Like a proper almost-Italian, he says, "I know a guy," and he takes me to his cousin's shop, where I get a nice mountain bike, a helmet, a lock and a basket for slightly less than fifty American dollars. Now I'm mobile in my new town of Ubud, or at least as mobile as I can safely feel on these roads, which are narrow and winding and badly maintained and crowded with motorcycles, trucks and tourist buses.

In the afternoon, I ride my bike down into Ketut's village, to hang out with my medicine man for our first day of . . . whatever it is we're going to be doing together. I'm not sure, to be honest. English lessons? Meditation lessons? Good old-fashioned porch-sitting? I don't know what Ketut has in mind for me, but I'm just happy to be invited into his life.

He's got guests when I arrive. It's a small family of rural Balinese who have brought their one-year-old daughter to Ketut for help. The poor little baby is teething and has been crying for several nights. Dad is a handsome young man in a sarong; he has the muscular calves of a Soviet war hero's statue. Mom is pretty and shy, looking at me from way below her timidly lowered eyelids. They have brought a tiny offering to Ketut for his services—2,000 rupiah, which is about 25 cents, placed in a handmade basket of palm fronds, slightly bigger than a hotel bar's ashtray. There is one flower blossom in the basket, along with the money and a few grains of rice. (Their poverty puts them in stark opposition to the richer family from the capital city of Denpesar who will come to see Ketut later in the afternoon, the mother balancing on her head a three-tiered basket filled with fruit and flowers and a roasted duck—a headgear so magnificent and impressive that Carmen Miranda would have bowed down in humility before it.)

Ketut is relaxed and gracious with his company. He listens to the parents explain their baby's troubles. Then he digs through a small trunk on his porch and pulls out an ancient ledger filled with tiny writing in Balinese Sanskrit. He consults this book like a scholar, looking for some combination of words that will suit him, talking and laughing with the parents the whole time. Then he takes a blank page from a notebook with a picture of Kermit the Frog on it, and writes what he tells me is "a prescription" for the little girl. The child is being tormented by a minor demon, he diagnoses, in addition to the physical discomforts of teething. For the teething, he advises the parents to simply rub the baby's gums with pressed red onion juice. To appease the demon, they must make an offering of a small killed chicken and a small pig, along with a little bit of cake, mixed with special herbs which their grandmother should definitely have access to from her own medicine garden. (This food won't be wasted; after the offering ceremony, Balinese families are always allowed to eat their own donations to the gods, since the offering is more metaphysical than literal. The way the Balinese see it, God takes what belongs to God—the gesture—while man takes what belongs to man—the food itself.)

After writing the prescription, Ketut turns his back to us, fills a bowl with water, and keens a spectacular, quietly chilling mantra above it. Then Ketut blesses the baby with the water he has just infused with sacred power. Even at one year old, the child already knows how to receive a holy blessing in the traditional Balinese manner. Her mother holds her, and the baby puts out her little plummy paws to receive the water, sips it once, sips it again and splashes the rest on top of her head—a perfectly executed ritual. She could not be less frightened of this toothless old man who is chanting at her. Then Ketut takes the rest of the holy water and pours it into a small plastic sandwich bag, ties the bag at the top and gives it to the family to use later. The mother carries this plastic bag of water away with her as she leaves; it looks like she has just won a goldfish at the state fair, only she forgot to take the goldfish with her.

Ketut Liyer has given this family about forty minutes of his undivided attention, for the fee of about twenty-five cents. If they hadn't any money at all, he would have done the same; this is his duty as a healer. He may turn nobody away, or the gods will remove his talent for healing. Ketut gets about ten visitors a day like this, Balinese who need his help or advice on some holy or medical matter. On highly auspicious days, when everyone wants a special blessing, he might have over one hundred visitors.

"Don't you get tired?"

"But this is my profession," he tells me. "This is my hobby—medicine man."

A few more patients come throughout the afternoon, but Ketut and I get some time alone together on the porch, too. I'm so comfortable with this medicine man, as relaxed as with my own grandfather. He gives me my first lesson in Balinese meditation. He tells me that there are many ways to find God but most are too complicated for Westerners, so he will teach me an easy meditation. Which goes, essentially, like this: sit in silence and smile. I love it. He's laughing even as he's teaching it to me. Sit and smile. Perfect.

"You study Yoga in India, Liss?" he asks.

"Yes, Ketut."

"You can do Yoga," he says, "but Yoga too hard." Here, he contorts himself in a cramped lotus position and squinches up his face in a comical and constipated-looking effort. Then he breaks free and laughs, asking, "Why they always look so serious in Yoga? You make serious face like this, you scare away good energy. To meditate, only you must smile. Smile with face, smile with mind, and good energy will come to you and clean away dirty energy. Even smile in your liver. Practice tonight at hotel. Not to hurry, not to try too hard. Too serious, you make you sick. You can calling the good energy with a smile. All finish for today. See you later, alligator. Come back tomorrow. I am very happy to see you, Liss. Let your conscience be your guide. If you have Western friends come to visit Bali, bring them to me for palm-reading. I am very empty in my bank since the bomb."

78

Here is Ketut Liyer's life story pretty much as he tells it:

"It is nine generations that my family is a medicine man. My father, my grandfather, my great-grandfather, all of them is a medicine man. They all want me to be medicine man because they see I have light. They see I have beautiful and I have intelligent. But I do not want to be medicine man. Too much study! Too much information! And I don't believe in medicine man! I want to be painter! I want to be artist! I have good talent with this.

"When I was still young man, I meet American man, very rich, maybe even New York City person like you. He like my painting. He wants to buy big painting from me, maybe one meter big, for lot of money. Enough money to be rich. So I start to painting this picture for him. Every day I painting, painting, painting. Even in night I painting. In this day, long time ago, no electric lightbulb like today, so I have lamp. Oil lamp, you understand? Pump lamp, have to pump it to make oil come. And I always make painting every night with oil lamp.

"One night, oil lamp is dark, so I pumping, pumping, pumping and it explode! Makes my arm on fire! I go to hospital for one month with burned arm, it make infection. Infection goes all the way to my heart. The doctor say I must to go to Singapore for cut off my arm, for amputation. This is not my cup of tea. But doctor says I must go to Singapore, have operation to cut arm off. I tell doctor—first I go home to my village.

"That night in village, I got dream. Father, grandfather, great-grandfather—all they come in my dream to my house together and tell me how to heal my burned arm. They tell me make juice from saffron and sandalwood. Put this juice on burn. Then make powder from saffron and sandalwood. Rub this powder on burn. They tell me I must do this, then I not lose my arm. So real this dream, like they in house with me, all of they together.

"I wake up. I don't know what to do, because sometimes dreams are just joking, you understand? But I make back to my home and I put this saffron and sandalwood juice on my arm. And then I put this saffron and sandalwood powder on my arm. My arm very infected, very ache, made big, very swell. But after juice and powder, become very cool. Became very cold. Start to feel better. In ten days, my arm is good. All heal.

"For that, I start to believe. Now I have dream again, with father, grandfather, great-grandfather. They tell me now I must be medicine man. My soul, I must give it to God. For do this, I must make fast for six days, understand? No food, no water. No drink. No breakfast. Not easy. I so thirsty from fast, I go to rice fields in morning, before sun. I sit in rice field with mouth open and take water from air. How you call this, the water in air in rice field in morning? Dew? Yes. Dew. Only this dew I eat for six days. No other food, only this dew. On number five day, I get unconscious. I see all yellow color everywhere. No, not yellow color—GOLD. I see gold color everywhere, even inside me. Very happy. I understand now. This gold color is God, also inside me. Same thing that is God is same thing inside me. Same-same.

"So now I must be medicine man. Now I have to learn medical books from great-grandfather. These books not made on paper, made on palm leaves. Called *lontars*. This is Balinese medical encyclopedia. I must learn all different plants on Bali. Not easy. One by one, I learn everything. I learn to take care of people with many problem. One problem is when someone is sick from physical. I help this physical sick with herbs. Other problem is when family is sick, when family always fighting. I help this with harmony, with special magic drawing, also with talking for helping. Put magic drawing in house, no more fighting. Sometimes people sick in love, not find right match. For Balinese and Western, too, always a lot of trouble with love, difficult to find right match. I fix love problem with mantra and with magic drawing, bring love to you. Also, I learn black magic, to help people if bad black magic spell on them. My magic drawing, you put in your house, bring you good energy.

"I still like to be artist, I like make painting when I have time, sell to gallery. My painting, always the same painting—when Bali was paradise, maybe one thousand years ago. Painting of jungle, animals, women with—what is word? Breast. Women with breast. Difficult for me to find time to make painting because of medicine man, but I must be medicine man. It is my profession. It is my hobby. Must help people or God is angry with me. Must deliver baby sometimes, do ceremony for dead man, or do ceremony for tooth-filing or wedding. Sometimes I wake up, three in morning, make painting by electric lightbulb—only time I can make painting for me. I like alone this time of day, good for making painting.

"I do true magic, not joking. Always I tell true, even if bad news. I must do good character always in my life, or I will be in hell. I speak Balinese, Indonesian, little bit Japanese, little bit English, little bit Dutch. During war, many Japanese here. Not so bad for me—I read palms for Japanese, make friendly. Before war, many Dutch here. Now many Western here, all speak English. My Dutch is—how you say? What that word you teach me yesterday? Rusty? Yes—rusty. My Dutch is rusty. Ha!

"I am in fourth caste in Bali, in very low caste like farmer. But I see many people in first caste not so intelligent as me. My name is Ketut Liyer. Liyer is name my grandfather gave me when I was little boy. It means 'bright light.' This is me."

79

I am so free here in Bali, it's almost ridiculous. The only thing I have to do every day is visit Ketut Liyer for a few hours in the afternoon, which is far short of a chore. The rest of the day gets taken care of in various nonchalant manners. I meditate for an hour every morning using the Yogic techniques my Guru taught me, and then I meditate for an hour every evening with the practices Ketut has taught me ("sit still and smile"). In between, I walk around and ride my bike and sometimes talk to people and eat lunch. I found a quiet little lending library in this town, got myself a library card, and now great, luscious portions of my life are spent reading in the garden. After the intensity of life in the Ashram, and even after the decadent business of zooming all over Italy and eating everything in sight, this is such a new and radically peaceful episode of my life. I have so much free time, you could measure it in metric tons.

Whenever I leave the hotel, Mario and the other staff members at the front desk ask me where I'm going, and every time I return, they ask me where I have been. I can almost imagine that they keep tiny maps in the desk drawer of all their loved ones, with markings indicating where everyone is at every given moment, just to make sure the entire beehive is accounted for at all times.

In the evenings I spin my bicycle high up into the hills and across the acres of rice terraces north of Ubud, with views so splendid and green. I can see the pink clouds reflected in the standing water of the rice paddies, like there are two skies—one up in heaven for the gods, and one down here in the muddy wet, just for us mortals. The other day, I rode up to the heron sanctuary, with its grudging welcome sign ("OK, you can see herons here"), but there were no herons that day, just ducks, so I watched the ducks for a while, then rode on into the next village. Along the way I passed men and women and children and chickens and dogs who all, in their own way, were busy working, but none so busy that they couldn't stop to greet me.

A few nights ago, on the top of one lovely rise of forest I saw a sign: "Artist's House for Rent, with Kitchen." Because the universe is generous, three days later I am living there. Mario helped me move in, and all his friends at the hotel gave me a tearful farewell.

My new house is on a quiet road, surrounded in all directions by rice fields. It's a little cottagelike place inside ivy-covered walls. It's owned by an Englishwoman, but she is in London for the summer, so I slide into her home, replacing her in this miraculous space. There is a bright red kitchen here, a pond full of goldfish, a marble terrace, an outdoor shower tiled in shiny mosaics; while I shampoo I can watch the herons nesting in the palm trees. Little secret paths lead through a truly enchanting garden. The place comes with a gardener, so all I have to do is look at the flowers. I don't know what any of these extraordinary equatorial flowers are called, so I make up names for them. And why not? It's my Eden, is it not? Soon I've given all the plants around here new monikers—daffodil tree, cabbage-palm, prom-dress weed, spiral show-off, tip-toe blossom, melancholy-vine and a spectacular pink orchid I have christened "Baby's First Handshake." The unnecessary and superfluous volume of pure beauty around here is not to be believed. I can pick papayas and bananas right off the trees outside my bedroom window. There's a cat who lives here who is enormously affectionate to me for the half hour every day before I feed him, then moans crazily the rest of the time like he's having Vietnam War flashbacks. Oddly, I don't mind this. I don't mind anything these days. I can't imagine or remember discontent.

The sound universe is also spectacular around here. In the evenings there's a cricket orchestra with frogs providing the bass line. In the dead of night the dogs howl about how misunderstood they are. Before dawn the roosters for miles around announce how freaking cool it is to be roosters. ("We are ROOSTERS!" they holler. "We are the only ones who get to be ROOSTERS!") Every morning around sunrise there is a tropical birdsong competition, and it's always a ten-way tie for the championship. When the sun comes out the place quiets down and the butterflies get to work. The whole house is covered with vines; I feel like any day it will disappear into the foliage completely and I will disappear with it and become a jungle flower myself. The rent is less than what I used to pay in New York City for taxi fare every month.

The word *paradise*, by the way, which comes to us from the Persian, means literally "a walled garden."

80

That said, I must be honest here and relay that it takes me only three afternoons of research in the local library to realize that all my original ideas about Balinese paradise were a bit misguided. I'd been telling people since I first visited Bali two years ago that this small island was the world's only true utopia, a place that has known only peace and harmony and balance for all time. A perfect Eden with no history of violence or bloodshed ever. I'm not sure where I got this grand idea, but I endorsed it with full confidence.

"Even the policemen wear flowers in their hair," I would say, as if that proved it.

In reality, though, it turns out Bali has had exactly as bloody and violent and oppressive a history as anywhere else on earth where human beings have ever lived. When the Javanese kings first immigrated here in the sixteenth century, they essentially established a feudal colony, with a strict caste system which—like all self-respecting caste systems—tended not to trouble itself with consideration for those at the bottom. The economy of early Bali was fueled by a lucrative slave trade (which not only preceded European participation in the international slave traffic by several centuries, but also outlived Europe's trafficking of human lives for a good long while). Internally, the island was constantly at war as rival kings staged attacks (complete with mass rape and murder) on their neighbors. Until the late nineteenth century, the Balinese had a reputation amongst traders and sailors for being vicious fighters. (The word *amok*, as in "running amok," is a Balinese word, describing a battle technique of suddenly going insanely wild against one's enemies in suicidal and bloody hand-to-hand combat; the Europeans were frankly terrified by this practice.) With a well-disciplined army of 30,000, the Balinese defeated their Dutch invaders in 1848, again in 1849 and once more, for good measure, in 1850. They collapsed under Dutch rule only when the rival kings of Bali broke ranks and betrayed each other in bids for power, aligning with the enemy for the promise of good business deals later. So to gauze this island's history today in a dream of paradise is a bit insulting to reality; it's not like these people have spent the last millennium just sitting around smiling and singing happy songs.

But in the 1920s and 1930s, when an elite class of Western travelers discovered Bali, all this bloodiness was ignored as the newcomers agreed that this was truly "The Island of the Gods," where "everyone is an artist" and where humanity lives in an unspoiled state of bliss. It's been a lingering idea, this dream; most visitors to Bali (myself on my first trip included) still endorse it. "I was furious at God that I was not born Balinese," said the German photographer George Krauser after visiting Bali in the 1930s. Lured by reports of otherworldly beauty and serenity, some really A-list tourists started visiting the island—artists like Walter Spies, writers like Noël Coward, dancers like Claire Holt, actors like Charlie Chaplin, scholars like Margaret Mead (who, despite all the naked breasts, wisely called Balinese civilization on what it truly was, a society as prim as Victorian England: "Not an ounce of free libido in the whole culture.")

The party ended in the 1940s when the world went to war. The Japanese invaded Indonesia, and the blissful expatriates in their Balinese gardens with their pretty houseboys were forced to flee. In the struggle for Indonesian independence which followed the war, Bali became just as divided and violent as the rest of the archipelago, and by the 1950s (reports a study called *Bali: Paradise Invented*) if a Westerner dared visit Bali at all, he might have been wise to sleep with a gun under his pillow. In the 1960s, the struggle for power turned all of Indonesia into a battlefield between Nationalists and Communists. After a coup attempt in Jakarta in 1965, Nationalist soldiers were sent to Bali with the names of every suspected Communist on the island. Over the course of about a week, aided by the local police and village authorities at every step, the Nationalist forces steadily murdered their way through every township. Something like 100,000 corpses choked the beautiful rivers of Bali when the killing spree was over.

The revival of the dream of a fabled Eden came in the late 1960s, when the Indonesian government decided to reinvent Bali for the international tourist market as "The Island of the Gods," launching a massively successful marketing campaign. The tourists who were lured back to Bali were a fairly high-minded crowd (this was not Fort Lauderdale, after all), and their attention was guided toward the artistic and religious beauty inherent in the Balinese culture. Darker elements of history were overlooked. And have remained overlooked since.

Reading about all this during my afternoons in the local library leaves me somewhat confused. Wait—why did I come to Bali again? To search for the balance between worldly pleasure and spiritual devotion, right? Is this, indeed, the right setting for such a search? Do the Balinese truly inhabit that peaceful balance, more than anyone else in the world? I mean, they *look* balanced, what with all the dancing and praying and feasting and beauty and smiling, but I don't know what's actually going on under there. The policemen really *do* wear flowers tucked behind their ears, but there's corruption all over the place in Bali, just like in the rest of Indonesia (as I found out firsthand the other day when I passed a uniformed man a few hundred bucks of under-the-table cash to illegally extend my visa so I could stay in Bali for four months, after all). The Balinese quite literally live off their image of being the world's most peaceful and devotional and artistically expressive people, but how much of that is intrinsic and how much of that is economically calculated? And how much can an outsider like me ever learn of the hidden stresses that might loiter behind those "shining faces"? It's the same here as anywhere else—you look at the picture too closely and all the firm lines start to melt away into an indistinct mass of blurry brushstrokes and blended pixels.

For now, all I can say for certain is that I love the house I have rented and that the people in Bali have been gracious to me without exception. I find their art and ceremonies to be beautiful and restorative; they seem to think so, as well. That's my empirical experience of a place that is probably far more complex than I will ever understand. But whatever the Balinese need to do in order to hold their own balance (and make a living) is entirely up to them. What

I'm here to do is work on my own equilibrium, and this still feels, at least for now, like a nourishing climate in which to do that.

81

I don't know how old my medicine man is. I've asked him, but he's not certain. I seem to remember, when I was here two years ago, the translator saying that he was eighty. But Mario asked him the other day how old he was and Ketut said, "Maybe sixty-five, not sure." When I asked him what year he was born, he said he didn't remember being born. I know he was an adult when the Japanese were occupying Bali during World War II, which could make him about eighty now. But when he told me the story about burning his arm as a young man, and I asked him what year that had happened, he said, "I don't know. Maybe 1920?" So if he was around twenty years old in 1920, then that makes him what now? Maybe a hundred and five? So we can estimate that he's somewhere between sixty and a hundred and five years old.

I've also noticed that his estimation of his age changes by the day, based on how he feels. When he's really tired, he'll sigh and say, "Maybe eighty-five today," but when he's feeling more upbeat he'll say, "I think I'm sixty today." Perhaps this is as good a way of estimating age as any—how old do you *feel*? What else matters, really? Still, I'm always trying to figure it out. One afternoon I got really simple, and just said, "Ketut—when is your birthday?"

"Thursday," he said.

"This Thursday?"

"No. Not this Thursday. A Thursday."

This is a good start . . . but is there no more information than that? A Thursday in what month? In what year? No telling. Anyway, the day of the week that you were born is more important in Bali than the year, which is why, even though Ketut doesn't know how old he is, he was able to tell me that the patron god of children born on Thursdays is Shiva the Destroyer, and that the day has two guiding animal spirits—the lion and the tiger. The official tree of children born on Thursday is the banyan. The official bird is the peacock. A person born on Thursday is always talking first, interrupting everyone else, can be a little aggressive, tends to be handsome ("a playboy or playgirl," in Ketut's words) but has a decent overall character, with an excellent memory and a desire to help other people.

When his Balinese patients come to Ketut with serious health or economic or relationship problems, he always asks on which day of the week they were born, in order to concoct the correct prayers and medicines to help them. Because sometimes, Ketut says, "people are sick in the birthday," and they need a little astrological adjustment in order to set them in balance again. A local family brought their youngest son to see Ketut the other day. The child was maybe four years old. I asked what the problem was and Ketut translated that the family was concerned about "problems with very aggressive this boy. This boy not take orders. Bad behave. Not pay attention. Everyone in house tired from the boy. Also, sometimes this boy too dizzy."

Ketut asked the parents if he could hold the child for a moment. They put their son in Ketut's lap and the boy leaned back against the old medicine man's chest, relaxed and unafraid. Ketut held him tenderly, placed a palm on the child's forehead, shut his eyes. He then placed a palm on the boy's belly, shut his eyes again. He was smiling and speaking gently to the child the whole time. The examination was quickly over. Ketut handed the boy back to his parents, and the people left soon after with a prescription and some holy water. Ketut told me he'd asked the parents about the circumstances of the boy's birth and had discovered the child had been born under a bad star and on a Saturday—a day of birth which contains elements of potentially bad spirits, like crow spirit, owl spirit, rooster spirit (this is what makes the child a fighter) and puppet spirit (this is what's causing his dizziness). But it was not all bad news. Being born on Saturday, the boy's body also contained rainbow spirit and butterfly spirit, and these could be strengthened. A series of offerings would have to be made and the child would be brought into balance once more.

"Why did you hold your hand on the boy's forehead and stomach?" I asked. "Were you checking for fever?"

"I was check his brain," Ketut said. "To see if he had evil spirits in his mind."

"What kind of evil spirits?"

"Liss," he said. "I am Balinese. I believe from black magic. I believe evil spirits come out rivers and hurt people."

"Did the boy have evil spirits?"

"No. He is only sick in his birthday. His family will make sacrifice. This will be OK. And you, Liss? You are practice Balinese meditation every night? Keep mind and heart clean?"

"Every night," I promised.

"You learn to smile even in your liver?"

"Even in my liver, Ketut. Big smile in my liver."

"Good. This smile will make you beautiful woman. This will give you power of to be very pretty. You can use this power—pretty power!—to get what you want in life."

"Pretty power!" I repeat the phrase, loving it. Like a meditating Barbie. "I want pretty power!"

"You are still practice Indian meditation, too?"

"Every morning."

"Good. Don't forget your Yoga. Beneficial to you. Good for you to keep practice both ways of meditation—Indian and Balinese. Both different, but good in equal way. Same-same. I think about religion, most of it is same-same."

"Not everybody thinks so, Ketut. Some people like to argue about God."

"Not necessary," he said. "I have good idea, for if you meet some person from different religion and he want to make argument about God. My idea is, you listen to everything this man say about God. Never argue about God with him. Best thing to say is, 'I agree with you.' Then you go home, pray what you want. This is my idea for people to have peace about religion."

Ketut keeps his chin lifted all the time, I've noticed, his head held a little bit back, sort of quizzical and elegant at the same time. Like a curious old king, he looks at the whole world from above his nose. His skin is lustrous, golden brown. He's almost totally bald, but makes up for it with exceptionally long and feathery eyebrows which look eager to take flight. Except for his missing teeth and his burn-scarred right arm, he seems in perfect health. He told me that he was a dancer in his youth, for the temple ceremonies, and that he was beautiful back then. I believe it. He eats only one meal a day—a typically simple Balinese dish of rice mixed with either duck or fish. He likes to drink one cup of coffee with sugar every day, mostly just to celebrate the fact that he can afford coffee and sugar. You, too, could easily live to a hundred and five on this diet. He keeps his body strong, he says, by meditating every night before sleep and by pulling the healthy energy of the universe into his core. He says that the human body is made of nothing more or less than the five elements of all creation—water (*apa*), fire (*tejo*), wind (*bayu*), sky (*akasa*) and earth (*pritiwi*)—and all you have to do is concentrate on this reality during meditation and you will receive energy from all of these sources and you will stay strong. Demonstrating his occasionally very accurate ear for English idiom, he said, "The microcosm becomes the macrocosm. You—microcosm—will become same as universe—macrocosm."

He was so busy today, crowded with Balinese patients who were stacked up all over his courtyard like cargo crates, all of them with babies or offerings in their laps. He had farmers and businessmen there, fathers and grandmothers. There were parents with babies who weren't keeping food down, and old men haunted by black magic curses. There were young men tossed by aggression and lust, and young women looking for love matches while suffering children complained about their rashes. Everyone out of balance; everyone needing equilibrium restored.

The mood of the courtyard of Ketut's home is always one of total patience, though. Sometimes people must wait for three hours before Ketut gets a chance to take care of them, but they never so much as tap their feet or roll their eyes in exasperation. Extraordinary, too, is the way the children wait, leaning up against their beautiful mothers, playing with their own fingers to pass the time. I'm always amused later when it turns out that these same tranquil children have been brought over to see Ketut because the mother and father have decided that the child is "too naughty" and needs a cure. *That* little girl? That little three-year-old girl who was sitting silently in the hot sun for four straight hours, without complaint or snack or toy? She's *naughty*? I wish I could say, "People—you want to see naughty, I'll take you to America, show you some kids that'll have you believing in Ritalin." But there's just a different standard here for good behavior in children.

Ketut treated all the patients obligingly, one after another, seemingly unconcerned by the passage of time, giving all exactly the attention they needed regardless of who was waiting to be seen next. He was so busy he didn't even get his one meal at lunchtime, but stayed glued to his porch, obliged by his respect for God and his ancestors to sit there for hours on end, healing everyone. By evening, his eyes looked as tired as the eyes of a Civil War field surgeon. His last patient of the day had been a deeply troubled middle-aged Balinese man complaining that he had not slept well in weeks; he was being haunted, he said, by a nightmare of "drowning in two rivers at the same time."

Until this evening, I still wasn't sure what my role was in Ketut Liyer's life. Every day I've been asking him if he's really sure he wants me around, and he keeps insisting that I must come and spend time with him. I feel guilty taking up so much of his day, but he always seems disappointed when I leave at the end of the afternoon. I'm not teaching him any English, not really. Whatever English he already learned however many decades ago has been cemented into his mind by now and there isn't much space for correction or new vocabulary. It's all I can do to get him to say, "Nice to see you," when I arrive, instead of "Nice to meet you."

Tonight, when his last patient had left and Ketut was exhausted, looking ancient from the weariness of service, I asked him whether I should go now and let him have some privacy, and he replied, "I always have time for you." Then he asked me to tell him some stories about India, about America, about Italy, about my family. That's when I realized that I am not Ketut Liyer's English teacher, nor am I exactly his theological student, but I am the merest and simplest of pleasures for this old medicine man—I am his company. I'm somebody he can talk to because he enjoys hearing about the world and he hasn't had much of a chance to see it.

In our hours together on this porch, Ketut has asked me questions about everything from how much cars cost in Mexico to what causes AIDS. (I did my best with both topics, though I believe there are experts who could have answered with more substance.) Ketut has never been off the island of Bali in his life. He has spent very little time, actually, off this porch. He once went on a pilgrimage to Mount Agung, the biggest and most spiritually important volcano on Bali, but he said the energy was so powerful there he could scarcely meditate for fear he might be consumed by sacred fire. He goes to the temples for the big important ceremonies and he is invited to his neighbors' homes to perform weddings or coming-of-age rituals, but most of the time he can be found right here, cross-legged upon this bamboo mat, surrounded by his great-grandfather's palm-leaf medical encyclopedias, taking care of people, mollifying demons and occasionally treating himself to a cup of coffee with sugar.

"I had a dream from you last night," he told me today. "I had a dream you are riding your bicycle anywhere."

Because he paused, I suggested a grammatical correction. "Do you mean, you had a dream that I was riding my bicycle *every-where*?"

"Yes! I dream last night you are riding your bicycle anywhere *and* everywhere. You are so happy in my dream! All over world, you are riding your bicycle. And I following you!"

Maybe he wishes he could . . .

"Maybe you can come see me someday in America, Ketut," I said.

"Can't, Liss." He shook his head, cheerfully resigned to his destiny. "Don't have enough teeth to travel on airplane."

82

As for Ketut's wife, it takes me a while to align myself with her. Nyomo, as he calls her, is big and plump with a stiff-hip limp and teeth stained red by chewing on betel nut tobacco. Her toes are painfully crooked from arthritis. She has a shrewd eye. She was scary to me from the first sight. She's got that fierce old lady vibe you see sometimes in Italian widows and righteous black churchgoing mamas. She looks like she'd whup your hide for the slightest of misdemeanors. She was blatantly suspicious of me at first—*Who is this flamingo traipsing through my house every day?* She would stare at me from inside the sooty shadows of her kitchen, unconvinced as to my right to exist. I would smile at her and she'd just keep staring, deciding whether she should chase me out with a broomstick or not.

But then something changed. It was after the whole photocopy incident.

Ketut Liyer has all these piles of old, lined notebooks and ledgers, filled with tiny little handwriting, of ancient Balinese-Sanskrit mysteries about healing. He copied these notes into these notebooks way back in the 1940s or 1950s, sometime after his grandfather died, so he would have all the medical information recorded. This stuff is beyond invaluable. There are volumes of data about rare trees and leaves and plants and all their medicinal properties. He's got some sixty pages of diagrams about palm-reading, and more notebooks full of astrological data, mantras, spells and cures. The only thing is, these notebooks had been through decades of mildew and mice and they're shredded almost to bits. Yellow and crumbling and musty, they look like disintegrating piles of autumn leaves. Every time he turns a page, he rips the page.

"Ketut," I said to him last week, holding up one of his battered notebooks, "I'm not a doctor like you are, but I think this book is dying."

He laughed. "You think is dying?"

"Sir," I said gravely, "here is my professional opinion—if this book does not get some help soon, it will be dead within the next six months."

Then I asked if I could take the notebook into town with me and photocopy it before it died. I had to explain what photocopying was, and promise that I would only keep the notebook for twenty-four hours and that I would do it no harm. Finally, he agreed to let me take it off the porch property with my most passionate assurances that I would be careful with his grandfather's wisdom. I rode into town to the shop with the Internet computers and photocopiers and I gingerly duplicated every page, then had the new, clean photocopies bound in a nice plastic folder. I brought the old and the new versions of the book back the next day before noon. Ketut was astonished and delighted, so happy because he's had that notebook, he said, for fifty years. Which might literally mean "fifty years," or might just mean "a really long time."

I asked if I could copy the rest of his notebooks, to keep that information safe, too. He held out another limp, broken, shredded, gasping document filled with Balinese Sanskrit and complicated sketches.

"Another patient!" he said.

"Let me heal it!" I replied.

This was another grand success. By the end of the week, I'd photocopied several of the old manuscripts. Every day, Ketut called his wife over and showed her the new copies and he was overjoyed. Her facial expression didn't change at all, but she studied the evidence thoroughly.

And the next Monday when I came to visit, Nyomo brought me hot coffee, served in a jelly jar. I watched her carry the drink across the courtyard on a china saucer, limping slowly on the long journey from her kitchen to Ketut's porch. I assumed the coffee was intended for Ketut, but, no—he'd already had his coffee. This was for me. She'd prepared it for me. I tried to thank her but she looked annoyed at my thanks, kind of swatted me away the way she swats away the rooster who always tries to stand on her outdoor kitchen table when she's preparing lunch. But the next day she brought me a glass of coffee and a bowl of sugar on the side. And the next day it was a glass of coffee, a bowl of sugar and a cold boiled potato. Every day that week, she added a new treat. This was starting to feel like that childhood car trip alphabet-memory game: "I'm going to Grandma's house, and I'm bringing an apple . . . I'm going to Grandma's house and I'm bringing an apple and a balloon . . . I'm going to Grandma's house and I'm bringing an apple, a balloon, a cup of coffee in a jelly glass, a bowl of sugar and a cold potato . . ."

Then, yesterday, I was standing in the courtyard, saying my goodbyes to Ketut, and Nyomo came shuffling past with her broom, sweeping and pretending not to be paying attention to everything that happens in her empire. I had my hands clasped behind my back as I was standing there, and she came up behind me and took one of my hands in hers. She fumbled through my hand like she was trying to untumble the combination on a lock and she found my index finger. Then she wrapped her whole big, hard fist around that finger and gave me this deep, long squeeze. I could feel her love pulsing through her power grip, right up into my arm and all the way down into my guts. Then she dropped my hand and limped away arthritically, saying not a single word, continuing her sweeping as though nothing had happened. While I stood there quietly drowning in two rivers of happiness at the same time.

83

I have a new friend. His name is Yudhi, which is pronounced "You-Day." He's Indonesian, originally from Java. I got to know him because he rented my house to me; he's working for the Englishwoman who owns the place, looking after her property while she's away in London for the summer. Yudhi is twenty-seven years old and stocky in build and talks kind of like a southern California surfer. He calls me "man" and "dude" all the time. He's got a smile that could stop crime, and he's got a long, complicated life story for somebody so young.

He was born in Jakarta; his mother was a housewife, his father an Indonesian fan of Elvis who owned a small air-conditioning and refrigeration business. The family was Christian—an oddity in this part of the world, and Yudhi tells entertaining stories about being mocked by the neighborhood Muslim kids for such shortcomings as "You eat pork!" and "You love Jesus!" Yudhi wasn't bothered by the teasing; Yudhi, by nature, isn't bothered by much. His mom, however, didn't like him hanging around with the Muslim kids, mostly on account of the fact that they were always barefoot, which Yudhi also liked to be, but she thought it was unhygienic, so she gave her son a choice—he could either wear shoes and play outside, or he could stay barefoot and remain indoors. Yudhi doesn't like wearing shoes, so he spent a big chunk of his childhood and adolescence life in his bedroom, and that's where he learned how to play the guitar. Barefoot.

The guy has a musical ear like maybe nobody I've ever met. He's beautiful with the guitar, never had lessons but understands melody and harmony like they were the kid sisters he grew up with. He makes these East-West blends of music that combine classical Indonesian lullabies with reggae groove and early-days Stevie Wonder funk—it's hard to explain, but he should be famous. I never knew anybody who heard Yudhi's music who didn't think he should be famous.

Here's what he always wanted to do most of all—live in America and work in show business. The world's shared dream. So when Yudhi was still a Javanese teenager, he somehow talked himself into a job (speaking hardly any English yet) on a Carnival Cruise Lines ship, thereby casting himself out of his narrow Jakarta environs and into the big, blue world. The job Yudhi got on the cruise ship was one of those insane jobs for industrious immigrants—living belowdecks, working twelve hours a day, one day off a month, cleaning. His fellow workers were Filipinos and Indonesians. The Indonesians and the Filipinos slept and ate in separate quarters of the boat, never mingling (Muslims vs. Christians, don't you know), but Yudhi, in typical fashion, befriended everybody and became a kind of emissary between the two groups of Asian laborers. He saw more similarities than differences between these maids and custodians and dishwashers, all of whom were working bottomless hours in order to send a hundred dollars or so a month back to their families at home.

The first time the cruise ship sailed into New York Harbor, Yudhi stayed up all night, perched on the highest deck, watching the city skyline appear over the horizon, heart hammering with excitement. Hours later, he got off the ship in New York and hailed a yellow cab, just like in the movies. When the recent African immigrant driving the taxi asked where he'd like to go, Yudhi said, "Anywhere, man—just drive me around. I want to see everything." A few months later the ship came to New York City again, and this time Yudhi disembarked for good. His contract was up with the cruise line and he wanted to live in America now.

He ended up in suburban New Jersey, of all places, living for a while with an Indonesian man he'd met on the ship. He got a job in a sandwich shop at the mall—again, ten-to-twelve-hour days of immigrant-style labor, this time working with Mexicans, not Filipinos. He learned better Spanish those first few months than English. In his rare moments of free time, Yudhi would ride the bus into Manhattan and just wander the streets, still so speechlessly infatuated with the city—a town he describes today as "the place which is the most full of love in the entire world." Somehow (again—that smile) he met up in New York City with a crowd of young musicians from all over the world and he took to playing guitar with them, jamming all night with talented kids from Jamaica, Africa, France, Japan . . . And at one of those gigs, he met Ann—a pretty blonde from Connecticut who played bass. They fell in love. They got married. They found an apartment in Brooklyn and they were surrounded by groovy friends who all went on road trips together down to the Florida Keys. Life was just unbelievably happy. His English was quickly impeccable. He was thinking about going to college.

On September 11, Yudhi watched the towers fall from his rooftop in Brooklyn. Like everyone else he was paralyzed with grief at what had happened—how could somebody inflict such an appalling atrocity on the city that is the most full of love of anywhere in the world? I don't know how much attention Yudhi was paying when the U.S. Congress subsequently passed the Patriot Act in response to the terrorist threat—legislation which included draconian new immigration laws, many of which were directed against Islamic nations such as Indonesia. One of these provisions demanded that all Indonesian citizens living in America register with the Department of Homeland Security. The telephones started ringing as Yudhi and his young Indonesian immigrant friends tried to figure out what to do—many of them had overstayed their visas and were afraid that registering would get them deported. On the other hand, they were afraid to *not* register, thereby behaving like criminals. Presumably the fundamentalist Islamic terrorists roaming around America ignored this registration law, but Yudhi decided that he did want to register. He was married to an American and he wanted to update his immigration status and become a legal citizen. He didn't want to live in hiding.

He and Ann consulted all kinds of lawyers, but nobody knew how to advise them. Before 9/11 there would have been no problems—Yudhi, now married, could just go to the immigration office, update his visa situation and begin the process of gaining citizenship. But now? Who knew? "The laws haven't been tested yet," said the immigration lawyers. "The laws will be tested on you." So Yudhi and his wife had a meeting with a nice immigration official and shared their story. The couple were told that Yudhi was to come back later that same afternoon, for "a second interview." They should have been wary then; Yudhi was strictly instructed to return without his wife, without a lawyer, and carrying nothing in his pockets. Hoping for the best, he did return alone and empty-handed to the second interview—and that's when they arrested him.

They took him to a detention center in Elizabeth, New Jersey, where he stayed for weeks amongst a vast crowd of immigrants, all of whom had recently been arrested under the Homeland Security Act, many of whom had been living and working in America for years, most of whom didn't speak English. Some had been unable to contact their families upon their arrests. They were invisible in the detention center; nobody knew they existed anymore. It took a near-hysterical Ann days to find out where her husband had been taken. What Yudhi remembers most about the detention center was the dozen coal-black, thin and terrified Nigerian men who had been found on a freight ship inside a steel shipping crate; they had been hiding in that container at the bottom of that ship for almost a month before they were discovered, trying to get to America—or anywhere. They had no idea now where they were. Their eyes were so wide, Yudhi said, it looked like they were still being blinded with spotlights.

After a period of detention, the U.S. government sent my Christian friend Yudhi—now an Islamic terrorist suspect, apparently—back to Indonesia. This was last year. I don't know if he's ever going to be allowed anywhere near America again. He and his wife are still trying to figure out what to do with their lives now; their dreams hadn't called for living out their lives in Indonesia.

Unable to cope with Jakarta's slums after having lived in the first world, Yudhi came to Bali to see if he could make a living here, though he's having trouble being accepted into this society because he isn't Balinese—he's from Java. And the Balinese don't like the Javanese one bit, thinking of them all as thieves and beggars. So Yudhi encounters more prejudice here—in his own nation of Indonesia—than he ever did back in New York. He doesn't know what to do next. Maybe his wife, Ann, will come and join him here. Then again—maybe not. What's here for her? Their young marriage, conducted now entirely by e-mail, is on the rocks. He's so out of place here, so disoriented. He's more of an American than he is anything else; Yudhi and I use the same slang, we talk about our favorite restaurants in New York and we like all the same movies. He comes over to my house in the evenings and I get him beers and he plays me the most amazing songs on his guitar. I wish he were famous. If there was any fairness, he would be so famous by now.

He says, "Dude—why is life all crazy like this?"

84

"Ketut, why is life all crazy like this?" I asked my medicine man the next day.

He replied, *"Bhuta ia, dewa ia."*

"What does that mean?"

"Man is a demon, man is a god. Both true."

This was a familiar idea to me. It's very Indian, very Yogic. The notion is that human beings are born, as my Guru has explained many times, with the equivalent potential for both contraction and expansion. The ingredients of both darkness and light are equally present in all of us, and then it's up to the individual (or the family, or the society) to decide what will be brought forth—the virtues or the malevolence. The madness of this planet is largely a result of the human being's difficulty in coming into virtuous balance with himself. Lunacy (both collective and individual) results.

"So what can we do about the craziness of the world?"

"Nothing." Ketut laughed, but with a dose of kindness. "This is nature of world. This is destiny. Worry about your craziness only— make you in peace."

"But how should we find peace within ourselves?" I asked Ketut.

"Meditation," he said. "Purpose of meditation is only happiness and peace—very easy. Today I will teach a new meditation, make you even better person. Is called Four Brothers Meditation."

Ketut went on to explain that the Balinese believe we are each accompanied at birth by four invisible brothers, who come into the world with us and protect us throughout our lives. When the child is in the womb, her four siblings are even there with her—they are represented by the placenta, the amniotic fluid, the umbilical cord and the yellow waxy substance that protects an unborn baby's skin. When the baby is born, the parents collect as much of these extraneous birthing materials as possible, placing them in a coconut shell and burying it by the front door of the family's house. According to the Balinese, this buried coconut is the holy resting place of the four unborn brothers, and that spot is tended to forever, like a shrine.

The child is taught from earliest consciousness that she has these four brothers with her in the world wherever she goes, and that they will always look after her. The brothers inhabit the four virtues a person needs in order to be safe and happy in life: intelligence, friendship, strength and (I love this one) *poetry*. The brothers can be called upon in any critical situation for rescue and assistance. When you die, your four spirit brothers collect your soul and bring you to heaven.

Today Ketut told me that he's never taught any Westerner the Four Brothers Meditation yet, but he thinks I am ready for it. First, he taught me the names of my invisible siblings—Ango Patih, Maragio Patih, Banus Patih and Banus Patih Ragio. He instructed me to memorize these names and to ask for the help of my brothers throughout my life, whenever I need them. He says I don't have to be formal when I speak to them, the way we are formal when we pray to God. I'm allowed to speak to my brothers with familiar affection, because "It just your family!" He tells me to say their names as I'm washing myself in the morning, and they will join me.

Say their names again every time before I eat, and I will include my brothers in the enjoyment of the meal. Call on them before I go to sleep, saying, "I am sleeping now, so you must stay awake and protect me," and my brothers will shield me through the night, stop demons and nightmares.

"That's good," I told him, "because I have a problem sometimes with nightmares."

"What nightmares?"

I explained to the medicine man that I've been having the same horrible nightmare since childhood, namely that there is a man with a knife standing next to my bed. This nightmare is so vivid, the man is so real, that it sometimes makes me scream out in fear. It leaves my heart pounding every time (and has never been fun for those who share my bed, either). I've been having this nightmare every few weeks for as long as I can remember.

I told this to Ketut, and he told me I had been misunderstanding the vision for years. The man with the knife in my bedroom is not an enemy; he's just one of my four brothers. He's the spirit brother who represents strength. He's not there to attack me, but to guard me while I sleep. I'm probably waking up because I'm sensing the commotion of my spirit brother fighting away some demon who might be trying to hurt me. It is not a knife my brother is carrying, but a *kris*—a small, powerful dagger. I don't have to be afraid. I can go back to sleep, knowing I am protected.

"You lucky," Ketut said. "Lucky you can see him. Sometimes I see my brothers in meditation, but very rare for regular person to see like this. I think you have big spiritual power. I hope maybe someday you become medicine woman."

"OK," I said, laughing, "but only if I can have my own TV series."

He laughed with me, not getting the joke, of course, but loving the idea that people make jokes. Ketut then instructed me that whenever I speak to my four spirit brothers, I must tell them who I am, so they can recognize me. I must use the secret nickname they have for me. I must say, "I am Lagoh Prano."

Lagoh Prano means "Happy Body."

I rode my bicycle back home, pushing my happy body up the hills toward my house in the late afternoon sun. On my way through the forest, a big male monkey dropped out of a tree right in front of me and bared his fangs at me. I didn't even flinch. I said, "Back off, Jack—I got four brothers protecting my ass," and I just rode right on by him.

85

Although the next day (protective brothers notwithstanding) I did get hit by a bus. It was sort of a smallish bus, but nevertheless it did knock me off my bicycle as I was cruising down the shoulderless road. I got tossed into a cement irrigation ditch. About thirty Balinese people on motorcycles stopped to help me, having witnessed the accident (the bus was long gone), and everyone invited me to their house for tea or offered to drive me to the hospital, they all felt so bad about the whole incident. It wasn't that serious a wreck, though, considering what it might have been. My bicycle was fine, although the basket was bent and my helmet was cracked. (Better the helmet than the head in such cases.) The worst of the damage was a deep cut on my knee, full of bits of pebbles and dirt, that proceeded—over the next few days in the moist tropical air—to become nastily infected.

I didn't want to worry him, but a few days later I finally rolled up my pants leg on Ketut Liyer's porch, peeled off the yellowing bandage, and showed my wound to the old medicine man. He peered at it, concerned.

"Infect," he diagnosed. "Painful."

"Yes," I said.

"You should go see doctor."

This was a little surprising. Wasn't *he* the doctor? But for some reason he didn't volunteer to help and I didn't push it. Maybe he doesn't administer medication to Westerners. Or maybe Ketut just had a secret hidden master plan, because it was my banged-up knee that allowed me, in the end, to meet Wayan. And from that meeting, everything that was meant to happen . . . happened.

86

Wayan Nuriyasih is, like Ketut Liyer, a Balinese healer. There are some differences between them, though. He's elderly and male; she's a woman in her late thirties. He's more of a priestly figure, somewhat more mystical, while Wayan is a hands-on doctor, mixing herbs and medications in her own shop and taking care of patients right there on the premises.

Wayan has a little storefront shop in the center of Ubud called "Traditional Balinese Healing Center." I'd ridden my bike past it many times on my way down to Ketut's, noticing it because of all the potted plants outside the place, and because of the blackboard with the curious handwritten advertisement for the "Multivitamin Lunch Special." But I'd never gone into the place before my knee got messed up. After Ketut sent me to find a doctor, though, I remembered the shop and came by on my bicycle, hoping somebody there might be able to help me deal with the infection.

Wayan's place is a very small medical clinic and home and restaurant all at the same time. Downstairs there's a tiny kitchen and a modest public eating area with three tables and few chairs. Upstairs there's a private area where Wayan gives massages and treatments. There's one dark bedroom in the back.

I limped into the shop with my sore knee and introduced myself to Wayan the healer—a strikingly attractive Balinese woman with a wide smile and shiny black hair down to her waist. There were two shy young girls hiding behind her in the kitchen who smiled when I waved to them, then ducked away again. I showed Wayan my infected wound and asked if she could help. Soon Wayan had water and herbs boiling up on the stove, and was making me drink *jamu*— traditional Indonesian homemade medicinal concoctions. She placed hot green leaves on my knee and it started to feel better immediately.

We got to talking. Her English was excellent. Because she is Balinese, she immediately asked me the three standard introductory questions—*Where are you going today? Where are you coming from? Are you married?*

When I told her I wasn't married ("Not yet!") she looked taken aback.

"Never been married?" she asked.

"No," I lied. I don't like lying, but I generally have found it's easier not to mention divorce to the Balinese because they get so upset about it.

"Really never been married?" she asked again, and she was looking at me with great curiosity now.

"Honestly," I lied. "I've never been married."

"You sure?" This was getting weird.

"I'm totally sure!"

"Not even once?" she asked.

OK, so she can see through me.

"Well," I confessed, "there was that one time . . ."

And her face cleared like: *Yes, I thought as much.* She asked, "Divorced?"

"Yes," I said, ashamed now. "Divorced."

"I could tell you are divorced."

"It's not very common here, is it?"

"But me, too," said Wayan, entirely to my surprise. "Me too, divorced."

"You?"

"I did everything I could," she said. "I try everything before I got a divorce, praying every day. But I had to go away from him."

Her eyes filled up with tears, and next thing you knew, I was holding Wayan's hand, having just met my first Balinese divorcée, and I was saying, "I'm sure you did the best you could, sweetie. I'm sure you tried everything."

"Divorce is too sad," she said.

I agreed.

I stayed there in Wayan's shop for the next five hours, talking with my new best friend about her troubles. She cleaned up the infection in my knee as I listened to her story. Wayan's Balinese husband, she told me, was a man who "drink all the time, always gamble, lose all our money, then beat me when I don't give him more money for to gamble and to drink." She said, "He beat me into the hospital many times." She parted her hair, showed me scars on her head and said, "This is from when he hit me with motorcycle helmet. Always, he was hitting me with this motorcycle helmet when he is drinking, when I don't make money. He hit me so much, I go unconscious, dizzy, can't see. I think it is lucky I am healer, my family are healers, because I know how to heal myself after he beats me. I think if I was not healer, I would lose my ears, you know, not be able to hear things anymore. Or maybe lose my eye, not be able to see." She left him, she told me, after he beat her so severely "that I lose my baby, my second child, the one in my belly." After which incident their firstborn child, a bright little girl with the nickname of Tutti, said, "I think you should get a divorce, Mommy. Every time you go to the hospital you leave too much work around the house for Tutti."

Tutti was four years old when she said this.

To exit a marriage in Bali leaves a person alone and unprotected in ways that are almost impossible for a Westerner to imagine. The Balinese family unit, enclosed within the walls of a family compound, is merely everything—four generations of siblings, cousins, parents, grandparents and children all living together in a series of small bungalows surrounding the family temple, taking care of each other from birth to death. The family compound is the source of strength, financial security, health care, day care, education and—most important to the Balinese—spiritual connection.

The family compound is so vital that the Balinese think of it as a single, living person. The population of a Balinese village is traditionally counted not by the number of individuals, but by the number of compounds. The compound is a self-sustaining universe. So you don't leave it. (Unless, of course, you are a woman, in which case you move only once—out of your father's family compound and into your husband's.) When this system works—which it does in this healthy society almost all the time—it produces the most sane, protected, calm, happy and balanced human beings in the world. But when it doesn't work? As with my new friend Wayan? The outcasts are lost in airless orbit. Her choice was either to stay in the family compound safety net with a husband who kept putting her in the hospital, or to save her own life and leave, which left her with nothing.

Well, not exactly *nothing*, actually. She did take with her an encyclopedic knowledge of healing, her goodness, her work ethic and her daughter Tutti—whom she had to fight hard to keep. Bali is a patriarchy to the end. In the rare case of a divorce, the children automatically belong to the father. To get Tutti back, Wayan had to hire a lawyer, whom she paid with every single thing she had. I mean—*everything*. She sold off not only her furniture and jewelry, but also her forks and spoons, her socks and shoes, her old washcloths and half-burned candles—everything went to pay that lawyer. But she did get her daughter back, in the end, after a two-year battle. Wayan is just lucky Tutti was a girl; if she'd been a boy, Wayan never would have seen the kid again. Boys are much more valuable.

For the last few years now, Wayan and Tutti have been living on their own—all alone, in the beehive of Bali!—moving from place to place every few months as money comes and goes, always sleepless with worry about where to go next. Which has been difficult because every time she moves, her patients (mostly Balinese, who are all on hard times themselves these days) have trouble finding her again. Also, with every move, little Tutti has to be pulled out of school. Tutti was always first in her class before, but has slipped since the last move down to twentieth out of fifty children.

In the middle of Wayan's telling me this story, Tutti herself came charging into the shop, having arrived home from school. She's eight years old now and a mighty exhibition of charisma and fireworks. This little cherry bomb of a girl (pigtailed and skinny and excited) asked me in lively English if I'd like to eat lunch, and Wayan said, "I forgot! You should have lunch!" and the mother and daughter rushed into their kitchen and—with the help of the two shy young girls hiding back there—produced sometime later the best food I'd tasted yet in Bali.

Little Tutti brought out each course of the meal with a bright-voiced explanation of what was on the plate, wearing a huge grin, generally just being so totally peppy she should've been spinning a baton.

"Turmeric juice, for keep clean the kidneys!" she announced.

"Seaweed, for calcium!"

"Tomato salad, for vitamin D!"

"Mixed herbs, for not get malaria!"

I finally said, "Tutti, where did you learn to speak such good English?"

"From a book!" she proclaimed.

"I think you are a very clever girl," I informed her.

"Thank you!" she said, and did a spontaneous little happy dance. "You are a very clever girl, too!"

Balinese kids aren't normally like this, by the way. They're usually all quiet and polite, hiding behind their mother's skirts. Not Tutti. She was all show-biz. She was all show *and* tell.

"I will see you my books!" Tutti sang, and hurtled up the stairs to get them.

"She wants to be an animal doctor," Wayan told me. "What is the word in English?"

"Veterinarian?"

"Yes. Veterinarian. But she has many questions about animals, I don't know how to answer. She says, 'Mommy, if somebody brings me a sick tiger, do I bandage its teeth first, so it doesn't bite me? If a snake gets sick and needs medicine, where is the opening?' I don't know where she gets these ideas. I hope she can go to university."

Tutti careened down the stairs, arms full of books, and zinged herself into her mother's lap. Wayan laughed and kissed her daughter, all the sadness about the divorce suddenly gone from her face. I watched them, thinking that little girls who make their mothers live grow up to be such powerful women. Already, in the space of one afternoon, I was so in love with this kid. I sent up a spontaneous prayer to God: *May Tutti Nuriyasih someday bandage the teeth of a thousand white tigers!*

I loved Tutti's mother, too. But I'd been in their shop now for hours and felt I should leave. Some other tourists had wandered into the place, and were hoping to be served lunch. One of the tourists, a brassy older broad from Australia, was loudly asking if Wayan could please help cure her "god-awful constipation." I was thinking, *Sing it a little louder, honey, and we can all dance to it . . .*

"I will come back tomorrow," I promised Wayan, "and I'll order the multivitamin lunch special again."

"Your knee is better now," Wayan said. "Quickly better. No infection anymore."

She wiped the last of the green herbal goo off my leg, then sort of jiggled my kneecap around a bit, feeling for something. Then she felt the other knee, closing her eyes. She opened her eyes, grinned and said, "I can tell by your knees that you don't have much sex lately."

I said, "Why? Because they're so close together?"

She laughed. "No—it's the cartilage. Very dry. Hormones from sex lubricate the joints. How long since sex for you?"

"About a year and a half."

"You need a good man. I will find one for you. I will pray at the temple for a good man for you, because now you are my sister. Also, if you come back tomorrow, I will clean your kidneys for you."

"A good man and clean kidneys, too? That sounds like a great deal."

"I never tell anybody these things before about my divorce," she told me. "But my life is heavy, too much sad, too much hard. I don't understand why life is so hard."

Then I did a strange thing. I took both the healer's hands in mine and I said with the most powerful conviction, "The hardest part of your life is behind you now, Wayan."

I left the shop, then, trembling unaccountably, all jammed up with some potent intuition or impulse that I could not yet identify or release.

87

Now my days are divided into natural thirds. I spend my mornings with Wayan at her shop, laughing and eating. I spend my afternoons with Ketut the medicine man, talking and drinking coffee. I spend my evenings in my lovely garden, either hanging out by myself and reading a book, or sometimes talking with Yudhi, who comes over to play his guitar. Every morning, I meditate while the sun comes up over the rice fields, and before bedtime I speak to my four spirit brothers and ask them to watch over me while I sleep.

I've been here only a few weeks and I feel a rather mission-accomplished sensation already. The task in Indonesia was to search for balance, but I don't feel like I'm searching for *anything* anymore because the balance has somehow naturally come into place. It's not that I'm becoming Balinese (no more than I ever became Italian or Indian) but only this—I can feel my own peace, and I love the swing of my days between easeful devotional practices and the pleasures of beautiful landscape, dear friends and good food. I've been praying a lot lately, comfortably and frequently. Most of the time, I find that I want to pray when I'm on my bicycle, riding home from Ketut's house through the monkey forest and the rice terraces in the dusky late afternoons. I pray, of course, not to be hit by another bus, or jumped by a monkey or bit by a dog, but that's just superfluous; most of my prayers are expressions of sheer gratitude for the fullness of my contentment. I have never felt less burdened by myself or by the world.

I keep remembering one of my Guru's teachings about happiness. She says that people universally tend to think that happiness is a stroke of luck, something that will maybe descend upon you like fine weather if you're fortunate enough. But that's not how happiness works. Happiness is the consequence of personal effort. You fight for it, strive for it, insist upon it, and sometimes even travel around the world looking for it. You have to participate relentlessly in the manifestations of your own blessings. And once you have achieved a state of happiness, you must never become lax about maintaining it, you must make a mighty effort to keep swimming upward into that happiness forever, to stay afloat on top of it. If you don't, you will leak away your innate contentment. It's easy enough to pray when you're in distress but continuing to pray even when your crisis has passed is like a sealing process, helping your soul hold tight to its good attainments.

Recalling these teachings as I ride my bike so freely in the sunset through Bali, I keep making prayers that are really vows, presenting my state of harmony to God and saying, "This is what I would like to hold on to. Please help me memorize this feeling of contentment and help me always support it." I'm putting this happiness in a bank somewhere, not merely FDIC protected but guarded by my four spirit brothers, held there as insurance against future trials in life. This is a practice I've come to call "Diligent Joy." As I focus on Diligent Joy, I also keep remembering a simple idea my friend Darcey told me once—that all the sorrow and trouble of this world is caused by unhappy people. Not only in the big global Hitler-'n'-Stalin picture, but also on the smallest personal level. Even in my own life, I can see exactly where my episodes of unhappiness have brought suffering or distress or (at the very least) inconvenience to those around me. The search for contentment is, therefore, not merely a self-preserving and self-benefiting act, but also a generous gift to the world. Clearing out all your misery *gets you out of the way*. You cease being an obstacle, not only to yourself but to anyone else. Only then are you free to serve and enjoy other people.

At the moment, the person I'm enjoying the most is Ketut. The old man—truly one of the happiest humans I've ever encountered—is giving me his full access, the freedom to ask any lingering questions about divinity, about human nature. I like the meditations he has taught me, the comic simplicity of "smile in your liver" and the reassuring presence of the four spirit brothers. The other day the medicine man told me that he knows sixteen different meditation techniques, and many mantras for all different purposes. Some of them are to bring peace or happiness, some of them are for health, but some of them are purely mystical—to transport him into other realms of consciousness. For instance, he said, he knows one meditation that takes him "to up."

"To up?" I asked. "What is to up?"

"To seven levels up," he said. "To heaven."

Hearing the familiar idea of "seven levels," I asked him if he meant that his meditation took him up through the seven sacred chakras of the body, which are discussed in Yoga.

"Not chakras," he said. "Places. This meditation takes me seven places in universe. Up and up. Last place I go is heaven."

I asked, "Have you been to heaven, Ketut?"

He smiled. Of course he had been there, he said. Easy to go to heaven.

"What is it like?"

"Beautiful. Everything beautiful is there. Every person beautiful is there. Everything beautiful to eat is there. Everything is love there. Heaven is love."

Then Ketut said he knows another meditation. "To down." This down meditation takes him seven levels below the world. This is a more dangerous meditation. Not for beginning people, only for a master.

I asked, "So if you go up to heaven in the first meditation, then, in the second meditation you must go down to . . . ?"

"Hell," he finished the statement.

This was interesting. Heaven and hell aren't ideas I've heard discussed very much in Hinduism. Hindus see the universe in terms of karma, a process of constant circulation, which is to say that you don't really "end up" anywhere at the end of your life—not in heaven or hell—but just get recycled back to the earth again in another form, in order to resolve whatever relationships or mistakes you left uncompleted last time. When you finally achieve perfection, you graduate out of the cycle entirely and melt into The Void. The notion of karma implies that heaven and hell are only to be found here on earth, where we have the capacity to create them, manufacturing either goodness or evil depending on our destinies and our characters.

Karma is a notion I've always liked. Not so much literally. Not necessarily because I believe that I used to be Cleopatra's bartender—but more metaphorically. The karmic philosophy appeals to me on a metaphorical level because even in one lifetime it's obvious how often we must repeat our same mistakes, banging our heads against the same old addictions and compulsions, generating the same old miserable and often catastrophic consequences, until we can finally stop and fix it. This is the supreme lesson of karma (and also of Western psychology, by the way)—take care of the problems now, or else you'll just have to suffer again later when you screw everything up the next time. And that repetition of suffering—that's hell. Moving out of that endless repetition to a new level of understanding—there's where you'll find heaven.

But here Ketut was talking about heaven and hell in a different way, as if they are real places in the universe which he has actually visited. At least I think that's what he meant.

Trying to get clear on this, I asked, "You have been to hell, Ketut?"

He smiled. Of course he's been there.

"What's it like in hell?"

"Same like heaven," he said.

He saw my confusion and tried to explain. "Universe is a circle, Liss."

I still wasn't sure I understood.

He said. "To up, to down   all same, at end."

I remembered an old Christian mystic notion: *As above, so below.* I asked. "Then how can you tell the difference between heaven and hell?"

"Because of how you go. Heaven, you go up, through seven happy places. Hell, you go down, through seven sad places. This is why it better for you to go up, Liss." He laughed.

I asked, "You mean, you might as well spend your life going upward, through the happy places, since heaven and hell—the destinations—are the same thing anyway?"

"Same-same," he said. "Same in end, so better to be happy on journey."

I said, "So, if heaven is love, then hell is . . ."

"Love, too," he said.

I sat with that one for a while, trying to make the math work.

Ketut laughed again, slapped my knee affectionately with his hand.

"Always so difficult for young person to understand this!"

88

So I was hanging out in Wayan's shop again this morning, and she was trying to figure out how to make my hair grow faster and thicker. Having glorious thick, shiny hair herself that hangs all the way down to her butt, she feels sorry for me with my wispy blond mop. As a healer, of course, she does have a remedy to help thicken my hair, but it won't be easy. First, I have to find a banana tree and personally cut it down. I have to "throw away the top of the tree," then carve the trunk and roots (which are still lodged in the earth) into a big, deep bowl "like a swimming pool." Then I have to put a piece of wood over the top of this hollow, so rainwater and dew don't get in. Then I will come back in a few days and find that the swimming pool is now filled with the nutrient-rich liquid of the banana root, which I then must collect in bottles and bring to Wayan. She will bless the banana root juice at the temple for me, then rub the juice into my skull every day. Within a few months I will have, like Wayan, thick, shiny hair all the way down to my butt.

"Even if you are bald," she said, "this will make you have hair."

As we're talking, little Tutti—just home from school—is sitting on the floor, drawing a picture of a house. Mostly, houses are what Tutti draws these days. She's dying to have a house of her own. There's always a rainbow in the backdrop of her pictures, and a smiling family—father and all.

This is what we do all day in Wayan's shop. We sit and talk and Tutti draws pictures and Wayan and I gossip and tease each other. Wayan's got a bawdy sense of humor, always talking about sex, busting me about being single, speculating on the genital endowments of all the men who pass by her shop. She keeps telling me she's been going to the temple every evening and praying for a good man to show up in my life, to be my lover.

I told her again this morning, "No, Wayan—I don't need it. My heart's been broken too many times."

She said, "I know cure for broken heart." Authoritatively, and in a doctorly manner, Wayan ticked off on her fingers the six elements of her Fail-Proof Broken-Heart Curing Treatment: "Vitamin E, get much sleep, drink much water, travel to a place far away from the person you loved, meditate and teach your heart that this is destiny."

"I've been doing everything but the vitamin E."

"So now you cured. And now you need a new man. I bring you one, from praying."

"Well, I'm not praying for a new man, Wayan. The only thing I'm praying for these days is to have peace with myself."

Wayan rolled her eyes, like *Yeah, right, whatever you claim, you big white weirdo,* and said, "That's because you have bad memory problem. You don't remember anymore how nice is sex. I used to have bad memory problem, too, when I was married. Every time I saw a handsome man walking down the street, I would forget I had a husband back home."

She nearly fell over laughing. Then she composed herself and concluded, "Everybody need sex, Liz."

At this moment, a great-looking woman came walking into the shop, smiling like a lighthouse beam. Tutti leapt up and ran into her arms, shouting, "Armenia! Armenia! Armenia!" Which, as it turned out, was the woman's name—not some kind of strange nationalist battle cry. I introduced myself to Armenia, and she told me she was from Brazil. She was so dynamic, this woman—so Brazilian. She was gorgeous, elegantly dressed, charismatic and engaging and indeterminate in age, just *insistently* sexy.

Armenia, too, is a friend of Wayan's, who comes to the shop frequently for lunch and for various traditional medical and beauty treatments. She sat down and talked with us for about an hour, joining our gossiping, girlish little circle. She's in Bali for only another week before she has to fly off to Africa, or maybe it's back to Thailand, to take care of her business. This Armenia woman, it turns out, has had just the teensiest bit of glamorous life. She used to work for the United Nations High Commissioner on Refugees. Back in the 1980s she had been sent into the El Salvadoran and Nicaraguan jungles during the height of war as a negotiator of peace, using her beauty and charm and wits to get all the generals and rebels to calm down and listen to reason. (Hello, pretty power!) Now she runs a multinational marketing business called Novica, which supports indigenous artists all over the world by selling their products on the Internet. She speaks about seven or eight languages. She's got the most fabulous pair of shoes I've seen since Rome.

Looking at us both, Wayan said, "Liz—why do you never try to look sexy, like Armenia? You such a pretty girl, you have good capital of nice face, nice body, nice smile. But always you wear this same broken T-shirt, same broken jeans. Don't you want to be sexy, like her?"

"Wayan," I said, "Armenia is *Brazilian*. It's a completely different situation."

"How is it different?"

"Armenia," I said, turning to my new friend. "Can you please try to explain to Wayan what it means to be a Brazilian woman?"

Armenia laughed, but then seemed to consider the question –seriously and answered, "Well, I always tried to look nice and be feminine even in the war zones and refugee camps of Central America. Even in the worst tragedies and crisis, there's no reason to add to everyone's misery by looking miserable yourself. That's my philosophy. This is why I always wore makeup and jewelry into the jungle—nothing too extravagant, but maybe just a nice gold bracelet and some earrings, a little lipstick, good perfume. Just enough to show that I still had my self-respect."

In a way, Armenia reminds me of those great Victorian-era British lady travelers, who used to say there's no excuse for wearing clothes in Africa that would be unsuited for an English drawing room. She's a butterfly, this Armenia. And she couldn't stay for too long at Wayan's shop because she had work to do, but that didn't stop her from inviting me to a party tonight. She knows another Brazilian expat in Ubud, she told me, and he's hosting a special event at a nice restaurant this evening. He'll be cooking a *feijoada*—a traditional Brazilian feast consisting of massive piles of pork and black beans. There will be Brazilian cocktails, as well. Lots of interesting expatriates from all over the world who live here in Bali. Would I care to come? They might all go out dancing later, too. She doesn't know if I like parties, but . . .

Cocktails? Dancing? Piles of pork?

Of course I'll come.

89

I can't remember the last time I got dressed up, but this evening I dug out my one fancy spaghetti-strap dress from the bottom of my backpack and slithered it on. I even wore lipstick. I can't remember the last time I wore lipstick, but I know it wasn't anywhere near India. I stopped at Armenia's house on the way over to the party, and she draped me in some of her fancy jewelry, let me borrow her fancy perfume, let me store my bicycle in her backyard so I could arrive at the party in her fancy car, like a proper adult woman.

The dinner with the expatriates was great fun, and I felt myself revisiting all these long-dormant aspects of my personality. I even got a little bit drunk, which was notable after all the purity of my last few months of praying at the Ashram and sipping tea in my Balinese flower garden. And I was flirting! I hadn't flirted in ages. I'd only been hanging around with monks and medicine men lately, but suddenly I was dusting off the old sexuality again. Though I couldn't really tell who I was flirting with. I was kind of spreading it around everywhere. Was I attracted to the witty Australian former journalist sitting next to me? ("We're all drunks here," he quipped. "We write *references* for other drunks.") Or was it the quiet intellectual German down the table? (He promised to lend me novels from his personal library.) Or was it the handsome older Brazilian man who had cooked this giant feast for all of us in the first place? (I liked his kind brown eyes and his accent. And his cooking, of course. I said something very provocative to him, out of nowhere. He was making a joke at his own expense, saying, "I'm a full catastrophe of a Brazilian man—I can't dance, I can't play soccer and I can't play any musical instruments." For some reason I replied, "Maybe so. But I have a feeling you could play a very good Casanova." Time stopped solid for a long, long moment, then, as we looked at each other frankly, like, *That was an interesting idea to lay on this table.* The boldness of my statement hovered in the air around us like a fragrance. He didn't deny it. I looked away first, feeling myself blush.)

His *feijoada* was amazing, anyway. Decadent, spicy and rich— everything you can't normally get in Balinese food. I ate plate after plate of the pork and decided that it was official: I can never be a vegetarian, not with food like this in the world. And then we went out dancing at this local nightclub, if you can call it a nightclub. It was more like a groovy beach shack, only without the beach. There was a live band of Balinese kids playing good reggae music, and the place was mixed up with revelers of all ages and nationalities, expats and tourists and locals and gorgeous Balinese boys and girls, all dancing freely, unself-consciously. Armenia hadn't come along, claiming she had to work the next day, but the handsome older Brazilian man was my host. He wasn't such a bad dancer as he claimed. Probably he can play soccer, too. I liked having him nearby, opening doors for me, complimenting me, calling me "darling." Then again, I noticed that he called everyone "darling"—even the hairy male bartender. Still, the attention was nice . . .

It had been so long since I'd been in a bar. Even in Italy I didn't go to bars, and I hadn't been out much during the David years, either. I think the last time I'd gone dancing was back when I was married . . . back when I was *happily* married, come to think of it. Dear God, it had been ages. Out on the dance floor I ran into my friend Stefania, a lively young Italian girl I'd met recently in a meditation class in Ubud, and we danced together, hair flying everywhere, blond and dark, spinning merrily around. Sometime after midnight, the band stopped playing and people mingled.

That's when I met the guy named Ian. Oh, I really liked this guy. Right away I really liked him. He was very good-looking, in a kind of Sting-meets-Ralph-Fiennes's-younger-brother sort of way. He was Welsh, so he had that lovely voice. He was articulate, smart, asked questions, spoke to my friend Stefania in the same baby Italian that I speak. It turned out that he was the drummer in this reggae band, that he played bongos. So I made a joke that he was a "bonga-leer," like those guys in Venice, but with percussion instead of boats, and somehow we hit it off, started laughing and talking.

Felipe came over then—that was the Brazilian's name, Felipe. He invited us all to go out to this funky local restaurant owned by European expatriates, a wildly permissive place that never closes, he promised, where beer and bullshit are served at all hours. I found myself looking to Ian (*did he want to go?*) and when he said yes, I said yes, also. So we all went to the restaurant and I sat with Ian and we talked and joked all night, and, oh, I really liked this guy. He was the first man I'd met in a long while who I really liked *in that way*, as they say. He was a few years older than me, had led a most interesting life with all the good résumé points (liked *The Simpsons*, traveled all over the world, lived in an Ashram once, mentioned Tolstoy, seemed to be employed, etc.). He'd started his career in the British Army in Northern Ireland as a bomb squad expert, then became an international mine-field detonation guy. Built refugee camps in Bosnia, was now taking a break in Bali to work on music . . . all very alluring stuff.

I could not believe I was still up at 3:30 AM, and not to meditate, either! I was up in the middle of the night and wearing a dress and talking to an attractive man. How terribly radical. At the end of the evening, Ian and I admitted to each other how nice it had been to meet. He asked if I had a phone number and I told him I didn't, but that I did have e-mail, and he said, "Yeah, but e-mail just feels so . . . ech . . ." So at the end of the night we didn't exchange anything but a hug. He said, "We'll see each other again when they"—pointing to the gods up in the sky—"say so."

Just before dawn, Felipe the handsome older Brazilian man offered me a ride home. As we rode up the twisting back roads he said, "Darling, you've been talking to the biggest bullshitter in Ubud all night long."

My heart sank.

"Is Ian really a bullshitter?" I asked. "Tell me the truth now and save me the trouble later."

"Ian?" said Felipe. He laughed. "No, darling! Ian is a serious guy. He's a good man. I meant *myself.* I'm the biggest bullshitter in Ubud."

We rode along in silence for a while.

"And I'm just teasing, anyway," he added.

Then another long silence and he asked, "You like Ian, don't you?"

"I don't know," I said. My head wasn't clear. I'd been drinking too many Brazilian cocktails. "He's attractive, intelligent. It's been a long time since I thought about liking anybody."

"You're going to have a wonderful few months here in Bali. You wait and see."

"But I don't know how much more socializing I can do, Felipe. I only have the one dress. People will start to notice that I'm wearing the same thing all the time."

"You're young and beautiful, darling. You only need the one dress."

90

Am I young and beautiful?

I thought I was old and divorced.

I can barely sleep at all this night, so unaccustomed to these odd hours, the dance music still thrumming in my head, my hair smelling of cigarettes, my stomach protesting the alcohol. I doze a bit, then wake as the sun comes up, just as I am accustomed to. Only this morning I am not rested and I am not at peace and I'm in no condition whatsoever for meditation. Why am I so agitated? I had a nice night, didn't I? I got to meet some interesting people, got to dress up and dance around, had flirted with some men . . .

MEN.

The agitation gets more jagged at the thought of that word, turning into a minor panic assailment. *I don't know how to do this anymore.* I used to be the biggest and boldest and most shameless of flirts when I was in my teens and twenties. I seem to remember that it was once fun, meeting some guy, spooling him in toward me, spooning out the veiled invitations and the provocations, casting all caution aside and letting the consequences spill how they will.

But now I am feeling only panic and uncertainty. I start blowing the whole evening up into something much huger than it was, imagining myself getting involved with this Welsh guy who hadn't even given me an e-mail address. I can see all the way into our future already, including the arguments over his smoking habit. I wonder if giving myself to a man again will ruin my journey/writing/life, etc. On the other hand—some romance would be nice. It's been a long, dry time. (I remember Richard from Texas advising me at one point, vis-à-vis my love life, "You need a *droughtbreaker*, baby. Gotta go find yo'self a *rainmaker.*") Then I imagine Ian zooming over on his motorbike with his handsome bomb-squad torso to make love to me in my garden, and how nice that would be. This not-entirely-unpleasant thought somehow screeches me, however, into a horrible skid about how I just don't want to go through any heartache again. Then I start to miss David more than I have in months, thinking, *Maybe I should call him and see if he wants to try getting together again . . .* (Then I receive a very accurate channeling of my old friend Richard, saying, *Oh, that's genius, Groceries—didja get a lobotomy last night, in addition to gettin' a little tipsy?*) It's never a far leap from ruminating about David to obsessing about the circumstances of my divorce, and so soon I start brooding (just like old times) about my ex-husband, my divorce . . .

I thought we were done with this topic, Groceries.

And then I start thinking about Felipe, for some reason—that handsome older Brazilian man. He's nice. *Felipe.* He says I am young and beautiful and that I will have a wonderful time here time in Bali. He's right, right? I should relax and have some fun, right? But this morning it doesn't feel fun.

I don't know how to do this anymore.

91

"What is this life? Do you understand? I don't."

This was Wayan talking.

I was back in her restaurant, eating her delicious and nutritious multivitamin lunch special, hoping it would help ease my hangover and my anxiety. Armenia the Brazilian woman was there, too, looking, as always, like she'd just stopped by the beauty parlor on her way home from a weekend at a spa. Little Tutti was sitting on the floor, drawing pictures of houses, as usual.

Wayan had just learned that the lease on her shop was going to come up for renewal at the end of August—only three months from now—and that her rent would be raised. She would probably have to move again because she couldn't afford to stay here. Except that she only had about fifty dollars in the bank, and no idea where to go. Moving would take Tutti out of school again. They needed a home—a real home. This is no way for a Balinese person to live.

"Why does suffering never end?" Wayan asked. She wasn't crying, merely posing a simple, unanswerable and weary question. "Why must everything be repeat and repeat, never finish, never resting? You work so hard one day, but the next day, you must only work again. You eat, but the next day, you are already hungry. You find love, then love go away. You are born with nothing—no watch, no T-shirt. You work hard, then you die with nothing—no watch, no T-shirt. You are young, then you are old. No matter how hard you work, you cannot stop getting old."

"Not Armenia," I joked. "She doesn't get old, apparently."

Wayan said, "But this is because Armenia is *Brazilian*," catching on now to how the world works. We all laughed, but it was a fair breed of gallows humor, because there's nothing funny about Wayan's situation in the world right now. Here are the facts: Single mom, precocious child, hand-to-mouth business, imminent poverty, virtual homelessness. Where will she go? Can't live with the ex-husband's family, obviously. Wayan's own family are rice farmers way out in the countryside and poor. If she goes and lives with them, it's the end of her business as a healer in town because her patients won't be able to reach her and you can pretty much forget about Tutti ever getting enough education to go someday to Animal Doctor College.

Other factors have emerged over time. Those two shy girls I noticed on the first day, hiding in the back of the kitchen? It turns out that these are a pair of orphans Wayan has adopted. They are both named Ketut (just to further confuse this book) and we call them Big Ketut and Little Ketut. Wayan found the Ketuts starving and begging in the marketplace a few months ago. They were abandoned there by a Dickensian character of a woman—possibly a relative—who acts as a sort of begging child pimp, depositing parentless children in various marketplaces across Bali to beg for money, then picking the kids up every night in a van, collecting their proceeds and giving them a shack somewhere in which to sleep. When Wayan first found Big and Little Ketut, they hadn't eaten for days, had lice and parasites, the works. She thinks the younger one is maybe ten and the older one might be thirteen, but they don't know their own ages or even their last names. (Little Ketut knows only that she was born the same year as "the big pig" in her village; this hasn't helped the rest of us establish a timeline.) Wayan has taken them in and cares for them as lovingly as she does her own

Tutti. She and the three children all sleep on the same mattress in the one bedroom behind the shop.

How a Balinese single mother facing eviction found it in her heart to take in two extra homeless children is something that reaches far beyond any understanding I've ever had about the meaning of compassion.

I want to help them.

That was it. This is what that trembling feeling was, which I'd experienced so profoundly after meeting Wayan for the first time. I wanted to help this single mother with her daughter and her extra orphans. I wanted to valet-park them into a better life. It's just that I hadn't been able to figure out how to do it. But today as Wayan and Armenia and I were eating our lunch and weaving our typical conversation of empathy and chops-busting, I looked over at little Tutti and noticed that she was doing something rather odd. She was walking around the shop with a single, small square of pretty cobalt blue ceramic tile resting on the palms of her upturned hands, singing in a chanting sort of way. I watched her for a while, just to see what she was up to. Tutti played with that tile for a long time, tossing it in the air, whispering to it, singing to it, then pushing it along the floor like it was a Matchbox car. Finally she sat upon it in a quiet corner, eyes closed, singing to herself, buried in some mystical, invisible compartment of space all her own.

I asked Wayan what this was all about. She said that Tutti had found the tile outside the construction site of a fancy hotel project down the road and had pocketed it. Ever since Tutti had found the tile, she kept saying to her mother, "Maybe if we have a house someday, it can have a pretty blue floor, like this." Now, according to Wayan, Tutti often likes to sit perched on that one tiny blue square for hours on end, shutting her eyes and pretending she's inside her own house.

What can I say? When I heard that story, and looked at that child deep in meditation upon her small blue tile, I was like: *OK, that does it.*

And I excused myself from the shop to go take care of this intolerable state of affairs once and for all.

92

Wayan once told me that sometimes when she's healing her patients she becomes an open pipeline for God's love, and she ceases even thinking about what needs to be done next. The intellect stops, the intuition rises and all she has to do is permit her God-ness to flow through her. She says, "It feels like a wind comes and takes my hands."

This same wind, maybe, is the thing that blew me out of Wayan's shop that day, that pushed me out of my hung-over anxiety about whether I was ready to start *dating* again, and guided me over to Ubud's local Internet café, where I sat and wrote—in one effortless draft—a fund-raising e-mail to all my friends and family across the world.

I told everyone that my birthday was coming up in July and that soon I would be turning thirty-five. I told them that there was nothing in this world that I needed or wanted, and that I had never been happier in my life. I told them that, if I were home in New York, I would be planning a big stupid birthday party and I would make them all come to this party, and they would have to buy me gifts and bottles of wine and the whole celebration would get ridiculously expensive. Therefore, I explained, a cheaper and more lovely way to help celebrate this birthday would be if my friends and family would care to make a donation to help a woman named Wayan Nuriyasih buy a house in Indonesia for herself and her children.

Then I told the whole story of Wayan and Tutti and the orphans and their situation. I promised that whatever money was donated, I would match the donation from my own savings. Of course I was aware, I explained, that this is a world full of untold suffering and war and that everyone is in need right now, but what are we to do? This little group of people in Bali had become my family, and we must take care of our families wherever we find them. As I wrapped up the mass e-mail, I remembered something my friend Susan had said to me before I left on this world journey nine months ago. She was afraid I would never come home again. She said, "I know how you are, Liz. You're going to meet somebody and fall in love and end up buying a house in Bali."

A regular Nostradamus, that Susan.

By the next morning, when I checked my e-mail, $700 had already been pledged. The next day, donations passed what I could afford to match.

I won't go through the entire drama of the week, or try to explain what it feels like to open e-mails every day from all over the world that all say, "Count me in!" Everyone gave. People whom I personally knew to be broke or in debt gave, without hesitation. One of the first responses I got was from a friend of my hairdresser's girlfriend, who'd been forwarded the e-mail and wanted to donate $15. My most wise-ass friend John had to make a typically sarcastic comment, of course, about how long and sappy and emotional my letter had been ("Listen—next time you feel the need to cry about spilled milk, make sure it's condensed, will ya?"), but then he donated money anyway. My friend Annie's new boyfriend (a Wall Street banker whom I'd never even met) offered to double the final sum of whatever was raised. Then that e-mail started whipping around the world, so that I began to receive donations from perfect strangers. It was a global smothering of generosity. Let's just wrap up this episode by saying that—a mere seven days after the original plea went out over the wires—my friends and my family and a bunch of strangers all over the world helped me come up with almost $18,000 to buy Wayan Nuriyasih a home of her own.

I knew that it was Tutti who had manifested this miracle, through the potency of her prayers, willing that little blue tile of hers to soften and expand around her and to grow—like one of Jack's magic beans—into an actual home that would take care of herself and her mother and a pair of orphans forever.

One last thing. I'm embarrassed to admit that it was my friend Bob, not me, who noticed the obvious fact that the word "Tutti" in Italian means "Everybody." How had I not realized that earlier? After all those months in Rome! I just didn't see the connection. So it was Bob over in Utah who had to point it out to me. He did so in an e-mail last week, saying, along with his pledge to donate toward the new house, "So that's the final lesson, isn't it? When you set out in the world to help yourself, you inevitably end up helping . . . *Tutti*."

93

I don't want to tell Wayan about it, not until all the money has been raised. It's hard to keep a big secret like this, especially when she's in such constant worry about her future, but I don't want to get her hopes up until it is official. So for the whole week, I keep my mouth shut about my plans, and I keep myself occupied having dinner almost every night with Felipe the Brazilian, who doesn't seem to mind that I own only one nice dress.

I guess I have a crush on him. After a few dinners, I'm fairly certain I have a crush on him. He's more than he appears, this self-proclaimed "bullshit master" who knows everyone in Ubud and is always the center of the party. I asked Armenia about him. They've been friends for a while. I said, "That Felipe—he's got more depth than the others, doesn't he? There's something more to him, isn't there?" She said, "Oh, yes. He's a good, kind man. But he's been through a hard divorce. I think he's come to Bali to recover."

Ah—now this is a subject I know *nothing* about.

But he's fifty-two years old. This is interesting. Have I truly reached the age where a fifty-two-year-old man is within my realm of dating consideration? I like him, though. He's got silver hair and he's balding in an attractively Picassoesque manner. His eyes are warm and brown. He has a gentle face and he smells wonderful. And he is an actual grown man. The adult male of the species—a bit of a novelty in my experience.

He's been living in Bali for about five years now, working with Balinese silversmiths to make jewelry from Brazilian gemstones for export to America. I like the fact that he was faithfully married for almost twenty years before his marriage deteriorated for its own multicomplicated plethora of reasons. I like the fact that he has already raised children, and that he raised them well, and that they love him. I like that he was the parent who stayed home and tended to his children when they were little, while his Australian wife pursued her career. (A good feminist husband, he says, "I wanted to be on the correct side of social history.") I like his natural Brazilian over-the-top displays of affection. (When his Australian son was fourteen years old, the boy finally had to say, "Dad, now that I'm fourteen, maybe you shouldn't kiss me on the mouth anymore when you drop me off at school.") I like the fact that Felipe speaks four, maybe more, languages fluently. (He keeps claiming he doesn't speak Indonesian, but I hear him talking it all day long.) I like that he's traveled through over fifty countries in his life, and that he sees the world as a small and easily managed place. I like the way he listens to me, leaning in, interrupting me only when I interrupt myself to ask if I am boring him, to which he always responds, "I have all the time in the world for you, my lovely little darling." I like being called "my lovely little darling." (Even if the waitress gets it, too.)

He said to me the other night, "Why don't you take a lover while you're in Bali, Liz?"

To his credit, he didn't just mean himself, though I believe he might be willing to take on the job. He assured me that Ian—that good-looking Welsh guy—would be a fine match for me, but there are other candidates, too. There's a chef from New York City, "a great, big, muscular, confident fellow," whom he thinks I might like. Really there are all sorts of men here, he said, all of them floating through Ubud, expatriates from everywhere, hiding out in this shifting community of the planet's "homeless and assetless," many of whom would be happy to see to it, "my lovely darling, that you have a wonderful summer here."

"I don't think I'm ready for it," I told him. "I don't feel like going through all the effort of romance again, you know? I don't feel like having to shave my legs every day or having to show my body to a new lover. And I don't want to have to tell my life story all over again, or worry about birth control. Anyway, I'm not even sure I know how to do it anymore. I feel like I was more confident about sex and romance when I was sixteen than I am now."

"Of course you were," Felipe said. "You were young and stupid then. Only the young and stupid are confident about sex and romance. Do you think any of us know what we're doing? Do you think there's any way humans can love each other without complication? You should see how it happens in Bali, darling. All these Western men come here after they've made a mess of their lives back home, and they decide they've had it with Western women, and they go marry some tiny, sweet, obedient little Balinese teenage girl. I know what they're thinking. They think this pretty little girl will make them happy, make their lives easy. But whenever I see it happen, I always want to say the same thing. *Good luck.* Because you still have a woman in front of you, my friend. And you are still a man. It's still two human beings trying to get along, so it's going to become complicated. And love is always complicated. But still humans must try to love each other, darling. We must get our hearts broken sometimes. This is a good sign, having a broken heart. It means we have tried for something."

I said, "My heart was broken so badly last time that it *still* hurts. Isn't that crazy? To still have a broken heart almost two years after a love story ends?"

"Darling, I'm southern Brazilian. I can keep a broken heart going for ten years over a woman I never even kissed."

We talk about our marriages, our divorces. Not in a petty way, but just to commiserate. We compare notes about the bottomless depths of post-divorce depression. We drink wine and eat well together and we tell each other the nicest stories we can remember about former spouses, just to take the sting out of all that conversation about loss.

He says, "Do you want to do something with me this weekend?" and I find myself saying yes, that would be nice. Because it *would* be nice.

Twice now, dropping me off in front of my house and saying goodnight, Felipe has reached across the car to give me a goodnight kiss, and twice now I've done the same thing—allowing myself to be pulled into him, but then ducking my head at the last moment and tucking my cheek up against his chest. There, I let him hold me for a while. Longer than is necessarily merely friendly. I can feel him press his face into my hair, as my face presses somewhere against his sternum. I can smell his soft linen shirt. I really like the way he smells. He has muscular arms, a nice wide chest. He was once a champion gymnast back in Brazil. Of course that was in 1969, which was the year I was born, but still. His body feels strong.

My ducking my head like this whenever he reaches for me is a kind of hiding—I'm avoiding a simple goodnight kiss. But it's also a kind of not-hiding, too. By letting him hold me at all during those long quiet moments at the end of the evening, I'm letting myself be *held*.

Which hasn't happened for a long time.

94

I asked Ketut, my old medicine man, "What do you know about romance?"

He said, "What is this, romance?"

"Never mind."

"No—what it is? What this word means?"

"Romance." I defined. "Women and men in love. Or sometimes men and men in love, or women and women in love. Kissing and sex and marriage—all that stuff."

"I not make sex with too many people in my life, Liss. Only with my wife."

"You're right—that's not too many people. But do you mean your first wife or your second wife?"

"I only have one wife, Liss. She dead now."

"What about Nyomo?"

"Nyomo not really my wife, Liss. She the wife of my brother." Seeing my confused expression, he added, "This typical Bali," and explained. Ketut's older brother, who is a rice farmer, lives next door to Ketut and is married to Nyomo. They had three children together. Ketut and *his* wife, on the other hand, were unable to have any children at all, so they adopted one of Ketut's brother's sons in order to have an heir. When Ketut's wife died, Nyomo began living in both family compounds, splitting her time between the two households, taking care of both her husband and his brother, and tending to the two families of her children. She is in every way a wife to Ketut in the Balinese manner (cooking, cleaning, taking care of household religious ceremonies and rituals) except that they don't have sex together.

"Why not?" I asked.

"Too OLD!" he said. Then he called Nyomo over to relay the question to her, to let her know that the American lady wants to know why they don't have sex with each other. Nyomo about died laughing at the very thought of it. She came over and punched me in the arm, hard.

"I only had one wife," Ketut went on. "And now she dead."

"Do you miss her?"

A sad smile. "It was her time to die. Now I tell you how I find my wife. When I am twenty-seven years, I meet a girl and I love her."

"What year was that?" I asked, desperate as always to figure out how old he is.

"I don't know," he said. "Maybe 1920?"

(Which would make him about a hundred and twelve by now. I think we're getting closer to solving this . . .)

"I love this girl, Liss. Very beautiful. But not good character, this girl. She only want money. She chase other boy. She never tell truth. I think she had a secret mind inside her other mind, nobody can see inside there. She stop to loving me, go away with other boy. I am very sad. Broken in my heart. I pray and pray to my four spirit brothers, ask why she not anymore love me? Then one of my spirit brothers, he tell me the truth. He say, 'This is not your true match. Be patient.' So I be patient and then I find my wife. Beautiful woman, good woman. Always sweet for me. Never once we argue, have always harmony in household, always she smiling. Even when no money at home, always she smiling and saying how happy she is to see me. When she die, I very sad in my mind."

"Did you cry?"

"Only little bit, in my eyes. But I do meditation, to clean the body from pain. I meditate for her soul. Very sad, but happy, too. I visit her in meditation every day, even to kissing her. She the only woman I ever make sex with. So I do not know . . . what is new word, from today?"

"Romance?"

"Yes, romance. I do not know romance, Liss."

"So it's not really your area of expertise, eh?"

"What is this, *expertise*? What this word means?"

95

I finally sat down with Wayan and told her about the money I'd raised for her house. I explained about my birthday wish, showed her the list of all my friends' names, and then told her the final amount which had been raised: Eighteen thousand American dollars. At first she was shocked to such an extent that her face looked like a mask of grief. It is strange and true that sometimes intense emotion can cause us to respond to cataclysmic news in exactly the opposite manner logic might dictate. This is the absolute value of human emotion—joyful events can sometimes register on the Richter scale as pure trauma; dreadful grief makes us sometimes burst out laughing. This news I had just handed to Wayan was too much for her to take in, she almost received it as a cause for sorrow, so I sat there with her for a few hours, telling her the story repeatedly and showing her the numbers again and again, until the reality began to sink in.

Her first really articulate response (I mean, even before she burst into tears because she realized she was going to be able to have a garden) was to urgently say, "Please, Liz, you must explain to everyone who helped raise money that this is not Wayan's house. This is the house of everyone who helped Wayan. If any of these people comes to Bali, they must never stay in a hotel, OK? You tell them they come and stay at my house, OK? Promise to tell them that? We call it Group House . . . the House for Everybody . . ."

Then she realized about the garden, and started to cry.

Slowly, though, happier realizations come to her. It was like she was a pocketbook shaken upside down and emotions were spilling all over the place. If she had a home, she could have a small library, for all her medical books! And a pharmacy for her traditional remedies! And a proper restaurant with real chairs and tables (because she had to sell all her old good chairs and tables to pay the divorce lawyer). If she had a home, she could finally be listed in *Lonely Planet*, who keep wanting to mention her services, but never can do so, because she never has a permanent address that they can print. If she had a home, Tutti could have a birthday party someday!

Then she got very sober and serious again. "How can I thank you, Liz? I would give you anything. If I had husband I loved, and you needed a man, I would give you my husband."

"Keep your husband, Wayan. Just make sure Tutti goes to university."

"What would I do if you never came here?"

But I was *always* coming here. I thought about one of my favorite Sufi poems, which says that God long ago drew a circle in the sand exactly around the spot where you are standing right now. I was never not coming here. This was never not going to happen.

"Where are you going to build your new house, Wayan?" I asked.

Like a Little Leaguer who's had his eye on a certain baseball glove in the shop window for ages, or a romantic girl who's been designing her wedding dress since she was thirteen, it turned out that Wayan already knew exactly the piece of land she would like to buy. It was in the center of a nearby village, was connected to municipal water and electricity, had a good school nearby for Tutti, was nicely located in a central place where her patients and customers could find her on foot. Her brothers could help her build the home, she said. She'd all but picked out the paint chips for the master bedroom already.

So we went together to visit a nice French expatriate financial adviser and real estate guy, who was kind enough to suggest the best way to transfer the money. His suggestion was that I keep it easy and just wire the money directly from my bank account into Wayan's bank account and let her buy whatever land or home she wants, so I don't have to mess around with owning property in Indonesia. As long as I didn't wire over amounts bigger than $10,000 at a time, the IRS and CIA wouldn't suspect me of laundering drug money. Then we went to Wayan's little bank, and talked to the manager about how to set up a wire transfer. In neat conclusion, the bank manager said, "So, Wayan. When this wire transfer goes through, in just a few days, you should have about 180 million rupiah in your bank account."

Wayan and I looked at each other and sparked off into a ridiculous riot of laughter. Such an enormous sum! We kept trying to pull ourselves together, since we were in some fancy banker's office, but we couldn't stop laughing. We stumbled out of there like drunks, holding on to each other to not fall over.

She said, "Never have I seen a miracle happen so fast! All this time, I was begging God to please help Wayan. And God was begging Liz to please help Wayan, too."

I added, "And Liz was begging her friends to please help Wayan, too!"

We returned to the shop, found Tutti just home from school. Wayan dropped to her knees, grabbed her girl, and said, "A house! A house! We have a house!" Tutti executed a fabulous fake faint, swooning cartoonishly right to the floor.

While we were all laughing, I noticed the two orphans watching this scene from the background of the kitchen, and I could see them looking at me with something in their faces that resembled . . . *fear.* As Wayan and Tutti galloped around in joy, I wondered what the orphans were thinking. What were they so afraid of? Being left behind, maybe? Or was I now a scary person to them because I'd produced so much money out of nowhere? (Such an *unthinkable* amount of money that maybe it's like black magic?) Or maybe when you've had such a fragile life as these kids, any change is a terror.

When there was a lull in the celebration I asked Wayan, just to be sure: "What about Big Ketut and Little Ketut? Is this good news for them, too?"

Wayan looked over at the girls in the kitchen and must have seen the same uneasiness I had seen, because she floated over to them and herded them into her arms and whispered some reassuring words into the crowns of their heads. They seemed to relax into her. Then the phone rang, and Wayan tried to pull away from the orphans to answer it, but the skinny arms of the two Ketuts clung on to their unofficial mother relentlessly, and they buried their heads in her belly and armpits, and even after the longest time they refused—with a fierceness I'd never seen in them before—to let her go.

So I answered the phone, instead.

"Balinese Traditional Healing," I said. "Stop by today for our giant close-out moving sale!"

96

I went out with Brazilian Felipe again, twice over the weekend. On Saturday I brought him to meet Wayan and the kids, and Tutti made drawings of houses for him while Wayan winked suggestively behind his back and mouthed, "New boyfriend?" and I kept shaking my head, "No, no, no." (Though I'll tell you what—I'm not thinking about that cute Welsh guy anymore.) I also brought Felipe to meet Ketut, my medicine man, and Ketut read his palm and pronounced my friend, no fewer than seven times (while fixing me with a penetrating stare), to be "a good man, a very good man, a very, very good man. Not a bad man, Liss—*a good man.*"

Then on Sunday, Felipe asked me if I'd like to spend a day at the beach. It occurred to me that I'd been living here in Bali for two months already and had not yet seen the beach, which now seemed like sheer idiocy, so I said yes. He picked me up at my house in his jeep and we drove an hour to this hidden little beach in Pedangbai where hardly any tourists ever go. This place that he took me to, was as good an imitation of paradise as anything I'd ever seen, with blue water and white sand and the shade of palm trees. We talked all day, interrupting our talking only to swim and nap and read, sometimes reading aloud to each other. These Balinese women in a shack behind the beach grilled us freshly caught fish, and we bought cold beers and chilled fruit. Dallying in the waves, we told each other whatever was left of the life story details which we hadn't yet covered in the past few weeks of evenings spent out together in the quietest restaurants in Ubud, talking over bottles and bottles of wine.

He liked my body, he told me, after the initial viewing at the beach. He told me that Brazilians have a term for exactly my kind of body (of *course* they do), which is *magra-falsa*, translating as "fake thin," meaning that the woman looks slender enough from a distance, but when you get up close, you can see that she's actually quite round and fleshy, which Brazilians consider a good thing. God bless Brazilians. As we lay out on our towels talking, he would reach over sometimes and brush sand off my nose, or push a mutinying hair out of my face. We talked for about ten solid hours. Then it was dark, so we packed up our things and went for a walk through the not-very-well-lit dirt road main street of this old Balinese fishing village, linked comfortably arm-in-arm under the stars. That's when Felipe from Brazil asked me in the most natural and relaxed of ways (almost as if he were wondering if we should get a bite to eat), "Should we have an affair together, Liz? What do you think?"

I liked everything about the way this was happening. Not with an action—not with an attempted kiss or a daring move—but with a question. And the correct question, too. I remembered something my therapist had said to me over a year ago before I'd left on this journey. I'd told her that I thought I wanted to remain celibate for this whole year of traveling, but worried, "What if I meet someone I really like? What should I do? Should I get together with him or not? Should I maintain my autonomy? Or treat myself to a romance?" My therapist replied with an indulgent smile, "You know, Liz—all this can be discussed at the time the issue actually arises, with the person in question."

So here it all was—the time, the place, the issue and the person in question. We proceeded to have a discussion about the idea, which came out easily, during our friendly, linked arm-in-arm walk by the ocean. I said, "I would probably say yes, Felipe, under normal circumstances. Whatever *normal circumstances* are . . ."

We both laughed. But then I showed him my hesitation. Which was this—that as much as I might enjoy to have my body and heart folded and unfolded for a while in the expert hands of an expat lover, something else inside me has put in a serious request that I donate the entirety of this year of traveling all to myself. That some vital transformation is happening in my life, and this transformation needs time and room in order to finish its process undisturbed. That basically, I'm the cake that just came out of the oven, and it still needs some more time to cool before it can be frosted. I don't want to cheat myself out of this precious time. I don't want to lose control of my life again.

Of course Felipe said that he understood, and that I should do whatever's best for me, and that he hoped I would forgive him for bringing up the question in the first place. ("It had to be asked, my lovely darling, sooner or later.") He assured me that, whatever I decided, we would still keep our friendship, since it seemed to be so good for both of us, all this time we spent together.

"Although," he went on, "you do need to let me make my case now."

"Fair enough," I said.

"For one thing, if I understand you correctly, this whole year is about your search for balance between devotion and pleasure. I can see where you've been doing a lot of devotional practices, but I'm not sure where the pleasure has come in so far."

"I ate a lot of pasta in Italy, Felipe."

"Pasta, Liz? *Pasta?*"

"Good point."

"For another thing, I think I know what you're worried about. Some man is going to come into your life and take everything from you again. I won't do that to you, darling. I've been alone for a long time, too, and I've lost a great deal in love, just like you have. I don't want us to take anything from each other. It's just that I've never enjoyed anyone's company as much as I enjoy yours, and I'd like to be with you. Don't worry—I'm not going to chase you back to New York when you leave here in September. And as for all those reasons you told me a few weeks ago that you didn't want to take a lover . . . Well, think of it this way. I don't care if you shave your legs every day, I already love your body, you've already told me your entire life story and you don't have to worry about birth control— I've had a vasectomy."

"Felipe," I said, "that's the most appealing and romantic offer a man has ever made me."

And it was. But still I said no.

He drove me home. Parked in front of my house, we shared a few sweet, salty, sandy day-at-the-ocean kisses. It was lovely. Of course it was lovely. But still, and again, I said no.

"That's fine, darling," he said. "But come over to my house tomorrow night for dinner, and I'll make you a steak."

Then he drove off and I went to bed alone.

I have a history of making decisions very quickly about men. I have always fallen in love fast and without measuring risks. I have a tendency not only to see the best in everyone, but to assume that everyone is emotionally capable of *reaching* his highest potential. I have fallen in love more times than I care to count with the highest potential of a man, rather than with the man himself, and then I have hung on to the relationship for a long time (sometimes far too long) waiting for the man to ascend to his own greatness. Many times in romance I have been a victim of my own optimism.

I married young and quick, from a place of love and hope, but without a lot of discussion over what the realities of marriage would mean. Nobody advised me on my marriage. I had been raised by my parents to be independent, self-providing, self-deciding. By the time I reached the age of twenty-four, it was assumed by everyone that I could make all my own choices, autonomously. Of course the world was not always like this. If I'd been born during any other century of Western patriarchy, I would've been considered the property of my father, until which time he passed me over to my husband, to become marital property. I would've had precious little say in the major matters of my own life. At one time in history, if a man had been my suitor, my father might have sat that man down with a long list of questions to establish whether this would be an appropriate match. He would have wanted to know, "How will you provide for my daughter? What is your reputation in this community? How is your health? Where will you take her to live? What are your debts and your assets? What are the strengths of your character?" My father would not have just given me away in marriage to anybody for the mere fact that I was in love with the fellow. But in modern life, when I made the decision to marry, my modern father didn't become involved at all. He would have no more interfered with that decision than he would have told me how to style my hair.

I have no nostalgia for the patriarchy, please believe me. But what I have come to realize is that, when that patriarchic system was (rightfully) dismantled, it was not necessarily replaced by another form of protection. What I mean is—I never thought to ask a suitor the same challenging questions my father might have asked him, in a different age. I have given myself away in love many times, merely for the sake of love. And I've given away the farm sometimes in that process. If I am to truly become an autonomous woman, then I must take over that role of being my own guardian. Famously, Gloria Steinem once advised women that they should strive to become like the men they had always wanted to marry. What I've only recently realized is that I not only have to become my own husband, but I need to be my own father, too. And this is why I sent myself to bed that night alone. Because I felt it was too soon for me to be receiving a gentleman suitor.

That said, I woke up at 2:00 AM with a heavy sigh and a physical hunger so deep I didn't have any idea of how to satisfy it. The lunatic cat who lives in my house was howling mournfully for some reason and I told him, "I know exactly how you feel." I had to do *something* about my longing, so I got up, went to the kitchen in my nightgown, peeled a pound of potatoes, boiled them up, sliced them, fried them in butter, salted them generously and ate every bite of them—asking my body the whole while if it would please accept the satisfaction of a pound of fried potatoes in lieu of the fulfillment of lovemaking.

My body replied, only after eating every bite of the food: "No deal, babe."

So I climbed back into bed, sighed in boredom and commenced to . . .

Well. A word about masturbation, if I may. Sometimes it can be a handy (forgive me) tool, but other times it can be so acutely unsatisfying that it only makes you feel worse in the end. After a year and half of celibacy, after a year and a half of calling my own name in my bed-built-for-one, I was getting a little sick of the sport. Still, tonight, in my restless state—what else could I do? The potatoes hadn't worked. So I had my way with myself yet again. As usual, my mind paged through its backlog of erotic files, looking for the right fantasy or memory that would help get the job done fastest. But nothing was really working tonight—not the firemen, not the pirates, not that pervy old Bill Clinton standby scene that usually does the trick, not even the Victorian gentlemen crowding around me in their drawing room with their task force of nubile young maids. In the end, the only thing that would satisfy was when I reluctantly admitted into my mind the idea of my good friend from Brazil climbing into this bed with me . . . on me . . .

Then I slept. I woke to a quiet blue sky and an even quieter bedroom. Still feeling unsettled and unbalanced, I took a long stretch of my morning and chanted the entire 182 Sanskrit verses of the Gurugita—the great, purifying fundamental hymn of my Ashram in India. Then I meditated for an hour of bone-tingling stillness until I finally felt it again—that specific, constant, clear-sky, unrelated-to-anything, never-shifting, nameless and changeless perfection of my own happiness. That happiness which is better, truly, than anything I have ever experienced anywhere else on this earth, and that includes salty, buttery kisses and even saltier and more buttery potatoes.

I was so glad I had made the decision to stay alone.

97

So I was kind of surprised the next night when—after he'd made me dinner at his house and after we'd sprawled on his couch for several hours and discussed all manner of subjects and after he'd unexpectedly leaned into me for a moment and sunk his face toward my armpit and pronounced how much he loved the marvelous dirty stink of me—Felipe finally put his palm against my cheek and said, "That's enough, darling. Come to my bed now," and I *did*.

Yes, I did come to his bed with him, in that bedroom with its big open windows looking out over the nighttime and the quiet Balinese rice fields. He parted the sheer, white curtain of mosquito netting that surrounded his bed and guided me in there. Then he helped me out of my dress with the tender competence of a man who had obviously spent many comfortable years getting his children ready for bathtime, and he explained to me his terms—that he wanted absolutely nothing from me whatsoever except permission to adore me for as long as I wanted him to. Were those terms acceptable to me?

Having lost my voice somewhere between the couch and the bed, I only nodded. There was nothing left to say. It had been a long, austere season of solitude. I had done well for myself. But Felipe was right—that was enough.

"OK," he replied, smiling as he moved some pillows out of our way and rolled my body under his. "Let's get ourselves organized here."

Which was actually pretty funny because that moment marked an end to all my efforts at organization.

Later, Felipe would tell me how he had seen me that night. He said that I seemed so young, not in the least bit resembling the self-assured woman he'd come to know in the daylight world. He said I seemed terribly young but also open and excited and relieved to be recognized and so tired of being brave. He said it was obvious I hadn't been touched in such a long time. He found me teeming with need but also grateful to be allowed to express that need. And while I can't say that I remember all *that,* I do take his word for it because he seemed to be paying awfully close attention to me.

What I mostly remember about that night is the billowy white mosquito netting that surrounded us. How it looked to me like a parachute. And how I felt like I was now deploying this parachute to escort me out the side exit of the solid, disciplined airplane which had been flying me during these few years out of A Very Hard Time in My Life. But now my sturdy flying machine had become obsolete right there in midair, so I stepped out of that single-minded single-engine airplane and let this fluttering white parachute swing me down through the strange empty atmosphere between my past and my future, and land me safely on this small, bed-shaped island, inhabited only by this handsome shipwrecked Brazilian sailor, who (having been alone himself for far too long) was so happy and so surprised to see me coming that he suddenly forgot all his English and could only manage to repeat these five words every time he looked at my face: *beautiful, beautiful, beautiful, beautiful* and *beautiful.*

98

We didn't sleep at all, of course. And then, it was ridiculous—I had to *go.* I had to go back to my house stupidly early the next morning because I had a date to meet my friend Yudhi. He and I had long ago planned that this was the very week we were going to leave on a big cross-Balinese road trip together. This was an idea we'd come up with one evening at my house when Yudhi said that, aside from his wife and Manhattan, what he most missed about America was driving—just taking off with a car and some friends and going on an adventure across those great distances, on all those fabulous interstate highways. I told him, "OK, so we'll go on a road trip here in Bali together, American-style."

This had struck us both as irresistibly comic—there's no way you can do an American-style road trip in Bali. There are no great distances, first of all, on an island the size of Delaware. And the "highways" are horrible, made surreally dangerous by the dense, mad prevalence of Bali's version of the American family minivan—a small motorcycle with five people crowded on it, the father driving with one hand while holding the newborn infant with the other (football-like) while Mom sits sidesaddle behind him in her tight sarong with a basket balanced on her head, encouraging her twin toddlers not to fall off the speeding motorbike, which is probably traveling on the wrong side of the road and has no headlight. Helmets are rarely worn but are frequently—and I never did find out why—*carried*. Imagine scores of these heavily laden motorcycles, all speeding recklessly, all weaving and dodging across each other like some kind of crazy motorized maypole dance, and you have life on the Balinese highways. I don't know why every single Balinese person hasn't been killed already in a road accident.

But Yudhi and I decided to do it anyway, to take off for a week, rent a car and drive all over this tiny island, pretending that we are in America and that both of us are free. The idea charmed me when we came up with it last month, but the timing of it now—as I am lying in bed with Felipe and he's kissing my fingertips and forearms and shoulders, encouraging me to linger—seems unfortunate. But I have to go. And in a way, I do want to go. Not only to spend a week with my friend Yudhi, but also as a repose after my big night with Felipe, to get my head around the new reality that, as they say in the novels: *I have taken a lover.*

So Felipe drops me off at my house with one last passionate embrace and I have just enough time to shower and pull myself together when Yudhi arrives with our rental car. He takes one look at me and says, "Dude—what time'd you get home last night?"

I say, "Dude—I *didn't* get home last night."

He says, "Duuuuuuude," and starts laughing, probably remembering the conversation we'd had only about two weeks earlier wherein I'd seriously posited that I might never, actually, have sex again for the rest of my life, ever. He says, "So you gave in, huh?"

"Yudhi," I replied, "let me tell you a story. Last summer, right before I left the States, I went to visit my grandparents in upstate New York. My grandfather's wife—his second wife—is this really nice lady named Gale, in her eighties now. She hauled out this old photo album and showed me pictures from the 1930s, when she was eighteen years old and went on a trip to Europe for a year with her two best friends and a guardian. She's flipping through these pages, showing me these amazing old photographs of Italy, and suddenly we get to this picture of this really cute young Italian guy, in Venice. I go, 'Gale—who's the hottie?' She goes, 'That's the son of the people who owned the hotel where we stayed in Venice. He was my boyfriend.' I go, 'Your *boyfriend*?' And my grandfather's sweet wife looks at me all sly and her eyes get all sexy like Bette Davis, and she goes, 'I was tired of looking at churches, Liz.' "

Yudhi gives me a high five. "Rock on, dude."

We set off for our fake American road trip across Bali, me and this cool young Indonesian musical genius in exile, the back of our car filled with guitars and beer and the Balinese equivalent of American road trip food—fried rice crackers and dreadfully flavored indigenous candies. The details of our journey are a bit blurry to me now, smudged over my distracting thoughts of Felipe and by the weird haziness that always accompanies a road trip in any country of the world. What I do remember is that Yudhi and I speak American the entire time—a language I hadn't spoken in so long. I'd been speaking English a lot during this year, of course, but not *American,* and definitely not the sort of hip-hop American Yudhi likes. So we just indulge it, turning ourselves into MTV-watching adolescents as we drive along, razzing each other like teenagers in Hoboken, calling each other *dude* and *man* and sometimes—with great tenderness—*homo*. A lot of our dialogue revolves around affectionate insults to each other's mothers.

"Dude, what'd you do with the map?"

"Why don't you ask your mother what I did with the map?"

"I would, man, but she's too fat."

And so forth.

We don't even penetrate the interior of Bali; we just drive along the coast, and it's beaches, beaches, beaches for a whole week. Sometimes we take a little fishing boat out to an island, see what's going on out there. There are so many kinds of beaches in Bali. We hang out one day along the long southern California–style groovy white sand surf of Kuta, then head up to the sinister black rocky beauty of the west coast, then we pass that invisible Balinese dividing line over which regular tourists never seem to go, up to the wild beaches of the north coast where only the surfers dare to tread (and only the crazy ones, at that). We sit on the beach and watch the dangerous waves, watch the lean brown and white Indonesian and Western surf-cats slice across the water like zippers ripping open the backs of the ocean's blue party dress. We watch the surfers wipe out with bone-breaking hubris against the coral and rocks, only to go back out again to surf another wave, and we gasp and say, "Dude, that is totally MESSED UP."

Just as intended, we forget for long hours (purely for Yudhi's benefit) that we are in Indonesia at all as we tool around in this rented car, eating junk food and singing American songs, having pizza everywhere we can find it. When we are overcome by evidence of the Bali-ness of our surroundings, we try to ignore it and pretend we're back in America. I'll ask, "What's the best route to get past this volcano?" and Yudhi will say, "I think we should take I-95," and I'll counter, "But that'll take us right through Boston in the middle of rush-hour traffic . . ." It's just a game, but it sort of works.

Sometimes we discover calm stretches of blue ocean and we swim all day, permitting each other to start drinking beer at 10:00 AM ("Dude—it's medicinal"). We make friends with everyone we encounter. Yudhi is the kind of guy who—when he's walking down the beach and he sees a man building a boat—will stop and say, "Wow! Are you building a boat?" And his curiosity is so perfectly winning that the next thing you know we've been invited to come live with the boat-builder's family for a year.

Weird things happen in the evenings. We stumble on mysterious temple rituals in the middle of nowhere, let ourselves get hypnotized by the chorus of voices, drums and gamelan. We find one small seaside town where all the locals have gathered in a darkened street for a birthday ceremony; Yudhi and I are both pulled out of the crowd (honored strangers) and invited to dance with the prettiest girl in the village. (She's enveloped in gold and jewels and incense and Egyptian-looking makeup; she's probably thirteen years old but moves her hips with the soft, sensual faith of a creature who knows she could seduce any god she wanted.) The next day we find a strange family restaurant in the same village where the Balinese proprietor announces that he's a great chef of Thai food, which he decidedly is not, but we spend the whole day there anyhow, drinking icy Cokes and eating greasy pad thai and playing Milton Bradley board games with the owner's elegantly effeminate teenage son. (It occurs to us only later that this pretty teenage boy could well have been the beautiful female dancer from the night before; the Balinese are masters of ritual transvestism.)

Every day I call Felipe from whatever outback phone I can find, and he asks, "How many more sleeps until you come back to me?" He tells me, "I'm enjoying falling in love with you, darling. It feels so natural, like it's something I experience every second week, but actually I haven't felt this way about anyone in nearly thirty years."

Not there yet, not yet to that place of a free fall into love, I make hesitant noises, little reminders that I am leaving in a few months. Felipe is unconcerned. He says, "Maybe this is just some stupid romantic South American idea, but I need you to understand—darling, for you, I am even willing to suffer. Whatever pain happens to us in the future, I accept it already, just for the pleasure of being with you now. Let's enjoy this time. It's marvelous."

I tell him, "You know—it's funny, but I'd been seriously thinking before I met you that I might be alone and celibate forever. I was thinking maybe I would live the life of a spiritual contemplative."

He says, "Contemplate this, darling . . . ," and then proceeds to detail with careful specificity the first, second, third, fourth and fifth things he is planning to do with my body when he gets me alone in his bed again. I wobble away from the phone call a little woozy in the knees, amused and bamboozled by all this new passion.

The last day of our road trip, Yudhi and I lounge on a beach someplace for hours, and—as often happens with us—we start talking about New York City again, how great it is, how much we love it. Yudhi misses the city, he says, almost as much as he misses his wife—as if New York is a person, a relative, whom he has lost since he got deported. As we're talking, Yudhi brushes off a nice clean patch of white sand between our towels and draws a map of Manhattan. He says, "Let's try to fill in everything we can remember about the city." We use our fingertips to draw in all the avenues, the major cross-streets, the mess that Broadway makes as it leans crookedly across the island, the rivers, the Village, Central Park. We choose a thin, pretty seashell to stand for the Empire State Building, and another shell is the Chrysler Building. Out of respect, we take two sticks and put the Twin Towers back at the base of the island, back where they belong.

We use this sandy map to show each other our favorite spots in New York. This is where Yudhi bought the sunglasses he's wearing right now; this is where I bought the sandals I'm wearing. This is where I first had dinner with my ex-husband; this is where Yudhi met his wife. This is the best Vietnamese food in the city, this is the best bagel, this is the best noodle shop ("No way, homo—*this* is the best noodle shop"). I sketch out my old Hell's Kitchen neighborhood and Yudhi says, "I know a good diner up there."

"Tick-Tock, Cheyenne or Starlight?" I ask.

"Tick-Tock, dude."

"Ever try the egg creams at Tick-Tock?"

He moans, "Oh my God, I know . . ."

I feel his longing for New York so deeply that for a moment I mistake it for my own. His homesickness infects me so completely that I forget for an instant that I am actually free to go back to Manhattan someday, though he is not. He fiddles a bit with the two sticks of the Twin Towers, anchors them more solidly in the sand, then looks out at the hushed, blue ocean and says, "I know it's beautiful here . . . but do you think I'll ever see America again?"

What can I tell him?

We slump into silence. Then he pops out of his mouth the yucky Indonesian hard candy he's been sucking on for the last hour and says, "Dude, this candy tastes like *ass*. Where'd you get it?"

"From your mother, dude," I say. "From your mother."

99

When we return to Ubud, I go straight back to Felipe's house and don't leave his bedroom for approximately another month. This is only the faintest of exaggerations. I have never been loved and adored like this before by anyone, never with such pleasure and single-minded concentration. Never have I been so unpeeled, revealed, unfurled and hurled through the event of lovemaking.

One thing I do know about intimacy is that there are certain natural laws which govern the sexual experience of two people, and that these laws cannot be budged any more than gravity can be negotiated with. To feel physically comfortable with someone else's body is not a decision you can make. It has very little to do with how two people think or act or talk or even look. The mysterious magnet is either there, buried somewhere deep behind the sternum, or it is not. When it isn't there (as I have learned in the past, with heart-breaking clarity) you can no more force it to exist than a surgeon can force a patient's body to accept a kidney from the wrong donor. My friend Annie says it all comes down to one simple question: "Do you want your belly pressed against this person's belly forever—or not?"

Felipe and I, as we discover to our delight, are a perfectly matched, genetically engineered belly-to-belly success story. There are no parts of our bodies which are in any way allergic to any parts of the other's body. Nothing is dangerous, nothing is difficult, nothing is refused. Everything in our sensual universe is—simply and thoroughly—complemented. And, also . . . *complimented*.

"Look at you," Felipe says, taking me to the mirror after we've made love again, showing me my nude body and my hair that looks like I just came through a NASA space-training centrifuge. He says, "Look how beautiful you are . . . every line of you is a curve . . . you look like sand dunes . . ."

(Indeed, I do not think my body has looked or felt this relaxed in its life, not since I was maybe six months old and my mother took snapshots of me all blissed-out on a towel on the kitchen counter after a nice bath in the kitchen sink.)

And then he leads me back to the bed, saying, in Portuguese, *"Vem, gostosa."*

Come here, my delicious one.

Felipe is also the endearment master. In bed he slips into adoring me in Portuguese, so I have graduated from being his "lovely little darling" to being his *queridinha.* (Literal translation: "lovely little darling.") I've been too lazy here in Bali to try to learn Indonesian or Balinese, but suddenly Portuguese is coming easily to me. Of course I'm only learning the pillow talk, but that's a fine use of Portuguese. He says, "Darling, you're going to get sick of it. You're going to get bored of how much I touch you, and how many times a day I tell you how beautiful you are."

Try me, mister.

I'm losing days here, disappearing under his sheets, under his hands. I like the feeling of not knowing what the date is. My nice organized schedule has been blown away by the breeze. I finally do stop by to see my medicine man one afternoon after a long hiatus of no visiting. Ketut sees the truth on my face before I say a word.

"You found boyfriend in Bali," he says.

"Yes, Ketut."

"Good. Be careful not get pregnant."

"I will."

"He good man?"

"You tell me, Ketut," I said. "You read his palm. You promised that he was a good man. You said it about seven times."

"I did? When?"

"Back in June. I brought him here. He was the Brazilian man, older than me. You told me you liked him."

"Never did," he insisted, and there was nothing I could do to convince him otherwise. Sometimes Ketut loses things from his recollection, as you would, too, if you were somewhere between sixty-five and a hundred and twelve years old. Most of the time he's keen and sharp, but other times I feel like I've disturbed him out of some other plane of consciousness, out of some other universe. (A few weeks ago he said to me, completely out of nowhere, "You good friend to me, Liss. Loyal friend. Loving friend." Then he sighed, stared off into space and added mournfully, "Not like Sharon." Who the hell is *Sharon*? What did she do to him? When I tried asking him about it, he would give me no answer. Acted suddenly like he didn't know who I was even referring to. As if *I* were the one who'd brought up that thieving hussy Sharon in the first place.)

"Why you never bring boyfriend here to meet me?" he asked now.

"I did, Ketut. Really I did. And you told me you liked him."

"Don't remember. He a rich man, your boyfriend?"

"No, Ketut. He's not a rich man. But he has enough money."

"Medium rich?" The medicine man wants details, spreadsheets.

"He has enough money."

My answer seemed to irritate Ketut. "You ask this man for money, he can give to you, or not?"

"Ketut, I don't *want* money from him. I've never taken money from a man."

"You spend every night with him?"

"Yes."

"Good. He spoil you?"

"Very much."

"Good. You still meditate?"

Yes, I do still meditate every day of the week, slithering out of Felipe's bed and over to the couch, where I can sit in silence and offer up some gratitude for all of this. Outside his porch, the ducks quack their way through the rice paddies, gossiping and splashing all over the place. (Felipe says that these flocks of busy Balinese ducks have always reminded him of Brazilian women strutting down the beaches in Rio; chatting loudly and interrupting each other constantly and waggling their bottoms with such pride.) I am so relaxed now that I kind of slide into meditation like it's a bath prepared by my lover. Naked in the morning sun, with nothing but a light blanket wrapped over my shoulders, I disappear into grace, hovering over the void like a tiny seashell balanced on a teaspoon.

Why did life ever seem difficult?

I call my friend Susan back in New York City one day, and listen as she confides to me, over the typical urban police sirens wailing in the background, the latest details of her latest broken heart. My voice comes out in the cool, smooth tones of a late-nite, jazz-radio DJ, as I tell her how she just has to let go, man, how she's gotta learn that everything is just perfect as it is already, that the universe provides, baby, that it's all peace and harmony out there . . .

I can almost hear her rolling her eyes as she says over the sirens, "Spoken like a woman who already had four orgasms today."

100

But all the fun and games caught up with me after a few weeks. After all those nights of not sleeping and all those days of too much lovemaking, my body struck back and I got attacked by a nasty infection in my bladder. A typical affliction of the overly sexed, especially likely to strike when you're not used to being overly sexed anymore. It came up as fast as any tragedy can strike. I was walking through town one morning doing some chores when suddenly I was buckled over with burning pain and fever. I'd had these infections before, during my wayward youth, so I knew what it was. I panicked for a moment—these things can be awful—but then thought, "Thank God my best friend in Bali is a healer," and I ran into Wayan's shop.

"I'm sick!" I said.

She took one look at me and said, "You sick from making too much sex, Liz."

I groaned, buried my face in my hands, embarrassed.

She chuckled, said, "You can't keep secrets from Wayan . . ."

I was in godawful pain. Anyone who's ever had this infection knows the dreadful feeling; anyone who hasn't experienced this specific suffering—well, just make up your own torturous metaphor, preferably using the term "fire poker" someplace in the sentence.

Wayan, like a veteran firefighter or an ER surgeon, never moves fast. She methodically started chopping some herbs, boiling some roots, wandering back and forth between her kitchen and me, bringing me one warm, brown, toxic-tasting concoction after another, saying, "Drink, honey . . ."

Whenever the next batch boiled, she would sit across from me, giving me sly, dirty looks and using the opportunity to get nosy.

"You careful not to get pregnant, Liz?"

"Not possible, Wayan. Felipe has a vasectomy."

"Felipe has a *vasectomy*?" she asked, in as much awe as if she were asking, "Felipe has a villa in *Tuscany*?" (I feel the same way about it, by the way.) "Very difficult in Bali to get a man to do this. Always the woman problem, birth control."

(Although it is true that the Indonesian birth rates are down lately due to a brilliant recent birth control incentive program: the government promised a new motorcycle to every man who would volunteer to come in for a vasectomy . . . though I hate to think the guys had to ride their new bikes home *the same day*.)

"Sex is funny," Wayan mused as she watched me grimacing in pain, drinking more of her homemade medicine.

"Yeah, Wayan, thanks. It's hilarious."

"No, sex *is* funny," she went on. "Make people do funny things. Everyone gets like this, at the beginning of love. Wanting too much happiness, too much pleasure, until you make yourself sick. Even to Wayan this happens at beginning of love story. Lose balance."

"I'm embarrassed," I say.

"Don't," she said. Then she added in perfect English (and perfect Balinese logic), "To lose balance sometimes for love is part of living a balanced life."

I decided to call Felipe. I had some antibiotics at the house, an emergency stash I always travel with, just in case. Having had these infections before, I know how bad they can get, even traveling up into your kidneys. I didn't want to go through that, not in

Indonesia. So I called him and told him what had happened (he was mortified) and asked him to bring me over the pills. It wasn't that I didn't trust Wayan's healing prowess, it's just that this was really serious pain . . .

She said, "You don't need Western pills."

"But maybe it's better, just to be safe . . ."

"Give two hours," she said. "If I don't make you better, you can take your pills."

Reluctantly, I agreed. My experience with these infections is that they can take days to clear, even with strong antibiotics. But I didn't want to make her feel bad.

Tutti was playing in the shop and she kept bringing little drawings of houses over to cheer me up, patting my hand with an eight-year-old's compassion. "Mama Elizabeth sick?" At least she didn't know what I'd been doing to *get* sick.

"Did you buy your house yet, Wayan?" I asked.

"Not yet, honey. No hurry."

"What about that place you liked? I thought you were going to buy that?"

"Found out not for sale. Too expensive."

"Do you have any other places in mind?"

"Not worry about it now, Liz. For now, let me make you quickly feel better."

Felipe arrived with my medicine and a face full of remorse, apologizing to both me and Wayan for having inflicted me with this pain, or at least that's how he was seeing it.

"Not serious," said Wayan. "Not worry. I fix her soon. Quickly better."

Then she went into the kitchen and produced a giant glass mixing bowl full of leaves, roots, berries, something I recognized as turmeric, some shaggy mass of something that looked like witches' hair, plus eye of what I believe might have been newt . . . all floating in its own brown juice. There was about a gallon of it in the bowl, whatever it was. It stank like a corpse.

"Drink, honey," Wayan said. "Drink all."

I suffered it down. And in less than two hours . . . well, we all know how the story ends. In less than two hours I was fine, totally healed.

An infection that would have taken days to treat with Western antibiotics was gone. I tried to pay her for having fixed me up, but she only laughed. "My sister doesn't need to pay." Then she turned on Felipe, fake stern: "You be careful with her now. Only sleep tonight, no touching."

"You're not embarrassed to fix people for problems like this, from sex?" I asked Wayan.

"Liz—I'm healer. I fix all problems, with women's vaginas, with men's bananas. Sometimes for women, I even make fake penises. For making sex alone."

"Dildos?" I asked, shocked.

"Not everyone has Brazilian boyfriend, Liz," she admonished. Then she looked at Felipe and said brightly, "If you ever need help making stiff your banana, I can give you medicine."

I was busily assuring Wayan that Felipe needed not one bit of help with his banana, but he interrupted me—always the entrepreneur— to ask Wayan if this banana-stiffening therapy of hers could perhaps be bottled and marketed. "We could make a fortune," he said. But she explained, no, it's not like that. All her medicines must be made fresh each day in order to work. And they must be accompanied by her prayers. Anyway, internal medicine is not the only way Wayan can firm up a man's banana, she assured us; she can also do this with massage. Then, to our lurid fascination, she described the different massages she does for men's impotent bananas, how she grips around the base of the thing and kind of shakes it around for about an hour to encourage the blood to flow, while incanting special prayers.

I asked, "But Wayan—what happens when the man comes back every day and says, 'Still not cured, Doctor! Need another banana massage!' " She laughed at this bawdy idea, and admitted that, yes, she has to be careful not to spend too much time fixing men's bananas because it causes a certain amount of . . . strong feeling . . . within her, which she isn't sure is good for the healing energy. And sometimes, yes, the men get out of control. (As you would, too, if you'd been impotent for years and suddenly this beautiful mahogany-skinned woman with long black silky hair gets the engine to turn over again.) She told us about the one man who leapt up and started chasing her around the room during an impotency cure, saying: "I need Wayan! I need Wayan!"

But that's not all Wayan can do. Also, she told us, she is sometimes called upon to be a teacher of sex for a couple who are either struggling with impotence or frigidity, or who are having trouble making a baby. She has to draw magic pictures on their bedsheets and explain to them which sexual positions are appropriate for which time of the month. She said that if a man wants to make a baby he should make intercourse with his wife "really, really hard" and should shoot "water out from his banana into her vagina really, really fast." Sometimes Wayan has to actually be there in the room with the copulating couple, explaining just how hard and fast this must be done.

I ask, "And is the man able to shoot water out of his banana really hard and really fast with Dr. Wayan standing over him watching?"

Felipe imitates Wayan watching the couple: "Faster! Harder! You want this baby or not?"

Wayan says, yes, she knows it's crazy, but this is the job of the healer. Though she admits it requires a whole lot of purification ceremonies before and after this event in order to keep her sacred spirit intact, and she doesn't like to do it very often because it makes her feel "funny." But if a baby needs to be conceived, she will take care of it.

"And do these couples all have babies now?" I asked.

"*Have* babies!" she confirmed with pride. Of course they do.

But then Wayan confides something extremely interesting. She said that if a couple is not having any luck conceiving a child, she will examine both the man and the woman to determine who is, as they say, to blame. If it's the woman, no problem—Wayan can fix this with ancient healing techniques. But if it's the man—well, this presents a delicate situation here in the patriarchy of Bali. Wayan's medical options here are limited because it is beyond the pale of safety to inform a Balinese man that he is sterile; it cannot possibly be true. Men are *men*, after all. If no pregnancy is occurring, it has to be the woman's fault. And if the woman doesn't provide her husband with a baby soon, she could be in big trouble—beaten, shamed or divorced.

"So what do you do in that situation?" I asked, impressed that a woman who still calls semen "banana water" could diagnose male infertility.

Wayan told us all. What she does in the case of male infertility is to inform the man that his wife is infertile and needs to be seen privately every afternoon for "healing sessions." When the wife comes to the shop alone, Wayan calls some young stud from the village to come over and have sex with her, hopefully creating a baby.

Felipe was appalled: "Wayan! No!"

But she just calmly nodded. Yes. "It's the only way. If the wife is healthy, she will have baby. Then everybody happy."

Felipe immediately wanted to know, since he lives in this town, "Who? Who do you hire to do this job?"

Wayan said, "The drivers."

Which made us all laugh because Ubud is full of these young guys, these "drivers," who sit on every corner and harass passing tourists with the neverending sales pitch, "Transport? Transport?" trying to make a buck driving folks out of town to the volcanoes, the beaches or the temples. Generally speaking, this is a fairly good-looking crowd, what with their fine Gauguin skin, toned bodies and groovy long hair. You could make a nice bit of money in America operating a "fertility clinic" for women, staffed with beautiful guys like this. Wayan says the best thing about her infertility treatment is that the drivers generally don't even ask any payment for their sexual transport services, especially if the wife is really cute. Felipe and I agree that this is quite generous and community-spirited of the fellows. Nine months later a beautiful baby is born. And everyone is happy. Best of all: "No need to cancel the marriage." And we all know how horrible it is to cancel a marriage, especially in Bali.

Felipe said, "My God—what suckers we men are."

But Wayan is unapologetic. This treatment is only necessary because it's not possible to tell a Balinese man that he is infertile without risking that he will go home and do something terrible to his wife. If men in Bali weren't like this, she could cure their infertility in other ways. But this is the reality of the culture, so there it is. She doesn't have the tiniest shred of bad conscience about it but thinks it's just another way of being a creative healer. Anyway, she adds, it's sometimes nice for the wife to make sex with one of those cool drivers, because most husbands in Bali don't know how to make love to a woman, anyway.

"Most husbands, it's like roosters, like goats."

I suggested, "Maybe you should teach sex education class, Wayan. You could teach men how to touch women in a soft way, then maybe their wives would like sex more. Because if a man really touches you gently, caresses your skin, says loving things, kisses you all over your body, takes his time . . . sex can be nice."

Suddenly she blushed. Wayan Nuriyasih, this banana-massaging, bladder-infection-treating, dildo-peddling, small-time-pimp, actually blushed.

"You make me feel funny when you talk like that," she said, fanning herself. "This talking, it makes me feel . . . *different.* Even in my underpants I feel different! Go home now, you both. No more talk like this about sex. Go home, go to bed, but only sleeping, OK? Only SLEEPING!"

101

On the ride home Felipe asked, "Has she bought a house yet?"

"Not yet. But she says she's looking."

"It's been over a month already since you gave her the money, hasn't it?"

"Yeah, but the place she wanted, it wasn't for sale . . ."

"Be careful, darling," Felipe said. "Don't let this drag out too long. Don't let this situation get all Balinese on you."

"What does that mean?"

"I'm not trying to interfere in your business, but I've lived in this country for five years and I know how things are. Stories can get complicated around here. Sometimes it's hard to get to the truth of what's actually happening."

"What are you trying to say, Felipe?" I asked, and when he didn't answer immediately, I quoted to him one of his own signature lines: "If you tell me slowly, I can understand quickly."

"What I'm trying to say, Liz, is that your friends have raised an awful lot of money for this woman, and right now it's all sitting in Wayan's bank account. Make sure she actually buys a house with it."

102

The end of July came, and my thirty-fifth birthday with it. Wayan threw a birthday party for me in her shop, quite unlike any I have ever experienced before. Wayan had dressed me in a traditional Balinese birthday suit—a bright purple sarong, a strapless bustier and a long length of golden fabric that she wrapped tightly around my torso, forming a sheath so snug I could barely take a breath or eat my own birthday cake. As she was mummifying me into this exquisite costume in her tiny, dark bedroom (crowded with the belongings of the three other little human beings who live there with her), she asked, not quite looking at me, but doing some fancy tucking and pinning of material around my ribs, "You have prospect to marrying Felipe?"

"No," I said. "We have no prospects for marrying. I don't want any more husbands, Wayan. And I don't think Felipe wants any more wives. But I like being with him."

"Handsome on the outside is easy to find, but handsome on the outside *and* handsome on the inside—this not easy. Felipe has this."

I agreed.

She smiled. "And *who* bring this good man to you, Liz? *Who* prayed every day for this man?"

I kissed her. "Thank you, Wayan. You did a good job."

We commenced to the birthday party. Wayan and the kids had decorated the whole place with balloons and palm fronds and hand-written signs with complex, run-on messages like, "Happy birthday to a nice and sweet heart, to you, our dearest sister, to our beloved Lady Elizabeth, Happy Birthday to you, always peace to you and Happy Birthday." Wayan has a brother whose young children are gifted dancers in temple ceremonies, and so the nieces and nephews came and danced for me right there in the restaurant, staging a haunting, gorgeous performance usually offered only to priests. All the children were decked out in gold and massive headdresses, decorated in fierce drag queen makeup, with powerful stamping feet and graceful, feminine fingers.

Balinese parties as a whole are generally organized around the principle of people getting dressed up in their finest clothes, then sitting around and staring at each other. It's a lot like magazine parties in New York, actually. ("My God, darling," moaned Felipe, when I told him that Wayan was throwing me a Balinese birthday party, "it's going to be so *boring . . .*") It wasn't boring, though—just quiet. And different. There was the whole dressing-up part, and then there was the whole dance performance part, and then there was the whole sitting around and staring at each other part, which wasn't so bad. Everyone did look lovely. Wayan's whole family had come, and they kept smiling and waving at me from four feet away, and I kept smiling at them and waving back at them.

I blew out the candles of the birthday cake along with Little Ketut, the smallest orphan, whose birthday, I had decided a few weeks ago, would also be on July 18 from now on, shared with my own, since she'd never had a birthday or a birthday party before. After we blew out the candles, Felipe presented Little Ketut with a Barbie doll, which she unwrapped in stunned wonder and then regarded as though it were a ticket for a rocket ship to Jupiter—something she never, ever in seven billion light-years could've imagined receiving.

Everything about this party was kind of funny. It was an oddball international and intergenerational mix of a handful of my friends, Wayan's family and some of her Western clients and patients whom I'd never met before. My friend Yudhi brought me a six-pack of beer to wish me happy birthday, and also this cool young hipster screenwriter from L.A. named Adam came by. Felipe and I had met Adam in a bar the other night and had invited him. Adam and Yudhi passed their time at the party talking to a little boy named John, whose mother is a patient of Wayan's, a German clothing designer married to an American who lives in Bali. Little John—who is seven years old and who is *kind of* American, he says, because of his American dad (even though he himself has never been there), but who speaks German with his mother and speaks Indonesian with Wayan's children—was smitten with Adam because he'd found out that the guy was from California and could surf.

"What's your favorite animal, mister?" asked John, and Adam replied, "Pelicans."

"What's a pelican?" the little boy asked, and Yudhi jumped in and said, "Dude, you don't know what a pelican is? Dude, you gotta go home and ask your dad about that. Pelicans *rock*, dude."

Then John, the kind-of-American boy, turned to say something in Indonesian to little Tutti (probably to ask her what a pelican was) as Tutti sat in Felipe's lap trying to read my birthday cards, while Felipe was speaking beautiful French to a retired gentleman from Paris who comes to Wayan for kidney treatments. Meanwhile, Wayan had turned on the radio and Kenny Rogers was singing "Coward of the County," while three Japanese girls wandered randomly into the shop to see if they could get medicinal massages. As I tried to talk the Japanese girls into eating some of my birthday cake, the two orphans—Big Ketut and Little Ketut—were decorating my hair with the giant spangled barrettes they'd saved up all their money to buy me as a gift. Wayan's nieces and nephews, the child temple dancers, the children of rice farmers, sat very still, tentatively staring at the floor, dressed in gold like miniature deities; they imbued the room with a strange and otherworldly godliness. Outside, the roosters started crowing, even though it was not yet evening, not yet dusk. My traditional Balinese clothing was squeezing me like an ardent hug, and I was feeling like this was definitely the strangest— but maybe the happiest—birthday party I'd ever experienced in my whole life.

103

Still, Wayan needs to buy a house, and I'm getting worried that it's not happening. I don't understand why it's not happening, but it absolutely needs to happen. Felipe and I have stepped in now. We found a realtor who could take us around and show us properties, but Wayan hasn't liked anything we've shown her. I keep telling her, "Wayan, it's important that we buy *something*. I'm leaving here in September, and I need to let my friends know before I leave that their money actually went into a home for you. And you need to get a roof over your head before you get evicted."

"Not so simple to buy land in Bali," she keeps telling me. "Not like to walk into a bar and buy a beer. Can take long time."

"We don't have a long time, Wayan."

She just shrugs, and I remember again about the Balinese concept of "rubber time," meaning that time is a very relative and bouncy idea. "Four weeks" doesn't really mean to Wayan what it means to me. One day to Wayan isn't necessarily composed of twenty-four hours, either; sometimes it's longer, sometimes it's shorter, depending upon the spiritual and emotional nature of that day. As with my medicine man and his mysterious age, sometimes you count the days, sometimes you weigh them.

Meanwhile, it also turns out that I have completely underestimated how expensive it is to buy property in Bali. Because everything is so cheap here, you would assume that land is also undervalued, but that's a mistaken assumption. To buy land in Bali—especially in Ubud—can get almost as expensive as buying land in Westchester County, in Tokyo, or on Rodeo Drive. Which is completely illogical because once you own the property you can't make back your money on it in any traditionally logical way. You may pay approximately $25,000 for an *aro* of land (an *aro* is a land measurement roughly translating into English as: "Slightly bigger than the parking spot for an SUV"), and then you can build a little shop there where you will sell one batik sarong a day to one tourist a day for the rest of your life, for a profit of about seventy-five cents a hit. It's senseless.

But the Balinese value their land with a passion that extends beyond the reaches of economic sense. Since land ownership is traditionally the only wealth that Balinese recognize as legitimate, property is valued in the same way as the Masai value cattle or as my five-year-old niece values lip gloss: namely, that you cannot have enough of it, that once you have claimed it you must never let it go, and that all of it in the world should rightfully belong to you.

Moreover—as I discover throughout the month of August, during my Narnia-like voyage into the intricacies of Indonesian real estate—it's almost impossible to find out when land is actually for sale around here. Balinese who are selling land typically don't like other people to know that their land is up for sale. Now, you would think it might be advantageous to advertise this fact, but the Balinese don't see it that way. If you're a Balinese farmer and you're selling your land, it means you are desperate for cash, and this is humiliating. Also, if your neighbors and family find out that you actually sold some land, then they'll assume you came into some money, and everyone will be asking if they can borrow that money. So land becomes available for sale only by . . . rumor. And all these land deals are executed under strange veils of secrecy and deception.

The Western expatriates around here—hearing that I'm trying to buy land for Wayan—start gathering around me, offering cautionary tales based on their own nightmarish experiences. They warn me that you can never really be certain what's going on when it comes to real estate around here. The land you are "buying" may not actually "belong" to the person who is "selling" it. The guy who showed you the property might not even be the owner, but only the disgruntled nephew of the owner, trying to get one over on his uncle because of some old family dispute. Don't expect that the boundaries of your property will ever be clear. The land you buy for your dream house may later be declared "too close to a temple" to allow a building permit (and it's difficult, in this small country with an estimated 20,000 temples, to find any land that is not too close to a temple).

Also you must take into consideration that you're quite probably living on the slopes of a volcano and you might be straddling a fault line, as well. And not just a geological fault line, either. As idyllic as Bali seems, the wise keep in mind that this is, in fact, Indonesia— the largest Islamic nation on earth, unstable at its core, corrupt from the highest ministers of justice all the way down to the guy who pumps gas into your car (and who only pretends to fill it all the way up). Some kind of revolution will always be possible here at any moment, and all your assets may be reclaimed by the victors. Probably at gunpoint.

Negotiating all this dodgy business is not something I have any qualifications whatsoever to be doing. I mean—I went through a divorce proceeding in New York State and everything, but this is another page of Kafka altogether. Meanwhile, $18,000 of money donated by me, my family and my dearest friends is sitting in Wayan's bank account, converted into Indonesia rupiah—a currency that has a history of crashing without notice and turning to vapor. And Wayan is supposed to get evicted from her shop in September, which is around the time I leave the country. Which is in about three weeks.

But it's turning out to be almost impossible for Wayan to find a piece of land she deems appropriate for a home. Setting aside all the practical considerations, she has to examine the *taksu*—the spirit—of each place. As a healer, Wayan's sense of *taksu*, even by Balinese standards, is supremely acute. I found one place that I thought was perfect, but Wayan said it was possessed by angry demons. The next piece of land was rejected because it was too close to a river, which, as everyone knows, is where ghosts live. (The night after she saw that place, Wayan says, she dreamt of a beautiful woman in torn clothes, weeping, and that did it—we could not buy this land.) Then we found a lovely little shop near town, with a backyard and everything, but it was located on a corner, and only somebody who wants to go bankrupt and die young would ever live in a house located on a corner. As everyone knows.

"Don't even try talking her out of it," Felipe advised me. "Trust me, darling. Don't get between the Balinese and their *taksu*."

Then last week Felipe found a place that seemed to fit the criteria exactly—a small, pretty piece of land, close to central Ubud, on a quiet road, next to a rice field, plenty of space for a garden and well within our budget. When I asked Wayan, "Should we buy it?" she replied, "Don't know yet, Liz. Not too fast, for making decisions like this. I need talk to a priest first."

She explained that she would need to consult a priest in order to find an auspicious day upon which to purchase the land, if she does decide to buy it at all. Because nothing significant can be done in Bali before an auspicious day is chosen. But she can't even ask the priests for the auspicious date upon which to buy the land until she decides if she really wants to live there. Which is a commitment she refuses to make until she's had an auspicious dream. Aware of my dwindling days here, I asked Wayan, like a good New Yorker, "How soon can you arrange to have an auspicious dream?"

Wayan replied, like a good Balinese, "Cannot be rushed, this." Although, she mused, it might help if she could go to one of the major temples in Bali with an offering, and pray to the gods to bring her an auspicious dream . . .

"OK," I said. "Tomorrow Felipe can drive you to the major temple and you can make an offering and ask the gods to please send you an auspicious dream."

Wayan would love to, she said. It's a great idea. Only one problem. She's not permitted to enter any temples for this entire week.

Because she is . . . menstruating.

104

Maybe I'm not getting across how fun all this is. Truly, it's so much odd and satisfying fun, trying to figure all this out. Or maybe I'm just enjoying this surreal moment in my life so much because I happen to be falling in love, and that always makes the world seem delightful, no matter how insane your reality.

I always liked Felipe. But there's something about the way he takes on The Saga of Wayan's House that brings us together during the month of August like a real couple. It's none of his concern, of course, what happens to this trippy Balinese medicine woman. He's a businessman. He's managed to live in Bali for five years without getting too entwined in the personal lives and complex rituals of the Balinese, but suddenly here he is wading with me through muddy rice paddies and trying to find a priest who will give Wayan an auspicious date . . .

"I was perfectly happy in my boring life before you came along," he always says.

He *was* bored in Bali before. He was languid and killing time, a character from a Graham Greene novel. That indolence stopped the moment we were introduced. Now that we're together, I get to hear Felipe's version of how we met, a delicious story I never tire of hearing—about how he saw me at the party that night, standing with my back to him, and how I did not even need to turn my head and show him my face before he had realized somewhere deep in his gut, "That is my woman. I will do anything to have that woman."

"And it was easy to get you," he says. "All I had to do was beg and plead for weeks."

"You didn't beg and plead."

"You didn't notice me begging and pleading?"

He talks about how we went dancing that first night we met, and how he watched me get all attracted to that cute Welsh guy, and how his heart sank as he saw the scene unfolding, thinking, "I'm putting all this work into seducing this woman, and now that handsome young guy's just going to take her from me and bring so much complication into her life   if only she knew how much love I could offer her."

Which he *can*. He's a caregiver by nature, and I can feel him going into a kind of orbit around me, making me the key directional setting for his compass, growing into the role of being my attendant knight. Felipe is the kind of man who desperately needs a woman in his life—but not so that he can be taken care of; only so that he can have someone to care for, someone to consecrate himself to. Having lived without such a relationship ever since his marriage ended, he's been adrift in life recently, but now he is organizing himself around me. It's lovely to be treated this way. But it also scares me. I hear him downstairs sometimes making me dinner as I am lounging upstairs reading, and he's whistling some happy Brazilian samba, calling up, "Darling—would you like another glass of wine?" and I wonder if I am capable of being somebody's sun, somebody's everything. Am I centered enough now to be the center of somebody else's life? But when I finally brought up the topic with him one night, he said, "Have I asked you to be that person, darling? Have I asked you to be the center of my life?"

I was immediately ashamed of myself for my vanity, for having assumed that he wanted me to stay with him forever so that he could indulge my whims till the end of time.

"I'm sorry," I said. "That was a little arrogant, wasn't it?"

"A little," he acknowledged, then kissed my ear. "But not so much, really. Darling, of course it's something we have to discuss because here's the truth—I'm wildly in love with you." I blanched in reflex, and he made a quick joke, trying to be reassuring: "I mean that in a completely hypothetical way, of course." But then he said in all seriousness, "Look, I'm fifty-two years old. Believe me, I already know how the world works. I recognize that you don't love me yet the way I love you, but the truth is that I don't really care. For some reason, I feel the same way about you that I felt about my kids when they were small—that it wasn't their job to love me, it was my job to love them. You can decide to feel however you want to, but I love you and I will always love you. Even if we never see each other again, you already brought me back to life, and that's a lot. And of course, I'd like to share my life with you. The only problem is, I'm not sure how much of a life I can offer you in Bali."

This is a concern I've had, too. I've been watching the expatriate society in Ubud, and I know for a stone-cold fact this is not the life for me. Everywhere in this town you see the same kind of character—Westerners who have been so ill-treated and badly worn by life that they've dropped the whole struggle and decided to camp out here in Bali indefinitely, where they can live in a gorgeous house for $200 a month, perhaps taking a young Balinese man or woman as a companion, where they can drink before noon without getting any static about it, where they can make a bit of money exporting a bit of furniture for somebody. But generally, all they are doing here is seeing to it that nothing serious will ever be asked of them again. These are not bums, mind you. This is a very high grade of people, multinational, talented and clever. But it seems to me that everyone I meet here used to be something once (generally "married" or "employed"); now they are all united by the absence of the one thing they seem to have surrendered completely and forever: *ambition*. Needless to say, there's a lot of drinking.

Of course, the precious Balinese town of Ubud is not such a bad place to putter away your life, ignoring the passing of the days. I suppose in that way it's similar to places like Key West, Florida, or Oaxaca, Mexico. Most expats in Ubud, when you ask them how long they've lived here, aren't really sure. For one thing, they aren't really sure how much time has passed since they moved to Bali. But for another thing, it's like they aren't really sure if they *do* live here. They belong to nowhere, unanchored. Some of them like to imagine that they're just hanging out for a while, just running the engine on idle at the traffic light, waiting for the signal to change. But after seventeen years of that you start to wonder . . . does anybody ever *leave*?

There is much to enjoy in their lazy company, in these long Sunday afternoons spent at brunch, drinking champagne and talking about nothing. Still, when I am around this scene, I feel somewhat like Dorothy in the poppy fields of Oz. *Be careful! Don't fall asleep in this narcotic meadow, or you could doze away the rest of your life here!*

So what will become of me and Felipe? Now that there is, it seems, a "me and Felipe"? He told me not long ago, "Sometimes I wish you were a lost little girl and I could scoop you up and say, 'Come and live with me now, let me take care of you forever.' But you aren't a lost little girl. You're a woman with a career, with ambition. You are a perfect snail: you carry your home on your back. You should hold on to that freedom for as long as possible. But all I'm saying is this—if you want this Brazilian man, you can have him. I'm yours already."

I'm not sure what I want. I do know that there's a part of me which has always wanted to hear a man say, "Let me take care of you forever," and I have never heard it spoken before. Over the last few years, I'd given up looking for that person, learned how to say this heartening sentence to myself, especially in times of fear. But to hear it from someone else now, from someone who is speaking sincerely . . .

I was thinking about all this last night after Felipe fell asleep, and I was curled up beside him, wondering what would become of us. What are the possible futures? What about the geography question between us—where would we live? Then there's the age difference to consider. Though, when I called my mother the other day to tell her I'd met a really nice man, but—brace yourself, Mom!—"he's fifty-two years old," she was completely non-flummoxed. All she said was, "Well, I've got news for you, Liz. *You're* thirty-five." (Excellent point, Ma. I'm lucky to get *anyone* at such a withered age.) Truthfully, though, I don't really mind the age difference, either. I actually like that Felipe is so much older. I think it's sexy. Makes me feel kind of . . . *French.*

What will happen with us?

Why am I worrying about this, by the way?

What have I not yet learned about the futility of worry?

So after a while, I stopped thinking about all this and just held him while he slept. *I am falling in love with this man.* Then I fell asleep beside him and had two memorable dreams.

Both were about my Guru. In the first dream, my Guru informed me that she was closing down her Ashrams and that she would no longer be speaking, teaching or publishing books. She gave her students one final speech, in which she said, "You've had more than enough teachings. You have been given everything you need to know in order to be free. It's time for you to go out in the world and live a happy life."

The second dream was even more confirming. I was eating in a terrific restaurant in New York City with Felipe. We were having a wonderful meal of lamb chops and artichokes and fine wine and we were talking and laughing happily. I looked across the room and saw Swamiji, my Guru's master, deceased since 1982. But he was alive that night, right there in a snazzy New York restaurant. He was eating dinner with a group of his friends and they also seemed to be having a merry time of it. Our eyes met across the room and Swamiji smiled at me and raised his wineglass in a toast.

And then—quite distinctly—this small Indian Guru who had spoken precious little English during his lifetime mouthed this one word to me across the distance:

Enjoy.

105

I haven't seen Ketut Liyer in so long. Between my involvement with Felipe and my struggle to secure a home for Wayan, my long afternoons of aimless conversation about spirituality on the medicine man's porch have long since ended. I've stopped by his house a few times, just to say hello and to drop off a gift of fruit for his wife, but we haven't spent any quality time together since back in June. Whenever I try to apologize to Ketut for my absence, though, he laughs like a man who has already been shown the answers to every test in the universe and says, "Everything working perfect, Liss."

Still, I miss the old man, so I stopped by to hang out with him this morning. He beamed at me, as usual, saying, "I am very happy to meet you!" (I never was able to break him of that habit.)

"I am happy to *see* you, too, Ketut."

"You leaving soon, Liss?"

"Yes, Ketut. In less than two weeks. That's why I wanted to come over today. I wanted to thank you for everything you've given me. If it wasn't for you, I never would've come back to Bali."

"Always you were coming back to Bali," he said without doubt or drama. "You still meditate with your four brothers like I teach you?"

"Yes."

"You still meditate like your Guru in India teach you?"

"Yes."

"You have bad dreams anymore?"

"No."

"You happy now with God?"

"Very."

"You love new boyfriend?"

"I think so. Yes."

"Then you must spoil him. And he must spoil you."

"OK," I promised.

"You are good friend to me. Better than friend. You are like my daughter," he said. (*Not like Sharon . . .*) "When I die, you will come back to Bali, come to my cremation. Balinese cremation ceremony very fun—you will like it."

"OK," I promised again, all choked up now.

"Let your conscience be your guide. If you have Western friends come to visit Bali, bring them to me for palm-reading. I am very empty in my bank since the bomb. You want to come with me to baby ceremony today?"

And this is how I ended up participating in the blessing of a baby who had reached the age of six months, and who was now ready to touch the earth for the first time. The Balinese don't let their children touch the ground for the first six months of life, because newborn babies are considered to be gods sent straight from heaven, and you wouldn't let a god crawl around on the floor with all the toenail clippings and cigarette butts. So Balinese babies are carried for those first six months, revered as minor deities. If a baby dies before it is six months old, it is given a special cremation ceremony and the ashes are not placed in a human cemetery because this being was never human: it was only ever a god. But if the baby lives to six months, then a big ceremony is held and the child's feet are allowed to touch the earth at last and Junior is welcomed to the human race.

This ceremony today was held at the house of one of Ketut's neighbors. The baby in question was a girl, already nicknamed Putu. Her parents were a beautiful teenage girl and an equally beautiful teenage boy, who is the grandson of a man who is Ketut's cousin, or something like that. Ketut wore his finest clothes for the event—a white satin sarong (trimmed in gold) and a white, long-sleeved button-down jacket with gold buttons and a Nehru collar, which made him look rather like a railroad porter or a busboy at a fancy hotel. He had a white turban wrapped around his head. His hands, as he proudly showed me, were all pimped out with giant gold rings and magic stones. About seven rings in total. All of them with holy powers. He had his grandfather's shining brass bell for summoning spirits, and he wanted me to take a lot of photographs of him.

We walked over to his neighbor's compound together. It was a considerable distance and we had to walk on the busy main road for a while. I'd been in Bali almost four months, and had never seen Ketut leave his compound before. It was disconcerting watching him walk down the highway amid all the speeding cars and madcap motorcycles. He looked so tiny and vulnerable. He looked so *wrong* set against this modern backdrop of traffic and honking horns. It made me want to cry, for some reason, but I was feeling a little extra emotive today anyway.

About forty guests were there already at the neighbor's house when we arrived, and the family altar was heaped with offerings—piles of woven palm baskets filled with rice, flowers, incense, roasted pigs, some dead geese and chickens, coconut and bits of currency that fluttered around in the breeze. Everyone was decked out in their most elegant silks and lace. I was underdressed, sweaty from my bike ride, self-conscious in my broken T-shirt amid all this beauty. But I was welcomed exactly the way you would want to be if you were the white girl who'd wandered in inappropriately attired and uninvited. Everyone smiled at me with warmth, and then ignored me and commenced to the part of the party where they all sat around admiring each other's clothes.

The ceremony took hours, Ketut officiating. Only an anthropologist with a team of interpreters could tell you all that occurred, but some of the rituals I understood, from Ketut's explanations and from books that I had read. The father held the baby during the first round of blessings and the mother held an effigy of the baby—a coconut swaddled to look like an infant. This coconut was blessed and doused with holy water just like the real baby, then placed on the ground right before the baby's feet touch earth for the first time; this is to fool the demons, who will attack the dummy baby and leave the real baby alone.

There were hours of chants, though, before that real baby's feet could touch ground. Ketut rang his bell and sang his mantras endlessly, and the young parents beamed with pleasure and pride. The guests came and went, milling about, gossiping, watching the ceremony for a while, offering their gifts and then taking off for another appointment. It was all strangely casual amid all the ancient ritualistic formality, sort of backyard-picnic-meets-high-church. The mantras Ketut chanted to the baby were so sweet, sounding like a combination of the sacred and the affectionate. While the mother held the infant, Ketut waved before the child samples of food, fruit, flowers, water, bells, a wing from the roast chicken, a bit of pork, a cracked coconut . . . With each new item he would sing something to her. The baby would laugh and clap her hands, and Ketut would laugh and keep singing.

I imagined my own translation of his words:

"Ohhhh . . . little baby, this is roast chicken for you to eat! Someday you will love roast chicken and we hope you have lots of it! Ohhhhhhh . . . little baby, this is a chunk of cooked rice, may you always have all the chunks of cooked rice you could ever desire, may you be showered with rice for always. Ohhhhh . . . little baby, this is a coconut, isn't it funny how this coconut looks, someday you will eat lots of coconuts! Ohhhhhh . . . little baby, this is your family, do you not see how much your family adores you? Ohhhhh . . . little baby, you are precious to the whole universe! You are an A-plus student! You are our magnificent bunny! You are a yummy hunk of silly putty! Ooohhhhh little baby, you are the Sultan of Swing, you are our everything . . ."

Everyone was blessed again and again with flower petals dipped in holy water. The whole family took turns passing the baby around, cooing to her, while Ketut sang the ancient mantras. They even let me hold the baby for a while, even in my jeans, and I whispered my own blessings to her as everyone sang. "Good luck," I told her. "Be brave." It was boiling hot, even in the shade. The young mother, dressed in a sexy bustier under her sheer lace shirt, was sweating. The young father, who didn't seem to know any facial expression other than a massively proud grin, was also sweating. The various grandmothers fanned themselves, got weary, sat down, stood up, fussed with the roasted sacrificial pigs, chased away dogs. Everyone was alternately interested, not interested, tired, laughing, earnest. But Ketut and the baby seemed to be locked in their own experience together, riveted to each other's attention. The baby didn't take her eyes off the old medicine man all day. Who ever heard of a six-month-old baby not crying or fussing or sleeping for four straight hours in the hot sun, but just watching someone with curiosity?

Ketut did his job well, and the baby did her job well, too. She was fully present for her transformation ceremony from god-status to human-status. She was handling the responsibilities marvelously, like a good Balinese girl already—steeped in ritual, confident of her beliefs, obedient to the requirements of her culture.

At the end of all the chanting, the baby was wrapped in a long, clean white sheet that hung far below her little legs, making her look tall and regal—a veritable debutante. Ketut made a drawing on the bottom of a pottery bowl of the four directions of the universe, filled the bowl with holy water and set it on the ground. This hand-drawn compass marked the holy spot on earth where the baby's feet would first touch.

Then the whole family gathered by the baby, everyone seeming to hold her at the same time, and—*oop! there goes!*—they lightly dipped the baby's feet in this pottery bowl full of holy water, right above the magic drawing which encompassed the whole universe, and then they touched her soles to the earth for the first time. When they lifted her back up into the air, tiny damp footprints remained on the ground below her, orienting this child at last onto the great Balinese grid, establishing who she was by establishing *where* she was. Everyone clapped their hands, delighted. The little girl was one of us now. A human being—with all the risks and thrills which that perplexing incarnation entails.

The baby looked up, looked around, smiled. She wasn't a god anymore. She didn't seem to mind. She wasn't fearful at all. She seemed thoroughly satisfied with every decision she had ever made.

106

The deal fell through with Wayan. That property Felipe had found for her somehow didn't happen. When I ask Wayan what went wrong, I get some fuzzy reply about a lost deed; I don't think I was ever told the real story. What matters is only that it's a dead deal. I'm starting to get kind of panicked about this whole Wayan house situation. I try to explain my urgency to her, saying, "Wayan—I have to leave Bali in less than two weeks and go back to America. I can't face my friends who gave me all this money and tell them that you still don't have a home."

"But Liz, if a place has no good *taksu* . . ."

Everybody has a different sense of urgency in this life.

But a few days later Wayan calls over at Felipe's house, giddy. She's found a different piece of land, and this one she really loves. An emerald expanse of rice field on a quiet road, close to town. It has good *taksu* written all over it. Wayan tells us that the land belongs to a farmer, a friend of her father's, who is desperate for cash. He has seven *aro* total to sell, but (needing fast money) would be willing to give her only the two *aro* she can afford. She loves this land. I love this land. Felipe loves this land. Tutti—spinning across the grass in circles, arms extended, a little Balinese Julie Andrews—loves it, too.

"Buy it," I tell Wayan.

But a few days pass, and she keeps stalling. "Do you want to live there or not?" I keep asking.

She stalls some more, then changes her story again. This morning, she says, the farmer called to tell her he isn't certain anymore whether he can sell only the two-*aro* parcel to her; instead, he might want to sell the whole seven-*aro* lot intact . . . it's his wife that's the problem . . . The farmer needs to talk to his wife, see if it's OK with her to break up the land . . .

Wayan says, "Maybe if I had more money . . ."

Dear God, she wants me to come up with the cash to buy the whole chunk of land. Even as I'm trying to figure out how to raise a staggering 22,000 extra American dollars, I'm telling her, "Wayan, I can't do it, I don't have the money. Can't you make a deal with the farmer?"

Then Wayan, whose eyes are not exactly meeting mine anymore, crochets a complicated story. She tells me that she visited a mystic the other day and the mystic went into a trance and said that Wayan absolutely needs to buy this entire seven-*aro* package in order to make a good healing center . . . that this is destiny . . . and, anyway, the mystic also said that if Wayan could have the entire package of land, then maybe she could someday build a nice fancy hotel there . . .

A nice fancy hotel?

Ah.

That's when suddenly I go deaf and the birds stop singing and I can see Wayan's mouth moving but I'm not listening to her anymore because a thought has just come, scrawled blatantly across my mind: SHE'S FUCKING WITH YOU, GROCERIES.

I stand up, say good-bye to Wayan, walk home slowly and ask Felipe point-blank for his opinion: "Is she fucking with me?"

He has not ever commented upon my business with Wayan, not once.

"Darling," he says kindly. "Of *course* she's fucking with you."

My heart drops into my guts with a splat.

"But not intentionally," he adds quickly. "You need to understand the thinking in Bali. It's a way of life here for people to try to get the most money they can out of visitors. It's how everyone survives. So she's making up some stories now about the farmer. Darling, since when does a Balinese man need to talk to his *wife* before he can make a business deal? Listen—the guy is desperate to sell her a small parcel; he already said he would. But she wants the whole thing now. And she wants you to buy it for her."

I cringe at this for two reasons. First of all, I hate to think this could be true of Wayan. Second, I hate the cultural implications under his speech, the whiff of colonial White Man's Burden stuff, the patronizing "this-is-what-all-these-people-are-like" argument.

But Felipe isn't a colonialist; he's a Brazilian. He explains, "Listen, I grew up poor in South America. You think I don't understand the culture of this kind of poverty? You've given Wayan more money than she's ever seen in her life and now she's thinking crazy. As far as she's concerned, you're her miracle benefactor and this might be her last chance to ever get a break. So she wants to get all she can before you go. For God's sake—four months ago the poor woman didn't have enough money to buy lunch for her child and now she wants a *hotel*?"

"What should I do?"

"Don't get angry about it, whatever happens. If you get angry, you'll lose her, and that would be a pity because she's a marvelous person and she loves you. This is her survival tactic, just accept that. You must not think that she's not a good person, or that she and the kids don't honestly need your help. But you cannot let her take advantage of you. Darling, I've seen it repeated so many times. What happens with Westerners who live here for a long time is that they usually end up falling into one of two camps. Half of them keep playing the tourist, saying, 'Oh, those lovely Balinese, so sweet, so gracious . . . ," and getting ripped off like crazy. The other half get so frustrated with being ripped off all the time, they start to hate the Balinese. And that's a shame, because then you've lost all these wonderful friends."

"But what should I do?"

"You need to get back some control of the situation. Play some kind of game with her, like the games she's playing with you. Threaten her with something that motivates her to act. You'll be doing her a favor; she needs a home."

"I don't want to play games, Felipe."

He kisses my head. "Then you can't live in Bali, darling."

The next morning, I hatch my plan. I can't believe it—here I am, after a year of studying virtues and struggling to find an honest life for myself, about to spin a big fat lie. I'm about to lie to my favorite person in Bali, to someone who is like a sister to me, someone who has cleaned my *kidneys*. For heaven's sake, I'm going to lie to Tutti's mommy!

I walk into town, into Wayan's shop. Wayan goes to hug me. I pull away, pretending to be upset.

"Wayan," I say. "We need to talk. I have a serious problem."

"With Felipe?"

"No. With you."

She looks like she's going to faint.

"Wayan," I say. "My friends in America are very angry with you."

"With me? Why, honey?"

"Because four months ago, they gave you a lot of money to buy a home, and you did not buy a home yet. Every day, they send me e-mails, asking me, 'Where is Wayan's house? Where is my money?' Now they think you are stealing their money, using it for something else."

"I'm not stealing!"

"Wayan," I say. "My friends in America think you are . . . a bull-shit."

She gasps as if she's been punched in the windpipe. She looks so wounded, I waver for a moment and almost grab her in a reassuring hug and say, "No, no, it's not true! I'm making this up!" But, no, I have to finish this. But, Lord, she is clearly staggered now. *Bullshit* is a word that has been more emotionally incorporated into Balinese than almost any other in the English language. It's one of the very worst things you can call someone in Bali—"a bullshit." In this culture, where people bullshit each other a dozen times before breakfast, where bullshitting is a sport, an art, a habit, and a desperate survival tactic, to actually call someone out on their bullshit is an appalling statement. It's something that would have, in old Europe, guaranteed you a duel.

"Honey," she said, eyes tearing. "I am not a bullshit!"

"I know that, Wayan. This is why I'm so upset. I try to tell my friends in America that Wayan is not a bullshit, but they don't believe me."

She lays her hand on mine. "I'm sorry to put you in a pickle, honey."

"Wayan, this is a very big pickle. My friends are angry. They say that you must buy some land before I come back to America. They told me that if you don't buy some land in the next week, then I must . . . *take the money back.*"

Now she doesn't look like she's going to faint; she looks like she's going to die. I feel like one-half of the biggest prick in history, spinning this tale to this poor woman, who—among other things—obviously doesn't realize that I no more have the power to take that money out of her bank account than I have to revoke her Indonesian citizenship. But how could she know that? I made the money magically appear in her bankbook, didn't I? Couldn't I just as easily take it away?

"Honey," she says, "believe me, I find land now, don't worry, very fast I find land. Please don't worry . . . maybe in next three days this is finish, I promise."

"You must, Wayan," I say, with a gravity that is not entirely acting. The fact is, she *must*. Her kids need a home. She's about to get evicted. This is no time to be a bullshit.

I say, "I'm going back to Felipe's house now. Call me when you've bought something."

Then I walk away from my friend, aware that she is watching me but refusing to turn around and look back at her. All the way home, I'm offering up to God the weirdest prayer: "Please, let it be true that she's been bullshitting me." Because if she wasn't bullshitting, if she's genuinely incapable of finding herself a place to live despite an $18,000 cash infusion, then we're in really big trouble here and I don't know how this woman is ever going to pull herself out of poverty. But if she was bullshitting me, then in a way it's a ray of hope. It shows she's got some wiles, and she might be OK in this shifty world, after all.

I go home to Felipe, feeling awful. I say, "If only Wayan knew how deviously I was plotting behind her back . . ."

". . . plotting for her happiness and success," he finishes the sentence for me.

Four hours later—four measly hours!—the phone rings in Felipe's house. It's Wayan. She's breathless. She wants me to know the job is finished. She has just purchased the two *aro* from the farmer (whose "wife" suddenly didn't seem to mind breaking up the property). There was no need, as it turns out, for any magic dreams or priestly interventions or *taksu* radiation-level tests. Wayan even has the certificate of ownership already, in her very hands! And it's notarized! Also, she assures me, she has already ordered construction materials for her house and workers will start building early next week—before I leave. So I can see the project under way. She hopes that I am not angry with her. She wants me to know that she loves me more than she loves her own body, more than she loves her own life, more than she loves this whole world.

I tell her that I love her, too. And that I can't wait to be a guest someday in her beautiful new home. And that I would like a photocopy of that certificate of ownership.

When I get off the phone, Felipe says, "Good girl."

I don't know whether he's referring to her or me. But he opens a bottle of wine and we raise a toast to our dear friend Wayan the Balinese landowner.

Then Felipe says, "Can we go on vacation now, please?"

107

The place we end up going on vacation is a tiny island called Gili Meno, located off the coast of Lombok, which is the next stop east of Bali in the great, sprawling Indonesian archipelago. I'd been to Gili Meno before, and I wanted to show it to Felipe, who had never been there.

The island of Gili Meno is one of the most important places in the world to me. I came here by myself two years ago when I was in Bali for the first time. I was on that magazine assignment, writing about Yoga vacations, and I'd just finished two weeks of mightily restorative Yoga classes. But I had decided to extend my stay in Indonesia after the assignment was up, since I was already all the way over here in Asia. What I wanted to do, actually, was to find someplace very remote and give myself a ten-day retreat of absolute solitude and absolute silence.

When I look back at the four years that elapsed between my marriage starting to fall apart and the day I was finally divorced and free, I see a detailed chronicle of total pain. And the moment when I came to this tiny island all by myself was the very worst of that entire dark journey. The bottom of the pain and the middle of it. My unhappy mind was a battlefield of conflicted demons. As I made my decision to spend ten days alone and in silence in the middle of exactly nowhere, I told all my warring and confused parts the same thing: "We're all here together now, guys, all alone. And we're going to have to work out some kind of deal for how to get along, or else everybody is going to die together, sooner or later."

Which may sound firm and confident, but I must admit this, as well—that sailing over to that quiet island all alone, I was never more terrified in my life. I hadn't even brought any books to read, nothing to distract me. Just me and my mind, about to face each other on an empty field. I remember that my legs were visibly shaking with fear. Then I quoted to myself one of my favorite lines ever from my Guru: "Fear—who cares?" and I disembarked alone.

I rented myself a little cabin on the beach for a few dollars a day and I shut my mouth and vowed not to open it again until some-

339

thing inside me had changed. Gili Meno Island was my ultimate truth and reconciliation hearing. I had chosen the right place to do this—that much was clear. The island itself is tiny, pristine, sandy, blue water, palm trees. It's a perfect circle with a single path that goes around it, and you can walk the whole circumference in about an hour. It's located almost exactly on the equator, and so there's a changelessness about its daily cycles. The sun comes up on one side of the island at about 6:30 in the morning and goes down on the other side at around 6:30 PM, every day of the year. The place is inhabited by a small handful of Muslim fishermen and their families. There is no spot on this island from which you cannot hear the ocean. There are no motorized vehicles here. Electricity comes from a generator, and for only a few hours in the evenings. It's the quietest place I've ever been.

Every morning I walked the circumference of the island at sunrise, and walked it again at sunset. The rest of the time, I just sat and watched. Watched my thoughts, watched my emotions, watched the fishermen. The Yogic sages say that all the pain of a human life is caused by words, as is all the joy. We create words to define our experience and those words bring attendant emotions that jerk us around like dogs on a leash. We get seduced by our own mantras (*I'm a failure . . . I'm lonely . . . I'm a failure . . . I'm lonely . . .*) and we become monuments to them. To stop talking for a while, then, is to attempt to strip away the power of words, to stop choking ourselves with words, to liberate ourselves from our suffocating mantras.

It took me a while to drop into true silence. Even after I'd stopped talking, I found that I was still humming with language. My organs and muscles of speech—brain, throat, chest, back of the neck—vibrated with the residual effects of talking long after I'd stopped making sounds. My head shimmied in a reverb of words, the way an indoor swimming pool seems to echo interminably with sounds and shouts, even after the kindergartners have left for the day. It took a surprisingly long time for all this pulsation of speech to fall away, for the whirling noises to settle. Maybe it took about three days.

Then everything started coming up. In that state of silence, there was room now for everything hateful, everything fearful, to run across my empty mind. I felt like a junkie in detox, convulsing with the poison of what emerged. I cried a lot. I prayed a lot. It was difficult and it was terrifying, but this much I knew—I never didn't want to be there, and I never wished that anyone were there with me. I knew that I needed to do this and that I needed to do it alone.

The only other tourists on the island were a handful of couples having romantic vacations. (Gili Meno is far too pretty and far too remote a place for anyone but a crazy person to come visit solo.) I watched these couples and felt some envy for their romances, but knew, "This is not your time for companionship, Liz. You have a different task here." I kept away from everyone. People on the island left me alone. I think I threw off a spooky vibe. I had not been well all year. You can't lose that much sleep and that much weight and cry so hard for so long without starting to look like a psychotic. So nobody talked to me.

Actually, that's not true. One person talked to me, every day. It was this little kid, one of a gang of kids who run up and down the beaches trying to sell fresh fruit to the tourists. This boy was maybe nine years old, and seemed to be the ringleader. He was tough, scrappy and I would have called him street-smart if his island actually had any streets. He was beach-smart, I suppose. Somehow he'd learned great English, probably from harassing sunbathing Westerners. And he was on to me, this kid. Nobody else asked me who I was, nobody else bothered me, but this relentless child would come and sit next to me on the beach at some point every day and demand, "Why don't you ever talk? Why are you strange like this? Don't pretend you can't hear me—I know you can hear me. Why are you always alone? Why don't you ever go swimming? Where is your boyfriend? Why don't you have a husband? What's wrong with you?"

I was like, *Back off, kid! What are you—a transcript of my most evil thoughts?*

Every day I would try to smile at him kindly and send him away with a polite gesture, but he wouldn't quit until he got a rise out me. And inevitably, he always got a rise out of me. I remember bursting out at him once, "I'm not talking because I'm on a friggin' spiritual journey, you nasty little punk—now go AWAY!"

He ran away laughing. Every day, after he'd gotten me to respond, he would always run away laughing. I'd usually end up laughing, too, once he was out of sight. I dreaded this pesky kid and looked forward to him in equal measure. He was my only comedic break during a really tough ride. Saint Anthony once wrote about having gone into the desert on silent retreat and being assaulted by all manner of visions—devils and angels, both. He said, in his solitude, he sometimes encountered devils who looked like angels, and other times he found angels who looked like devils. When asked how he could tell the difference, the saint said that you can only tell which is which by the way you feel after the creature has left your company. If you are appalled, he said, then it was a devil who had visited you. If you feel lightened, it was an angel.

I think I know what that little punk was, who always got a laugh out of me.

On my ninth day of silence, I went into meditation one evening on the beach as the sun was going down and I didn't stand up again until after midnight. I remember thinking, "This is it, Liz." I said to my mind, "This is your chance. Show me everything that is causing you sorrow. Let me see all of it. Don't hold anything back." One by one, the thoughts and memories of sadness raised their hands, stood up to identify themselves. I looked at each thought, at each unit of sorrow, and I acknowledged its existence and felt (without trying to protect myself from it) its horrible pain. And then I would tell that sorrow, "It's OK. I love you. I accept you. Come into my heart now. It's over." I would actually feel the sorrow (as if it were a living thing) enter my heart (as if it were an actual room). Then I would say, "Next?" and the next bit of grief would surface. I would regard it, experience it, bless it, and invite it into my heart, too. I did this with every sorrowful thought I'd ever had—reaching back into years of memory—until nothing was left.

Then I said to my mind, "Show me your anger now." One by one, my life's every incident of anger rose and made itself known. Every injustice, every betrayal, every loss, every rage. I saw them all, one by one, and I acknowledged their existence. I felt each piece of anger completely, as if it were happening for the first time, and then I would say, "Come into my heart now. You can rest there. It's safe now. It's over. I love you." This went on for hours, and I swung between these mighty poles of opposite feelings—experiencing the anger thoroughly for one bone-rattling moment, and then experiencing a total coolness, as the anger entered my heart as if through a door, laid itself down, curled up against its brothers and gave up fighting.

Then came the most difficult part. "Show me your shame," I asked my mind. Dear God, the horrors that I saw then. A pitiful parade of all my failings, my lies, my selfishness, jealousy, arrogance. I didn't blink from any of it, though. "Show me your worst," I said. When I tried to invite these units of shame into my heart, they each hesitated at the door, saying, "No—you don't want *me* in there . . . don't you know what I did?" and I would say, "I *do* want you. Even you. I *do*. Even you are welcome here. It's OK. You are forgiven. You are part of me. You can rest now. It's over."

When all this was finished, I was empty. Nothing was fighting in my mind anymore. I looked into my heart, at my own goodness, and I saw its capacity. I saw that my heart was not even nearly full, not even after having taken in and tended to all those calamitous urchins of sorrow and anger and shame; my heart could easily have received and forgiven even more. Its love was infinite.

I knew then that this is how God loves us all and receives us all, and that there is no such thing in this universe as hell, except maybe in our own terrified minds. Because if even one broken and limited human being could experience even one such episode of absolute forgiveness and acceptance of her own self, then imagine—just imagine!—what God, in all His eternal compassion, can forgive and accept.

I also knew somehow that this respite of peace would be temporary. I knew that I was not yet finished for good, that my anger, my sadness and my shame would all creep back eventually, escaping my heart, and occupying my head once more. I knew that I would have to keep dealing with these thoughts again and again until I slowly and determinedly changed my whole life. And that this would be difficult and exhausting to do. But my heart said to my mind in the dark silence of that beach: "I love you, I will never leave you, I will always take care of you." That promise floated up out of my heart and I caught it in my mouth and held it there, tasting it as I left the beach and walked back to the little shack where I was staying. I found an empty notebook, opened it up to the first page—and only then did I open my mouth and speak those words into the air, letting them free. I let those words break my silence and then I allowed my pencil to document their colossal statement onto the page:

"I love you, I will never leave you, I will always take care of you."

Those were the first words I ever wrote in that private notebook of mine, which I would carry with me from that moment forth, turning back to it many times over the next two years, always asking for help—*and always finding it*, even when I was most deadly sad or afraid. And that notebook, steeped through with that promise of love, was quite simply the only reason I survived the next years of my life.

108

And now I'm coming back to Gili Meno under notably different circumstances. Since I was last here, I've circled the world, settled my divorce, survived my final separation from David, erased all mood-altering medications from my system, learned to speak a new language, sat upon God's palm for a few unforgettable moments in India, studied at the feet of an Indonesian medicine man and purchased a home for a family who sorely needed a place to live. I am happy and healthy and balanced. And, yes, I cannot help but notice that I am sailing to this pretty little tropical island with my Brazilian lover. Which is—I admit it!—an almost ludicrously fairy-tale ending to this story, like the page out of some housewife's dream. (Perhaps even a page out of my own dream, from years ago.) Yet what keeps me from dissolving right now into a complete fairy-tale shimmer is this solid truth, a truth which has veritably built my bones over the last few years—I was not rescued by a prince; I was the administrator of my own rescue.

My thoughts turn to something I read once, something the Zen Buddhists believe. They say that an oak tree is brought into creation by two forces at the same time. Obviously, there is the acorn from which it all begins, the seed which holds all the promise and potential, which grows into the tree. Everybody can see that. But only a few can recognize that there is another force operating here as well—the future tree itself, which wants so badly to exist that it pulls the acorn into being, drawing the seedling forth with longing out of the void, guiding the evolution from nothingness to maturity. In this respect, say the Zens, it is the oak tree that creates the very acorn from which it was born.

I think about the woman I have become lately, about the life that I am now living, and about how much I always wanted to be this person and live this life, liberated from the farce of pretending to be anyone other than myself. I think of everything I endured before getting here and wonder if it was *me*—I mean, this happy and balanced *me*, who is now dozing on the deck of this small Indonesian fishing boat—who pulled the other, younger, more confused and more struggling me forward during all those hard years. The younger me was the acorn full of potential, but it was the older *me*, the already-existent oak, who was saying the whole time: "Yes—grow! Change! Evolve! Come and meet me here, where I already exist in wholeness and maturity! I need you to grow into me!" And maybe it was this present and fully actualized *me* who was hovering four years ago over that young married sobbing girl on the bathroom floor, and maybe it was this *me* who whispered lovingly into that desperate girl's ear, "Go back to bed, Liz . . ." Knowing already that everything would be OK, that everything would eventually bring us together *here*. Right here, right to this moment. Where I was always waiting in peace and contentment, always waiting for her to arrive and join me.

Then Felipe wakes up. We'd both been dozing in and out of consciousness all afternoon, curled in each other's arms on the deck of this Indonesian fisherman's sailboat. The ocean has been swaying us, the sun shining. While I lie there with my head pillowed on his chest, Felipe tells me that he had an idea while he was sleeping. He says, "You know—I obviously need to keep living in Bali because my business is here, and because it's so close to Australia, where my kids live. I also need to be in Brazil often, because that's where the gemstones are and because I have family there. And you obviously need to be in the United States, because that's where your work is, and that's where your family and friends are. So I was thinking . . . maybe we could try to build a life together that's somehow divided between America, Australia, Brazil and Bali."

All I can do is laugh, because, hey—why *not*? It just might be crazy enough to work. A life like this might strike some people as absolutely loony, as sheer foolishness, but it resembles me so closely. Of course this is how we should proceed. It feels so familiar already. And I quite like the poetry of his idea, too, I must say. I mean that literally. After this whole year spent exploring the individual and intrepid I's, Felipe has just suggested to me a whole new theory of traveling:

Australia, America, Bali, Brazil = A, A, B, B.

Like a classic poem, like a pair of rhyming couplets.

The little fishing boat anchors right off the shore of Gili Meno. There are no docks here on this island. You have to roll up your pants, jump off the boat and wade in through the surf on your own power. There's absolutely no way to do this without getting soaking wet or even banged up on the coral, but it's worth all the trouble because the beach here is so beautiful, so special. So me and my lover, we take off our shoes, we pile our small bags of belongings on the tops of our heads and we prepare to leap over the edge of that boat together, into the sea.

You know, it's a funny thing. The only Romance language Felipe doesn't happen to speak is Italian. But I go ahead and say it to him anyway, just as we're about to jump.

I say: *"Attraversiamo."*

Let's cross over.

FINAL RECOGNITION AND
REASSURANCE

A few months after I'd left Indonesia, I returned to visit loved ones and to celebrate the Christmas and New Year's holiday. My flight landed in Bali only two hours after Southeast Asia was struck by a tsunami of staggering destruction. Acquaintances all over the world contacted me immediately, concerned about the safety of my Indonesian friends. People seemed particularly consumed with this worry: "Are Wayan and Tutti OK?" The answer is that the tsunami did not impact Bali in any way whatsoever (aside from emotionally, of course) and I found everybody safe and sound. Felipe was waiting for me at the airport (the first of many times we would be meeting each other at various airports). Ketut Liyer was sitting on his porch, same as ever, making medicine and meditations. Yudhi had recently taken work playing guitar in some fancy local resort and was doing well. And Wayan's family was living happily in their beautiful new house, far away from the dangerous coastline, sheltered high in the rice terraces of Ubud.

With all the gratitude I can summon (and on Wayan's behalf), I would now like to thank everyone who contributed money to build that home:

Sakshi Andreozzi, Savitri Axelrod, Linda and Renee Barrera, Lisa Boone, Susan Bowen, Gary Brenner, Monica Burke and Karen Kudej, Sandie Carpenter, David Cashion, Anne Connell (who also, along with Jana Eisenberg, is a master of last-minute rescues), Mike and Mimi de Gruy, Armenia de Oliveira, Rayya Elias and Gigi Madl, Susan Freddie, Devin Friedman, Dwight Garner and Cree LeFavour, John and Carole Gilbert, Mamie Healey, Annie Hubbard and the almost-unbelievable Harvey Schwartz, Bob Hughes, Susan Kittenplan, Michael and Jill Knight, Brian and Linda Knopp, Deborah Lopez, Deborah Luepnitz, Craig Marks and Rene Steinke, Adam McKay and Shira Piven, Jonny and Cat Miles, Sheryl Moller, John Morse and Ross Petersen, James and Catherine Murdock (with Nick and Mimi's blessings), José Nunes, Anne Pagliarulo, Charley Patton, Laura Platter, Peter Richmond, Toby and Beverly Robinson, Nina Bernstein Simmons, Stefania Somare, Natalie Standiford, Stacey Steers, Darcey Steinke, The Thoreson Girls (Nancy, Laura and Miss Rebecca), Daphne Uviller, Richard Vogt, Peter and Jean Warrington, Kristen Weiner, Scott Westerfeld and Justine Larbalestier, Bill Yee and Karen Zimet.

Lastly, and on a different topic, I wish I could find a way to properly acknowledge my cherished Uncle Terry and my Aunt Deborah for all the help they gave me during this year of travel. To call it mere "technical support" is to diminish the importance of their contribution. Together they wove a net beneath my tightrope without which—quite simply—I would not have been able to write this book. I don't know how to repay them.

In the end, though, maybe we must all give up trying to pay back the people in this world who sustain our lives. In the end, maybe it's wiser to surrender before the miraculous scope of human generosity and to just keep saying thank you, forever and sincerely, for as long as we have voices.

A Note on the Author

Elizabeth Gilbert is the author of a short story collection, *Pilgrims* (a finalist for the Pen/Hemingway Award), a novel, *Stern Men* and a book of non fiction, *The Last American Man* (nominated for the National Book Award and a *New York Times* Notable Book for 2002). She is a writer-at-large for American *GQ* where she has received two National Magazine Award nominations for feature writing. Elizabeth Gilbert currently lives in New Jersey.

Read on to find out what happened after *Eat, Pray, Love* in
Elizabeth Gilbert's new book . . .

COMMITTED

CHAPTER ONE

Marriage and Surprises

MARRIAGE IS A FRIENDSHIP RECOGNIZED BY THE POLICE.

—*Robert Louis Stevenson*

$\mathcal{L}$ate one afternoon in the summer of 2006, I found myself in a small village in northern Vietnam, sitting around a sooty kitchen fire with a number of local women whose language I did not speak, trying to ask them questions about marriage.

For several months already, I had been traveling across Southeast Asia with a man who was soon to become my husband. I suppose the conventional term for such an individual would be "fiancé," but neither one of us was very comfortable with that word, so we weren't using it. In fact, neither one of us was very comfortable with this whole idea of matrimony at all. Marriage was not something we had ever planned with each other, nor was it something either of us wanted. Yet providence had interfered with our plans, which was why we were now wandering haphazardly across Vietnam, Thailand, Laos, Cambodia, and Indonesia, all the while making urgent—even desperate—efforts to return to America and wed.

The man in question had been my lover, my sweetheart, for over two years by then, and in these pages I shall call him Felipe. Felipe is a kind, affectionate Brazilian gentleman, seventeen years my senior, whom I'd met on another journey (an actual planned journey) that I'd taken around the world a few years earlier in an effort to mend a severely broken heart. Near the end of those travels, I'd encountered Felipe, who had been living quietly and alone in Bali for years, nursing his own broken heart. What had followed was attraction, then a slow courtship, and then, much to our mutual wonderment, love.

Our resistance to marriage, then, had nothing to do with an absence of love. On the contrary, Felipe and I loved each other unreservedly. We were happy to make all sorts of promises to stay together faithfully forever. We had even sworn lifelong fidelity to each other already, although quite privately. The problem was that the two of us were both survivors of bad divorces, and we'd been so badly gutted by our experiences that the very idea of legal marriage—with *anyone*, even with such nice people as each other—filled us with a heavy sense of dread.

As a rule, of course, most divorces are pretty bad (Rebecca West observed that "getting a divorce is nearly always as cheerful and useful an occupation as breaking very valuable china"), and our divorces had been no exception. On the mighty cosmic one-to-ten Scale of Divorce Badness (where one equals an amicably executed separation, and ten equals . . . well, an actual execution), I would probably rate my own divorce as something like 7.5. No suicides or homicides had resulted, but aside from that, the rupture had been about as ugly a proceeding as two otherwise well-mannered people could have possibly manifested. And it had dragged on for more than two years.

As for Felipe, his first marriage (to an intelligent, professional Australian woman) had ended almost a decade before we'd met in Bali. His divorce had unfolded graciously enough at the time, but losing his wife (and access to the house and kids and almost two decades of history that came along with her) had inflicted on this good man a lingering legacy of sadness, with special emphases on regret, isolation, and economic anxiety.

Our experiences, then, had left the two of us taxed, troubled, and decidedly suspicious of the joys of holy wedded matrimony. Like anyone who has ever walked through the valley of the shadow of divorce, Felipe and I had each learned firsthand this distressing truth: that every intimacy carries, secreted somewhere below its initial lovely surfaces, the ever-coiled makings of complete catastrophe. We had also learned that marriage is an estate that is very much easier to enter than it is to exit. Unfenced by law, the unmarried lover can quit a bad relationship at any time. But you—the legally married person who wants to escape doomed love—may soon discover that a significant portion of your marriage contract belongs to the State, and that it sometimes takes a very long while for the State to grant you your leave. Thus, you can feasibly find yourself trapped for months or even years in a loveless legal bond that has come to feel rather like a burning building. A burning building in which you, my friend, are handcuffed to a radiator somewhere down in the basement, unable to wrench yourself free, while the smoke billows forth and the rafters are collapsing . . .

I'm sorry—does all this sound unenthusiastic?

I share these unpleasant thoughts only to explain why Felipe and I had made a rather unusual pact with each other, right from the beginning of our love story. We had sworn with all our hearts to never, ever, under any circumstances, marry. We had even promised never to blend together our finances or our worldly assets, in order to avoid the potential nightmare of ever again having to divvy up an explosive personal munitions dump of shared mortgages, deeds, property, bank accounts, kitchen appliances, and favorite books. These promises having been duly pledged, the two of us proceeded forth into our carefully partitioned companionship with a real sense of calmness. For just as a sworn engagement can bring to so many other couples a sensation of encircling protection, our vow *never* to marry had cloaked the two of us in all the emotional security we required in order to try once more at love. And this commitment of ours—consciously devoid of official commitment—felt miraculous in its liberation. It felt as though we had found the Northwest Passage of Perfect Intimacy—something that, as García Márquez wrote, "resembled love, but without the problems of love."

So that's what we'd been doing up until the spring of 2006: minding our own business, building a delicately divided life together in unfettered contentment. And that is very well how we might have gone on living happily ever after, except for one terribly inconvenient interference.

The United States Department of Homeland Security got involved.

The trouble was that Felipe and I—while we shared many similarities and blessings—did not happen to share a nationality. He was a Brazilian-born man with Australian citizenship who, when we met, had been living mostly in Indonesia. I was an American woman who, my travels aside, had been living mostly on the East Coast of the United States. We didn't initially foresee any problems with our countryless love story, although in retrospect perhaps we should have anticipated complications. As the old adage goes: A fish and a bird may indeed fall in love, but where shall they live? The solution to this dilemma, we believed, was that we were both nimble travelers (I was a bird who could dive and Felipe was a fish who could fly), so for our first year together, at least, we basically lived in midair—diving and flying across oceans and continents in order to be together.

Our work lives, fortunately enough, facilitated such footloose arrangements. As a writer, I could carry my job with me anyplace. As a jewelry and gemstone importer who sold his goods in the United States, Felipe always needed to be traveling anyhow. All we had to do was coordinate our locomotion. So I would fly to Bali; he would come to

America; we would both go to Brazil; we would meet up again in Sydney. I took a temporary job teaching writing at the University of Tennessee, and for a few curious months we lived together in a decaying old hotel room in Knoxville. (I can recommend *that* living arrangement, by the way, to anyone who wants to test out the actual compatibility levels of a new relationship.)

We lived at a staccato rhythm, on the hoof, mostly together but ever on the move, like witnesses in some odd international protection program. Our relationship—though steadying and calm at the personal level—was a constant logistical challenge, and what with all that international air travel, it was bloody expensive. It was also psychologically jarring. With each reunion, Felipe and I had to learn each other all over again. There was always that nervous moment at the airport when I would stand there waiting for him to arrive, wondering, *Will I still know him? Will he still know me?* After the first year, then, we both began to long for something more stable, and Felipe was the one who made the big move. Giving up his modest but lovely cottage in Bali, he moved with me to a tiny house I had recently rented on the outskirts of Philadelphia.

While trading Bali for the suburbs of Philly may seem a peculiar choice, Felipe swore that he had long ago grown tired of life in the tropics. Living in Bali was too easy, he complained, with each day a pleasant, boring replica of the day before. He had been longing to leave for some time already, he insisted, even before he'd met me. Now, growing bored with paradise might be impossible to understand for someone who has never actually lived in paradise (I certainly found the notion a bit crazy), yet Bali's dreamland setting honestly had come to feel oppressively dull to Felipe over the years. I will never forget one of the last enchanting evenings that he and I spent together at his cottage there—sitting outside, barefoot and dewy-skinned from the warm November air, drinking wine and watching a sea of constellations flicker above the rice fields. As the perfumed winds rustled the palm trees and as faint music from a distant temple ceremony floated on the breeze, Felipe looked at me, sighed, and said flatly, "I'm so sick of this shit. I can't wait to go back to Philly."

So—to Philadelphia (city of brotherly potholes) we duly decamped! The fact is we both liked the area a lot. Our little rental was near my sister and her family, whose proximity had become vital to my happiness over the years, so that brought familiarity. Moreover, after all our collective years of travel to far-flung places, it felt good and even revitalizing to be living in America, a country which, for all its flaws, was still *interesting* to both of us: a fast-moving, multicultural, ever-evolving, maddeningly contradictory, creatively challenging, and fundamentally alive sort of place.

There in Philadelphia, then, Felipe and I set up headquarters and practiced, with encouraging success, our first real sessions of shared domesticity. He sold his jewelry; I worked on writing projects that required me to stay in one place and conduct research. He cooked; I took care of the lawn; every once in a while one of us would fire up the vacuum cleaner. We worked well together in a home, dividing our daily chores without strife. We felt ambitious and productive and optimistic. Life was nice.

But such intervals of stability could never last long. Because of Felipe's visa restrictions, three months was the maximum amount of time that he could legally stay in America before he would have to excuse himself to another country for a spell. So off he would fly, and I would be alone with my books and my neighbors while he was gone. Then, after a few weeks, he'd return to the United States on another ninety-day visa and we'd recommence our domestic life together. It is a testament to how warily we both regarded long-term commitment that these ninety-day chunks of togetherness felt just about perfect for us: the exact amount of future planning that two tremulous divorce survivors could manage without feeling too threatened. And sometimes, when my schedule allowed, I would join him on his visa runs out of the country.

This explains why one day we were returning to the States together from a business trip overseas and we landed—due to the peculiarity of our cheap tickets and our connecting flight—at the Dallas/Fort Worth International Airport. I passed through Immigration first, moving easily through the line of my fellow repatriating American citizens. Once on the other side, I waited for Felipe, who was in the middle of a long line of foreigners. I watched as he approached the immigration official, who carefully studied Felipe's bible-thick Australian passport, scrutinizing every page, every mark, every hologram. Normally they were not so vigilant, and I grew nervous at how long this was taking. I watched and waited, listening for the all-important sound of any successful border crossing: that thick, solid, librarian-like *thunk* of a welcoming visa-entry stamp. But it never came.

Instead, the immigration official picked up his phone and made a quiet call. Moments later, an officer wearing the uniform of the United States Department of Homeland Security came and took my baby away.

$\diagup\!\!\!\!\sim$

$\mathcal{T}$he uniformed men at the Dallas airport held Felipe in interrogation for six hours. For six hours, forbidden to see him or ask questions, I sat there in a Homeland Security waiting room—a bland, fluorescent-lit space filled with apprehensive people from all over the world, all of us equally rigid with fear. I had no idea what they were doing to Felipe back there or what they were asking from him. I knew that he had not broken any laws, but this was not as comforting a thought as you might imagine. These were the late years of George W. Bush's presidential administration: not a relaxing moment in history to have your foreign-born sweetheart held in government custody. I kept trying to calm myself with the famous prayer of the fourteenth-century mystic Juliana of

Norwich ("All shall be well, and all shall be well, and all manner of thing shall be well"), but I didn't believe a word of it. Nothing was well. Not one single manner of thing whatsoever was well.

Every once in a while I would stand up from my plastic chair and try to elicit more information from the immigration officer behind the bulletproof glass. But he ignored my pleas, each time reciting the same response: "When we have something to tell you about your boyfriend, miss, we'll let you know."

In a situation like this, may I just say, there is perhaps no more feeble-sounding word in the English language than *boyfriend*. The dismissive manner in which the officer uttered that word indicated how unimpressed he was with my relationship. Why on earth should a government employee ever release information about a mere *boyfriend*? I longed to explain myself to the immigration officer, to say, "Listen, the man you are detaining back there is far more important to me than you could ever begin to imagine." But even in my anxious state, I doubted this would do any good. If anything, I feared that pushing things too far might bring unpleasant repercussions on Felipe's end, so I backed off, helpless. It occurs to me only now that I probably should have made an effort to call a lawyer. But I didn't have a telephone with me, and I didn't want to abandon my post in the waiting room, and I didn't know any lawyers in Dallas, and it was a Sunday afternoon, anyhow, so who could I have reached?

Finally, after six hours, an officer came and led me through some hallways, through a rabbit warren of bureaucratic mysteries, to a small, dimly lit room where Felipe was sitting with the Homeland Security officer who had been interrogating him. Both men looked equally tired, but only one of those men was *mine*—my beloved, the most familiar face in the world to me. Seeing him in such a state made my chest hurt with longing. I wanted to touch him, but I sensed this was not allowed, so I remained standing.

Felipe smiled at me wearily and said, "Darling, our lives are about to get a lot more interesting."

Before I could respond, the interrogating officer quickly took charge of the situation and all its explanations.

"Ma'am," he said, "we've brought you back here to explain that we will not be allowing your boyfriend to enter the United States anymore. We'll be detaining him in jail until we can get him on a flight out of the country, back to Australia, since he does have an Australian passport. After that, he won't be able to come back to America again."

My first reaction was physical. I felt as if all the blood in my body had instantly evaporated, and my eyes refused to focus for a moment. Then, in the next instant, my mind kicked into action. I revved through a fast summation of this sudden, grave crisis. Starting long before we had met, Felipe had made his living in the United States, visiting several times a year for short stays, legally importing gemstones and jewelry from Brazil and Indonesia for sale in American markets. America has always welcomed international businessmen like him; they bring merchandise and money and commerce into the country. In return, Felipe had prospered in America. He'd put his kids (who were now adults) through the finest private schools in Australia with income that he'd made in America over the decades. America was the center of his professional life, even though he'd never lived here until very recently. But his inventory was here and all his contacts were here. If he could never come back to America again, his livelihood was effectively destroyed. Not to mention the fact that I lived here in the United States, and that Felipe wanted to be with me, and that—because of my family and my work—I would always want to remain based in America. And Felipe had become part of my family, too. He'd been fully embraced by my parents, my sister, my friends, my world. So how would we continue our life together if he were forever banned? What would we do? ("*Where will you and I sleep?*" go the lyrics to a mournful Wintu love song. *"At the down-turned jagged rim of the sky? Where will you and I sleep?"*)

"On what grounds are you deporting him?" I asked the Homeland Security officer, trying to sound authoritative.

"Strictly speaking, ma'am, it's not a deportation." Unlike me, the officer didn't have to try sounding authoritative; it came naturally. "We're just refusing him entrance to the United States on the grounds that he's been visiting America too frequently in the last year. He's never overstayed his visa limits, but it does appear from all his comings and goings that he's been living with you in Philadelphia for three-month periods and then leaving the country, only to return to the United States again immediately after."

This was difficult to argue, since that was precisely what Felipe had been doing.

"Is that a crime?" I asked.

"Not exactly."

"Not exactly, or no?"

"No, ma'am, it's not a crime. That's why we won't be arresting him. But the three-month visa waiver that the United States government offers to citizens of friendly countries is not intended for indefinite consecutive visits."

"But we didn't know that," I said.

Felipe stepped in now. "In fact, sir, we were once told by an immigration officer in New York that I could visit the United States as often as I liked, as long as I never overstayed my ninety-day visa."

"I don't know who told you that, but it isn't true."

Hearing the officer say this reminded me of a warning Felipe had given me once about international border crossings: "Never take it lightly, darling. Always remember that on any given day, for any given reason whatsoever, any given border guard in the world can decide that he does not want to let you in."

"What would you do now, if you were in our situation?" I asked.

This is a technique I've learned to use over the years whenever I find myself at an impasse with a dispassionate customer service operator or an apathetic bureaucrat. Phrasing the sentence in such a manner invites the person who has all the power to pause for a moment and put himself in the shoes of the person who is powerless. It's a subtle appeal to empathy. Sometimes it helps. Most of the time, to be honest, it doesn't help at all. But I was willing to try anything here.

"Well, if your boyfriend ever wants to come back into the United States again, he's going to need to secure himself a better, more permanent visa. If I were you, I would go about securing him one."

"Okay, then," I said. "What's the fastest way for us to secure him a better, more permanent visa?"

The Homeland Security officer looked at Felipe, then at me, then back at Felipe. "Honestly?" he said. "The two of you need to get married."

*M*y heart sank, almost audibly. Across the tiny room, I could sense Felipe's heart sinking along with mine, in complete hollow tandem.

In retrospect, it does seem unbelievable that this proposition could possibly have taken me by surprise. Had I never heard of a green card marriage before, for heaven's sake? Maybe it also seems unbelievable that—given the urgent nature of our circumstances—the suggestion of matrimony brought me distress instead of relief. I mean, at least we'd been given an option, right? Yet the proposition did take me by surprise. And it did hurt. So thoroughly had I barred the very notion of marriage from my psyche that hearing the idea spoken aloud now felt shocking. I felt mournful and sucker punched and heavy and banished from some fundamental aspect of my being, but most of all I felt *caught*. I felt we had both been caught. The flying fish and the diving bird had been netted. And my naïveté, not for the first time in my life, I'm afraid, struck me across the face like a wet slap: *Why had I been so foolish as to imagine that we could get away with living our lives as we pleased for-ever?*

Nobody spoke for a while, until the Homeland Security interrogation officer, regarding our silent faces of doom, asked, "Sorry, folks. What seems to be the problem with this idea?"

Felipe took off his glasses and rubbed his eyes—a sign, I knew from long experience, of utter exhaustion. He sighed, and said, "Oh, Tom, Tom, Tom . . ."

I had not yet realized that these two were on a first-name basis, though I suppose that's bound to happen during a six-hour interrogation session. Especially when the interrogatee is Felipe.

"No, seriously—what's the problem?" asked Officer Tom. "You two have obviously been cohabiting already. You obviously care about each other, you're not married to anyone else . . ."

"What you have to understand, Tom," explained Felipe, leaning forward and speaking with an intimacy which belied our institutional surroundings, "is that Liz and I have both been through really, really bad divorces in the past."

Officer Tom made a small noise—a sort of soft, sympathetic "*Oh* . . ." Then he took off his own glasses and rubbed his own eyes. Instinctively, I glanced at the third finger of his left hand. No wedding ring. From that bare left hand and from his reflexive reaction of tired commiseration I made a quick diagnosis: divorced.

It was here that our interview turned surreal.

"Well, you could always sign a prenuptial agreement," Officer Tom suggested. "I mean, if you're worried about going through all the financial mess of a divorce again. Or if it's the relationship issues that scare you, maybe some counseling would be a good idea."

I listened in wonder. *Was a deputy of the United States Department of Homeland Security giving us* marital advice? *In an interrogation room? In the bowels of the Dallas/Fort Worth International Airport?*

Finding my voice, I offered this brilliant solution: "Officer Tom, what if I just found a way to somehow *hire* Felipe, instead of marrying him? Couldn't I bring him to America as my employee, instead of my husband?"

Felipe sat up straight and exclaimed, "Darling! What a terrific idea!"

Officer Tom gave us each an odd look. He asked Felipe, "You would honestly rather have this woman as your boss than your wife?"

"Dear God, yes!"

I could sense Officer Tom almost physically restraining himself from asking, "What the hell kind of people *are* you?" But he was far too professional for anything like that. Instead, he cleared his throat and said, "Unfortunately, what you have just proposed here is not legal in this country."

Felipe and I both slumped again, once more in complete tandem, into a depressed silence.

After a long spell of this, I spoke again. "All right," I said, defeated. "Let's get this over with. If I marry Felipe right now, right here in your office, will you let him into the country today? Maybe you have a chaplain here at the airport who could do that?"

There are moments in life when the face of an ordinary man can take on a quality of near-divinity, and this is just what happened now. Tom—a weary, badge-wearing, Texan Homeland Security officer with a paunch—smiled at me with a sadness, a kindness, a luminous compassion that was utterly out of place in this stale, dehumanizing room. Suddenly, he looked like a chaplain himself.

"Oh no-o-o . . . ," he said gently. "I'm afraid things don't work that way."

Looking back on it all now, of course I realize that Officer Tom already knew what was facing Felipe and me, far better than we ourselves could have known. He well knew that securing an official United States fiancé visa, particularly after a "border incident" such as this one, would be no small feat. Officer Tom could foresee all the trouble that was now coming to us: from the lawyers in three countries—on three continents, no less—who would have to secure all the necessary legal documents; to the federal police reports that would be required from every country in which Felipe had ever lived; to the stacks of personal letters, photos, and other intimate ephemera which we would now have to compile to prove that our relationship was real (including, with maddening irony, such evidence as shared bank accounts—details we'd specifically gone through an awful lot of trouble in our lives to keep *separated*); to the fingerprinting; to the inoculations; to the requisite tuberculosis-screening chest X-rays; to the interviews at the American embassies abroad; to the military records that we would somehow have to recover of Felipe's Brazilian army service thirty-five years earlier; to the sheer expanse and expense of time that Felipe now would have to spend out of the country while this process played itself out; to—worst of all—the horrible uncertainty of not knowing whether any of this effort would be enough, which is to say, not knowing whether the United States government (behaving, in this regard, rather much like a stern, old-fashioned father) would ever even accept this man as a husband for me, its jealously guarded natural-born daughter.

So Officer Tom already knew all that, and the fact that he expressed sympathy toward us for what we were about to undergo was an unexpected turn of kindness in an otherwise devastating situation. That I never, prior to this moment, imagined myself praising a member of the Department of Homeland Security in print for his personal tenderness only highlights how bizarre this whole situation had become. But I should say here that Officer Tom did us one other kind deed, as well. (That is, before he handcuffed Felipe and led him off to the Dallas county jail, depositing him for the night in a cell filled with actual criminals.) The gesture that Officer Tom made was this: He left me and Felipe alone together in the interrogation room for two whole minutes, so that we could say our good-byes to each other in privacy.

When you have only two minutes to say good-bye to the person you love most in the world, and you don't know when you'll see each other again, you can become logjammed with the effort to say and do and settle everything at once. In our two minutes alone in the interrogation room, then, we made a hasty, breathless plan. I would go home to Philadelphia, move out of our rented house, put everything into storage, secure an immigration lawyer and start this legal process moving. Felipe, of course, would go to jail. Then he would be deported back to Australia—even if, strictly speaking, he wasn't being legally "deported." (Please forgive me for using the word "deported" through-out the pages of this book, but I'm still not sure what else to call it when a person gets thrown out of a country.) Since Felipe had no life in Aus-tralia anymore, no home or financial prospects, he would make arrange-ments as quickly as possible to go somewhere cheaper to live—Southeast Asia, probably—and I would join him on that side of the world once I got things rolling on my end. There, we would wait out this indefinite period of uncertainty together.

While Felipe jotted down the phone numbers of his lawyer, his grown children, and his business partners so that I could alert everyone to his situation, I emptied out my handbag, frantically looking for things I could give him to keep him more comfortable in jail: chewing gum, all my cash, a bottle of water, a photograph of us together, and a novel I had been reading on the airplane titled, aptly enough, *The People's Act of Love*.

Then Felipe's eyes filled with tears and he said, "Thank you for coming into my life. No matter what happens now, no matter what you decide to do next, just know that you've given me the two most joyful years I've ever known and I will never forget you."

I realized in a flash: *Dear God, the man thinks I might leave him now.* His reaction surprised me and touched me, but more than anything it shamed me. It had not crossed my mind, since Officer Tom had laid out the option, that I would *not* now marry Felipe and save him from exile—but apparently it had crossed *his* mind that he might now be ditched. He genuinely feared that I might abandon him, leaving him high and dry, broke and busted. Had I earned such a reputation? Was I really known, even within the boundaries of our small love story, as somebody who jumps ship at the first obstacle? But were Felipe's fears entirely unjustified, given my history? If our situations had been reversed, I would never have doubted for a moment the solidity of his loyalties, or his willingness to sacrifice virtually anything on my account. Could he be certain of the same steadfastness from me?

I had to admit that if this state of affairs had taken place ten or fifteen years earlier, I almost certainly would have bailed out on my endangered partner. I am sorry to confess that I possessed a scant amount of honor in my youth, if any, and behaving in a flighty and thoughtless manner was a bit of a specialty of mine. But being a person of character matters to me now, and matters only more as I grow older. At that moment, then—and I had only one moment left alone with Felipe—I did the only right thing by this man whom I adored. I vowed to him—drilling the words into his ear so he would grasp my earnestness—that I would not leave him, that I would do whatever it took to fix things, and that even if things could not somehow be fixed in America, we would always stay together anyhow, somewhere, wherever in the world that had to be.

Officer Tom came back into the room.

At the last instant, Felipe whispered to me, "I love you so much, I will even marry you."

"And I love *you* so much," I promised, "that I will even marry you."

Then the nice Homeland Security people separated us and handcuffed Felipe and led him away—first to jail and then off to exile.

$\mathcal{A}$s I flew home alone that night to our now-obsolete little existence in Philadelphia, I considered more soberly what I had just promised. I was surprised to find that I was not feeling weepy or panicky; somehow the situation seemed too grave for any of that. What I felt, instead, was a ferocious sense of focus—a sense that this situation must be addressed with the utmost seriousness. In the space of only a few hours, my life with Felipe had been neatly flipped upside down, as though by some great cosmic spatula. And now, it seemed, we were engaged to be married. This had certainly been a strange and rushed engagement ceremony. It felt more like something out of Kafka than out of Austen. Yet the engagement was nonetheless official because it needed to be.

Fine, then. So be it. I would certainly not be the first woman in my family's history who ever had to get married because of a serious situation—although my situation, at least, did not involve accidental pregnancy. Still, the prescription was the same: Tie the knot, and do it quickly. So that's what we would do. But here was the real problem, which I identified that night all alone on the plane back home to Philadelphia: I had no idea what marriage *was*.

I had already made this mistake—entering into marriage without understanding anything whatsoever about the institution—once before in my life. In fact, I had jumped into my first marriage, at the totally unfinished age of twenty-five, much the same way that a Labrador jumps into a swimming pool—with exactly that much preparation and foresight. Back when I was twenty-five, I was so irresponsible that I probably should not have been allowed to choose my own toothpaste, much less my own future, and so this carelessness, as you can imagine, came at a dear cost. I reaped the consequences in spades, six years later, in the grim setting of a divorce court.

Looking back on the occasion of my first wedding day, I'm reminded of Richard Aldington's novel *Death of a Hero*, in which he ponders his two young lovers on *their* ill-fated wedding day: "Can one tabulate the ignorances, the relevant ignorances, of George Augustus and Isabel when they pledged themselves together until death do us part?" I, too, was once a giddy young bride very much like Aldington's Isabel, about whom he wrote: "What she *didn't* know included almost the whole range of human knowledge. The puzzle is to find out what she *did* know."

Now, though—at the considerably less giddy age of thirty-seven—I was not convinced that I knew very much more than ever about the realities of institutionalized companionship. I had failed at marriage and thus I was terrified of marriage, but I'm not sure this made me an expert on marriage; this only made me an expert on failure and terror, and those particular fields are already crowded with experts. Yet destiny had intervened and was demanding marriage from me, and I'd learned enough from life's experiences to understand that destiny's interventions can sometimes be read as invitations for us to address and even surmount our biggest fears. It doesn't take a great genius to recognize that when you are pushed by circumstance to do the one thing you have always most specifically loathed and feared, this can be, at the very least, *an interesting growth opportunity*.

So it slowly dawned on me on the airplane out of Dallas—my world now turned back-to-front, my lover exiled, the two of us having effectively been sentenced to marry—that perhaps I should use this time to somehow make peace with the idea of matrimony before I jumped into it once again. Perhaps it would be wise to put a little effort into unraveling the mystery of what in the name of God and human history this befuddling, vexing, contradictory, and yet stubbornly enduring institution of marriage actually is.

So that is what I did. For the next ten months—while traveling with Felipe in a state of rootless exile and while working like a dog to get him back into America so we could safely wed (getting married in Australia or anywhere else in the world, Officer Tom had warned us, would merely irritate the Homeland Security Department and slow down our immigration process even more)—the only thing I thought about, the only thing I read about, and pretty much the only thing I talked about with anybody was the perplexing subject of matrimony.

I enlisted my sister back home in Philadelphia (who, conveniently, is an actual historian) to send me boxes of books about marriage. Wherever Felipe and I happened to be staying, I would lock myself up in our hotel room to study the books, passing untold hours in the company of such eminent matrimonial scholars as Stephanie Coontz and Nancy Cott—writers whose names I had never heard before but who now became my heroes and teachers. To be honest, all this studying made me a lousy tourist. During those months of travel, Felipe and I fetched up in many beautiful and fascinating places, but I'm afraid I didn't always pay close attention to our surroundings. This stretch of traveling never had the feeling of a carefree adventure anyhow. It felt more like an expulsion, a hegira. Traveling because you cannot go back home again, because one of you is not legally allowed to go home again, can never be an enjoyable endeavor.

Moreover, our financial situation was worrisome. *Eat, Pray, Love* was less than a year away from becoming a lucrative best seller, but that welcome development had not yet occurred, nor did we anticipate its ever occurring. Felipe was now completely cut off from his income source, so we were both living off the fumes of my last book contract, and I wasn't sure how long that would hold out. A while, yes—but not forever. I had recently begun working on a new novel, but my research and writing had now been interrupted by Felipe's deportation. So this is how we ended up going to Southeast Asia, where two frugal people can feasibly live on about thirty dollars a day. While I won't say that we exactly suffered during this period of exile (we were hardly starving political refugees, for heaven's sake), I will say that it was an extremely odd and tense way to live, with the oddness and tension only heightened by the uncertainty of the outcome.

We wandered for close to a year, waiting for the day when Felipe would be called to his interview at the American Consulate in Sydney, Australia. Flopping in the meantime from country to country, we came to resemble nothing more than an insomniac couple trying to find a restful sleeping position in a strange and uncomfortable bed. For many anxious nights, in many strange and uncomfortable beds indeed, I would lie there in the dark, working through my conflicts and prejudices about marriage, filtering through all the information I was reading, mining history for comforting conclusions.

I should clarify right away here that I limited my studies largely to an examination of marriage in Western history, and that this book will therefore reflect that cultural limitation. Any proper matrimonial historian or anthropologist will find huge gaps in my narrative, as I have left unexplored entire continents and centuries of human history, not to mention skipping over some pretty vital nuptial concepts (polygamy, as just one example). It would have been pleasurable for me, and certainly educational, to have delved more deeply into an examination of every possible marital custom on earth, but I didn't have that kind of time. Trying to get a handle on the complex nature of matrimony in Islamic societies alone, for instance, would have taken me years of study, and my urgency had a deadline that precluded such extended contemplation. A very real clock was ticking in my life: Within one year—like it or not, ready or not—I had to get married. That being the case, it seemed imperative that I focus my attention on unraveling the history of monogamous Western marriage in order to better understand my inherited assumptions, the shape of my family's narrative, and my culturally specific catalogue of anxieties.

I hoped that all this studying might somehow mitigate my deep aversion to marriage. I wasn't sure how that would happen, but it had always been my experience in the past, anyhow, that the more I learned about something, the less it frightened me. (Some fears can be vanquished, Rumpelstiltskin-like, only by uncovering their hidden, secret names.) What I really wanted, more than anything, was to find a way to somehow embrace marriage to Felipe when the big day came rather than merely swallowing my fate like a hard and awful pill. Call me old-fashioned, but I thought it might be a nice touch to be happy on my wedding day. Happy *and* conscious, that is.

This book is the story of how I got there.

And it all begins—because every story must begin somewhere—in the mountains of northern Vietnam.

Also available by Elizabeth Gilbert

STERN MEN

A *New York Times* Notable Book

On two remote islands off the coast of Maine, the local lobstermen have fought savagely for generations over the fishing rights to the ocean waters between them. Young Ruth Thomas is born into this feud, the daughter of one of the greediest lobstermen in Maine. Eighteen years old, as smart as a whip, and irredeemably unromantic, Ruth returns home from boarding school determined to throw her education overboard and join the 'stern-men'. As the feud escalates, she helps work the lobster boats, brushes up on her profanity, and eventually falls for a handsome young lobsterman. A funny, sparkling novel of unlikely friendships and family ties, *Stern Men* captures a feisty American spirit through this unforgettable heroine who is destined for greatness despite herself.

✻

'A wonderful novel about life, love and lobster fishing ...
Stern Men is high entertainment'
USA TODAY

'A mix of Annie Proulx and John Irving ... memorable and enjoyable'
THE TIMES

'Beautifully wrought and very funny ... finding an Austen heroine
in a lobster boat is one of [its] many delights'
MIRABELLA

✻

ISBN 978 0 7475 9824 4 · PAPERBACK · £7.99

B L O O M S B U R Y

PILGRIMS

A *New York Times* Notable Book

The cowboys, strippers, labourers and magicians of *Pilgrims* are all on their way to being somewhere, or someone, else. Some are browbeaten and world-weary, others are deluded and naïve, yet all seek companionship as fiercely as they can. A tough East Coast girl dares a western cowboy to run off with her; a matronly bar owner falls in love with her nephew; an innocent teenager falls hopelessly for the local bully's sister.

These are tough heroes and heroines, hardened by their experiences, who struggle for their epiphanies. Yet hope is never far away and though they may act blindly, they always act bravely. Sharply drawn and tenderly observed, *Pilgrims* is filled with Gilbert's inimitable humour and warmth.

✳

'Gilbert takes us on a grit-strewn ride into the heart of Country and Western territory: good old boys, cowgirls, dingy bars, the backwaters and empty plains of America'
SUNDAY TIMES

'This has all the hallmarks of a great writer: sympathy, wit, and an amazing ear for dialogue'
HARPER'S BAZAAR

'A superior collection of stories about women who are as tough as they look, though perhaps not quite as tough as they think they are'
GLAMOUR

✳

ISBN 978 0 7475 9825 1 · PAPERBACK · £7.99

BLOOMSBURY

COMMITTED

A SCEPTIC MAKES PEACE WITH MARRIAGE

The eagerly awaited sequel to the multi-million international bestseller *Eat, Pray, Love*

At the end of *Eat, Pray, Love* Elizabeth Gilbert fell in love with Felipe, a Brazilian-born man of Australian citizenship. Resettling in America, they swore eternal fidelity to each other, but also (each a survivor of a difficult divorce. Enough said) swore never, under any circumstances, to get married. But when providence intervened in the form of the US government, Elizabeth and Felipe find themselves with a stark choice: either marry, or Felipe would never be allowed in the country again.

Having been effectively sentenced to wed, Gilbert delved completely into the subject of marriage and the stunning result, which debunks myths, unthreads fears, celebrates love, suggests that sometimes even the most romantic of souls must trade in amorous fantasies for the humbling responsibility of adulthood.

✳

ISBN 9781408805763 · TRADE PAPERBACK · £12.99

THE SIGNATURE OF ALL THINGS

5th January 1800. At the beginning of a new century, Alma Whittaker is born into a perfect Philadelphia winter. Her father, Henry Whittaker, is a bold and charismatic botanical explorer whose vast fortune belies his lowly beginnings as a vagrant in Kew Gardens. Alma's mother, a strict woman from an esteemed Dutch family, is conversant in five living languages (and two dead ones) and her knowledge of botany is equal to any man's. An independent girl with a thirst for knowledge, it is not long before Alma comes into her own within the world of plants and science.

As Alma's careful studies of moss take her deeper into the mysteries of evolution, the man she comes to love draws her in the opposite direction – into the realm of the spiritual, the divine, and the magical. Alma is a clear-minded scientist; Ambrose is a Utopian artist. But what unites this couple is a shared passion for knowing – a desperate need to understand the workings of this world and the mechanisms behind all of life.

The Signature of All Things is a big novel, about a big century. It soars across the globe from London, to Peru, to Philadelphia, to Tahiti, to Amsterdam. Peopled with extraordinary characters – missionaries, abolitionists, adventurers, astronomers, sea captains, geniuses and the quite mad – most of all it has an unforgettable heroine in Alma Whittaker, a woman of the Enlightened Age who stands defiantly on the cusp of the modern.

ORDER BY PHONE: +44 (0)1256 302 699; BY EMAIL: DIRECT@MACMILLAN.CO.UK

DELIVERY IS USUALLY 3–5 WORKING DAYS. POSTAGE AND PACKAGING WILL BE CHARGED.

ONLINE: WWW.BLOOMSBURY.COM/BOOKSHOP

FREE POSTAGE AND PACKAGING FOR ORDERS OVER £20.

PRICES AND AVAILABILITY SUBJECT TO CHANGE WITHOUT NOTICE.

WWW.BLOOMSBURY.COM/ELIZABETHGILBERT

BLOOMSBURY

Praise for *Eat, Pray, Love*

'It is a testimony to Gilbert's writing skills, intellectual energy and self-deprecating wit that from the moment we meet her sobbing on her bathroom floor at 3am, we are rooting for her to find the peace and happiness she seeks' *Daily Mail*

'One of the most amazing autobiographies I've ever read. It's beautiful' Toni Collette

'*Eat, Pray, Love* has been passed from woman to woman like the secret of life ... The question is: why has it struck such a deep chord? A modern-day *A Room of One's Own* (a year of one's own?), it seems to be a call to arms for thirty-something females who, despite appearing to have tiptop lives – the job, the flat, the bloke, the handbags – are dogged by a vague spiritual dread, a lingering "what if?"' *Sunday Times*

'Every woman should read it' Elle Macpherson

'A true account of her search for happiness and sense of self'
Harper's Bazaar

'Be advised that the supremely entertaining *Eat, Pray, Love* – a mid-thirties memoir by the endlessly talented Elizabeth Gilbert – is not just for the ladies, fellas' *GQ*

'Warm, self-deprecating and filled with hope' *Marie Claire*

'A tender and funny account of a woman's search for happiness'
Closer

'Gilbert's wry, unfettered account of her extraordinary journey makes even the most cynical reader dare to dream of someday finding God deep within a meditation cave in India, or perhaps over a transcendent slice of pizza' *Los Angeles Times*

'I loved it' Hillary Clinton